Diaries
1969–1977

Peter Nichols

Diaries
1969–1977

London
NICK HERN BOOKS

www.nickhernbooks.demon.co.uk

A Nick Hern Book

Diaries 1969–1977
first published in Great Britain in 2000
by Nick Hern Books Limited
14 Larden Road, London W3 7ST

A CIP catalogue record for this book
is available from the British Library

ISBN 1 85459 474 5

Typeset by Country Setting, Kingsdown, Kent CT14 8ES

Printed by Biddles of Guildford

Illustrations

1   Abigail, Thelma, Dan, Peter, Louise (Bristol, 1968).

2   Albert Finney, Susan Alpern, Zena Walker (*Joe Egg*, New York 1968).
    Taking Abigail 'home'.

3   Arriving Berlin airport: Thelma, Peter, Werner Beyer.
    Valerie and Charles Wood, Thelma.

4   Joe Melia, Denis Quilley, *Privates on Parade:* 'Latin American Way' (Kobal Collection).
    Privates film rehearsal: Michael Blakemore, George Harrison (co-producer), John Cleese and the rest of us.

5   Blackheath on screen. *The Common*, 1974, including Peter Jeffrey, Denis Waterman, Vivien Merchant, Gwen Taylor.
    Blackheath reality: Thelma, her parents and daughters.
    The front garden: Dan and Louise.
    Back garden: Catherine and Louise.

6   Lynn Redgrave, Mervyn Johns, Jim Dale: *The National Health* film, 1973 (Kobal Collection).
    Joan Hickson sings 'There'll Always Be an England':
    Forget-me-not-Lane, 1971 (Zoe Dominic).

7   Chez Magnou, Dordogne.
    Thelma, Christopher Morahan, Anna Carteret.
    Thelma and M. Maze, the gardener and garden.
    Francis Hewlett painting the house.

8   The family, Old Rectory, Shropshire, 1980s.
    Geoffrey Nichols, Antoni Gaudi, Peter, El Capricho, Spain.

Introduction

Only Americans do introductions well, confidently shouting, 'Philip de Sousa Bolenczewiecz, I don't think you've met Marylou Felicia von Winterhalter.' And they can do this even without staring at the label pinned to your jacket. For them togetherness is all; for the English it's to be avoided.

I'm doing the native routine even now, avoiding the task with facetiousness and a meandering sidelong approach that suggests I'm somehow ashamed, that I don't *want* you to meet this selection from the diary I've kept on-and-off since my eighteenth year. In fact, there's been so much 'off' that, strictly speaking, it's not a diary at all, at times almost a memoir, not only because of the periods when it was let lapse altogether but for the irregular years before I began writing (as now) every next-morning about the day-before. So, in many of the forty or so volumes, events were recollected after a gap of weeks and may be as much a work of fiction as my plays or my alleged autobiography, *Feeling You're Behind* (Weidenfeld, 1984). This was a memoir of my first forty years as boy, man, aircraftsman, actor, teacher, husband, father and playwright, a *Life* cobbled together from memory, photographs, hearsay, my semi-fictional comedies and the journals. Only for the last twenty have these deserved that name, that's to say: being written on a daily basis, almost like a morning exercise or pianist's scales, recording not just the big events but the everyday trivia and casual encounters that comprise the true diary. Boswell told Johnson he was afraid he put into his journals too many little incidents.

'There is nothing, Sir,' was the expected put-down, 'too little for so little a creature as man. It is by studying little things that we attain the great art of having as little misery and as much happiness as possible.'

The originals of mine are now in the British Library's Theatre Archive, though their access is limited till after my death, or that of my wife, whichever's the later. This is more to avoid hurt feelings than a fear of litigation. There are, unfortunately, few scandals or juicy revelations.

From 1945 to 1948 they're in the form of letters home from India, Singapore, Malaya and Hong Kong, written to describe my national service years to my parents in Bristol. They're on scraps of notepaper, airmail forms, in pads and blocks of lined notepaper, mostly undated, but with chapter-numbers and fancy travelogue headings like 'Delhi, Utopia of India' or 'Tomorrow and Tomorrow'. From my release in 1948 to the start of a brief acting career in the early fifties, there are only occasional entries. Then a rough record begins again, now typed on loose sheets with two fingers (still my style in the year 2000). From '71 to '76, I used those day-by-day diaries sold by stationers, done in longhand. The longest lapse means there are only scraps and fragments from '76 till '83, when the page-a-days resume and run till '93. Since then I've kept them daily, religiously, using a series of word processors of increasing complexity and obtuseness. Much of my energy goes into shouting at their refusal to think for themselves instead of slavishly obeying my manual mistakes. So fiendish yet so fundamentally dim! But the advantages of the PC for a diarist are clear: the previous day can be scanned and altered, omitted events added later, mistakes corrected and on occasion shameful opinions deleted. This makes the entries more readable and detailed but even less reliable. Pen-and-ink has to stand. These electronic images can be erased without trace so easily that, at this stage in their evolution, huge screeds are lost at the touch of a wrong key. On one occasion twenty-five pages vanished in the works of a borrowed machine no-one knew how to cajole.

The processor changes diaries forever. Their authors can censor their own lives. I try not to make many restrospective emendations after a couple of days have elapsed, not looking again for a long time, perhaps years. On the other hand, published diaries are always edited, plums pulled from the pudding, 'life' so arranged and altered that they become an even greater lie than photographs. Both have to be interpreted to surrender their truths.

The present selection covers about ten years, taking up where the Memoir left off in New York in 1968. Our immediate family – I the father, Thelma the mother, two daughters Louise and Catherine, one son Dan, and Barbara, a German au pair – had gone there for the Broadway opening of my play *A Day in the Death of Joe Egg*, which had begun in Glasgow's Citizens' Theatre. Albert Finney and his producing partner Michael Medwin saw it and brought it to London. It was now, for the third time, successfully launched (on Broadway) by our close friend the director Michael Blakemore, with Albert replacing Joe Melia in the lead. Albert's name – and he was then a Great Store – was causing queues around the block. We waited awhile for Storedom to come to us too and, when it didn't, went visiting family and friends farther west in Illinois and Wisconsin.

Our voyage from England had been in the depth of a bitter winter on an ocean liner that had seen better days, plodding across a stormy Atlantic. Our first US visit over, we *flew* home from Chicago in a few hours and tried to resettle to the old life in Bristol.

Not for long. The royalties from Albert's three-month run meant we could afford to move to London to enjoy the Storedom we were still sure was waiting for us somewhere. We bought a detached (by a few feet) villa in Blackheath and, leaving the children in Bristol with the au pair, camped out on a sleeping-bag in one of the enormous empty rooms. That is where, in 1968, this selection starts. It ends at the point where I began to live more and set down less. This wasn't a conscious decision to avoid or hide from unbearable memories, as in Larkin's poem 'Forget What Did'. Life just became busier and for some time I lost the inexplicable habit of wanting to put it all down.

Most people have hobbies. Sad to say, this is mine. I've even asked to take it on my desert island along with the eight records.

A familiar hurdle in naturalistic playwriting is introducing – say – members of a family to an audience of strangers. To get over the necessary facts, there's usually a stretch known as The Exposition, where people who know each other perfectly well can sound as though they're all suffering amnesia as they explain to each other who their spouses or parents or children are, where they live and what jobs they do. Opening scenes try to tell The Story So Far without appearing to, a problem TV solves by saying 'Previously' and showing a few clips from last week's episode. A series also gains by the main characters being already familiar.

I've found a similar sort of difficulty cropping up with this volume and, rather than burden the text with notes, have added explanations that weren't in the original diary. When more's needed, or when I remember more than I noted at the time or consider a bit of hindsight would help, a modern commentary is shown in smaller, square-bracketed type and indented paragraphs.

I hope the contribution of my family is obvious from the diary itself. Even so, all my writing is made possible by Thelma, who has shared my life for forty years and without whom it would hardly be bearable.

Our adult children have had to watch distorted versions of their lives being acted on stage and screen and weren't even consulted in the matter. Their good natures must be due mostly to their mother. As the grandchildren grow, they may find explanations here but must be careful not to believe everything they read.

There was no obvious way to explain our long affinity with Charles Wood and my brother Geoffrey. Their wives Valerie and Mary were at Colston's Girls School in Bristol in the '40s with Thelma. The motto was 'Go and do thou likewise,' which they took to heart, Val and Thelma by marrying playwrights, Mary by becoming my sister-in-law. We're still good friends and relations.

Nick Hern looked into these pages long before there was any thought of making them public. He encouraged me to think they would interest others and has kept rekindling the fire when it was nearly out. So any blame is partly his.

July 2000

1968

May

The garden burgeoned like a floral mile, roses and lupins, sage and peonies and weeds choking the beds between. I borrowed a mower and cut the grass. The house was at first depressing, hardly worth the cheque I'd written the previous week for Eleven Thousand One Hundred and Twenty Two Pounds Only, completing the total of £12,250. It's redbrick with a pitch roof and bay windows, circa 1890, the sort one associates with H.G. Wells or the one Thomas Hardy built himself when he'd made some money. Badly thought out and so deep that the rooms on the ground floor are pitch dark where they meet halfway back. They don't build them like that any more. But it's big and solid and there are large gardens front and back, a playground for our two daughters and son after the cramped yard in Bristol.

Barbara brought them up by train. Odd how you could sometimes kill them after a week of no-one else – say, half-term or in a Manhattan hotel room – but, parted from them for a day, you're usually glad to see them again. They stood on the platform so shiny and gay and their faces were such pictures of happiness to see us!

[While work was done on the awkward house, making the rear room into a spacious kitchen and adding a bathroom to our bedroom floor, we stayed on in Bristol, not making the move until August. During these months, I talked to several people about the film of *Joe Egg*, met Robert Shaw in the Ritz and at Shepperton where Harold Pinter laughed forcefully at rushes of *The Birthday Party*.

I entertained Albert Finney and William Friedkin (*The French Connection*) in Bristol and lunched in Soho with executives from Columbia pictures and Sidney Lumet (*Twelve Angry Men*, *Network*) who talked mostly of oysters and wondered why in *Hadrian the Seventh* a Protestant craved to be Pope. A Jew he said he could understand. 'It's a good job, near the mountains for the wife and kids, a big town house. But for a goy?' For several very different reasons, nothing came of any of this.]

July

The weeks fly and I am a day off forty-one. Last night my latest play was the opening drama of Yorkshire Television. As I feared, it came over as an anthology of domestic trivia. I'd written it to order last year to fill a slot in a series under the umbrella heading *The Sex War*. Any such war finished for me in a truce some years ago and now there's only a long peace relieved by daily skirmishes. Due to my stage success, this was now seen as a creditable catch for the producer, so it went out with undeserved fuss and flourish.

The press was the best I've had for a TV play, far more highly praised than the BBC's expensive futuristic satire, shown at the same hour. The week's good reviews ended with young Stoppard in *The Observer*: 'Though nothing much "happens" in his plays, I can't think of many things more dramatic than the thought of ten million people sitting safe around their sets and discovering that someone has got them right between the eyes.'

Who could resist such a honeyed tongue?

August

Took passports to Petty France where I found Joe Melia ahead of me in the queue, off to Spain to appear in a film. We hadn't met since he'd refused to go to New York with the rest of the *Joe Egg* cast. A slight smell lingers around this episode but Joe the radical had certainly not been keen to meet all the Fascists he expected in that right-wing city.

'Is it all for Spain in this queue?' I asked the waiting people, 'all Fascists here?'

We afterwards walked and drank beer, and he insisted again that he'd never maligned Albert Finney in public and had indeed killed all press implication that he'd been dropped from the cast for Broadway.

'And the fact is, if I'd gone with it instead, you'd never have had your sell-out run and couldn't have bought a house in Blackheath. So mine's another pint, cheers!'

Mum and friend Jean came to stay, en route from a cut-price holiday in Cattolica, loaded with nasty toys for the children which broke almost at once. Dan cried 'I don't want this!' and Catherine pulled the voice from the belly of her crying doll. For herself Mum had bought dainty shoes, trinkets and a toy grand piano that played a Neapolitan song when the lid was lifted. Coming home in the car from the coach station, they seemed cheerful. Mum blew smoke in our faces at seven a.m., but we'd expected that and held our breath. As the days passed, her self-pity became uncontrollable. How can I condemn her when we're so alike? Life's not easy, even for us, the privileged, and those with our temperament must get on the winning side or we'll waste time lamenting our lot. Luckily I can use that feeling for my work, writing it out. Poor Mum just becomes a burden, a little girl who hasn't had her fair share of dolly mixtures.

September

Neither Thelma nor I much wanted to leave the kids in this house of mounting female excitement but our chance had come for a week on our own, the first ever. Louise cried as we drove off; the others waved happily. When they pointed this out to her, they told us later, she said, 'But they're too young to understand that Mummy and Daddy are going for a long time.'

A week for them can look like forever.

At Hanover we came down out of the clouds to follow flight corridors across East Germany to the isolated city of Berlin. As at no other airport I know, landings are made right into the urban centre. Buildings rise all around as you wait for touch-down. Sheep crop the grass, inured to the roaring engines. At passport control, an official tipped the wink to a photographer who started taking our pictures. Another first. No-one in New York gave us the celebrity treatment. In fact, we were mostly ignored and the general view was that Blakemore and Nichols were pseudonyms for Finney, who had also written and directed the play he was starring in.

His snaps taken, the photographer helped us with our luggage to the barrier where, he told us, Mrs Beyer of Schiller Theater would soon be meeting us. Mrs Beyer turned out to be thin on top and with a luxuriant beard and an injured finger encased in plaster, an apt introduction to the man who was to be our host for the week, drama-turg Werner Beyer, eager, smiling, respectful but stubborn. Thelma baptised him Noddy in recognition of this tireless reassuring gesture.

At our hotel beside the Schlosspark-Theater, a sort of annexe of the Schiller, we were met by Boleslaw Barlog, the general intendant or Big Cheese of the whole outfit. More photos, capturing us before a poster advertising *Ein Tag im Sterben von Joe Egg*. With a plethora of bows and handshakes, Herr Barlog assured us of his best intentions and hoped to see us next day at the eleven o'clock rehearsal.

In due course, Noddy let us sit in his posh secondhand Citroen with the adjustable suspension. 'Can you feel it going up and down?' he asked as we sat in the car park waiting to move. Eventually he took us to see Kurfurstendamm ('only Berliners must call it Ku'damm,' he warned us), Brandenburg Gate, Congress Hall, National Gallery, Philharmonie and Reichstag. In an hour, more impressive modern architecture than you'd find in the whole of London. But then, we realised, West Berlin is nearly all modern; the rest was destroyed. Mies van der Rohe's gallery was opened only three days before in time for the Festwochen, of which my little play is one of the events. The boulevards are as in the nineteenth century, designed – like those in Paris – by Baron Haussmann, broad and with generous promenades for pedestrians.

We walked up to the Wall, ugly and offensive, with barbed wire, in fact only one of several such walls that are hidden by the first. Noddy was unmoved by our sympathy that his city's so severed. He showed the nearby memorial to the Russian dead, guarded within the Western sector by Russian troops. Sometimes, he said, during anti-Soviet demos, these poor squaddies were far too easy a target for attack, so to avoid an international incident the British have built a camp alongside and stationed a detachment there to guard the Russians who are supposed to be our enemies.

The rehearsal was encouraging, though the worst errors weren't obvious at first: one, that the child's played by an adult actress and two, we couldn't see any affection in the way the parents handled her. The woman doing Joe has made a great effort imitating the physical distortions of a spastic child, a spectacle so repulsive that Herr Barlog has turned her wheelchair to face upstage. All this helps to create an atmosphere not so much homely as horrific. I thought of *UFA* and *The Cabinet of Dr Caligari*. The achievement of Mike's production was to show the mundane exchanges and routines that constitute life with such a daughter.

Useless to complain. They'd been in rehearsal for months and no criticism was expected or wanted. My visit was a public formality.

For Noddy and his wife Inke, the enemy's not Russia or the DDR but Axel Springer, reactionary press baron whose glass tower stands against the Wall as a symbolic up-you to the East. The uncles and oldies on all sides are the villains, if they're old in spirit. Werner had refused the application of some students to hire the theatre for a birthday party for one of their professors who's a spokesman for Nazi views.

We walked by the waters of the Wannsee and he pointed out Goering's villa.

'These people are not important. They can live quietly with their dogs and keep their country houses. But they shan't be heard. I told these students we could hurt their professor if we wanted but we don't want. They said How you could? And I said we could print in a programme for a Jewish play what this man said in 1933. Then they went to see Mister Barlog and of course he too throw them out.'

It seemed Barlog succeeded to his post because, when jobs came to be allotted after the war, he was the only eligible applicant who hadn't been a Nazi.

In Werner's lovely car, we floated to Charlottenburg Schloss, a cool baroque palace with formal ornamental gardens behind and lawns which no-one ever trampled. I suggested to Inke that it must have been one of the few old buildings left in Berlin.

'Oh, this is a reconstruction, built about 1948,' she told me, 'the original was gutted by fire-bombs.'

A jet airliner rose suddenly into the sky behind the classical marble statuary, carved in the last twenty years. The tearing rasp of its engines savaged the serenity of the park.

'Isn't that beautiful!' said Inke, meaning the aircraft. It wasn't the first or last example of a Berliner's gratitude for their lifeline.

I was shown first to the local press and TV film units and shared an interview with another visitor, the author of *Catch 22*, Joseph Heller who, despite his name, had no German either. I was somewhat awed by him but he was easy company, though not much better than I at keeping the talk rolling. The reporters were shy, Barlog explained, of asking questions and betraying the limits of their English.

[9]

Heller's only play was the other production on offer for the Festwochen, staged in the Schiller's main house. *We Bombed in New Haven* had become *Wir bombardieren Regensburg*. Behind us at the preview sat a young actor Max Unterzaucher, who pissed on it mercilessly. In the row in front sat Heller, muttering explanations over his shoulder to help us follow the action. We felt as Berliners must, trying to keep peace between two extremes. Max played the eponymous Kaspar in Peter Handke's monodrama in a club theatre on Ku'damm. It wasn't so much about the famous wolf-boy as the power of words to define the limits of our minds. Max and his wife and the producers of that event came for drinks at the Beyers'. All the things we'd hoped of New York were, to our surprise, happening here: intelligent people, decent company, generous entertainment and a respectful interest in us. Of course, they hadn't yet seen my play.

On Sunday morning at eleven I was called downstairs to the theatre where a full invited house was already watching the first act. During the social comedy of the second, which seemed to me to be getting its proper laughs, Barlog turned and put his face close to mine, his vile breath flooding my nostrils as he whispered:

'Next time, you write a comedy.'

Werner worked himself into a state about whether I should wear what-he-called 'a dinner chucket' to the mayoral opening of the festival that evening, at which I was to be the honoured guest. Perhaps, he thought, wearing a mere lounge suit would be construed as insolence. I said alright, it would have to be as I hadn't brought a dinner chucket.

'No,' Inke told her husband, 'as honoured guest and author of the play at Schlosspark he must make a scandal.'

'No, not that either,' I said. 'If they won't let us in. we come away without drawing attention. Not really very likely they will though, is it?'

'Ah, these occasions are absurd, a subject for farce,' said Werner, nodding and jumping from foot to foot.

'But why are you, a Communist, a radical, so bothered about wearing the right clothes for a mayoral beanfeast?'

'We must know our enemy,' and he tapped the side of his nose with the plaster finger.

He measured himself against me. 'I am about the same size but shorter in the arms and wider in the bellows. I shall go to the wardrobe of Schiller Theater and find a right-size dinner-chucket. A shirt, a tie and cummerbund. You say cummerbund?'

'Well, not often.'

But after a stroll with Inke to watch the dancing and ice-skating at Europa Centre, we came home to find he'd changed his strategy.

'If they don't let you in, I announce that the honoured author-guest is standing outside because of bourgeois follies.'

'So I'll go in my lounge suit?'

Evidently no spare chuckets in the Schiller's wardrobe.

The reception was at the Philharmonie. Werner found a place in the car park and was about to kill the engine when he cried 'No, wait! This is for the doctor only' and reversed to another. I stepped off in the dark across the lawn towards the main entrance.

'No, wait!' he called again, then, 'Ah, you are English so yes, you walk on the grass. Very well so shall I and we shall say it is the English way.'

The glass doors leading into the foyers were firmly closed against us. Werner pushed them all without any luck, not for a moment letting the smile die on his face. Some guests who were leaving early opened the door and we slipped in unnoticed.

'This was lucky,' he admitted and led us towards a gathering of several hundred people at the far end. By no means all were in dinner chuckets so a scandal was averted. After about ten minutes, we found some glasses on a table and busied ourselves with them like extras in a film left to improvise our own business.

'This might be a party for the workers of TWA,' Werner said.

'You don't know anyone?'

'No-one. That's the mayor over there but he doesn't know me.'

He did finally meet an elderly critic. Everyone in authority in the city was elderly, if not old. Through Werner, he warned us that my play would offend many people, then saw someone and made his escape. We were alone again. We helped ourselves to more drinks from a passing tray.

'Excuse me, sir,' said a voice behind me. I turned as a camera was raised towards me. By now almost used to this, I assumed a photogenic smile. 'Would you mind standing out of the way while I photograph Mister Bernstein?'

The maestro of the New York Phil, the *real* guest of honour, moved forward to meet the mayor, arms outstretched, cape flowing, a pint-sized Dracula.

[The first of several Bernstein semi-encounters over the next few decades till we finally did meet him in 1990 shortly before his death.]

It was easier getting out than in.

At the restaurant where they took us to eat, we saw, at a distant table, Heller dining with some of his actors. We felt we should say hullo.

'Hey, however d'you find me?' he said, assuming this was the end of a long search for us.

'How did it go?' asked Thelma.

'They seemed to like the actors but when I went on they booed me. I thought the show was fine and wanted to ask what the hell was the matter with it but I don't have any German.'

The next day, Monday, our last in the city, began with shopping and finished with the opening of my play. Max, the actor who played Kaspar in Handke's play, is Austrian, a foreigner, so can go into East Berlin. Werner and Inke, being Berliners, can't. First we bought flowers for the actresses then Max drove us in his battered Deux Chevaux to Checkpoint Charlie, a location familiar from Cold War films.

Max told the glowering borderguards that the newspaper I carried had been bought that morning to read a notice of Heller's play and also carried a photo from mine. The soldier pored over the print as if over a bit of hard-core porn and finally tore out the actors' picture and gave it to me. Thelma and I, unaccustomed to these rituals, found ourselves acting truculent, quarrelling with each other and producing all the wrong things. The torn piece of newsprint kept coming out, to Max's annoyance. We declared and counted out our currency, made lists of our passport numbers, home addresses, professions, Christ knows what, for all of which no pens were provided. Twenty yards from the US sector, the place was as tatty as wartime England, all cream paint and handwritten signs, prefab huts and ill-fitting uniforms. At another window we changed the obligatory five marks into the currency of the DDR. No books are allowed in but Thelma had brought along for light reading, in her smart Bergdorf-Goodman-5th-Avenue handbag, a paperback of Edmund Wilson's *To the Finland Station*. This brought no approving smile to the likenesses of Marx and Lenin staring from the walls. The woman flipped through and handed it back. Outside, another soldier went over the car, examining every bag and sweet-paper, poking about under the seats and scrutinising the underside with a mirror on a stick.

Quieter streets, hardly any cars and the few pedestrians staring curiously at us as we drove past the drab buildings. Max parked in Unter den Linden, far more easily than on Ku'damm. Shop-windows were full of porcelain for visitors to buy with their marks. The traditional stuff was pretty but anything modern was in a style not far from Woolworth's. Max was as depressed as we were by the absence of a modern manner. At the end, a confluence of empty boulevards became a group of public buildings that fronted a great square which Max seemed to be telling us was used for parrots. Well, after all, there was a train-station called Zoo in West Berlin so perhaps . . .

'You know – soldiers, bands and rockets.'

It was their Red Square, of course, used for shows of military strength, May Day parades.

He showed us The Berliner Ensemble, on Museum Island, explaining that the Deutsches Theater is now the one that counts. Brecht's is as much of a joke here as the Schiller is in the other half, both establishment symbols, like almost everything else in this city, like the city itself, which has no real power even as a capital. All real authority has passed to Bonn, Munich, Frankfurt and Stuttgart.

'It's hard to make contact with the people here. So much fear on both sides.'

Time was getting on and it began to rain. We walked back and found the Deux Chevaux being examined by two young men.

'They don't see many French cars,' Max said and started a conversation with the strangers who, without explaining, got into the back seat and sat beside Thelma. Some children came up and asked for chocolate, cigarettes and gum, as we had of GI's in wartime England. Max drove about the streets, talking to the young men in German so that I grasped only a few proper names – Tito, Cernik, Dubcek. He finally dropped them in a side-street where they shook hands sadly and went off.

'Interesting,' Max said. 'They're students. They don't agree with the regime, especially what happened in Prague. They wanted us to know.'

At the cream-coloured prefabs at Checkpoint Charlie, my newspaper photo was again scrutinised by the shy young soldiers. One examined my passport, staring at me and my mug-shot till I thought I should burst into inappropriate laughter. Was this the idea? Within minutes we were in the artificial bustle of Ku'damm.

[The play's opening went well. Laughter until the entrance of the child, then a respectful silence. At the end, strong applause and some cheers as the actors lined up. Berlin still held to a practice long abandoned in England, that the author should appear on first nights to share the credit. My orders were to get backstage in time for the fifth or so curtain. I was there in the wings but miscounted and Mister Barlog had to grab my jacket and pull me back when I was halfway on. He finally let me walk forward into the lights. There was a pause as they tried to decide who this myopic stranger could be, then a chorus of boos. So my play was as bad as Heller's? Like him, I lacked the German to ask who the hell they thought had won the war for Chrissake. The catcall was soon countermanded by stronger applause but not soon enough for me.

It was later explained, by Max I think, that this was all part of a protest movement. All English-language plays were catcalled on principle to promote the production of homegrown drama. The endemic secrecy of the place prevented anyone from warning us.]

Next morning some last-minute shopping for the children. No toy soldiers, Action Men, guardsmen, rockets or guns allowed. The military urge is discouraged and about time too, though playing with toy soldiers does not a warrior make. I did as a kid and was a pacifist at eighteen, as soon as the war ended. We were late at Werner's place and he was hopping from foot to foot. Over lunch, he gave us his translations of the first reviews, all good.

'Now we just go to Schiller Theater where Mr Bessing will want to say goodbye.'

'Will there be time before our plane leaves?'

We found Mr Bessing in the canteen. He was as unknown to us as we to him but as Werner's immediate boss had to be sure our minder was doing his job. He now drove to Tempelhof at high speed for a departure time I read as 3.40. He was taking things even more hectically than usual and we had to run to keep up as he arrived at check-out, where the girl telephoned and said they'd hold the plane.

'Again we are lucky,' he said, 'but it is close.'

'Close? Three-forty?'

'Three o'clock. It is about to leave.'

'No, look, in your own writing.'

'That's not four, it's aitch for hundred. Fifteen hundred hours.'

He danced from foot to foot, waved the hand with the plaster finger, shouting best greetings as we juggled with passports and scampered across the airstrip with our hand baggage. The doors were closed behind us. Minutes later we looked down on what Günter Grass calls 'the city closest to the realities of the age'.

Werner had thrust an envelope into my hand before we left his flat. Two shots of me and Heller talking and one of our arrival a week ago: Thelma and I trying to live up to expectations and Werner behind us, poised springheeled as though about to take off, exultant to have bagged us. On the envelope he'd written: 'to use whenever they doubt their Berlin adventure could have been reality'.

[During the next two months, I revised the first draft of the new stage play for Olivier and Tynan, based on the old television script *The End Beds* that had been rejected by every producer in the land, now retitled *The National Health*. Our new friends among the neighbours at Blackheath include John Grigg, who had disclaimed his Lord Altrincham handle to run for Parliament, and Michael Frayn, whose funny pieces we'd long enjoyed.]

I told Michael I'd been asked to appear on *Any Questions?* and wondered whether he had.

'Oh, don't tell that story,' said Gill his wife, covering face with hands, almost as embarrassed as himself.

'Well,' he began at once, 'they asked me, yes, and I said alright, just once, no more, I'm not going on every week, understand that. I think they must have because they've never asked me since. We were all eating and drinking in this pub in Devizes or somewhere – Boothby, Marghanita Laski – having a pretty good time by and large, when the producer came and told us first that President Kennedy had been shot at, not yet that he was dead. It sobered us a bit and we all turned to discussing him. The second bulletin said he'd been killed and of course we were all very shocked. We really were. But, you know, not enough to stop us eating and drinking. That wouldn't have helped anyone. We decided we shouldn't go on air and talk about the morality of mini-skirts or whatever it was and Boothby was delegated to phone the Controller, who said all scheduled broadcasts were being cancelled anyway, so we just went in front of the audience and made short speeches of regret.'

'You were awful,' Gill said, raising her face for a moment.

'I was terrible. I managed to say we'd all wanted Adlai Stevenson but were very sorry just the same . . . Oh God! . . . But Boothby was terribly moving. He broke down when it came to his turn. He said it wasn't just the death of a fine statesman and charismatic leader but – for him – the death of a friend. And we were all horrified. I mean, we'd been drinking and discussing Kennedy as a public figure and all the time Bob knew him *as a friend*. Tears were pouring down his cheeks. I went up as soon as we'd done and told him how sorry I was and it turned out they'd been once together on a TV show in America! Christ, what a bloody cheek!'

Life's changed a good deal for us recently. In the spring of last year we had to borrow £500 from Peggy and £250 from Charles Wood. This week I've turned down three film offers and heard that my share of the US tour of *Egg* is $2,000 a week. My new play's gone off to Tynan, who was eager to read it. But when I urged Peggy to send him *Egg*, she said he was far too busy. Charles, who was in favour for a few years, is out again. The military craze is over, John Lennon's given up wearing nineteenth-century uniforms and the Yanks have dropped Swinging London, in which by some strange process Charles got himself included. Our new accountant assesses our annual income as £24,000. I also employ a solicitor to look after the children's trust, lawyers to argue my film contracts, a mother's help, part-time gardener, daily woman, window-cleaner and team of builders.

Uncle Bert and Aunt Hattie came for Sunday dinner. Heather, our new help, drove me through the Blackwall Tunnel to Stratford-atte-Bowe to fetch them. We were minutes late arriving and they had coffee ready on a tray.

'We'd given you up for lost,' she snapped, 'I thought our reply hadn't reached you because Bert hadn't put Blackheath on it.'

In the car, she told me she'd only been through the tunnel once when she was a girl, on an outing to Margate and on that occasion she'd been sick. We crossed fingers and the charm worked.

'Look at the flats, Harriet,' Bert kept saying. They couldn't leave the subject of blocks of flats going up everywhere. Are they contemplating having to move from the jerry-built house they've lived in for eighty years? Perhaps the council has threatened eviction. Once at our house, they oo-er'ed and laughed at the sights. Eighty-seven-years-old Hattie climbed to the top to see everything. The number of bathrooms shocked her. At home, they only have an outside lav and hip-bath in front of the open fire. She's lived her long life in a state of nervous alarm yet survives all her brothers and sisters – my father Dick, Bea, Robb, Florrie and others I never knew. Only Bert remains.

Dinner at the Griggs; other guests the Sieffs (directors of M&S) and the Roses, international journalists. Sieff had seen *Manon* at The Garden last night and thought it dreary, the music nothing like as good as Puccini and even *he* never wrote a tune as good as 'Tea For Two'.

The table was candelit.

'Hullo!' said Sieff, 'has the electricity failed?'

Mrs Rose is an ex-actress now working in a rough school in Paddington. She looked too young to have given up the stage in 1942. She was in fact fifty-one at midnight, when we all drank her health.

I talked to her of India, saying I was perhaps lucky to have been there during the worst of post-war austerity at home. She said she'd liked that, it simplified life, eliminated all the many choices you must make these days.

'I used to just put down my ration book and say 'Give me what I'm due'. I liked the egalitarian aspect. You weren't nearly so aware of privilege. Britain's gone back in that way, rather than forward. Perhaps I'm basically a Puritan.'

I responded warmly to all this. Coming home from the East in '48, I never found austerity a trial. It wasn't abundance we craved but to be let do the work we'd chosen, without much thought of personal ambition. Certainly 'success' in the modern sense had little to do with it.

As Thelma and I undressed later, I passed this on.

'Yes, Patsy went on about being a Puritan too. It's all very well for them. Mrs Rose had on one of the world's most expensive perfumes.

Easy for Patsy too, dealing with shopgirls, when most people know she's really Lady Altrincham and she's got such a posh voice. I wonder what she'd think of the simple life if she had my voice to do it with. And Mrs Rose's dress didn't come from M&S and when her husband's finished his report on race relations, they're off for a working holiday in Indonesia. If that's the simple life, I'm a Puritan too.'

She went on to say how proud she was of me.

'What for?'

'Being so unabashed.'

'What about?'

'The way you followed the women out after the meal.'

'Followed them out?'

'It was obvious the men were staying behind for smokes and dirty stories so we went to sit in the living-room and when I turned round you were following us, with all these bewildered cigar-smoking men after you.'

'Christ, yes, of course. Grigg asked me if I wanted a pee after I'd refused a cigar. I've never been to a dinner where that happened. I should have known from novels.'

'Hullo, dear, Peggy here. Tynan's just rung. Likes the play very much and thinks it fuller and richer than *Joe Egg*. He's passed it to Sir Laurence, who of course is the laziest bastard in the world when it comes to reading *anything* so let's hope he gets round to it before Christmas.'

Relieved and at the same time embarrassed to think of this faulty play, of which I am so sick, being staged with all the attendant fuss at the National Theatre. I must next write an attractive comedy about People Like Us and resist all ghoulishness.

Walking to Charing Cross down Lower Regent Street, after shopping for clothes, we were nearly knocked down by a nasty little scarlet sports car coming from Panton Street and flashing its lights to tell us to jump back out of its way. Having avoided injury, as it passed I thumped the bodywork with the cardboard carrier containing my new coat. The driver stopped and jumped out, a small bald man with large aggressive glasses.

'D'you know there's such a thing in this country as a law of property?' he bawled.

'Also one against killing people.'

'I've been driving for forty years and never ever knocked anyone down, you silly cunt!'

'Then you've met with some fast-moving pedestrians.'

He was already halfway back to his car, which was now blocking the street. He charged off in his puerile vehicle, boiling with anger, honking and flashing lights at every crossing, the epitome of the man who sees himself as a safe driver.

Charles and Val Wood came with their children Katrina and John on Christmas Eve and we all went to a matinée of Sean Kenny's spectacular *Gulliver's Travels*. Kenny was near us on the aisle, making notes for future improvements. Catherine, who had as usual talked all through the show, now fell forward, cried and shouted, 'I want to go home!' I wish I'd been able to see the note Kenny made at this point.

Charles got down to serious boozing in the evening. It snowed in time to sprinkle the garden. From time to time we watched the Apollo 8's orbit of the moon. Cameras were trained on the earth and the astronauts told us how it looked.

'Time for supper, everyone,' said Val, coming from the kitchen.

'That's the earth we're watching!' Charles told her. 'I want to keep my eyes on it in case it blows up.'

'If it does,' she said, 'I shall watch it on the late news.'

Blakemore rang. Tynan does like the play but Sir Larynx Delivery thinks it only so-so and has no strong feelings either way. This somewhat dampened our festive spirits, though not too much, as *Joe Egg* has done the trick for me. Though I'd like another success, I'm not as hungry as I was. Charles's *H, or Monologues at Front of Burning Cities* is in rehearsal at the Old Vic. His optimism's tempered by four failures, at least with the public.

Boxing Night had us wondering why their young actor friend who'd come for drinks was such a success with women and where we go wrong. Val told of this bloke's enviable promiscuity and the way (on location in Turkey for the shooting of Charles's script of *The Charge of the Light Brigade*) he'd come down every morning and kissed the hand of whichever girl he'd slept with the night before. Thelma said I might do better if I hadn't such bad wind and Val mentioned Charles's habit of cleaning out his ears so that she can hear the wax move. Also they both agreed that our slippers weren't very alluring.

Thel and I sat at home on New Year's Eve while Heather, our mother's help, joined the gaiety in Trafalgar Square.

'Everyone was kissing everyone,' she told us next day in her native Bristol accent. 'It was smashing. I was kissed by hundreds of people. One little Pakistani kept coming back for more. I said, "Here, just a minute, you've had more than one already".'

She talks of kissing as though it were giving each other sweets and I'm none too sure she knows if there's anything to follow. She seems very innocent for twenty-five.

We were saying how much more was made of New Year in Bristol when suddenly a great discord filled the air and we realised the Thames was alive with horns and hooters. We went into the garden and the windows of flats and houses were open all around, our neighbours shouting good wishes. The noise didn't die away for half an hour.

1969

January

Working on my new play one morning, I saw a caterer's van deliver boxes and furniture to the Griggs'. The mother's-help grapevine reported a party for twenty people. That evening police cars and motorbike outriders blocked the street to escort Mrs Gandhi, here for The Commonwealth Prime Ministers' Conference.

'She usually comes to dinner while she's here,' Patsy told Thelma, 'but I'd no idea they were going to put on such an embarrassing show. And that's all it was, because nobody checked those enormous back gardens. The obvious route if anyone meant business.'

Clearing up the minibus today, I was accosted by a man of about sixty, dirty cloth cap, red nose, watery eyes behind NHS glasses, clear strong voice with an accent like my father's.

'You a landlord, guvnor? Own a house? Tell you why, you can give me a tip. I'm round the corner, one of those old houses, damp on the walls, shocking. I'm starving. I've had no dinner. But the owner's a nice coloured fellow, very decent man. Well, they're pulling them down. Condemned. They said, "You'll have to get out". I said, "I paid my rent for furnished accommodation, you'll have to find me somewhere else. I'm entitled." I went to the police, three stripes up, he said, "You'll have to go, mate." I said, "Sergeant? I was a sergeant before you was out of nappies – Royal Artillery – eff right, eff right, pick 'em up there, form fours, dressing by the right." I said, "The Law? Don't talk to me, you don't know the law." I walked out. Now the council says I'll have to go, the rent tribunal says I can stay. So who do you believe? Who *can* you believe? This other fellow in our place, they said, "We'll put you down The Centre" and like a fool he went. Workhouse style, down Peckham. He should have let his wife and kids go in The Centre but stayed where he was . . . This lot on the top floor used to go in the landlord's place at night and thieve his stuff. And suspicion fell on me because I'm a rough-looking man. But I lead a quiet life, breed canaries. How I met the landlord, I saw him painting his windows. He said, "You've been watching me a long time." I said, "Yes, I have and you're letting that paint dribble down the pane. Tell you what," I said, "You go inside, put a kiddle on, I got some tea in my pocket." When he come back, I'd done three. I done the whole place for him. His mates come in and said, "You had the builders?" He said, "Only a rough-looking man." They said, "Well, he knows his job." They call me Blackie. Or Yankee. I been to America. Been everywhere. I know the coloured people well. Understand them. Here's the form they give me at the council.'

He handed me a housing application.

'Windy, see? Got the wind up. They could see I knew the law, my rights.'

I wonder in such cases whether I could be more useful and help him get his disputed rights. But all I did was give him a few bob, filched his monologue for future use and sent him on his way. Wrong. A writer shouldn't expect more than he gives.

Olivier liked *The National Health* more on his second reading. Doesn't care for the rude jokes and wants the best one cut out. Mike went to see him to discuss actors and designers.

'Close the door, Michael. I don't want the gentleman doing the garden to hear what we're saying. Much as I admire the negro races, I'm no great admirer of their histrionic abilities. This play has a number of coloured characters. D'you think the regular girls in the company should black up? Joan, for instance?'

Tynan says they have another play that's been with them some time and are trying to decide between that and mine. Mike tells me the other is a Pinter double-bill, one of which is *Landscape*, the radio play with two people sitting absolutely still for an hour. And it's with the RSC but Harold's sick of waiting and is using it to bully the NT. For this they'd drop mine, written for the company and using its full resources, for the snob appeal of the Pinter name.

Saw *H* the other night. Some of the acting's barely adequate, but the resources of cash and stage skill are terrific. Olivier was wandering about in his pinstripe suit and bank-manager spectacles, giving a little touch of Larry in the night. Charles didn't introduce me so I couldn't raise the matter of my play.

The Writers' Guild are giving me the merit scroll for that TV play *The Gorge*.

'The what?' I said to the man who rang to tell me.

'Merit Scroll.'

'Oh, good.'

We never know about awards till we win them.

Thelma's Uncle Frank is staying for a few days. Tall and gaunt, his voice high-pitched and very South Welsh. He joined up just before the second war started and wasn't released till '45. He served at Dunkirk, in the abortive invasion of West Africa and in India when the Japanese reached Burma. His stories are all told with a profusion of apologetic or naughty-boy gestures and with no trace of resentment.

'On the front at Calais there was this big restaurant where I was lying among the tables, sheltering, when a sergeant said to me "Get these airforce uniforms in the boat, we don't want Jerry to get them." When I got on the boat there were all these poor devils lying in the hold in a terrible state. I went round giving them water and sharing out a tin of fags they'd given us buckshee so as Jerry wouldn't get them either. I was the only medic and then only by accident. Anyway years later, after I'd been trained and become a proper nurse like and was walking through a ward one of the patients calls out to me, "You were at Dunkirk. You gave me a drink of water."

'They called me Professor. Well, no-one else would do the work.

'I'd only just got back from overseas when they started issuing me with tropical kit. I thought: not again surely? I said to this captain, "I've only just come back." He said, "I can't help that." We marched miles in our Blighty kit carrying our k.d. and when we fell out for a smoke, I said to an oppo of mine, "He's mad, that officer." And – ' hand on mouth, more furtive tone of voice – 'he was just behind me! Later he bought us all a pint. He said to me, "I know I'm mad but have this on me".'

You feel he was worth more than all the bullies who browbeat him.

Evening at Broadbents, the local salon, on Croom's Hill. Cecil Day Lewis, notorious leftie, as he described himself at one point, 'Sissle' to his wife Jill Balcon, and Bernard Levin, Claire Tomalin and the Frayns. Lewis seemed nervous at our 'youthful' shoving and pushing and Levin is as pompous as on the page. The literary high life, which once seemed enviable and unattainable, is dull and slightly sickening.

Thelma, worried at not having spoken a word to the Poet Laureate, told him, as we walked with him and his wife Jill Balcon a few steps down the road to their redbrick Georgian house, that we'd be going home in the bus. He appeared worried and said we should have to take at least two, changing at Deptford. Then she pointed out our parked Bedford Dormobile.

In the dressing-room after the opening of *H*, the John Mortimers were wild with praise, Tom Stoppard was noncommittal and Tynan was saying they should have cut more boldly. Olivier came in asking for Charlie-boy and introduced Anthony Havelock-Allan, great grandson of the play's soldier-hero, and his ex-wife, and leered in his Richard III manner, 'Is known by another name'. A.H-A, the film-director had no such scruples and named her as Valerie Profumo. We all tried not to gape but the wives failed and stood frankly staring with open mouths.

Again no-one introduced me to Olivier. The Woods look reluctant to hand over their big trophy until the last possible moment.

The morning reviews were generally hostile and, whatever the play's qualities, picked out only its faults. Charles appeared for breakfast saying, 'You must be happy this morning then.' They left for Bristol, saying it had been the least miserable of the six first nights he's gone through.

Dan, opening his comic one Saturday, exclaimed with joy: 'They've put Bill and Ben instead of Jesus!'

It was this kind of fun we had at the Magritte show at the Tate. Dan laughed a good deal at a man's nose sinking into the bowl of his pipe, lighted candles wriggling along the shore and bowler-hatted men with apples for faces. The children's approach was to find the deliberate mistakes, as in What's Wrong With This Picture?

'That apple's too big,' Louise said, and 'Tubas don't burn.'

Albee's *A Delicate Balance* at the RSC. It all seemed pretty remote and ethnically vague, though the audience, sedated with hotel dinners and pre-theatre Scotch, purred in recognition whenever someone, usually Dame Peggy Ashcroft, pulled off a bit of Good Theatre. It had an air of instant classic and a strong whiff of déjà vu. A pantheon of past playwrights peered over his shoulder.

While waiting for curtain-up, we heard a man and woman in the row behind.

He: I saw *H* at the National Theatre.

She: Oh, yes, how long did it run?

He: It's still on.

She: No, I mean a friend of mine left after three hours and the third act hadn't even started.

He: Oh, I enjoyed it.

She: Good.

He: I saw *Hamlet* with Nicol Williamson. He's good.

She: Oh, very.

He: In a neurotic sort of way. But then it's a neurotic part. A neurotic play, too. And Richardson gave it a neurotic production.

She: Is my zip done up?

He: Your slip?

She: Zip.

He: Yes.

She: Oh, good.

To the Dorchester to collect this scroll thing for *The Gorge*.

The prize-giving began with radio awards, and two unknowns (to me anyway) were named for some forgotten feature on the problems of blindness. The presenter said this would be received by Mr Martin Esslin on behalf of the producer and writer who couldn't come. Esslin promptly went to the dais, took the statuette, said thanks and returned to his party, when some of us noticed two elderly people negotiating a path between the tables. A confused spotman turned his light and followed them, a tall woman in an unfashionable evening gown leading a blind man. They crossed the open bit of floor while Esslin hurried up again and met them at the steps. On the platform they were about to announce the next category. Esslin then did his own mini-presentation, turned them about-face and started them on their long and bewildered journey back to their table. We all kept applauding as best we could, as it was evidently their big moment.

Frankie Howerd came lurching up our front path, as he does onstage, advancing on the audience. Olivier had asked him to play Barnet the ward orderly in *The National Health*.

'I'm sorry I wasn't home when you dropped in at my place,' he said over tea, 'only I was having a portrait sitting with Madame Vivienne.'

'She the one who still uses a hood over the camera?'

'Now you're being unkind.'

'No, really. I saw it in a film.'

'Well, of course, she doesn't like the look of everyone.'

My delicate task here was to dissuade him from playing it. He was obviously of that mind anyway, talking about his image and (a favourite word) 'following' and how they'd hate him in the part and what the coach-parties expected and how little money he'd make at the National. But he wanted to do a play and at least in this one he wouldn't be on all night, only popping in now and then. I praised him with all sincerity but agreed it would hardly be worth his while, wondering whether someone of his skill and brilliance would be the best thing for the play. He asked if I couldn't see my way to cleaning up the dialogue somewhat.

Even so, as he retreated to his chauffeur-driven Bentley, I wasn't sure he hadn't wanted to be persuaded.

We heard yesterday that Aunt Harriet ('Hats') had died on Friday after a heart attack and subsequent stroke. Bert's gone to live with Dora, my spinster cousin, now responsible for two old men – her father and uncle. I spoke to Bert by phone and he cried there and then, saying they'd been together for so long, she was eighty-seven, then pulled himself together and asked after our children.

Rang Mum in Bristol to say I'd drive her to the funeral. With the zeal of her death-loving generation she went through the rituals of bereavement. I doubt if there's anyone in the world she disliked more than Hats, yet here she was saying, 'Ah, poor Hattie, I am sorry.'

She and Geoff came up Wednesday evening, and I drove them and Thelma to Stratford, where my uncle and aunt had lived since child-hood, without electricity, hot water, inside toilet, bath, telephone or television. As we turned into Gurney Road, a white car shot from a kerb and blocked our way. The elderly-looking man inside was attempting a three-point turn, grinding gears and shooting back and forth several times without any appreciable difference in his position.

I blew my horn to make him pause and, passing, we recognised the flushed and incompetent driver as cousin Frank, who's only a few years older than me.

The mourners sat together in the tiny back parlour with its coal-fire and ancient trappings: Brother Bert, three surviving Motts from Ilford (Bert and cousins Dora and Frank), Frank's wife Betty and ourselves, nine altogether. Not one friend or acquaintance. When the undertakers came, there was some spirited argument between the Motts about who should go in which car. Geoff, Thelma and I were assigned to Frank but consoled ourselves that the cortège would keep him slow and it was only a short step to the cemetery. The hearse was first, then a black limousine with the other mourners, then Frank grinding gears behind. Two undertakers, silk toppers with crepe bands held in hands, walked in the road looking about as if to proclaim this death to the unknown neighbours. The street, debased in their lifetime, now contains a dog-meat factory and infants' school. Holes in the terraces made by bombing have been stopped with new flats. Turning into the graveyard, I thought that all Hattie's rides in Bentleys and Daimlers had been to funerals.

At the grave, a vicar who never met her droned through the obsequies. A sexton shuffled forward and sprinkled dry soil or sand over the hole he'd dug. All of it was carried away by a light breeze and none fell on the coffin.

There was hot soup and cold collation back at No. 3, made by Dora and Betty. Bert said it would be an easy job leaving the house, as he'd only have to give a week's notice. For sixty years and more he'd paid rent, probably buying the place many times over. He thinks it will now be condemned as it's so damp. Dora took Geoff into the tiny front room and asked him if he wanted any pieces. He said Mary had always admired the china figurines and she said brother Frank had already laid claim to those. And everything else of any worth, no doubt. There were things we'd have liked too but I wasn't joining that flock of vultures. It was Frank who'd come to Dad's funeral with an empty car expecting a terrific haul of the old man's gramophone records. Every time I moved in any direction, the chains of gas mantles lightly brushed my hair. Bert's life must now be better at Dora's. Only Harriet's fears and superstitions kept him from watching television, as he did incessantly when he stayed with us.

There was no more I could do to *The National Health* until I'd seen how an operating theatre works. Roy Meadow, the paediatrician, took me to various observation galleries at Guy's, looking down directly on to the tables. In a locker room we had first to take off all our clothes except socks and underwear, putting on instead light sleeveless shirts, trousers, caps and white Wellingtons. Roy scanned a list on the wall and asked which operations might interest me. Most frequent were prostatectomies and vaginal terminations.

'Abortions,' he explained. 'There used to be one or two a month but since The Act . . . look, four this afternoon!'

A young surgeon came from theatre.

'Murder Mile,' he said, not looking for a laugh. 'We're killing them all day.'

These lines and sentiments went to Barnet the orderly in *Health*, who was made to say 'All morning we save the old, all afternoon we kill the young.' Some of the visual details I noted that day went into the hospital soap-opera play-within-the-play.

We watched an abdominal operation being sewn up and an elaborate job by a dental surgeon on someone's gums. When a woman was wheeled in with shaved genitals and knees tied upwards and apart, I said I'd seen enough. In these conditions, the human form's unseductive but not without beauty. The theatre staff looked curiously sexy in their white outfits, the women's eyes peering shyly from over their muslin yashmaks, underwear outlined under their flimsy tunics. Constrained movement too; an avoidance of the tactile, no formal gestures indicating lack of sexual intent, like shaking hands. One began to see the advantage of less overt physical behaviour.

One of the prostatecomies was an old man's. The surgeon probed and prodded and clamped the skin aside as though opening a flower's white outer petals to reveal the violently red inside. A sister hung the swabs on a rack, to count when the time came to sew him up. That row of bloody rags was a visually exciting prop but no use to me as the op in my play is in the TV soap-opera and they're always anaemic in black and white, with solemn figures, eyes meeting over masks and all in a theatrical silence, whereas here – in *this* theatre – everyone chatted freely and laughed aloud.

Roy Meadow and wife came to dinner with the Frayns and Stoppards. A very pleasant evening. Tom's so charming. His wife Josie was strange, though, threatening to leave because of a cold that made her sniff. Michael and Tom hit it off at once and had to be prised apart.

Before Tom left, I asked him about working under Olivier.

'I look on him as a kind of cheery uncle. I don't take his opinion seriously. Only Tynan's.'

I walked them down the garden to the front gate. Tom looked back, checking that he'd done all that courtesy required.

'I do congratulate you on the house.'

Michael Blakemore, having been asked to meet Olivier fifteen minutes before I was due, arranged to see me fifteen minutes before *that*. All his life is like this – a farce of concealments and intricate deceptions. Having left him at Waterloo Bridge, I walked about for fifteen minutes before turning up at Aquinas Street where the offices of the National Theatre are crammed into government-issue prefabs among terraces of two-storey artisan housing. Olivier had outflanked Mike's intrigue by not arriving at all, leaving Ken to keep us happy. Ken gave me whisky and apologised for Larry, said to be at a wig-fitting. We all talked of the new theatre to be built to Denys Lasdun's design near the Festival Hall. Is it likely or just another mirage? The Queen Mother had already un-veiled several foundation-stones in various places. Ken was hopeful.

After half an hour and a good deal of Scotch, Ken lost patience and said it must be quite some wig. At which moment, a Rolls was man-oeuvred through the narrow opening and parked in the yard.

There was a flutter of myrmidons and the little man I'd seen at Charles's rehearsals bustled in, holding out his hand.

'I've never been more sorry in my life.'

For some minutes he alternated apology with disposing of the busi-ness accrued in his absence, mostly arrangements to bring a film pro-ducer from LA, requiring subtraction sums for the lost hours.

'I apologise abjectly for being late then attend to anything but your play!' he exclaimed, took off the pinstripe suit-jacket, sat at the table and drank some of the Scotch we'd left.

We went through the cast of twenty-two characters, matching them to the available actors. His opinions of his company were unimpressed, even brutal.

[29]

'No, he can't play Foster because he's not staying.' This was evidently news to Tynan. 'No. Boring man. Drinks too much and is always slapping me on the back and asking me to supper with his family. No.'

Discussing the negro contingent of nurses, chaplain, etc, Michael raised the name of Cy Grant [handsome actor and popular calypso singer of the time.] 'Cy Grant,' said Olivier, 'so large and strong! When Vivien and I were managing the St James's, now alas! vanished, we took a boat party for the whole numerous company, down the river. I, as befits the manager, held aloof, though seeming to join the fun and games. My lovely prop-men and carpenters, strong as oxen every man-jack, carried off the drunks on stretchers. Cy was seen disappearing in the direction of the Bishop's Palace of Lambeth. At a word from me, off went the boys and down went Grant in a great flurry of arms and legs . . . ' – here he used the swirling movements with snaky hands from the opening soliloquy of Richard III – ' . . . when suddenly from under this hefty scrimmage Grant's voice rang across the forecourt "FUCK Sir Laurence Oh–liv–ee–ay" – ' and this was with all the stops out and one hand flung across his forehead. Then the sudden diminuendo on – 'I never worked with him again but followed his career with in–ter–rest and was happy at his success.'

The advantage a famous actor has is the history he carries with him. I, now fairly far gone on subsidised whisky, saw not only a sixty-year-old man with toothbrush moustache, bank-manager glasses, suit and club tie, but Maxim de Winter confessing he hadn't loved Rebecca, Heathcliffe on the moor, Darcy, Henry V, Richard III, Hamlet, Archie Rice, Astrov, Titus Andronicus, Coriolanus, Antony, The Duke of Altair, the waiter in *Carrie*, etc., so I'd been watching him much of my life in the flesh or on film.

'Well, I don't know what else we have to discuss.' As he poured another glass, this seemed to be our exit-cue, but Tynan asked where I stood on euthanasia and this began a further hour's discussion. I put my own confused and watery arguments for allowing the helplessly defective to die, based on our own firstborn. Tynan argued the liberal case against this and Olivier got the best of both worlds by saying we shouldn't be so squeamish about life itself and in a few years we'd all be standing on each other's heads and then it would be too late for such sentiments, people who were no use should be helped out, then at once told us that when the doctors warned him his daughter may not survive, she had only a five-per-cent chance, he'd said, 'Save her! Save her!' I hope he didn't do this with quite the panache he used in telling us or the doctors' hands must have shaken with fear. 'You see? I wanted to save my child, though I knew she might not be whole.' His eyes were burning bright as he roared: 'I was a female tiger.'

As we walked away later, Michael pointed out that Tynan, for all his egalitarian posturing, has lived a life devoted to excelling and becoming élite, whereas Olivier exemplifies in his vigorous person and his willingness to face the crowd again and again, a reason for living. He's hugely enriched my own. Views differ, of course, and Francis Hewlett told me he went to see his *Othello* with a very intelligent black African, who rocked with laughter all through.

At the Griggs' met Arthur Koestler, a disagreeable little man with a pretty younger wife. He still speaks with a heavy Hungarian accent and, of course, carries the weight of that extraordinary life and life's work: the death sentence in Spain, the spells in prison, the disillusion with Communism, the political novels and popularising scientific histories. He and John talked public affairs and about an article they're writing on Gandhi. Patsy and John, remembering how last time I disturbed the after-dinner ritual, firmly let me know I was to remain at table when the ladies left. It was done, like everything they do, with tact and courtesy.

Koestler, celebrated ex-Lefty, told John, champion of race relations, that allowing the immigration of coloured people is a grave social error.

'Why d'you think that, Arthur?'

'I don't want them living next to me in Chester Square. They have different cultures. They'll be eating different food.'

[No mention in Diary of how, as we were in the hall and about to leave, he led me aside to tell a dirty joke. It was as though a saint had recited Eskimo Nell.]

The Stoppards live in a thatched Edwardian villa on an exclusive estate near the river at Cookham. It's like the first-scene setting for a pantomime, The Village Green, with a shallow and lifeless stream running through the garden, a croquet lawn, a magnolia, a boat moored beside a shed (also thatched) where Tom writes, and road-barriers to keep out the unwashed. Josie's pregnant, burnt the roast and slept much of the afternoon.

Catherine's a sexy child, more than either of the others. She likes lying on her back and giggling. Otherwise she's garrulous, bright and loud.

Louise goes in for tantrums and stormy exits. If not watched, she beats the others mercilessly. Eldest of the survivors, she has to cope with having a vegetable elder sister and being displaced by first Dan, then Cath. People like her tend to do better when they're older.

Dan's tall and broad with pink skin and blonde hair, a gruff voice and a fondness for rolling on the ground. He has a prompt imagination, frowning as soon as a story starts, seeing it clearly, already worrying over the outcome.

Heather, their nurse, is a boisterous twenty-six year old who shouts intimacies across the street and involves the neighbouring girls in her apparently crowded life. In fact, it's mostly sound and fury. The others get engaged and she's still on the shelf. Whenever a man gets fresh and makes advances, she says she doesn't indulge. We have to cool her down a good deal before we go out for an evening or she follows us into the garden shouting 'Enjoy yourselves!' and 'Don't do anything I wouldn't do!' When we set off for Hattie's funeral, she yelled 'Have a good time!'

I seem not to have mentioned Peter Medak before, a sleepy young Hungarian who'll be directing the *Joe Egg* film. David Deutsch, the noisy, ineffective man who produced *Catch Us If You Can*, the Dave Clark film that subsidised the writing of the play, will do that job again. After a year of prevarication, these two will make a film I'd hoped would attract the best people in the trade.

Dinner at the Deutsch's with the Medaks and the Carl Foremans. The louder David shouted, the quieter his wife Claire became.

Carl had just been down on the farm.

'How much did you lose?'

'Six pounds.'

'Great!' shouted David.

In weight, of course, and a few hundred pounds sterling into the bargain, for carrots and lemon juice. Farms nowadays starve you;

factories feed. And to think Foreman once had a reputation as a liberal, even a Communist, one of those blacklisted by the McCarthy hearings!

Medak's alright, though sluggish in mind and body. Got out of Hungary after the abortive revolt, running across a frozen lake with other refugees, not believing he'd reached Austria, running back again and then once more before finally realising he'd made his escape. That drama seems to have exhausted his capacity for action.

[This lethargy was deceptive. Peter had what energy was required to sustain a career. Behind the Magyar charm and 'Yes, doorlink' endearments, he was a sharp operator. I showed him 'my' Bristol, where the action was set, took him to tea with my mother, Grace in the script; toured the undistinguished houses that the teacher-hero could afford to buy and that should be the film location, showed him the usual tourist sights and visited Abigail in her mental hospital.]

Our daughter has declined a great deal since we last saw her nine months ago. Her legs are withering entirely with lack of use. You can almost circle them at the calf with thumb and middle finger. She cried a few times while Thelma nursed her. The other inmates sat in their invalid chairs or on seats around the walls, watching us or busy with their own repetitive gestures. One pretty child rhythmically struck the back of her head against the padded chair-back with a violence that could have been either suicidal or therapeutic. Glum-faced, the sister told us Abo wasn't so well.

'She's going down, I'm afraid.'

I can't say I was overjoyed but certainly felt some cold comfort from knowing she won't have to survive this much longer. Of course, one can't help being haunted by the thought that she feels and knows far more than she can tell. Why else cry so bitterly, sedated and anaesthetised as she is? Is her consciousness like her mother's during her birth? A point I failed to make in the film. This is my last chance to say what I have to on the subject of our poor daughter, whose misfortune has given us a certain fame and a safe future but who can't share either.

Peter and I walked in the grounds while Thelma sat nursing her daughter. Children in the furthest wing were penned behind wirenetting, like zebras in a zoo.

We left poor Abo, hoping as usual that we shouldn't see her alive again. Or I did. Could Thelma really wish such a thing?

On Friday morning I delivered the finished film-script to Peggy's office and Medak rang on Sunday to say he thought it was fine and didn't really want to change anything. The call came while Michael Frayn and I were walking on the heath with all my children. A relief to talk to a sane man after all these film-business hot-heads. It was worth coming to live here, if only to meet him and Gill. We get on really well with them and their daily round is as like ours as we gathered and hoped from his columns.

Uncle Bert came to stay for a week. His empty life can't have long to run surely? I seem to be advocating death for everyone, but of course in his case that's only a statement of fact. Since his violent time at the front in the Great War, when he was wounded in action, nothing much has happened. He's never even been abroad. His only holidays were with our family, at the end of which he always palmed me half-a-crown, as uncles should. No marriage, no career, no family life, no hobbies. A gaslit life relieved by a few flutters on the stock market.

During his week with us, he helped us read novels, plays and essays by inmates of HM Prisons from Scotland to Dartmoor, entrants for the Koestler Awards.

[This scheme was devised and begun by AK in 1962, after he'd served prison sentences in Seville, Vichy and as an alien in Pentonville. It was in recognition of the importance of relieving the tedium by offering chances for creative activity. It now covers 53 categories, from matchstick modelling to poetry. We dealt with fiction.]

Frayn and I were conned into this by John Grigg as part of his programme to encourage those born without silver spoons. I'd expected one or two smallish pieces to browse through at my leisure but John accosted me in the street, led me back to his house and handed me an immense parcel, asking if I could get through it in the coming week. No two ways about it, as that's when we were off to holiday in Portugal and taking this lot with me on the plane would have used up all my baggage allowance. Bert helped and between us we reduced the pile to three or four. The entries ranged from a preview of decimal coinage, all arithmetic calculations, to a four-volume vindication of the character of Richard Crouchback. We also ruled out a first-person day-in-the-life of a Persian cat and the story of a monster who turned out to be Davy Jones, fresh from his locker. The judgement was hasty and biased, though we tried to be fair. We leaned over backwards to enjoy *A Junk Triptych*, wincing our way through a scene in a phone booth where a junkie tries to ram a needle into his vein, fails and finally effects his fix with a broken matchstick. Michael even persevered for some time with 'Thoughts on being an octogenarian' but threw it angrily across the room when it transpired the first person subject wasn't eighty at all.

Spring

Lisbon on its great estuary glowed in the afternoon sun as we flew over. Not long after, we stepped from our pressurised cabin into the warmth of Faro airport. We were twice welcomed, by the Avis man and by Arnold Cawthrow, present tenant of Michael Medwin's villa but moving out next day to make way for our family. Short and stout, dark brown tan, camp voice and a recurrent gesture of seeming to bite the quicks of his fingernail with his front teeth.

'Follow my car,' he said, taking Heather and Lou, 'you can't miss it, the number's SPY 999 because I'm Big Chief I-Spy of the *Daily Mail*.'

Coping with a strange car, left-hand drive and a manual gear column, I could tell we were abroad by the bright sun, donkeys, black-dressed peasants, plants we see only in the vestibules of banks, the white cottages and boldly curious stares. More than all these, by the empty roads.

The kids were soon naked in the pool. This is a spec. development for English émigrés, each house different but all white stucco with elaborate chimneys made by a craftsman on the Faro road. Throughout our stay, a gang of men have chipped away at the road with tiny picks. Is this more sensible than our system where millions of unemployed are supported in idleness by those with jobs?

Along a track beyond the end of the long beach road there's a freshwater lagoon, resalted by every tide, and here the bathing's warm. The ocean's exciting, with a terrific undertow, but too cold for enjoyable bathing. Fishermen go out in strange kits of black mackintosh to catch cockles. Sometimes a herd of goats comes from inland and the goatherd looks for a bather, native or tourist, to carry him across the lagoon. His animals, black, white and brown, are the most beautiful of local sights. Towards Quartiera itself, on an outcrop of sandy cliffs, is a white fort guarded desultorily by coastguards or conscripts who patrol the beach with rifles. Taken by surprise, they stand up among the bushes, their women remaining on the ground.

On the roadside near Lagos are a number of pieces of carved marble, perhaps masonry from some demolished villa. Beside them, two disintegrating stagecoaches stand on the verge unattended, still not past restoration, their horsehair upholstery spilling from tears in the leather, ironwork rusty but glass screens intact. Great forts dominate all the towns and from the road out of Lagos you look back to see ramparts surrounding the old city, the sparkling harbour beyond. We got out to look more closely at a miniature fortress built out into the estuary, a drawbridge joining it to the quay and a number of eroded inscriptions on marble slabs over the pointed entrance. I could make out little more than its date in the seventeenth century. Dan loved this place and wasn't as upset as I was to discover its function. A folly? A toy castle built by some besotted king for a pet prince? Sea-defences? None of these, but Europe's earliest slave-market.

At Monchique, an old spa some way inland, a blare of loudspeaker music followed us everywhere, filling the town, its source hard to locate until we climbed high above to look down on the reccy where young men were playing football to this ceaseless din. Imagine retiring here to find peace and quiet in a mountain retreat and having to install double-glazing to keep out Herman's Hermits.

We'd been stared at like royalty in the car: walking the streets we were film-stars. Heather particularly, taller than any of their men, drew their astonished gaze and helpless titters. To be quite honest with you, as she would say, her skirts are short even in London. I'm always catching inadvertent glimpses of her knickers as she bends over to load the washing-machine. In the staid society of Algarve, she must have seemed a Martian. (Or Marchioness?)

The church is in what I now know to be the Manueline style: stone tendrils twisted like those plaited loaves baked for harvest festivals. Women gathered at the church-door muttered about the outrageous foreign senoras, so Thelma put on a head-scarf and we took Dan and Catherine to see the interior. Golden madonna, candlelit at the far end, old men kneeling on their handkerchiefs and, drowning their muttered prayers, Cliff Richard from the distant tannoy. No young people. The locals seem to be irreligious and anti-clerical.

Climbing the steep streets, we added two local girls to our party. They led us past the outlying houses to a lane through a forest of acacia, eucalyptus and cork. The last have curious shapes after their useful bark has been cut off in great sections, as if from a cheese. The girls led us through the porch of the ruined church, strewn with hay, and pushed open the great door into the nave. Chickens scattered and from some chapel or sacristy came the bleat of a donkey. When our eyes grew accustomed to the dark, we saw not only the donkey but two bullocks. The choir was a roost for poultry, the screen a crude trellis with handfuls of fodder stuck between the slats. Rabbits bred in a hutch beside the West Door. What remained of the roof was in a Moorish manner. We climbed the unreliable tower to gaze down on the town, dazzling in the afternoon sun.

Chief I-Spy came back after some days and told about the English he'd met in Albufeira, golfing people with RAF moustaches. He went to see some dancing at a fiesta, but it was 'disaster'.

'All they wanted to do, these young men, was ride in my car, pull up with a screech of brakes and get out in front of the most glamorous drinking-place, that's the BP garage, slamming all the doors. That's the big thing here, slamming car doors. By the time we reached the dancing it was finito.'

He favours words like 'disaster' and 'drama'.

'Oh, yes,' he'll say of the gas-oven, 'there were disasters last year too.'

'Goodbye, donkeys!' shouted Louise as we drove to Faro.

'Goodbye, witches!' their name for the black-dressed peasants.

'Goodbye, white houses,' from Thelma.

'Goodbye, water-wheels,' called Cath.

'Goodbye, cars,' from Dan.

'We've got cars in England,' Louise snarled at him.

'Alright, goodbye, horses and carts!'

'And goodbye, donkeys!'

'We've *had* donkeys!'

At Heathrow we waited half-an-hour for a bus to take us to our parked car. On the M4, a burnt-out lorry caused a tail-back a mile long, more cars joining the end every minute. Newspaper placards proclaimed 'The Agony of Liz Taylor' and 'Free Pub Crawl!' We were home.

The opening of the Koestler Award Exhibition. Frayn had gone to Israel and the Griggs to Spain to attend a brother who was ill, leaving us to deal with this alone. At the lunch after the announcements, a strange group met in John's club in Mayfair. Lord Stonham, the Home Secretary, William Douglas-Home who made a facetious speech about all his family having been inside, Iris Murdoch, her husband John Bailey and Julian Trevelyan. I sat by him and saw at once that stroke had impaired his speech. At first it was no easy task understanding him but he was so interesting and intelligent that it finally didn't matter. I had a pee with Bailey and Thelma said that Iris, in the Ladies', tried on all the hats, giggling like a schoolgirl on open day.

Louise came into the bathroom after a hot day in the garden, took a daisy from between her toes and flushed it down the lavatory.
    'There,' she said, 'now Angela's dad will see that.'
    'Angela's dad. Why?'
    'He goes down the sewers.'
    'Angela Dunn?'
    'No. Angela Kirkham, who d'you think?'
    'Why should I know? Why shouldn't Angela Dunn's dad go down the sewers?'
    'Because he's got enough to do up here, looking after her!'

Yesterday, July 16th, will go down in history, they tell us. Another blazing day, the hottest for a year, 86 Fahrenheit. After breakfast, Thelma left to catch the Bristol train. Abigail nearly died last week and her ward sister asked Thelma to visit. There'd been no detectable pulse for some time and we hourly expected to hear of her death. Uncle Frank, the male nurse, was sent to see her and reported her to be pathetically wasted. We all hoped they wouldn't strive too officiously to keep her alive.
    I drove to Guy's, where Michael Blakemore was joining me for his first glimpse of the operating theatres. His labyrinthine adulteries put him out of touch for some days, while I was eager to work.
    After garbing in white, we watched a young girl undergoing an operation on her heart. On the anaesthetist's side of the protective

screen, her sweet face with the unspoilt child's hair, so healthy after the pallid adult's faces; on the other side, a shambles of blood and puckered flesh. The anaesthetist gently laid his hand on her brow, which I thought a lovely and reassuring gesture, then realised he was noting the pulse in her temple.

In the pub later, a TV screen showed Apollo nearing lift-off. The drinkers left their pints and papers to watch. The launch went as smoothly as expected, and we now wait with undisguised patience for the lunar landing.

I drove back through the chaotic London streets while astronauts zoomed through space at inconceivable speeds.

Thelma had been in Abigail's ward when blast-off was due. Sister suddenly said: 'It's on telly and I've forgot to put it on.'

The nurses started a chorus: 'We've forgot to put it on.'

One of the inmates called, 'What's that, Sister?'

'Those men are going to the moon and I forgot.'

'Oh, my God, and you forgot!'

When the picture at last came through, they lay watching it with their partial minds and Thelma nursed her dying daughter.

'What's the date?' she asked this morning, having already forgotten yesterday which will, according to the Pope and Nixon, be remembered as long as there are men on earth to do so.

We watched the landing last night, or rather heard that gabble that meant they were there. There followed an anthology of songs and poems about the moon. In fact, they weren't about the moon at all but the effect of reflected sunlight. We've all known for ages that it's a rocky sphere, but that makes no difference to moonlight. Rainbows are no less beautiful for being sun refracted through vapour.

While 600,000,000 were watching the first moon-walk, almost that number of journalists were rushing to cover the week's other event of global significance – Edward Kennedy's having driven his car into a Connecticut river and left a drowned secretary inside. Good news for Tricky Dick, who was otherwise the laugh of the world, appearing in inset while the moon-men tried to stand to attention on the dust.

The Royal Tournament at Earl's Court also had rocketry and radar among the Mounties and massed bands. Heath took the salute and an old-boy commentator delivered a stream of right-wing patter that was heard in stony silence by an audience perhaps more than half of which were trades unionists and Labour supporters. Tories always take it for granted that the people are behind them, as Beaverbrook did in 1945, not seeing that Churchill was on the way out.

John Schlesinger asked me to do some work on a film script that wasn't quite right yet. Fatter, greyer, but otherwise just as he was in 1947.

> [The famed director had been a conjuror in our entertainments unit in Singapore, not in my particular party but one which starred Barri Chatt, the original of my character Terris Dennis in *Privates on Parade*. John had lived a semi-civilian life in the equatorial city, writing and broad-casting, passing the time till his number came up.]

'The idea for this story's mine, very personal, and I perhaps divulged it to the wrong writer. Penelope Gilliatt's brilliant and I'm not but her brand of superior upper-middle-class left-wing humbug rubs me up the wrong way. All the characters know themselves so well and they're all buttoned up and in control and sit there smiling like Cheshire cats and discussing pre-Columbian art until I want to take my knickers down and *fart!*'

> [I took the script home and read it with admiration and later told John I had no idea what to do with it. He should go back to Gilliatt and tell her to make it better. This he did and the result was filmed as *Sunday Bloody Sunday*. I regret not having had enough gall to begin what might have been a happy association. His producer Jo Janni was with him and, whenever he put in his twopenn'orth, John would round on him like a shrewish wife and tell him he was a fucking old organ-grinder or ice-cream vendor.]

Dinner at Frayns' and a first meeting with the amazing Jonathan Miller and his smiling wife Rachel. Michael was at once on his mettle, trying to keep up if not outwit him. Jonathan fenced with the three other male guests like Errol Flynn in those old films, taking us all on on our own ground and sending each in turn toppling downstairs, careering backwards through a window, disappearing head first down a well. Michael knew about Wittgenstein and Russell; Simon Broadbent's in computers and advertising and could cope with arguments about serial-ism and McLuhan's attacks on sequential methods of communication;

I tried to match his mimicry and just about kept up with his showbiz gossip. There were no challengers in his other fields – medicine, current affairs, physics and biology. Pre-Columbian art perhaps? What would Schlesinger do? What did *we*? Tried to compete and then, having acknowledged his Protean eminence, sat and listened.

What was the purpose of dreams? To clear the decks and classify information as in a computer.

'So many dreams defy all but the most logical constructions. For example, Alan Bennett and I were riding great stallions down the staircase of some splendid country house. It had a square spiral, as yours has here, Michael, and as I turned the corner I realised that Alan had somehow got his mount inextricably entangled with the banisters' – superb ungainly mime – 'and as he struggled to free this beast from the stair-rail, he said calmly, "You go on". And I was riding on across a landscape but not – I was surprised to find – on a horse now but on Patrick Wymark, who was interested to hear I was doing a film on Oliver Cromwell but asked' – instantly perfect imitation – ' "Yes, but have you got the quintessentially Cromwellian spirit?" When I looked again, I found I was now riding Peter Finch.'

He found this inexplicable but I wish a Freudian had been among us.

Our wives brought up the hot topic: Kennedy and Chappaquiddick. Jonathan, of course, had dined with Jacqui and met Bobby.

'She's surprisingly voluptuous in person, not petite as in photographs. There were eight at this dinner, including the Soviet ambassador, who was rather touching and had brought along a speech which had been bolted together in the basement of his embassy, with some very Russian jokes. And he brought out Havana cigars saying, "I sink you find some problem getting zeze over here." And he had this amazing Pop Art wife, all hair and smiles, lobbing food into her mouth.

'Bobby wasn't a guest, he came later. A footman pulled up a chair for him and he sat awhile with each guest, working his way round to the ambassador, pointing his finger, very cold and Puritanical. I didn't take to him. One felt one was mere dressing, invited to make up the numbers so that Bobby could suggest a hot-line to Moscow to by-pass LBJ.'

Being asked to make up the numbers must be a recurrent nightmare, one he wouldn't divulge as freely as his riding dream.

He was of the opinion people there are about ready to overturn the Kennedy apple-cart. Alright, Jack, then Bobby, both gone, but why is it taken for granted Teddy will succeed them? Maybe he'll have to carry the can for the womanising of the other two. For instance, Bobby and Marilyn Monroe – '

'What?' shouted Michael, 'No!'

'Oh, common knowledge.'

'I had absolutely no idea. Hell's bells!'

'The last phone-call she made on the night she killed herself was said to be to him.'

'But nobody can know that,' said Rachel, still smiling.

'I'd absolutely no idea,' said Michael. 'Marilyn Monroe?'

On Monday my play was read in a dusty rehearsal room at the Old Vic, a space very like the hospital ward in which it's set. Open windows let in air but also traffic noise from Waterloo Road so that much of what we wanted to hear was inaudible. Michael and I then talked it over and I left him for some days to set the moves that he and I had planned down to the last detail.

[This we had to do as there was a cast of thirty, six beds and lockers, screens, earphones, all the paraphernalia of a ward. It was the sort of production that best suited Michael's staging skills, which finally went a long way towards hiding the play's faults.]

Later in the week I talked to the actors about the real-life people their characters were based on. They're very willing, but only the author and director can really have an overall idea of the play and they must use any sleight of hand they can to see it fleshed out as they imagine.

Thelma and I took a day away and walked part of the Pilgrim's Way after motoring to near Guildford. My dislike of The Car is part of a sense of what we're losing. Of course, some of the natural world's still there, quite close too, if we make an effort to find it: quiet woods, cool and shady after violent sun, gardens of wild flowers on heathland, bees humming in swarms, plentiful caterpillars becoming butterflies and making the meadows shimmer. At one point, a roe deer froze at our approach then bounded off between the trees.

First act run-through. A few of my worst fears laid to rest. Jim Dale, especially, looks like being as good as we could reasonably hope. Questions hang over Robert Lang and Charles Kay, the real leads. I thought Bob, being Bristolian, would find Ash easy but he tends to revert to the same inflexions again and again. Kay plays Loach with a Midlands accent because he's not confident in Cockney. Michael and I both know he's bound to miss that feeling of the Kipling tommy bearing the white man's burden out India way. A wrong dialect can ruin dialogue as properly heard as this was: where Cockney would be funny, pathetic and boisterous, Brummagem's depressing. There seems to be no fight in the man, only a sinister resentment.

Otherwise the play works. I mean, as a piece of carpentry the pieces fit and action dovetails well with dialogue, even in the intricate scenes of bed-removal when anyone dies. There are moments of real originality and seeing it up there onstage will probably be a strange experience.

Because Jim was so surprisingly good, I gave him another speech at the end, written over the weekend, a farewell to the audience in doggerel rhymed couplets:

A double-wedding ends our pantomime
Four hearts transplanted in the nick of time.

This will give everyone a chance to bow (as in a panto finale) while rubbing in the meaning a bit: the fictional people living happy ever after, Matron as the Queen depending on her darkies and the patients loyally waving their Union Jacks. Crude perhaps but true in its broad outlines. The play doesn't commit to being an exact metaphor or siding with one point of view. A couple I might share are held in tension in the last episode of Act One when Foster advocates equality and a naïve Socialism while Mackie, the cancerous engineer, makes a speech that begins coherently with the case for euthanasia and ends in a crackpot quasi-Fascism.

Spent a week in Swansea and persuaded Michael and Gill Frayn to join us for the bank-holiday week-end.

[Thelma had grown up in South Wales but her family came to Bristol in the 1930s when there was no longer any work at home. Her father assembled aero-engines in the Filton factories and finally bought a suburban semi less than a mile from ours.]

[43]

Her Aunt Millie was entertaining over ham and chicken supper in her tiny dining-room, remembering the war. Her vivid use of metaphor. People come alive.

'This woman was an absolute dragon. Well, at the age of eighty she died falling downstairs lighting one cigarette from another. I had to pick her up: stone dead she was.'

'During the first raid we were down the cellar in the pitch dark and we heard the bells of Sketty church. Invasion, we thought. That's torn it. Then we heard these footsteps, clump-clump-clump. We were terrified but it was only the ARP men. And, d'you know, not one of them thought to shout "You alright, Win?"'

'I was coming home one night down the crescent, this soldier shouted, "Who-goes-there?" I said, "Only me". He said, "Who's that?" I said, "Me, Millie Reed!" Stupid boy, he knew me as well as I know you. I told my father and he said the soldier was right because it could have been a Nazi making out he was me.'

We lay in bed later, recreating in low voices the scene at Gestapo HQ when Stormtrooper Hoffmann gets commended for his Millie Reed voice and his improvised 'Vos only me, dummkopf!'

'You remember Winnie Smith, Thelma? Cashier at Benn Evans? She was terrible in the raids. Spent every minute sitting in the toilet but, come the all-clear, she was down in Swansea looking at the corpses.'

'I was standing in the street outside Calder's when a warden came up and said, "What d'you think you're doing then?" I said, "Waiting for a bus." He said, "You won't catch one here. You're standing on a land-mine."'

When the Frayns joined us, there were five adults and six children in the cramped semi. Yet Thelma said that during the war *four* families lived there.

Michael's a decent, intelligent and agreeable (one of his favourite words) man but also extremely competitive.

'When I played tennis as a boy in the garden, I'd go on until I literally couldn't stand up. I had to crawl from the lawn on my hands and knees.'

October

Ten days from the official opening and a week from the first public dress. Yesterday techs began, our first time on a stage. Smooth enough, though we didn't get through Act One. Jim Dale brings a breezy efficiency to the amiable Old Vic muddle. The composer doesn't know the models he's supposed to parody, the choreographer's never seen a cakewalk and can't suggest anything else, the hospital noises-off could be a tube-train arriving . . . And under all the expensive clutter what's happened to the play I wrote, which we'd been so concerned with in rehearsal? The drama of the patients has retreated almost out of sight, the TV soap parodies and music-hall monologues, being downstage and spotlit, come on strong and threaten to overwhelm the subtler, more naturalistic ward scenes. What to do?

On Tuesday, Thelma came to our first Dress. The cakewalk has still to be set and Michael, due partly to my anxiety, has at last insisted they find the proper music and a choreographer who knows how to direct 'modern' dances rather than galliards and sarabands. Within an hour, the right score was found and a hoofer from showbiz watched from the stalls and later showed them an effective routine, within their scope. We sat in the circle and Thelma wept at Rees's death, which Gerald James plays beautifully. Downstairs sweeties from wardrobe bellowed with laughter at their friends and kept silent through Jim Dale's solos, as he's a new boy and not yet accepted by their clique. I'm told Olivier won't allow this in-group business during his rehearsals, saying they're not laughing at what the audience will find funny but the antics of their chums.

Olivier was in a red shirt and a new grey beard, Vershinin from the film he's making of *Three Sisters*. Our week's rehearsals had gone well, calmly and efficiently, and I sat upstairs with a pleasurable sense of expectation that died almost as soon as the play began. The company responded to LO's presence in the worst way possible, decorating their already slow portrayals with pauses and gestures that leave the play dead or dying. Truth is, they were auditioning for next season, saying, 'Sir, look at me!'

Still, I'm not offering alibis or scapegoats. Next morning, writing this as coldly as I can, it's impossible to avoid admitting that the thing doesn't work. Olivier wanted the whole balcony scene cut, a good quarter of an hour. He said again how little he admires 'the histrionic ability of our coloured brethren'. Those who watched him told me he hardly smiled. Michael's asked him to see how it goes with an audience. Tonight there's an invited house of friends and associates. But by now I hardly care. I'd sooner have it succeed, of course, but I've always felt there's a hole at the centre, caused by the removal of that politician's story, which Michael had thought too explicit [in a version never seen called *The Hysterical Fugue*, which centred on a Labour minister's decision to be treated in a public ward instead of some privileged private hospital]. Now that we've seen it through Olivier's critical eyes, the truth won't be baulked. However attractive, saucy, coarse and entertaining the thing may be in its parts, it simply doesn't come off the way it should, with an urgency of action that carries the audience along. I've not been able to enter the characters. They're people seen in passing. I must stick to my own in future. Maybe I'll have to limit myself to autobiography. It's nasty to learn after so much work that this one's a washout.

The invited audience lifted everyone's spirits. The actors played faster, finding where the laughs might come, and we listened carefully for coughs of boredom. A partisan but not particularly bright crowd, they roared at the farts but missed the cleverer lines. Tonight's paid preview house will probably laugh less but take in more and the company's mood will plummet again.

[I'm surprised Diary doesn't mention how we'd tried to rehearse the farting scenes, Harry Lomax as the old man Flagg pushing down on a rubber bladder, none of the actors able to carry on without corpsing. MB's sensible decision was that, if it made the actors laugh, it would the patients, so they should give way to their reflexes and enjoy. When this was played, the scene brought the house down and – particularly – elegant women in the stalls would, some minutes later, suddenly start laughing again at the memory. One of the surviving taboos.]

Olivier goes about saying 'Told you so' for decisions mostly made by him. He really is an appalling autocrat. Left to him, the National's repertoire would consist of high-toned revivals. It very nearly does anyway, and only Tynan has been any counter-balance, insisting on plays by Osborne, Tom, Charles and me.

[46]

Peggy Ramsay believes we have the chance of something unusually good.

'Darling, it's almost a work of art.' As it is, she says, we won't have a failure but might, if we keep working, yet have a success. Knowing her form as a critic, I fear the worst.

First public preview. Our mothers, Uncle Frank, Tom Stoppard, John Osborne and his wife Jill Bennett both wearing scowls as they made for their Rolls.

Asked each other whether the scowl was a good omen for us.

The day of the opening we drove to the theatre late afternoon and struggled about backstage putting a present (whisky, chocolates or cigarettes) in each dressing-room. By now I expected to be calm but in the event was terrified all over again. Why? What can they do but ruin you? The first night audience is always somehow different from the others – more expectant, reluctant, slow to warm, easily distracted. By the end there was pin-drop silence for my new lines and the applause was muted but encouraging. Jim lost his way and cut a page of text. Albert Finney kept me talking in the stalls, explaining why the reception hadn't been as warm as we might have hoped, kindly preparing me to face a failure. At last I arrived onstage, where Mike and I were greeted by the assembled company and the wedding march being played on the speakers and were presented with a cornucopia of flowers and fruit spilling from a chamber-pot on which was inscribed a line from the play: 'There's a clever boy!' Big Chief-I-Spy had found us an antique bedpan to give Mike. I was enjoying the general relief and euphoria when Thelma shouted at me to fetch the car to the stage door because Mike's wife, Shirley, had hurt her leg, so I went off walking the streets in my velvet suit, carrying a gift bottle of wine and wondering why. It began to drizzle. By the time I got back, people were drinking in Bob Lang's room and Shirley was enjoying herself in an armchair. Thelma later explained that she'd got caught in the crossfire between these two and Mike had shouted at her to get Shirley to the car.

Olivier embraced me and called me a genius.

I finally ushered them all off to the Café Royal where we enjoyed a good supper. The Hewletts had come from Cornwall and Francis told me he'd waved at Anouk Aimee under the impression she was one of his students at Falmouth Art College. He was glad he'd had no chance to ask her what she was up to these days.

Mike had predicted a split press, but the morning papers were unanimous in our favour. They tended to assume I was attacking doctors and hospitals and saying the NHS wasn't good enough, but I was relieved they'd enjoyed, if not understood, it. You can't have everything.

On Saturday brother Geoff and sister-in-law Mary arrived from Bristol, with her sister Cath and husband John. We slipped in to see the end of the show and basked in the general sense of pleasure as in a scented bath. We'd left the children with our new mother's help, Sylvia, who is a negative of Heather – quiet, neat, undemonstrative, with a Stoke-on-Trent accent and a Polish surname.

A last late supper at home with our family and friends, and I prompted Francis to repeat a few of his funniest turns: the Grosvenor Square peace protests (his face pressed against the flanks of a police-horse and shouting 'Ho-Ho-Ho-Chi Minh!); the concrete-poetry recital; the Nancecuke nerve-gas fiasco using balloons to demonstrate how this poison could drift across Cornwall, though in the event they all blew out to sea. And so to bed with aching throats and diaphragms.

[As I select these entires in early 2000, it's been revealed that the health of over forty workers at Nancecuke nuclear research station was damaged during their experiments. Despite the wayward balloons, the Hewletts were right to demonstrate.]

Hobson's *Sunday Times* review named the play of the week as Brian Rix's *She's Done It Again* and ended his notice of ours: 'The passion of Mr Nichols's hatred of life is interesting but it is saddening also. I am afraid that it is no good asking him to change his outlook. If he did so, I think that there would be nothing left.' Frank Marcus's in the *Telegraph* finished: 'Operation Successful, Play Dead'.

Ronald Bryden devoted several columns in *The Observer* to us. 'In jokiness he robs his play of a spine. Still, he's gathered up in his bleak microcosm, more of modern Britain, its clichés, hypochondria and mild shabby decency than we've seen in the theatre since Osborne's *The Entertainer* and Michael Blakemore's production confirms that he's the liveliest rising director on the scene.'

Still, it's depressing to be so insulted in public with no chance of redress so I challenged Geoff to tennis on the public courts, knowing he was a novice and had a slipped disc. He still managed to beat me hollow so Sunday wasn't my favourite day of the week.

Though the mood at the theatre matches the rare sunny weather, my own fluctuated as reviews in the weeklies began to confirm that Marcus's view was general. Numerically, we held our own but the posh papers weren't on our side.

Pro: *The Stage*, *Punch*, *Illustrated London News* and *What's On*.

Con: *Listener*, *New Statesman*, *Vogue* and *Spectator*.

The last was the most telling, as Robert Cushman saw that my talent is for naturalistic detail, which has been sacrificed (by myself as much as anyone) for the sake of theatrical effect. 'The last ten minutes include some of the ugliest writing I remember, ' he writes.

[Some years later, the same critic saw the Parisian production of *Santé Publique* at Théâtre de la Ville. 'Mr Nichols's humanity, which I thought unalterably English, has crossed the Channel undamaged.' I always admire a critic who admits to second thoughts.]

On Friday I found a full house, standing room only, enjoying the show a great deal, a fact the reviewers must ignore. I certainly would.

Charles Wood and family came to stay on Saturday. He's having a bad time just now and my play's reception, which from a Bristol viewpoint seemed better than from here, obviously didn't help reconcile him to his inability (so far) to appeal to wide audiences. Next morning there was mist and incessant rain and we'd booked lunch at the Post Office Tower. We could barely see our hands in front of us, leave alone the view from the thirtieth floor. We've now seen the Isle of Wight and Soho in the rain and Bream Sands in a hurricane. We talked of hiring ourselves out as Rentacloud for areas struck by drought.

Evening: to Ewan Hooper's new Greenwich Theatre, a ten-minute walk down Croom's Hill. A smashing hall holding 420 people in considerable comfort, all with good views of the projecting stage. For ten years, he and his friends (including John Hale, another Bristol alumnus) have worked at rebuilding this former theatre. And what have Charles and I done in that time? Written a few scripts. No comparison. Anyway, he wants me to do a play for him.

26 October

Monday morning, blazing sunshine. I'm back at the desk with the sheet of paper. Time to start again.

30 October

A wonderful exchange in *The Listener*. D.A.N. Jones, the drama critic, laid into my play on ideological grounds. Michael Frayn picked up the grenade and chucked it back. Jones caught it before it exploded and tossed it over again.

Frayn: His solemn denunciation is a classic. It's like one of those outbursts from some local worthy complaining that *Macbeth* is disrespectful about monarchy or an insult to Scottish womanhood.

Jones: Michael Frayn's letter is intended to wound and I am indeed wounded.

Jones scuppers any cool debate (which he seemed to want) by quoting, not from the play, but from a *Daily Express review* of it, 'to illustrate the effect it might have on a receptive audience'.

For me, this amusing exchange was an early case of the confusion of fiction with fact, provocation with real issue. Sonia Orwell also found *Health* reactionary. As usual, no-one came to the theatre with an open mind. I should hope not.

13 November

The day before we were due in Paris to see rehearsals of *Un jour dans la mort de Joe Egg*, the translator Claude Roy called to tell me that the actress Marthe Keller, playing Sheila, had opened an old operation scar when carrying the child onstage and was in hospital. We decided to go anyway and hope for the best. It would be a break at least.

Thelma, the world's worst sailor, seems to want to try every ship in the world before she accepts flying. Few passengers either on Golden Arrow or cross-channel ferry. Claude met us at Gare du Nord, carrying his copy of *Plays and Players* as arranged. Paris was an inferno of traffic and, even allowing for Claude's taking a wrong route, this was hardly an encouraging glimpse of a city we remembered for its charm. There seemed to be no restriction at all on parking: along both sides of even the narrowest streets, across pavements, on raised islands of trees . . . After eating in a bistro, we were driven to Montparnasse where he left the car up a cul-de-sac (the arse of a bag?). The Gaite is a tiny theatre where, twenty years ago, on my first visit to the city (with my mother!) I saw the amazing Grenier-Hussenot company. Claude confirmed this, adding that in middle age M. Hussenot, with six children, has left his wife for another man. I hadn't remembered how small it is, mostly stage with a few rows of stalls and one shallow circle. A second circle is a fake, occupied only by lights. Half the former auditorium was chopped off at some point by a voracious speculator. How can they ever make it pay? We met Michel Fagadu, the Romanian director, who speaks better English than Claude but was naturally depressed by the illness of his leading lady. Except for having a chat and trying to cheer him, there was nothing to do that night. Claude's car was now boxed in by a Citroen which we bounced out of the way, common practice here. Back in St Germain, Claude left his in the courtyard of his apartment in Rue Dauphine. As we walked through, Thelma recognised Rue de Seine, the street where she'd stayed as a girl of seventeen when as an art-student she'd won a holiday there as part of MGM's promotion of *An American in Paris*. We had a coffee in Café Flore opposite Deux Magots and Hotel Tarrano, where I'd put up on a later visit. 'Adamov lived there for a long time,' Claude told us. We watched the narcissists going in and out. Must be a long while since Sartre or de Beauvoir put their noses anywhere near.

Back at the hotel, pleasant sex for the ten-year-marrieds.

11 November

A remembrance holiday as at home. Nice, bright and sunny. Sex again and café complet. At the theatre, the actors were waiting for us and we met Mlle Keller, still unable to move about. They recited the text while I tried to follow. Was it Claude's fault that it took so much longer in French? Some of my stuff was cut and ideas of his own had been added. Perhaps it takes longer to say the same things but when I raised the point, he denied it and said (if memory serves) 'au contraire'.

The acting was volatile and amazingly accomplished, a show of fireworks that wasn't any mirror of their offstage behaviour, which was no different from that of a company at home. I suffered again the humiliation of not being able to speak or even understand their language, though they all made a good attempt at ours. At about teatime, they started moving about but Marthe wasn't well enough and they rang her husband, film director Phillipe de Broca, to take her home to rest. The actors dispersed in despair and Jean Rochefort, the leading man, took us to dinner, the most enjoyable meal we had – great company and good eating. A tank of healthy fish near our table was now and then approached by a waiter with a net. After a short decisive struggle, he'd return to the kitchen with his thrashing catch, the lucky survivors swimming on till another order was placed.

Fagadu's not given to unjustified enthusiasm. When I asked if he thought Parisians would take to the play, he said 'I don't think so, no, not at all.'

Storms had struck Southern England and the Channel, though France was sunny all the way. The ferry was lurching horribly even before they cast off. A noise of hearty welcome announced the arrival on board of Peter Finch, who was at once escorted to a cabin.

'Always bring good weather, doneye?' he shouted in his native tongue. Now and then throughout the crossing I saw him in his cabin with some young friends, drinking heavily and roaring with laughter.

The ship pitched and tossed all the way and Thelma, as usual, made for the rest-room at once and lay there in the care of an English Mme Defarge who cursed the weather as it meant we'd probably arrive late and she'd miss the bus to Folkestone.

In the train to London middle-aged English were saying they hadn't had a decent cup of tea for weeks and that the continentals had gone tea-bag mad. When the pots finally came, of course, they were made with bags. Finch had a separate compartment on the train too and the hearty laughter went on for some time. At Victoria, he emerged very much more sober. Even so, would he have been able to carry Jonathan Miller across that plain?

[There's little more mention of the Paris *Egg*. Fagadu was unduly pessimistic, as it played at the Gaite for a year and twenty years later he himself revived it there. Rochefort has become one of the strengths of French cinema and Keller made her inevitable way to Hollywood. It was the first of three adaptations of my stuff by Claude. He and his wife, the actress Loleh Bellon, became for some years good friends of ours.]

Went with the actor John Woodnutt (so good in *The Gorge*) to hear his brother, MP (Con) for the Isle of Wight, ask two questions in the Commons.

You go in by St Stephen's entrance and, surrounded by mock-Gothic stone and oil-paint, climb steps to a corridor which passes Westminster Hall on the left, the only ancient part of the whole palace, with a replica of Richard II's hammerbeam roof above and the large empty space below, like a tithe-barn in the middle of London, now used only for state lyings-in. Soon we were made to stand clear and someone shouted, 'Hats off, strangers!', and those few wearing them, mostly staff, took them off as the Sergeant-at-Arms came in bearing the mace, followed by the Speaker in his archaic drag, turned sharp right and made for the House itself.

We were bullied on to green leather benches upstairs and repeatedly told to 'Close up'. I'd not been ordered about so much since those long cinema queues of the early fifties. At Home Secretary Callaghan's question-time, John's brother asked two questions: whether he would (a) consider re-introducing the death penalty for offences against police officers and (b) transfer top-security prisoners when trouble was known to be brewing. Both got negative replies. Then Prime Minister Wilson's began, at which the front benches filled with ministers and opposition. From the gallery, one's struck by the shortage of dark hair on either side. Wilson and Heath cancel each other with greyness and Andrew Faulds is a backbench thicket but elsewhere there's an awful lot of skin. Nor can you long escape the feeling they're overgrown boys recreating their public- and grammar-school debating societies. If government has to be seen to be done (pretty questionable anyway), it's probably as good a system as any and most parliaments follow its general pattern, but the speeches are forgettable, made only for the record, to refer to when there's some future need to justify their salaries. Wilson's replies to left-wing backbenchers about the Vietnam

War avoided criticism of the US but praised the American press for making public facts that would have been suppressed under communism. He spoke fluently but in that unpleasant monotone that turns me off as soon as he starts. Sandys countered by hoping the PM would make clear to Mr Nixon that many British were grateful to him for containing the Red menace.

In the dreary little bar afterwards, Mark bought us Scotch and let us know how good it was of him to spare us a few moments. I felt some pity for poor John, faced at every turn by this boor braying about how much bigger The House was than its members. What a quasi-religious atmosphere these Tories live in! Mark's to the right of his party, aligned with Sandys and the hangers, pathetic in a deeper way than John, who at least has self-knowledge. He tells me their parents were shabby-genteel and filled the boys' childhood with tales of the noble families they'd known in better days. They're both actors really but Mark, being more obtuse, is a little more successful.

For the Bristol home of Bri and Sheila in the *Egg* film, Medak has chosen Freeland Place, a choice Regency location overlooking Hotwells, where only TV producers can afford to live. In the same call, I was told that Janet Suzman's already been signed. So, as Thelma said, they have their way about everything. I told Peggy how I felt and, going to see Van Eyssen of Columbia, said it wasn't the best time to discuss the film rights of *The National Health* as I was very unhappy. He at once rang Deutsch and ticked him off for prettifying the film and said he'd never wanted views of Clifton. David was furious that I'd tried to interfere. But Medak, ringing the next day, didn't even mention these events. 'Hey listen, doorlink, really, . . . everysing's great I tell you . . . simply great.'

Could there be a better example of a Hungarian going into a revolving-door after you and coming out ahead?

In the morning we heard from Hortham that Abigail's worse again. She can't last much longer, they say. So shall we go down tomorrow, sit by her bed and hope she won't recover yet again? No wonder I've written two plays about sickness and my latest TV describes a funeral. She'll soon be nine, if she makes it.

The unanimous praise in Paris still hadn't managed to attract audiences but now we've been sent an Italian magazine with pictures of the

Rome production where the action takes place in a marble palazzo with chandeliers, ornate inlaid ceiling, and old-master paintings. Peggy said: 'And you're complaining about a tumbledown Georgian cottage in Clifton!'

Charles met us at Temple Meads [the Bristol Great Western station] and drove us in bright sunshine along the short stretch of motorway to Hortham Hospital, offering a flask of brandy to fortify our spirits. We stayed at our daughter's bedside from 11 a.m. to 3.30 p.m. She can't be moved without causing her to cry. The slightest disturbance hurts and upsets her. The bedclothes were at first pulled up to her chin but, after she'd wet herself, the nurses had to change her sheets and nightdress and there was no hiding the pitiful twisted body. Her ribcage juts through skin stretched like a membrane, merely a bag keeping in the organs. It's muscles that make us attractive. Her thighs are bone with a thin covering of flesh and, everywhere the bones touch the bed, she's sore. One elbow's bandaged. Her legs are doubled up and have to be disposed so as to inflict the minimum discomfort. She made a good deal of noise and cried whenever Thelma moved her too abruptly.

In the opposite bed is a pretty girl, some years younger than Abo but obviously damaged in similar ways. Having seen our daughter's decline over the last two years, we know this child will end like her. She has a future of only pain and misery. Johnnie, the hydrocephalic, looked more horrible than ever, his head now inflated surely – please! – as far as it will go, his eyes pulled apart by the growth of his skull. All day long he plays with a plastic toy. In the far corner, a child beats the railings of her cot or bangs against the hardboard partition with hands clenched like hammerheads.

Some cases are more bearable than these: the hunchback mongol pushing herself about the floor on her knees at least finds a lot to smile about; a fat bald woman in a wheelchair who likes to propel herself; and a handsome boy who's clever enough to go to 'school', which probably means that hall I visited where they assemble the lids of bubble-blowers.

Above these, the slightly happier, are those capable of helping nurse the others, young women obsessed with the hospital's social calendar, bossing one another, flaring into quick resentments. One of sixty-three was sick of the place and made repeated attempts to walk out during our visit.

'She's as high as a kite,' a nurse said, 'her nerves are gone.'

'I'm not staying here.'

'Where are you off to, dear? You can't go out now, just as you're about to have a bath.'

They stopped her at the door and put her into a bath. In no time she was dressed again, outdoor shoes, hat and coat on, heading for the exit.

'Where you going now?'

'I'm not staying here. I've had enough.'

'Listen to the wireless. Have a smoke.'

She came to me. 'Can I have a light, sir? My fag's gone out. Thank you, sir. They won't let us have matches, see. That's why I'm not staying.'

She could be one of those who were institutionalised, committed here before sedative drugs were common, leave alone psychiatric treatment, so now incapable of making her way in the world.

Above the level of capable patients are the nurses themselves, brusque, jocular, doing a job few of us would consider but themselves not able to decide it would be best not to save these people from their living deaths. They content themselves with mundane grumbling about the injustices of hospital admin and their low pay.

'I can't give anything to the Christmas Club for them as well,' one said, 'there's too many and – let's face it – I haven't got the money.'

'Just some chocolates or something.'

'For all that lot? Where's the money to come from?'

One of the kids was, we found, the son of a woman who had written to me about *Joe Egg*, telling me both her children are handicapped. One's at Hortham, one waiting for a place. So much for the lies they told us about disability never striking in the same place twice.

As I walked outside, smoking, a few of the trusties, helping load the laundry, shouted at passing staff till they got a response.

'Hullo, Mrs Davis! Mrs Davis! Mrs Davis! Hullo!'

In the wire pen, semi-caged humans performed their inexplicable movements. Beyond the wall, some way off, the motorway traffic streaked past. I wanted Harold Hobson to take the guided tour and then look at his notice again.

[Penelope Gilliatt made the famous joke about the sound of a typical English Sunday morning being Hobson barking up the wrong tree.

[56]

This was never more true than when he allowed his own experience to distort his view of *Joe Egg*. He was lame and walked with sticks, due to his parents having trusted Christian Science to cure his infantile polio. He allowed that I'd 'taken a limiting case', as though I'd gone shopping for it, but thought I had too easily scorned The Laying-On of Hands. 'Miracles do sometimes happen' he wrote, then went on to exemplify his own history (presumably) where a doctor had said he'd never be able to earn his living and that child 'went on subsequently to earn about £6,000 a year more than the doctor ever did. But I admit the author has *chosen* (my italics) an instance graver than this.'

I kept quiet at the time, his review probably costing us the audience we might have had if he'd been more honest. He was, as we've seen, even more intolerant of my next play, though here his view was muddied by his family relations with Lord Chandos (né Lyttelton), Chairman of the Board and prime opponent of the play.]

The matron apologised for calling us.

'You never know. She seems to be dead. For days there isn't a even a pulse then suddenly she revives like this.'

We've decided not to visit again until we hear the good news that she's gone. This trip at least convinced Thelma we can't have her home. She can't even bear being moved a few inches but must lie there being fed and bathed and revived by drugs and brandy (yes!) until the mechanism finally overcomes their cruel and crazy efforts to keep it working. Someone give me permission and a painless sedative and I'll kill her without a qualm.

Since our first meeting, I've lost the admiration – no, hero-worship – I've always felt for Olivier. Last night he was on TV proposing the toast to Coward on his seventieth birthday. Most viewers must have felt like Victorian urchins with noses pressed against the windows of a great house, seeing but not sharing or understanding the grandeur inside. Coward replied modestly but by that time many had surely turned to other channels. He's an original and brilliant entertainer but the talent's spread thinly over a wide field, making up in versatility what it lacks in depth. But, according to friend Larry, he's Sheridan, Wilde, Kean, Astaire, Caruso, G & S, Cole Porter and Judy Garland rolled into one. It was a chilling glimpse of the world he inhabits and respects, that tough little clique at the top, survivors and mutual flatterers who sit smiling on the shoulders of those who lack their luck or favour or ruthlessness. I'd like to think they're the last of their kind but there are always new elites waiting to snatch up the ermine capes where they've been dropped. Tynan and Osborne hold their courts. Let's hear it for the clay-footed.

But my immediate task is to stop Olivier cutting my play to suit himself and Chandos and also to keep it in the repertoire.

I finished a new TV comedy about Dad's funeral, called *Hearts and Flowers*. Unsatisfactory. I'm bursting to resume the stage play I suspended halfway through. This feeling of urgency, comes probably from having lost or wasted my youth.

I was correcting Faber's proofs of *The National Health* when Thelma brought an envelope. 'I hope this is worth having. A man's just delivered it by hand from Fleet Street.'

It was from the *Evening Standard* to tell me *TNH* has been voted best of the year. *Egg* got that in 1967 and I'm surprised they found no way out of giving me two in three years but 1969 hasn't been that dazzling .

Tynan rang to say that, whatever happens, I must be there this time to receive the statuette, otherwise Olivier will, and he couldn't bear that, given his persistent opposition. Ken says the old man's told him he hopes he's ashamed to have championed such a nasty piece of work. Lord Chandos is having a rough time being snubbed or berated by members of his club. I'd never realised any of that sort went to the National. Aren't they more often at the opera or Brian Rix?

Michael Frayn and I spent a day parking for presents: a brooch for Gill, a ring for Thelma. The wives, on the other hand, were swept up in a tidal wave of spending, struggling with the new ten-shilling coins (Fifty New Pence?), coming back sick and angry from the West End. Thelma gradually filled the spare room with, first, toys, cardigans and bath salts in their ordinary packages, then with yards of wrapping paper from an arty-crafty shop, finally bringing these two elements together, ending up after some days of Sellotaping, with a roomful of toys, cardigans and bath salts wrapped in arty paper. I happened to mention that I hadn't bought her anything 'from' the children and she flew into one of her passions. I slammed out of the house, drove across to Blackheath village, bought a number of pins, needles, thimbles and bath salts and soon afterwards put in my own hour or so with Sellotape and arty paper. She relaxed to hear me at it. The god of retailing had been appeased for another twelvemonth.

25 December

All this and more we packed into the Peugeot, left at six a.m. and were at the Woods' in Bristol before either Charles or John were up. Later we limbered up for the real event by dropping off presents at Geoff and Mary's new house in Clifton. But next day came the real trial of strength. After a late breakfast, the Woods and Nicholses swapped what we'd bought and wrapped a few days earlier. The arty paper was ripped off to reveal dressing-up sets for the children: commando's, nurse's and Indian squaw's; dolls for the girls; books for the dads; body-decorations for the wives; six football annuals for John without a duplication.

The next lap was picking up my mother and driving her to Thelma's parents' tiny semi-det, bulging with food, drink and people. Hardly inside before Reg and Millie began handing out the ties, books, spinning tops, plastic spiders and drawing books. Sherry was followed by the enormous dinner, from prawn soup through turkey to pudding with Liebfraumilch and Graves. The sixpences were a disaster: Millie and Win got two each, Catherine and Thelma none. A scene was avoided in the nick of time by Uncle Frank dropping his into Catherine's dish before she'd quite finished. Others did the same and she soon found she had three, which caused cries of 'Unfair!' from Lou and Dan.

With the onset of TV pantomimes, I as the only male smoker was detailed to provide the scent of cigar. At breaking point, I suggested a stroll to Frank and we took Dan and Cath to the swings on Purdown. This field is part of my childhood. There was always the risk of rough boys spoiling our games of being rough boys but later came the allure of seeing GI's having girls beside every hedge. The great manors, now mental homes, stretch away towards the spire of Stapleton Church. Eastville Park's now partly hidden by the embankment of a new motorway which will cut through and obliterate the district where my grandma lived. The farm's still there, in private ownership. A radar dish is on the site of the old anti-aircraft unit where, during the war, mother and I entertained the troops.

Back in the roomful of furniture and family, we sit watching Petula Clark singing 'Holy Night', Val Doonican crooning a lullaby to Wendy Craig, the Young Generation dancing the life of Jesus. The children are shouted at every time they block an adult's view. They want to play with the toys they've been given, not grasping that the important part, the giving, is over for another year and they should sit like grateful mutes and let us watch our favourite stars.

Charles's place felt enormous afterwards and, indeed, the whole area of the Reeds' would have gone into his front room.

26 December

Boxing Day was lunch at the Unicorn. Then tea with Geoff's family. Arriving at their house, Thelma discovered she'd lost the ring I gave her. Half an hour's misery before I found it on the floor of the car. Tea with paper crackers then ping-pong and table-football. I gave Mum her cheque and heard her complaints about the other tenants of her block. Mary at one point stilled the merriment by breathing, 'Peter, you should be the happiest man in the world.' And certainly I should, having achieved all I aimed at when I was thirty. Still I'd like to free myself from the domestic clutter, bitter fights with Thelma, threats to leave home, find a carefree lover, get a steady job, all hollow but sincerely meant.

27 December

Today was our tenth anniversary. I'd forgotten and had to be reminded. No presents.

We washed and polished the children to take them visiting at Tormarton, John Grigg's home whither Patsy had invited us for tea. The house stands alone, across the road from the village church, a mile or so from the motorway, which at present peters out on the Altrincham land. From the gravel forecourt, the front door is off-centre of a long gabled façade. A marbled lobby leads to a central hall, the earliest part of the house, the wings being added in the eighteenth century. After

Patsy and Alexander received us, John came from one of the many rooms wearing tweed knickerbockers. The children were taken off by nannie, while his mother, Lady Altrincham, fussed around them with suggestions.

In the long narrow living-room overlooking lawns which, beyond a wall, give way to a paddock and stables, we met the other guests: Kenneth Rose, a biographer whose latest subject is Curzon, and Fred Gollings, a jolly historian from Santa Barbara whose voice is a hoarse whisper. They had a heated disagreement over the personality of Beaverbrook.

[Throughout the years we've known them, I've never felt entirely at ease with John's acquaintance with the century's top people. His father really did know Lloyd George and John rode piggy-back on the famous Welshman's shoulders.]

Hide-and-seek was organised and John returned to childhood with relish, as he'd done on Guy Fawkes' Night. Alexander and Dan were first to get lost and eight of us hunted them.

Looking from his library window, John said of the motorway: 'It'll affect the village, yes, it already has. From being far off the beaten track, suddenly we're right on it. In many ways it'll be a good thing. Motorways do less violence to landscape than the railways, about which everyone's now so sentimental.'

The short day turned to twilight and we seemed to be in an M.R. James ghost story. I found myself in upstairs passages hunting the boys and discovering, behind every door, four-posters or nurseries full of huge doll's houses and almost lifesize rocking-horses. This is where the classic children's literature takes place, not among our semis and terraces, not on the by-pass or M5. In such a house Alice chased the rabbit, Lucy found Narnia beyond the wardrobe, the Borrowers took refuge and the posher Nesbit children slipped through time, while on warmer days and nights outside there were secret gardens and lakes where statues swam. The parvenu snobbery of middle and upper-middle-lower-class writers has compounded aristocratic advantage.

I found Dan and Alexander in the music room behind a chair. Giggles showed where Thelma and John were under a grand piano.

As the game went on, there always seemed to be somewhere else to hide. Was it their discreet way of showing us round the house? In the wing that went off by the servants' quarters were numerous cosy parlours, habitat of various retainers we found in kitchens and sculleries, drying dishes, talking to men in outdoor clothes. At the farthest reach of this wing, John and Catherine hid behind a pile of leather-bound volumes in a junk-room large enough to lose a tennis-table in, among mounds of toys, clothes, furniture, chests and signed photographs of past and present royals.

I stood on a gallery surrounding the main hall and saw John entering from one room, Patsy another, Nannie from the lobby and Thelma descending the staircase, between walls hung with ancestral portraits, including one of John as a boy against an idealised glade.

As he was passing, his mother said, 'Shouldn't we now play hunt-the-slipper?'

'In a minute.'

'There's always time to change the game.'

'Yes, but not while everyone's enjoying this one.'

When darkness fell, other guests arrived through a dense but penetrable fog. Dogs of all colours slouched about and John appeared with champagne to drink the continued health of our marriage.

In the car, at 35 m.p.h. while others passed at 50, Thelma told me how John admires her father.

'He hasn't met him,' I said.

'No but he liked the character you made of him in *The Gorge* and approves of all I say about him. I suppose he seems a figure of incorrigible working-class values.'

'And John, for all his liberalism, deeply respects the status quo and is glad to hear of anyone who's loyal to his class.'

'Perhaps I should introduce them?'

'How about next Christmas – in Reg's house?'

'I'd like to see how many hiding places he could find there.'

1970

[The award for *Joe Egg* in 1967 had been accepted on my behalf by Michael B, as I was on the storm-tossed Bremen in mid-Atlantic en route for New York. I hadn't realised that this prize was a career event of some importance, as only a statuette was on offer, not a cheque. This time we'd been warned.]

14 January

As guests leave the luncheon, copies of the *Evening Standard* are given away, carrying their ready-made scoop, set up before the party began. If some absolute disaster happened – their critic assassinated by an aggrieved actor, etc – it would be too late to abort the edition. What then? The other papers almost ignore the event altogether.

Under a row of photographs of sweeties hugging each other was a report of the prizewinners, only excepting me. But *The Times* makes up for that this morning: 'Appropriately the best speech yesterday came from the author of the Best Play. He pointed out the valuable contribution of his director and itemised where other thanks were due: a string of hospitals where he'd been treated, an apocalyptic circular received through the post and his wife for eavesdropping in the supermarket. This self-effacing performance contrasted sharply with some of the more extravagant and lengthy speeches.'

This meant those of Alan Brien and Nicol Williamson. The first was a model of misjudgement and finished with an irrelevant joke with the tag-line 'Like a prick but smaller'.

Ginger Rogers was not amused. A well-preserved fifty-seven, tee-total, clean-minded and a staunch Republican. She was seated beside me.

'Are you nervous about your speech?' she asked before I went up. 'When I went to get my Oscar, I don't remember walking to the dais. It's some seconds out of my life.'

What do you say to Ginger Rogers? I of course asked why the Hollywood musical was in such a bad way.

'I think it's because romance is dead.'

She ate nothing and drank orange juice.

Tynan had been giving in his coat as I gave mine and told me he'd just noticed my play's not in the current programme. 'I'll have something to say, let me tell you.' It's the only one not in the Christmas season as well as being the most successful show since Tom's [*Rosencrantz and Guildenstern*].

Last year there'd been a noticeable falling-back by the press and much reloading of flashbulbs after our names were brayed by the frog footman. This time they had me on their bits of paper. 'Nice smile, Pete, that's it.' Ken introduced me to Antonia Fraser, and we exchanged icy pleasantries. I knew she'd opposed *Joe Egg* as winner on the grounds that it was 'generally inferior'.

Olivier said 'Where's the boy?' and clasped my hand in both of his. Joan [Plowright] said, 'After all these years!' though we'd had a conversation not long ago at Aquinas Street.

Jim Dale, eager to be on time, had overdone it, arriving yesterday and asking for the ballroom, to be told he'd be all alone.

Frankie Howerd did a marvellous fifteen minutes. 'Sir Max Aitken, you see, he's all for the open air, yachting and shooting, not a bit like us. He never gets to the theatre but every year on this occasion he does have a go. You hear him using words like "camp" and "drag". He hasn't a clue what they mean but he tries, that's the main thing.'

To Bristol to observe shooting. We lunched on location at Freeland Place, the quaint terrace where they've chosen to set their picturesque, TV-commercial version of *Joe Egg*. The hundred or so miserable members of the unit queued in a yard for food which they ate on trestle-tables in an abandoned shop. Surely film technicians are the most dispiriting people on earth? Among the pasty faces, Alan Bates's, made up for colour, glowed orangely. The kids ate with us and were afterwards taken off to Weston by their Grandpa. I did interviews – with *Points West* for TV and with some boys from the Royal College of Art who were making a film about making a film. These zealous lads had me sitting in a mini-Moke careering through the wind and rain and saying why the action should be shot in Bristol, this is where it took place and is set and where the play was written. Medak, in a fur coat, smooth and benign as ever, gave the impression all was going according to his own inscrutable plan.

'Some of this stuff is beautiful, doorlink. There is one moment when she brings the baby back from the hospital and she just wipes away a tear . . . my God, it's the whole bloody play in one shot!'

But not the play I wrote.

I see now what he's turning it into: *Georgy Girl* with tears.

[In 1965 I'd done three weeks' revision of the script for this extremely successful weepie, enough to earn me a credit as co-author with Margaret Forster the author of the book. The result was a bit of 1960s camp about a fat girl who finds love. At a preview, the director asked me, 'Who the hell's gonna pay to see this?' 'All the fat girls?' I suggested.

That proved to be so and made somebody a zillion dollars. It is still the only work I'm known by in much of America.]

I asked to see rushes and Medak said there weren't any that day. We afterwards heard some chippies in the hotel lift telling each other where and when they were being shown.

I'd expected Thornbury Castle to be a Victorian folly, but it looked real enough as we drove through the gatehouse and found the three wings forming a courtyard and floodlit behind extensive lawns. Having parked at the rear, we walked in a light rain to a door at one corner and inside passed through heavy drapes to a lofty hall where a refectory table was set out for our party alone, before a hearth of blazing logs. Varnished copies of Caravaggio decorated roughstone walls. Unobtrusive waiters came and went through a tapestry arras. By candlelight we read the menu, partly a history of the house from Athelstan in the tenth century to 1840 when it was rebuilt. The whole cost per head came to less than our lunch at the Post Office Tower. Columbia, the film company, was of course footing the bill.

Our party was the host David Deutsch, his wife Claire, Peter Medak, Alan Bates, Janet Suzman, Peter Bowles, Sheila Gish and ourselves. Peter said this was the first time since coming on location that he'd had to put in an appearance.

Janet's husband Trevor Nunn arrived later and was seated the other side of Sheila. He was over-respectful to me and I had no idea how to deal with this as so far the only show of his I'm aware of seeing is *Much Ado* and didn't much care for it. Surely he couldn't have thought as much of me as he made out. Supporting Janet, I suppose, as it's no secret I wanted Zena to do the part again.

'Oh, Peter,' he said as we munched our way through the delicious venison, 'what a play! How I wish you'd sent it to us first – the Royal Shakespeare!'

'Oh, Trevor,' I answered, 'I did. And we didn't even get a reply.'

5 *February*

Through the coloured screen, we see Biafra surrender, Dubcek relieved of his post by the Soviets, Australia nickel shares boom and a late member of the Bristol Co-op arrested for spying for East Germany.

Meeting about the proposed film of *The National Health* in Columbia's building off Oxford Street. Present: the film executives, Michael Blakemore, Peggy Ramsay and I.

In a coffee-bar afterwards, Peggy waved her arms at Michael and me and wrote my deal, as she understood it, on a paper napkin. We were again in the Land Of Noughts. I'm now very calm when faced with a row of such figures because I know I'm the prime mover of a minor industry. Out of any money paid to a fiction called Peter Nichols Limited, I help support The National Theatre, Margaret Ramsay Ltd., Harbottle and Lewis (solicitors), Vallance Lodge (accountants) and the inland revenue, before even arriving at a figure from which to pay rates, road tax, water, power and national insurance. Expenditure on ourselves isn't much more than it ever was. I have (as stores-wallahs put it) suits (3), jackets [sports] (1). Trousers (prs 2), shoes (prs 6), overcoats (1) and mac (1).

I visited Stage H where Albert Finney's making *Scrooge*. Inside the great factory, previously a silent stage, they'd built the kind of film-set one always imagines but hardly ever sees, representing two streets of an idealised but detailed Dickensian London. Carts and stalls stood about with prop sides of beef and hung poultry, milliners and cobblers, smiths and chandlers. Beyond the tops of nearby buildings, cunningly diminished roofs and steeples stood against a cycloramic sky flooded with wintry light. The whole effect is of a greetings card sparkling with tinsel, though in fact this snow is made of seven tons of Epsom Salts which will be swept clean before every take, where in fact it would have been blackened by soot and yellowed by horse-shit. When this reaches our screens next year, there won't be a turd in sight.

Albert, complete with mangy wig, said he was enjoying all this show-business and certainly seemed cheerful and popular with the crew and extras. 'Oh, yes, I've worked with Albie. A real pro. No side to him. Talk to anyone.'

I watched him do an exit four times, the last two of which they printed. Naïve of me, but I hadn't realised they record all the songs first and mime the action to a loud playback.

8 February

Arnold Cawthrow told us about the Big Chief I-Spy who preceded him,

[This successful series in the *Daily Mail* was pseudo-educational, sharpening up children's observation of everyday life in nature and society. The figurehead was an invented Indian Chief, currently embodied by Arnold.]

who became obsessed and took his new wife on their honeymoon in a teepee. Arnold himself has to carry a feathered headdress and tomahawk in the boot of his car. The well-intentioned project has lately been misconstrued and the paper's offices have been getting strange calls from children who say they are spying on the married woman next door who seems to have a lot of men staying with her when hubbie's away; or that a white girl's been seen kissing a brown boy and that a strict I-Spy is being kept on her. The Gestapo would have had no difficulty recruiting agents.

1 March

An interview alone with John Van Eyssen, the executive director of Columbia UK. He managed to assure me that, not only am I the greatest living writer but nearly as good-looking as Alan Bates and as strong in personality as Carl Foreman, who is spoken of to produce *The Nat Health*. I'm suggesting he's the wrong man and so doctrinaire he'll bully us into making a film with a message like Illness Hurts. John spent an hour and a half persuading me he'd be the best possible person to help Michael Blakemore through his first crack at the movies.

To Paris, France, for the 100th performance of *Egg*. Felt randy in the hotel room and walked about nude. I wanted her but by the time she wanted me, it was too late, we had to leave.

The performance was quietly received by a two-thirds house. A decent shot though by no means a bull's-eye. The French theatre seems to have no relation to French life. Their behaviour offstage is more rhetorical than ours but nothing like as explosive as they make it appear onstage. The accuracy of the author is cancelled by their extravagance. Marthe Keller's performance was the most faithful and, of course, she isn't French but German-Swiss. Her accent worries French listeners and she told us that, until two years ago, she knew nothing of the language and still can't understand the scenes she isn't in.

We ate afterwards in a Russian restaurant run by an aged critic, who seemed to be responsible for getting Michel Fagadu a prize for Best Direction. He called for silence, pinned a medal on him and kissed him on both cheeks. We all clapped. This was re-enacted later, clapping and all, for a camera team making a film about Marthe's life for television. The actors became grotesquely animated whenever the lights went on. Even Claude Roy, the austere and eminent translator and man of French letters, acquired an extra brilliance as soon as the cameras turned over.

We visited Versailles, a Chagall exposition at the Grand Palais, the Louvre, Place des Vosges, and walked a good deal around the Left Bank and along the banks, north and south, of the swollen Seine. Riverside roads were submerged, making traffic worse than ever. At the Chagall an English woman, after looking for a while, said 'He was fond of animals, wasn't he?'

Claude insisted that we see *Operetta* by Witold Gombrowicz, which has had an unexpected succés d'estime at the TNP. Waiting for curtain-up, we heard a voice call our name and it was Tynan with the Oliviers. In the interval, Joan and Ken were very affable and Sir (as the actors all call him) was struggling to pull the cork from a champagne bottle, using teeth, fingers, anything, and looking angry and unhappy. I offered to shake his hand, realising too late that he had none free. He seemed florid and old beyond his years and I felt, as ever, that I'd somehow offended him. Is it his fault or my nervousness?

The first act was disappointing and, though Ken had the script for a crib, I'd been briefed by Claude and was able to identify which character was based on Sartre, and that saved the day for me.

'The French do get on your wick a bit,' Ken declaimed amid a lobbyful of sophisticated natives who understood only too well. 'All that showing-off! There's never been a realistic period in their theatre and nothing they do there has any relation to life offstage.'

What could I say? It was exactly what I'd felt about their version of my play.

Joined the commuting crowd homeward on Friday afternoon and sprayed diesel fumes over a few gardens in West London, shattered the peace at Kew and made teacups rattle in Windsor Castle and thousands of suburban semis. Our taxi-driver was fortyish, a Lewisham man in a windcheater and shades.

'Bitter cold, eh? I don't like it. Give me the old Spain any day. I love holidays abroad, do you? I do. When I had the old Merc, we went down Malaga, loaded with tins and all the gear 'cause I can't stomach foreign food.

'Did seven hundred a day. My wife says, " 'Ere, take it easy." I said, "You drive then." She said, "I ain't gonna drive." She don't like driving. So that was the end of that.

'We're all dockers, our family. I hate the Germans, mind, do you? We sorted one of them out. He was going on in German, the way they do, but we knew enough. "Dirty English pigs." I liked that too. So we done him up a bit. Not that the French is any better. I said to one, "You call on us next time you got a war you want winning." So that was the end of that.

'Mind, we are saucy, the English, don't you think? *I* think we are. We're only a little country but we have a go. And what I know of history, we've always liked a war. We met this kraut in Malaga, had a few drinks. I thought to myself, I'll show off a bit with the old Merc. I offered to go for a stroll with him, through the car park like, and when we got to the Merc, I'd say it was mine. Well, when we was out and on the way he showed me his. Only a Silver Cloud. When we got to mine, he said, "Oh, you got the old Merc then?" So that was the end of that.

'My girls are nearly off-hand now. Well, they keep you poor, don't they? I've often reckoned I'd go off alone for a bit, get the boat across, poodle down through France in the Merc. I'd like that, long as I didn't have to eat the food. I was going once with my brother. He asked his old woman. She said, "What, and leave me here with the kids? No bloody fear." So she told my old woman and they got together and stopped it. He said, "You want to learn to control your wife." I said, "*My* wife? What about *your* wife?" So that was the end of that.'

15 *March*

Read two novels by Kurt Vonnegut: *Slaughterhouse Five* and *Mother Night*, the last of which Medwin's suggesting I turn into a screenplay. He's one of the few writers trying to find a new form to describe modern experience. His subjects show this: the bombing of Dresden, to which he was witness; a ruined Europe; a spoilt America; counter-espionage, time-travel, blue movies, the mad and bigotted poor. I find the preoccupations of, say, David Mercer, oddly old-fashioned beside his, good as David's plays are. Doctrinaire ideology and hair-splitting over forms of Socialism seem more like intellectual games than attempts to wrestle with the problems of a poisoned world. Vonnegut's at least in there trying. Having come from sci-fi and admitting that authors in that genre don't write very well, he still prefers their clumsy failures to those that go on safely exploring tiny lives with traditional brilliance.

To *Tiny Alice*, a play by Albee at the Aldwych full of very classy writing and high-toned metaphors. It meant nothing to me, but Thelma deciphered something about Jesus being killed to satisfy the church. We left after two long acts and walked across Waterloo Bridge, arriving in time to see the modified final scenes of *TNH*. It's back in the season after a sizeable break and we've cut as much as the actors will let us without going out on strike. The fact that The Old Vic full house were enjoying themselves more than the Aldwych lot were means nothing. They'd probably have had an even better time at *She's Done It Again*.

Theatre's a vulgar form by definition. Hundreds of spectators coughing like seals, some bellowing with laughter, others wondering out loud why they've come, all seriously affecting one another's enjoyment, these are the conditions under which even the most austere text is acted. I'm happy to be counted among the champions of a more popular, less high-altar, form of theatre.

Mood of elation backstage and Joan Plowright was especially friendly. Olivier introduced me to Lilli Palmer, one of the idols of my youth and still beautiful (at 56), who said she'd appreciated the evening, as her father had been a surgeon.

'In Vienna?' I said.

Olivier, whose antennae are always at full stretch, caught this sotto-voce remark.

'The boy's being polite! You're not Austrian. You're a German, aren't you, dear? A bloody Kraut?'

'Oh, me, I'm Boche through and through.'

He invited us for drinks in the Lilian Baylis suite. I realised he was pretty pissed when he knocked over a bottle of Scotch and let a quarter of it run into the carpet. Whenever we meet, he seems to be having trouble with bottles.

[What would Miss Baylis, the temperance advocate, have made of this pungent smell of whisky in her commemorative room? Her prime reason for starting the Old Vic Company was to get the men off the streets and out of the pubs.]

Tynan's asked me to write a sketch for his erotic review *Oh, Calcutta!* ('Oh, quel cul tu as!'). Having no amusing ideas on this, I sent for a book that had been advertised by a circular through my door, an American way of distributing pornography, which has led to some pious denunciation in Parliament, by the likes of John Woodnutt's brother. *Variations on a Sexual Theme* arrives under plain cover, an octavo hardback containing forty or so photographs of a nude man and woman in various coital positions, with explanatory text beneath. An informative and inoffensive thing with not a genital in sight and even the models' faces discreetly turned away, like drug-addicts in a TV documentary. After a while, I found some comic mileage in the thought of a husband trying to bring back the magic to his marriage with this book and the minimal equipment required. Spent a day writing what we both thought an amusing ten minutes, showing a couple in a cold bedroom standing on piles of encyclopaedias, etc. Tynan thought it funny too and is glad because there's nothing else like it in the material they have so far. Clifford Williams, the director, would have the final word. After weeks, Williams sent a nasty note to say he wouldn't be using it as it's too much like another they already have.

My television play *Hearts and Flowers* is with the BBC and they're taking their time about saying yes or no. I asked Thelma, 'Am I out again?', always aware that any success one has is temporary, that those who invent the stuff are at the mercy of the entrepreneurs who run the business.

To cocktails at Tom Maschler's house and to meet Vonnegut, over here to launch the *Slaughterhouse* novel. I've since read another, *God Bless You, Mister Rosewater*. He stood, tall and mild-mannered, with back to mantelpiece while various pilgrims (including me) approached to pay respects. His wife sat on a sofa nearby and told Thelma they'd lived a quiet life for twenty years in a dormitory village of commuting businessmen and never met a writer. Suddenly he's being lionised and this back-to-the-wall posture is his way of coping. To me, he seemed to be enjoying himself but maybe that was part of the performance and he was really longing to be back at the desk, because writers mostly feel they're disappointing after their books.

Maschler seemed nicer than the wheelers-and-dealers of *our* trade.

[This was our only meeting with the famous publisher until 1990 when we went to view his maisonette in Belsize Park and his face appeared at the third floor front door, telling us to keep climbing. We bought the flat at the crest of a price-boom and have lived in it happily for ten years, no thanks to him. I'll write nothing more here for fear of a storm of litigation, perhaps even more determined than the one we had over the coal-effect gas-fire.]

Saw the assembled *Joe Egg* film material so far. It's likely to depress rather than illuminate. Where we cast light, he's found only shadows.

1 April

Dreamt last night I was examining one of Dad's shirts, striped blue and white, with no collar but white cuffs that needed links. I thought it splendid and decided to buy some collars and wear it with his suit, an expensive worsted, which his weren't in life. The mood was a warm and comforting sadness, such as I seldom or never feel when awake.

Woke up and lay dazed and mystified by the dream's intensity. Daniel and Louise came galumphing into the room and shouted, 'Someone's left the taps on and the bathroom's flooded.'

'Who? What?' I blurted out, still half-asleep.

'Don't know who. But everywhere's soaking.'

'Then it's nothing to laugh at. Have you turned it off?'

'April Fool!' they yelled and ran off to work out more jokes.

Dad's birthday, always so appropriate for a man who spent so much of his life fooling about. Five years now since his death, a few years before his eightieth.

I've been thinking about him more lately, trying as I am to write a play that describes my adolescence and his part in it. His scenes come most vividly alive – grandiloquent, pathetic, likeable, insufferable, nagging, priggish, a real stage-sized character. The stage of a variety theatre is where he saw himself as belonging, except that he lacked the gift. Or only the opening?

But what does it mean? Most lives make no sense and his didn't.

Turned out of my study by plumbers, I have no calendar to find the date of this entry. The central heating system, which cost a fortune when we moved in two years ago, has never worked properly on the upper floor. The cowboy who installed those radiators has now gone out of business so we're paying other men to raise the pressure tank and replace the narrow-bore copper piping. This reminds me somewhat of the doctor who delivered Abigail and has never spoken to us from that day to this.

Poor Abo, our parcel of faulty goods, lives on, despite repeated promises. The Euthanasia Bill, which I supported, was defeated in the Lords and *The Times* rejoiced. Our next door neighbour, Doctor Alan Norton, in his book *New Dimensions in Medicine* agrees. In person, he told me it would do more harm than good to alter the vague conditions in which doctors are able to help the dying out of their misery. Alright,

I argued, but it's in places like Hortham that one looks for courage and mercy from the outside world. What's easier than to sweep those poor idiots under the carpet and forget them? By sustaining such lives, society is relieved of the guilt of their deaths. It's the Harold Hobson view that's such an ugly lie: that their horrible existence in any way resembles the life of the *Sunday Times* drama critic.

Before going off to Tunisia to visit oases, Peggy R rang to say the BBC has accepted *Hearts and Flowers* and envisage a production in the autumn. Tynan apologised for the balls-up over *Neither Up Nor Down*, my sketch for *Oh, Calcutta*, and says they're still thinking. My new stage play's difficult. Too early to say much yet. It amuses *me* but is so personal that it may well only bore or mystify others. I've had some exhilarating moments in the writing though and think it may be my best so far, if I can only be truthful. My other things all seem to have a nasty element of cajolery, trying to talk to audiences in ways they understand.

My feeling is that the first act's mostly funny, amusing memories of the war with some comic sex-play, but the second will be harder for me to control. I'll have to stretch myself farther than I know I can go. If the first is about uninformed, uncomprehending adolescence, the second shows the same people twenty-five years on, the actor who played Young Frank now Young Frank's son. It's all about time and how it creeps or gallops. A North Bristolian Proust.

Shall I call it *Down Memory Lane*? I like that but Thelma thinks it's too much a cliché.

25 April

Catherine's favourite game is *Kind* Cowboys and Indians, by which she means 'no fighting'.

'Nice and short,' said Thelma as we applauded *Medea* at Greenwich last night. I'd dozed off once or twice and, though it was a creditable effort, I can't believe these plays can ever grip a modern audience. We've none of the poetry, song, dance or sharing of monumental passions and crimes under an open sky in a great stone crescent. A clever set of steel spars and a lot of amplified chanting can't do the trick.

My new one's nearly done and, of course, it's a disappointment. Anyway, a sort of paper chain and later I may be able to hang some lanterns on it.

10 May

The Koestler Awards to be judged again and Hugh Casson asked Michael Frayn and me to do the fiction. We'd recommended more prisoners be given typewriting facilities and the Home Office said they'd advise the various governors to do so. In the event, there are just as many as ever in longhand.

[We awarded the novel prize the year before to Tony Hoar, who came to see us on his release, to thank us for helping him abandon his previous career in thieving and GBH and take up writing for television. His experience made him one of the most required scenarists for the burgeoning cops-and-villains market and we could chalk him up as the one real success of our stint as Koestler judges.

Tony told us governors and ordinary screws won't agree to allowing typewriters, as they're afraid they'll be used to smuggle out decently-written and persuasive petitions to MPs and Lord Longford.]

Even though we gave the big prize last year to a novel about robbery, this is still officially discouraged and the HM-issue-exercise books in which many of the entries are written have a list of proscribed subjects on their covers. The first item is 'Your Own Life' and Michael and I couldn't think of any work we admired that didn't fall into that subversive category. Tony Hoar told us that letters home are officially written on prison notepaper, sent through the proper channels and censored. Their *real* mail's on unofficial paper and smuggled out, the screws turning a blind eye.

Prison officers can hardly be blamed for being unimaginative. They're only doing their jobs. But the conditions attached to this competition mean nothing much can come of it. What more interesting than to read an essay by Myra Hindley, secretary, now in Holloway for her part in the Moors Murders? But 'Reflections' begins as it goes on for pages:

'Winter is the season of memories, a rich harvest which I can reap at leisure, memories gleaned from the past which can be savoured nostalgically. I remember particularly those snug times I have spent in my study . . . etc., etc. . . . the first time I heard this call of the hills was at the age of eleven, spending my very first holiday away from the grimy, semi-slum environment in which I had been born and raised. I was staying for a week on a small farm in The Lake District and, immediately upon arriving there, determined I would not spend a minute away from the farm itself for I was a confirmed animal-lover and was in my element among the cows and chickens, pigs and sheep, all surrounded by their tender offspring.'

But this is getting dangerously close to Her Own Life and in no time she's off (on her tutor's advice?) on another pantheistic rhapsody.

26 May

Stole a few days from work on the script of *Nat Health* film and flew to Bordeaux with Thelma and Catherine to look at farms and cottages in south-western France, with a view to buying a holiday home. A jam caused by an overturned lorry made us an hour late at Heathrow. Otherwise an easy, uneventful journey. A Renault 16 was waiting and I drove without much difficulty through the city and sixty miles eastward to the market town of Ribérac, where we put up at the Hotel de France and Cath revelled in her new bed and bathroom. The country round about didn't strike me as especially beautiful, though Claude Roy and others had told us it was their favourite region of France. This of course was only the Dordogne departement but not the river, almost Charente, in fact, and watered by another river altogether, The Dronne.

Next day we drove north-east to Bourdeilles, a riverside village boasting a beautiful buttressed bridge and two chateaux high above. Picnicked on the bank before driving on to Brantôme, where the limestone cliffs were perforated with square holes, shuttered or draped, the windows and doors of modern cave-dwellings. The eroded rocks overhang the roads like roofs and allow the natural shapes to serve as houses.

[In Knightsbridge, some days before, we'd been shown by a Hooray or Sloane, some slides of available properties we could afford. He was the English end of an association with a local agent who now showed us round, speeding from one village to another.]

M. Varaillon spoke no English and we met no-one who was able to eke out our pitiable French. This at least meant I had to make a real effort to talk. My grammar-school way of thinking had me wondering whether to try cases and tenses or stick to blurting out verb infinitives, which is all most foreigners manage. I even tried a joke or two. As some bikers sped past in black leather, I asked 'Les anges d'enfer?' 'Comment?' said Varaillon, the usual response to any attempt to cope with their ludicrous lingo. Had he ever even heard of Hell's Angels? An Italian will say 'Parla benissimo,' if you so much as blurt out a few words. The French see anything less than perfection as an affront. Their many qualities don't include being lovable, or wanting to be.

The properties were large and dilapidated, often lacking floors or stairs; some damp, some larger than we needed, most had extensive land, once small-holdings the family had abandoned as a bad job. Some were remote, a few situated in villages, one was part of another house. The most expensive comprised not only an impressive farmstead but a middle-aged couple who still tended the land and would act as *gardiens* when we're not there.

The natives are leaving in droves. We gradually gathered that it's a national dilemma, how to encourage people to stay in the farms and work the land. The young have already gone or going. In one room, in a dark corner, there was even a very old man lying on what was evidently his death-bed.

These mostly nineteenth-century houses appear sound and sturdy, needing only superficial renovation to be habitable. There are enormous barns, the size of churches, like rural folk museums, complete with great bullock-carts, yokes and wine-presses. In upper granaries, maize-cobs lie rotting in heaps. A youngish family in possession looked like the most underprivileged slum-dwellers, the woman, almost certainly younger than Thelma, had blackened and swollen legs and a crone's face; her children's skin was hideous with untreated sores. Varaillon spoke to them brusquely and ordered them about, as though dealing with an inferior species. We saw for the first time what the word 'peasant' could mean to a townsman, even from a town as small as Ribérac. A mere estate-agent had someone to look down on. But mostly the houses were empty and one we liked at once was a one-storey farm standing alone on its own two hectares, with a massive barn, a well, an orchard of overgrown cherries, a walled vegetable garden and a fish-pond. This would come to less than £4,000.

[This part of the diary strongly tempts me to jump the gun. Hindsight tells me this was Chez Magnou, the house we bought, that for ten years was to be our second home for spring and summer school holidays and even, but not often, midwinter excursions.

There'd been a programme of rural state subsidy a hundred years and more ago, to encourage agriculture, when these farms were built, and little had been done since to bring all this into line with modern methods. When we arrived, they still ploughed with oxen and broadcast grain by hand from a heap held in an apron, as in the drawing in my school Bible illustrating the parable of the good seed.

The invasion of English buyers was soon spoken of as a Second Hundred Years' War, but the locals were all eager to sell up and move into breezeblock bungalows. During the years we visited the place, the native way of life changed from bullocks to tractors, from Deux Chevaux to Simca saloons. The houses were put in better order, power and mains water installed, marshy citernes made into swimming-pools, all employing local labour and ensuring these craftspeople stayed. Those who came in hordes from the north, not only us but Dutch, Belgians and Scandinavians, were mostly modest professionals with a little cash to spare, eager to drink cheap wine and cook fresh produce grown in their own restored orchards and vegetable gardens, tended by local men in their long years of retirement.]

We spent two of our four days house-hunting and on the last drove south-east towards the Dordogne to see the cave-paintings at Lascaux. Thelma read out the fulsome descriptions from our guide-book while we travelled through fine weather on the empty roads of Perigord. Finally, reaching and climbing the hill, following signs to the grotte, we were surprised at how few tourists there were at such a world-famous attraction. A car-park deep in the woods had only one vehicle on it, presumably belonging to the man setting out picture postcards of prehistoric paintings on a table. By getting off in good time, we told each other, we'd beaten the crowds. I asked the way to the caves and we tried to understand his reply. We must be translating it all wrong. Thelma was first to accept the truth. They'd been closed for seven years.

Everyone knows now, of course, when we tell the story. Oh, yes, algae began growing and the Ministry of Culture closed it down before too much damage was done and the hot breath of tourists destroyed what had been there for ten thousand years, etc etc.

Drove instead to Les Eyzies, where Cro-Magnon man was discovered. Here we found some caves at last and were shown round by two giggling girls, one clearly an official guide, easy to tell by the formal pedantry the French bring to this job, at whatever level. Her spiel, little of which we could understand anyway, kept changing from a precise recital of statistics and eulogy, to a gabble of private jokes with her friend, while we gazed at the exhibits. Nothing was made at all of the limestone formations which are all they have at Cheddar. No Devils' Curtain or Castle in a Lake. All the attention here was on the remarkable drawings of buffalo, horse and deer. In photographs, one can't feel the size and extent or the way the pictures use the rockface contours or, most surprising, the strange luminosity that makes them far more apparent by indirect light than when a torch is shone directly at them.

We were the last of that morning's tourists and sat eating peaches and Camembert as the girl-guides parted with one last giggle, to go home for *déjeuner*. A school party arrived too late and had to wait for the girls to come back. It began to rain and we left them sheltering and sharing their food beneath the trees.

Bordeaux on our return was crammed with traffic. Almost at once we passed a three-car collision. The central park is only for cars and above it rises an immense winged statue, like an ironic comment on our inability to deal with the problems of locomotion.

The minicab driver took us through the Friday rush-hour on King's Road, Chelsea. This was the end of a day that had begun with breakfast in Ribérac, taking in the prehistoric caves, the Dordogne valley and vineyards of St Emilion. Our species *could* be going in the right direction but today it doesn't seem likely.

Since then, work with Michael on the script, mostly in Carl Foreman's office but with one or two research visits to the Whittington hospital. Matron, refined and antiseptic, chaffed some West Indian nurses and, as we moved off, explained to us: 'We don't encourage colour prejudice here because, you see, we *need* them.' Later, in the kitchens: 'Sometimes the coloured women are cleaning the vegetables, sun coming in behind the windows, a charming scene. I think it would appeal to your artistic sense.' Michael said, as she turned away to inspect a surface, that the effect would have been even finer with banjos and tap-dancing.

Sensing perhaps that her picture was too sweet to be true, she told us they'd had a nasty case where a deranged mortuary attendant had had dreams of being a great surgeon. After he'd gone, complaints began to come in of loved ones being delivered at funerals with missing limbs. Police paid him a visit and found the arms, legs and feet scattered about his bed-sitting-room.

Party at Tynans'. Kathleen in a see-through dress that I didn't notice, though she's a great-looking girl. Thelma said later you could see her pubic hair. Why did she look? Must be true women dress to please each other, not men. Harold Clurman had been to *Health* and enjoyed it.

> [This director and critic had been one of the prime movers of the Group Theatre (1931-41) in the USA and author of its history *The Fervent Years*, a formative book for me in the post-war period. I couldn't then imagine a better way of life than belonging to such a company and doing that sort of original and creative work, the first stagings of work by Odets, Saroyan, Irwin Shaw, etc, played by actors like Franchot Tone, John Garfield and the Adlers. For the NY *Nation*, he'd written the most perceptive review ever of *Joe Egg*. He saw that my play was 'a new wrench to the proverbial British "stiff upper lip".']

David Mercer arrived at this party with a petition for the release of Bolivian political prisoners and bothered some lords till one lent him a biro so that they could all sign.

The Oliviers also came and were friendly. In this week's Honours List he was made a life peer.

We left early to see Carol Channing's new show at Drury Lane and afterwards eat with her and her husband. We've been mystified by her interest in me and wondered if she wants to do a musical of *Egg* and, if so, which part she'd play, mother or child. The show was lively, high-powered and mindless. She never misses a performance and makes the kind of appeal that athletes do. Some Americans in the audience applauded the first lines of songs because they recognised them.

Afterwards reported to her dressing-room and waited while other guests paid their respects and left. We sat on, no drinks were offered, no move made towards supper. At last, out of a heavy silence, the husband rose and said, 'Well, we'll meet on Monday and have the pleasure of taking you and Miss Ramsay to dine afterwards.' Thelma'd got the date wrong and now it was too late to eat anywhere. We left like scalded cats. On top of all this, we now had to spend more time with them when it had been sticky enough already. Our hearts sank.

Dressed for society the following week, the star of *Hello, Dolly* cut quite a figure: nearly six feet tall, with bleached hair (a rug?), clownish circles of rouge on cheeks and nose, vermilion lips, a yachting cap at a jaunty angle, a navy-blue-and-white sailor's style dress and white stockings with high-heeled shoes. We'd been warned she'd bring her own food but weren't prepared for her driver rushing in and out of The Inigo Jones with various black leather containers.

'What's this?' Peggy demanded.

'I only eat organic food.'

'Is that the same as macrobiotic? How terribly interesting!'

Nothing else she did quite equalled her appearance or eating habits. Whenever the husband/manager seemed close to suggesting some possible songs and dances for *Egg*, Peggy put on a display of distractions that was exciting in itself. She talked at length about the importance of footwork for comedians and advised them to watch Ernie Wise's feet. Channing looked nervous, as though she'd never thought about that, and the husband asked us to change the subject or she might suddenly think of feet onstage and fall over.

We refused their offer of a lift and walked through the busy fruit and vegetable market [Covent Garden, now a theme park and shopping centre!] and along streets still warm at two a.m., then under the porch of St Paul's Church, where meths-drinkers and other vagrants slept in rows. Peggy, in a golden dress, picked her way between the bodies and declaimed her view of the Channing duo and pictured us taking up their invitation to join them this summer at Las Vegas.

Saw the *Egg* film at last, at the end of a week when it had transpired that everyone in London had seen some part of it, except me. I asked Medak if I should wait till it came to the local Odeon, if it really was that difficult to arrange. Even Blakemore had seen a couple of reels. We were invited to a Wardour Street viewing-theatre and sat with Van Eyssen, Deutsch, Medak, the editor, Peggy and some girls from

Columbia's typing-pool to give us the female point of view. I praised it wherever I found something that could be praised. I *was* pleasantly surprised at times, only because my expectations had been so low. Melodrama instead of light comedy. He's denied any possibility of living a decent life with a handicapped child. Of course, the play too failed to state that case well enough but at least it tried. I'd have done better to understate the difficulties than exaggerate them.

The confounding of opinion polls is some, but not much, consolation for the return of a Conservative government, including four old Etonians, a Scottish laird as Foreign Secretary and a hanging-flogging woman as Education Minister [the first diary mention of Margaret Thatcher, though unnamed]. John Grigg, also fooled by the polls, spent much of an evening persuading Iris Murdoch and me that we'd be wrong to vote for Wilson. He claims you may expect more from Heath, an essentially progressive man pretending to be reactionary, than from Wilson, the polar opposite. Iris was voting, she said, on principle because *any* Labour government must represent social justice and fair shares better than one that is, by definition, on the side of the status quo. Then she corrected herself. She wouldn't be voting at all, as husband John's a Tory so they'll be paired. Bailey's main concern is to save the party from degenerating into Fascism. Out of office, he said, he feared extremists would take over and force them to the right. But what we all feared before the polls did happen and Powellites were put in everywhere. Small-c conservatives of all classes voted to keep the wogs out. And the others? Who knows? Wanted a change or to cheer up the underdog because Heath seemed nice and Wilson was complacent, already talking about his next summit in Moscow. John's wife, Patsy, says Heath's always very nice to Alexander so perhaps the country's in good hands after all.

Mum arrived from Bristol, excited at the prospect of her latest holiday in Vancouver with her brother Harold and his child-like wife. Where has the traditional (fictional?) grandmother gone? Her mother, our Nan, was one, always taking over the children so that Vi could go to her whist drives, travellers' balls or trips to Belgium and Scotland. But now it's difficult to get Vi to occupy Dan and Catherine for an hour while Louise is taken to a piano lesson. She starts on about washing her hair.

I said no doubt they've got water in Canada and made her laugh herself out of that particular laziness but she's not at all a type-cast grannie.

She couldn't find a single book on our shelves to read in bed at night We'd already put most of our light reading in her room, but she found nothing there either. At the air-terminal Wymans, she chose a historical romance. 'That looks alright.' A bit of crap about milady with poke-bonnets and crinolines to escape into from her stratospheric DC10 while zooming over the north pole, literary equivalent of the muzak that will soothe the turbulence. Not music or literature, but paste art, lacking the vitality of kitsch, an aspirin, an industrial product. In days when life was cruel, a shelter from the stormy blast was really desirable because so hard to find. Now what's elusive is the raw and real. A Comet crashed last night in Spain and a hundred died, though they probably knew very little about it, listening to Mantovani and reading Frank Yerby.

The production of Michael Frayn's evening of one-act plays opened at Cambridge and we went up on Friday. There's nothing I can usefully say about a first visit to the town. It's like Venice in being exactly as you expect it to be. Michael says his undergraduate years here were the happiest of his life. He enjoyed every minute. Christ but I envy him going there at the right time. If only I'd known what universities *were*. I thought Cambridge was a team of oarsmen and knew the other place only as the location for *A Yank at Oxford,* in which Robert Taylor routed all the stuck-up limeys.

Later Michael punted us away from Scudamore's boatyard, standing on the platform at the back. Not long after, he invited me to take a turn. Dreading a disaster, overturning the punt or left clinging to the pole and arriving at the hotel in wet clothes like Trevor Howard in *Brief Encounter*, I nonetheless rolled up my sleeves and took hold. With the advantage of a downstream current, I made a good enough crack, though it's impossible to tell with the Frayns, they're so adept at playing down their own skills and praising other people's. If I manage to return the ball in tennis, he never fails to says what a brilliant cross-court volley it was or may shout, 'Fantastic shot, Peter!', despite – or because of? – his regularly thrashing me 6–2, 6–1. So now with punt-ing. Gill and he lay on blue plastic cushions saying what amazing natural ability I had. The first time he'd been out, he said, he'd had to be rescued by the boatman after circling five times before settling on a direction. Most of the other boats today were full of noisy French youths. Tired Americans stared blankly from bridges as I tried to make out this was all in a day's work.

He showed us over his alma mater, Emmanuel, with its pleasant garden and pond, into which, one summer night many moons ago, he was thrown by the rugger team for having invented for a varsity paper an undergraduate hearty called Mr Plod.

'I swam up and down a couple of times, to show I didn't mind, then got out and bowed to their applause. They were jolly decent about it and insisted I join them for a drink.'

Is this role playing, I wondered. Wasn't it like saying 'Unaccustomed as I am to public speaking'? And from one of the wittiest men in England, with an ear so well-tuned and sceptical that I was at first afraid to speak in his presence? I can't avoid a suspicion (hope?) that he's limited as a novelist and (more so) a dramatist by a lack of seriousness at the crunch, a decency bred of having spent four years in this urbane place, around these quiet courts, Fellows' gardens, the supreme Perpendicular chapel, these tepid pools and streams. The four plays didn't disprove this, though were brilliant in their way and well performed by Lynn Redgrave and Richard Briers.

11 July

Alan Bennett read a selection of prose and poetry on TV, beginning with a bit from *Put Out More Flags*, perhaps Waugh's most offensive and snobbish novel, even including *Brideshead*. Alan said all his choices would be from minor authors like him and much of their effect would come from the snobbery of the English class system. He liked class and élitism, especially that of dons, the Cambridge sort best of all. His favourites included several books Michael had mentioned, such as *Private View* by Gwen Raverat, whose house we saw from the punt. I'm ambidextrous about this. Class is, after all, only an aspect of Money. The rich can afford to pay lower- and lower-middle-class comics to perform for them and idealise them for all the other parvenus to admire.

Such people as Nancy Mitford's uncle, the second Baron Redesdale, is tremendous fun, of course, but no reins restricted his eccentricity. He never had to fear unemployment or dismissal or loss of face. His voice would have signalled 'toff' to anyone about to arrest or impede him. My father shared Redesdale's penchant for Galli-Curci and played records of her in just the same way. Had Dad known about Papism, he'd have been as funny about Friar Lawrence: 'That damned padre was the cause of the trouble.' Mitford's old men are more attractive than, say, Micawber or Pritchett's Mister Beluncle because of her lightness of touch, in itself a manner that comes from the privilege earned by inherited land or – more often nowadays – industrial shares.

Humiliating game of tennis with Grigg. By obvious cheating, he managed to let me win one game out of twelve. I pulled a muscle trying to get the ball back and am in cruel pain when I turn from the waist.

The sketch for *Oh! Calcutta*, after being accepted, rejected and accepted again, has now finally been rejected. We're claiming the fifty pounds originally promised by Tynan, as some small consolation for the insult. I hear Tennessee Williams has been treated the same way.

19 July

Reading Henri Troyat's monumental life of Tolstoy. No fictional character could be quite such a shit as he was at his worst or such a genius at his best. The only role he never tired of, it seems, was landowner. Even as he blathered on about freeing the serfs and giving them their share of the land, he was acquiring vast acreages to add to Yasnaya Polyana. He gambled the whole estate away and sold serfs on a regular basis to pay for his losses at cards. Affronted by some insult, he vowed to leave and live in England, writing at once to his aunt here to establish contacts with the aristocracy so that he could move at once in the best circles. Despite his levelling educational theories, his children were all sent to the poshest schools.

But the sheer industry! After *War and Peace*, he spent a period he thought of as idling time away, which meant helping with the harvest, writing a 700-page manual on education, hunting, planning a novel on Peter the Great, learning Greek and outlining a translation of Homer, as well as reading the entire works of Schopenhauer.

The time's out of joint for protean figures. Discussed this with Alan Bates when he came to dinner. He'd only met one: Moyshe Dayan's daughter, who apart from being (like Tolstoy) soldier and novelist, speaks six languages and does her share of international diplomacy as all Israelis do. A society like that would force more out of you than a lazy place like ours. They look to the future, we to the past. Alan says he tries any number of things – playing the flute, working out at the gym, gardening, learning Italian – but can't keep any going long enough to become proficient.

Hearing this, Tony Garnett [celebrated producer of much of the best television drama of the sixties – including *Cathy, Come Home, Edna, Up the Junction* and my own *The Gorge* as well as feature films like *Kes*] said yes, Tolstoy okay, but what about all the others? Was he in any way typical? Are the energy and sweep of his stories part of the zeitgeist of his Russia? To what extent did his individual force derive from his world? Judging from Chekhov's (which of course are from somewhat later), I'd say people then were as idle as we are, though not, of course, Chekhov himself, whose languor was due to TB.

Listing Tolstoy's busy-ness, I left out the incessant diary-writing, the hilarious reciprocal journals of him and Sonya, where they corrected and made addenda to each others' entries, just as Dad did when he read mine. My own inertia's only too obvious from the negligence in keeping this so-called journal. Two pages a week, if we're lucky. Certainly no prompt day-by-day reports while the memory's warm.

To the Infant section of the children's state primary school, Morden Mount, to hear the headmaster address a parents' meeting. Louise and Dan go there at present and Cath will start next autumn. This was an hour of euphemisms. 'Encountering difficulties' means 'backward' or 'dim'. 'Not everyone can profit from an academic education' equals 'we'll always need shelf-stackers and shit-shovellers'. Comical and also sad that they feel they must use these dishonest pretensions to equality in a field where everything consists of differences. Louise and Dan probably aren't exceptionally bright but Lou (and her friend Rhadni, daughter of an HMI from Lahore) have already been through all the reading books and now have to mark time until they move up to Junior level where they'll start on them all over again, probably so as not to humiliate anyone encountering difficulties.

Finished revisions of *Hearts and Flowers*, a nice quiet little play that should pass an interesting hour, then turned to revising the screenplay of *Health*, now approved by Columbia. Michael [Blakemore] rang and suggested we work this week in Carl Foreman's office, halfway between Blackheath and Hampstead. We did a day on Tuesday, starting at 11.30. I was a little late, having had a call from Medak as I was leaving, but Mike still hadn't arrived and, when he did, it was with some cock-and-bull story about waiting for a script to come, when he'd told me previously he was seeing Shirley off on a holiday in Nice with Conrad. Mike's already had his, in Spain, without them. To put it mildly, he's obsessive, niggling over the food in restaurants as though expecting to find animal turds in the lettuce, devouring newspapers as if they were ambrosia, never passing a cinema without turning aside to look at the stills, often asking me to cross busy streets to peer at pictures in a strip-club doorway. Thelma says that if you want to hold or win back his attention, you must drop in at random words like 'breast' and naked'.

When we left, he suggested we meet next day at twelve, because he had an interview earlier. In that case, I said, why not the day after? No, we'd get a lot done after noon. I submitted, but later Thelma told me I should have insisted on a day's work or none at all. Next morning, he called to say he was seeing a doctor after the interview and could we make it the afternoon. When I let him know I was pretty fed up with this, as this week's work had been his idea, he burst out:

'Now just a minute! I put off a production so that you could go to France. Alright, forget it.' And slammed down the receiver.

Later, while I was fetching the kids from school, he rang saying he'd come out to Blackheath in the morning to air his grievances and wanted Thelma there too.

I was doing Diary when he arrived and finally came down to find them chatting over coffee. I joined in, and it became harder to imagine how he'd turn round this congenial conversation. But he did.

'Frankly, Pete, I have the impression you're behaving in a rather spoilt fashion. I'm the last to deny your writing stands on its own. *The Gorge* worked wonderfully and I had nothing to do with that. But you must agree that many of the formal qualities of *Joe Egg* owed a good deal to me. I think I made a real contribution to that and *National Health*.'

[87]

'I've never denied that.'

'In private, yes, but it's odd that you never mention it in interviews. On that broadcast, as soon as the critic asked about the work we did together on the script, you said you didn't want to discuss it. I could hardly say *I* did but it struck me as ungrateful.'

He went on, awkwardly, almost apologetically, to list my inconsiderate acts for some years past. Some were just, some not. I've always praised and recognised his share of the credit or blame for the stuff, in public and in private. This was one of those cases where critics came between workers. It wasn't my fault that my tributes were left out. Journalism thrives on 'names' and neither Morahan's nor his are starry enough yet to add glamour to their columns, so however often I sing their praises, they don't appear. I reminded him of my speech at the awards lunch which insisted the trophy was as much his as mine.

Thelma took the chance to round on me as well, giving vent to a few long-felt resentments, and it was almost pleasurable to let their abuse wash over me. The peace of martyrdom. I said I was sorry he'd got that impression and promised to do better in future.

28 July

In New York City, sufferers from heart and chest conditions are advised to stay indoors when pollution counts are high. Tokyo traffic policemen use oxygen respirators. I was woken this morning by a sound like some demented god splitting open the sky: a jet plane circling above. While I shaved, it came through the skylight and while I dressed through the window. Eating breakfast, trying to concentrate on news of Salazar's death and reviews of *Oh! Calcutta*, the din roared on around the kitchen. As I write this in my attic study, the plane sounds close to the chimneys. Only Berliners could find this beautiful.

To enable us to work on the script, Michael stayed over a night. At home, without Shirley, he let the dishes pile up unwashed for her return and, when they were all dirty, took to eating out. He makes any place his own in no time. In the evening, while I was practising elementary Bach and Mozart on *my* piano while he sat in *my* armchair watching *my* television, he lost his rag and asked *my* wife how much longer I'd keep it up. When she refused to ask me to stop, he strode about slamming all the doors. Most of us conform to one or two demands of

[88]

courtesy, feeling we shouldn't grumble at what we receive but be truly thankful. Not him.

'You're absolutely sure this is home-made marmalade? Good, I'll have that. It's no reflection on your excellent tea if you see me pouring more water into the kettle or boiling it again.'

Of course, he's as bad at home. We remember the handwritten signs left for Shirley on suspect foodstuff in the fridge: 'Out!' He has an enviable (I suppose) knack of making women do as he tells them. Thelma was about to marshal Louise across the road on some errand when he insisted she switch the extension through so that he could make a call. That the child got across unharmed was no thanks to him. He then remained on the phone for an hour while I waited to run him to Lewisham station, ten minutes' walk away. He could have been *with* the woman if he'd left straight away.

His directorial brilliance is partly due to voyeurism and he was among the first in line to see a preview of *Calcutta*. Having devoured the notices this morning, he said I was well out of it, as the writing had been slated in every paper.

Working with him in the living-room overlooking the street, I was facing into the room when he suddenly plunged forward, transfixed by something he'd seen through the bay windows. Alarmed, I jumped up and rushed to see, imagining an accident. Our neighbour, an attractive middle-aged wife and mother, was walking past. Her head shot round at my sudden appearance and I had to smile and wave like someone in a farce.

Half-past ten as I finish typing this and the jet-plane's still circling. Using up fuel before coming in on a wing and a prayer? Few cities I've seen have so much dangerous traffic in their skies.

1 August

At five past midnight, I remembered I was forty-three. Michael Frayn was giving a party at a restaurant in Kennington for the Griggs and us after the West End opening of his one-act plays. They'd gone well but not *very* well. Thelma said Irving Wardle looked sour. Noël Coward sat in front of us. He laughed a good deal and repeatedly raised his arm to scratch his bald pate. Rachel Kempson was beside me, called him darling and leaned across to kiss him, nearly breaking my leg in the process. Nervous for her daughter Lynn, who again acquitted herself very well.

The morning reviews were cool and we heard that some were hostile. I spoke to Michael later and he sounded shaken, though philosophic, seeing it as an experience one had to go through, like being ducked in the Cam.

Blakemore told me of the occasion when he took his mistress to an exhibition of cartoons at the National Portrait Gallery. She was late for their covert assignation and, while waiting, he noticed several distinctly inartistic-looking men with cameras standing in a huddle by the entrance. When the woman finally arrived, Mike and she tried to sidle in but were welcomed at the ticket-office by an official who said, 'You are the five thousandth person to visit this exhibition and we hope you'll join us and receive a present from Dr Roy Strong the director.'

While Mike tried to hide his face and hers, pressmen flashed their bulbs, unaware of the Feydeau possibilities. Mike had packed off his wife and son, claiming pressure of work. To add a pinch more savour, Strong had written a hostile notice of *National Health* in *Queen* magazine. They forced down the complimentary sherry and were presented with a Giles cartoon by the artist.

My doctor has an article on pox in one of the Sundays, claiming that non-specific urethritis is the commonest form of VD, is confined to males, has more nuisance value than real danger and suggests it's due solely to promiscuity. I must put him straight on this.

To Club Row animal market in Bethnal Green. Amazing, the East End on Sunday morning, a Jewish Saturday atmosphere, despite there being far fewer Jews than when I came as a child with Auntie Lil to Petticoat Lane.

'Ere yar, Alsatians arf-price!' shouted a bored woman over a box of struggling puppies.

'Labradors 'ere, guaranteed,' said another.

Parrots, mynah-birds, canaries, budgies, white doves and finches perched in cages; minuscule and multicoloured tropical fish swam in plastic bags. Tubby Isaacs sold eels, dead and jellied, under the sign 'We lead, others follow'.

'We're out of Malayan Angelfish,' said an assistant in the only shop in a permanent structure, around which the other stalls cluster. The people look savage with each other, tender with their pets.

> A singing bird in a cage
> Puts all heaven in a rage.

[I agree with Blake and see Cockneys as sentimental and cruel, especially in their supposed love of dogs like Rottweilers and pit-bulls. My distrust of them comes from being more Bristolian than East End, even though my father was born and brought up east of Whitechapel.]

16 August

On a fine Sunday evening, we're sitting in Thelma's Auntie Millie's front room. We just dropped her off at her friend Phyllis's place, a mile or two closer in to Swansea itself.

[These spinster friends were of that generation that came of age in the 1920s. The Great War (never WW1 or World War One to anyone who remembered it) had diminished the stock of eligible men, and our families were typical in the number of unmarried women always about, with whispered legends of their fiancés having been killed in Flanders.]

Phyllis showed us colour transparencies of their holidays in a light-up viewer held together with rubber bands.

'This is Salzburg, the fountain where Julie Andrews danced with the children.'

I praised her spacious house.

'Far too large for me alone. Four rooms on this floor, three on the next and two attics where I haven't been for months.'

And Millie, her inseparable friend, lives alone in the semi-det halfway round the bay to Mumbles. Why do they keep themselves to themselves? Thelma says their houses are their only claim on their families' continuing interest, enabling them to offer free rooms for holidays by the sea. Without that treat to dangle, the nieces and nephews might never bring their children to visit.

We drove down yesterday through crawling holiday traffic, bright sun giving way to rain as we reached Wales and to tempests by Derwen Fawr.

Small rooms, with every surface strewn with knick-knacks, tokens from bewildered relatives, or souvenirs of coach-tours in Spain, Austria or Scotland; ash-trays so tiny they're full after the first tap, in ultramarine glass or green ceramic; models of yachts, gondolas and feluccas; bowls held in the antlers of Disney deer; stylised yellow Scotties; a humorous cross-eyed donkey holding two barrels for salt and pepper; a plastic watering-can beside a ball-point pen in a holder marked Muscular Dystrophy Research. On the walls a reproduction Canaletto and an old art photograph of Thelma, an entry for some Miss Wind-and-Rain competition. If she didn't win, it's hard to see why. The rooms are congested with armchairs and uprights; the bedroom suites are in Aztec varnished wood; ballet-scenes edge Iberian bulls off the glass-topped dressing-tables; travel-agents' brochures lie in piles in Lloyd-Loom linen baskets. A museum of token gifts to a woman who never lets you forget her birthday, her busy and untutored mind racing ahead, presuming the next affront, mitigating the last barbed remark.

'Mrs Beynon had a bit of a shock, got the sack. Well, she was rude to The Board. No-one ever thought they'd give her the boot, she was the best buyer Benn Evans ever had.'

(The names in her monologues are either those of relatives or the Swansea shops where she's worked as cashier – Calders, Evans, Sidney Heath.)

'Anyway she found herself a bit hard up and starting letting rooms to darkies. She went on holiday a fortnight ago and while she was away, two Pakistanis murdered a woman and her daughter in the upstairs front. Blood all up the walls. Not very nice to come home to.'

The house depresses me and Thelma's at her worst while we're there. But the children love the beaches along the coast, as beautiful as you find anywhere. At twilight we went to Rotherslade to see the hut Millie's hired for the week. Children care about nothing if they have sea, sand, a steady flow of Coca-Cola and a light fall of bacon-flavoured crisps.

We were the only people there. Even in oilskins and boots, it finally defeated us and we came home to Millie's and a weather forecast promising thunderstorm and flood.

The weather lifted briefly so we took an hour on a hard court behind the beach-huts and had a good knock, before the tide rose and we had to hurry down to see Louise's great trench filling up. The sun was low but strong and we lay with backs against the rocks watching all three kids cavorting in the waves. Dan stood on a rock chanting continuously 'Sea, sea, you can't touch me!', his version of the Canute legend I'd told him earlier. It was perfect, this long moment, almost euphoric, lasting while the tide reached its high point among large pebbles near the concrete shelter.

In the evening, we two walked across the golf-course beyond Mumbles Road and some way along the beach as an immense moon rose over the bay, cause of the high tides, while she talked of her family history and I grumbled inside my head. These people mean nothing to me and I've never cared much for families, starting with my own. Same time, I admit she's a far saner, more effective person than I'll ever be. My kind of melancholic madness is only useful to an overfed and indulgent society. Her nature's more essential and practical. She'd get things going anywhere. Optimistic, so that rain's a challenge to her, not an excuse to stay home. She hates bed, except for reading and sleeping, won't lie in. I love and hate her, and her hometown aggravates my feelings of alarm, jealousy and scorn. Fears of falling back into the undistinguished lives of our families rise like ghouls to strengthen the awful depression that's hung around me these last few months. By most criteria, I'm a rich man with a deposit account standing at over £20,000, a house in London, another in France, a trust for the children that also owns property in Bristol. I'm a reputable playwright with a wife he finds cruelly attractive, three healthy kids, some bright friends . . . depressed? But think of Tolstoy, how much more he had, how much more titanically depressed. Money to me means being free of economic pressure, being able to write as I like. But so far none of my plays has been more than decorative, clever and entertaining. Useful they aren't. I know selfishness is the worst sin and carries its own punishments (see Blakemore) but all manner of rational argument can't cancel one's character. I'm a selfish man trying not to be.

Still, I get very little return for the apparently enviable position I'm in. If Thelma has her French house, why shouldn't I have a flat in Town, perhaps one she doesn't know about? Wouldn't it help us both if I had a private life, left off bothering her for demonstrations of a sexual pleasure she doesn't feel? I'm suggesting a safety-valve so as to avoid a disastrous explosion.

She and I left Kate looking after the tots and drove back yesterday, stopping at Abergavenny for a good lunch of pasta with rosemary, and pigeon in red wine. [Our first time in the now-celebrated Walnut Tree, though Diary doesn't name it.] After Severn Bridge and motorway, we always take the road through Tormarton, the Griggs' village, and here, passing the public playground, saw Lady Altrincham [his mother] pushing two children back and forth on swings. I'd have stopped to talk but left it too late. A strange sight, this woman drawn as a young beauty by Sargent, a likeness that hangs over the Griggs' hearth, now standing by a roadside trying to amuse two – what? grandchildren? The progeny of family retainers?

Thelma's indifference has made me think about my new stage play in a different way. Shouldn't it happen after the husband has left home to live on his own? Then his monologue's a soliloquy and the arguments only in his head, mulling over his past actions, quarrelling with his alibis, trying to discredit the views of others. He has something to talk *about*: having left his wife. In thinking this out as fiction, I might help myself solve the problem. Perhaps it should be set in that hypothetical flat I proposed just now?

Dropped in on Peggy Ramsay at her office in the alley Goodwin's Court, while Thelma went shopping with Patsy Grigg. Found Jenny the secretary filing her nails, Peggy reading the paper. We talked for over an hour without the phone ringing. So business is quiet. Thel joined us later and Peggy suggested meatless lunch at the Vega in Panton St, which was as bad as we feared. Shared a table with a timid-looking spinster munching her way through some nutty fritter.
    'Well, darling, Marcus has got Parkinson's,' declaimed my (and Frank Marcus's) agent, 'can't stop his head nodding like a lunatic. He takes these tablets but they don't do any good, though everyone says they're aphrodisiac. Well, dear, I hope he's getting some good fucks because his head still nods.'

The other woman kept her eyes on her plate and left as soon as she could.

'D'you think she *knows* Marcus, darling?' Peggy wondered aloud, 'perhaps his best friend?'

Lazed through the day, except for Thelma's driving-lesson and a session with John G, who came to translate some documents to do with the purchase of our farm. Listened to records I bought that morning of Bechet, Beiderbecke and Waller, now on LP's, greatly improved and with no discernible surface hiss. Watched television while she began Trollope's autobiography which John had tipped as a good read. To bed quite early, reflecting again on the length of days not dominated by the needs of children.

[The purchase of Chez Magnou had been bewildering in more ways than fathoming legalistic (*ancien?*) French. The price we actually agreed and paid was higher than that appearing on the vending documents. We first thought we were being cheated by the vendor and her agent but learned in the long run that this was a Gallic shrug at the taxman. Declaring less is common practice there, an understood way of short-changing the revenue.]

Saw Maggie Smith as Hedda Gabler. The setting for Bergman's production, a few screens, reflected the walls of the Cambridge Theatre's auditorium. Enjoyed very much this non-naturalistic version and thought Maggie wonderful, funny as you'd expect but also weird and pathetic. Bergman had managed what few English directors can, that's subdue her Kenneth Williams side. I took the view that the play would be better without the tragically conventional suicide at the end. Worse surely to have to go on living with Tesman and Brack?

Went round. First time we'd spoken for years. Husband Bob Stephens also came in. A burglar alarm had rattled all night on a nearby building and was driving 'Miss Neurosis' (as Ken always called her) into a near-hysterical state. She also feels she's being exploited for the American tourist trade and I, of course, am equally angry that I'm not. *The National Health* plays that theatre for a few evenings in September.

They were both scathing about the planned *Guys and Dolls* later this year with Olivier as Nathan.

'They've got a room down the Waterloo Road,' said Bob, 'crammed with advance bookings.'

'And he can't imitate anybody,' said Mags, 'let alone a Broadway bum. What he has got is a tin ear – and two left feet.'

30 August

Left Greenwich 5.30 a.m., the five Frayns in their VW, we six in our Renault 16, eleven beings unable to move without taking half our homes with us. A great dome of luggage on our roof, the boot full of bulky sleeping-bags, tennis rackets, rainwear, espadrilles, frying pans, a gas cooker, cutlery, medicine and lotions, a transistor radio, Thelma's first consignment of goods for the holiday farm. A Green Card I'd spent a week trying to collect was not at Dover but we took the first ferry to Boulogne nonetheless.

'Have two sausages,' said the British Rail matelot in the cafeteria, 'you're entitled.'

At midday we picnicked on the banks of the Somme. Michael led us a roundabout way to Chartres where we ran about in the rush-hour trying to find enough hotel rooms for *onze personnes* and, once that was done, unloaded much of our load in a drizzle and up two flights of stairs to tiny cubby-holes crammed with beds and broken toilet fittings. This was the lowest point. I gazed about, remembering my spacious bedroom at home, my books, armchair, shelves of drink. After dinner that night, I came close to fainting in the restaurant, saved by Michael telling me to put my head between my legs, a gesture nobody stopped to stare at or offer to help, probably thinking I was drunk.

31 August

Next morning, duly astonished at cathedral rose-window and at women in folk-costume outside selling souvenirs.

Drove south, eating lunch on banks of Loire.

Put up for our stay at the Hotel France at Ribérac, had a relaxing dinner and watched local majorettes high-stepping to a band in the square.

[96]

1 September

No agent available but, too eager to wait, visited the farm anyway, a drive through beautiful partly wooded landscape, at last reaching Siorac village, where the postmistress, preparing lunch, directed us to what-she-called Mme Boisseau's house. Would it ever be *ours*?

Full of anxiety after a tiring and stressful journey, I couldn't see how we were ever to make use of a place so far away. How often could we face the drive, overnight ferry, and more driving, and what would this place offer us that we couldn't find at home? This was soon answered.

The waist-high grass had been scythed since our first and only visit and was spread about the barn, in case we wanted to use it as hay. The lofty beamed roof, the old cart and antique agricultural implements were as I remembered. The house itself was better. We pushed open doors that scraped the floors. There was even a single room upstairs we hadn't been shown by the agent but the shutter couldn't be opened here as it pressed against the unpruned branch of an apple-tree. On a rotting rope, we drew a bucketful of water from forty feet down the well, clear, cold and sparkling.

Of course, there was dilapidation, the wood nearly all worm-eaten, some rotted, cobwebs at every corner, a great frog staring from the middle of the room, as though searching for the right phrase to order us out, lizards scattered as we turned shutters on rusty hinges. The twin outside privy – His and Hers? – had collapsed, its dividing wall warped as though from the blast of a titanic fart. The huge barn doors were off their pivots and the floor was strewn with stuff that seemed to have been dropped at a moment's notice – in 1939? A pair of sabots, home-made basket, milking stool, bridle and other tackle. The tools were from a distant kind of life: harrows, ploughs, portable mangers, hoes, forks, saws. Evidence of more recent habitation were instant-coffee tins, glasses, a coffee-mill, dead Pschitt bottles. Although the last calendar was of 1967, no money seemed to have been spent anywhere for about fifty years. The air of neglect contrasted sharply with the hopes of the original houses, solid masonry, only the wood decayed.

In the hedged orchard and garden, apple and cherry trees were past their best, the fruit worm- or bird-eaten but, where we could taste any, sweet and good. Blackberries abounded. Gill tried nuts from the hazels but found them bitter. A vine over the back door bore green and black

[97]

grapes. Plops from the pond I'd at first thought denoted fish were more plump frogs. There were water-snakes a foot long. The ground shimmered and hummed with butterflies and cicadas.

We'd been told the house across the chemin vicinal (the width of one car) was used as a hunting lodge by a businessman from Perigueux but through the windows we saw dilapidation as serious as our own. Otherwise the nearest house was some way off.

'We've met our neighbours,' Thelma reported, 'they're English and they've got that farm we saw near the main road. He's a retired surveyor from Bromley and they live here all the year round. They say the family in the next farm shout at each other day and night.'

We'd glimpsed a woman bawling at a stunned-looking peasant while she took in the washing and later nagging their boy who stared at our car with the impassive curiosity of people who live in seclusion.

Immensely relieved to find the farm so promising, I saw months of happy pottering away from home. Sad, too, that the smallholdings had been abandoned, whole villages empty, roofs gone, fruit left to the birds, a Chekhovian scene, but better that we should come with our cheques from the Banque Nationale Populaire than that this decay should continue till nothing remained. The peasants were obsolescent, like megalosauruses, unable to modernise their agriculture. Apart from metal tools, this appears to have been a stone-age culture, with the well, bread-ovens and sinks all masonry and the only metal domestic appliance a hook in the chimney for smoking hams.

We'd heard about a pleasure ground some way beyond Siorac-de-Ribérac and found a sizeable lake approached through a plantation of pines and young oaks. Water gleamed between the dark frame of trees. Cafés and bars enhanced the place and a *grand bal* was advertised at a disco hall. Sometimes a French or English pop song blared from the speakers, but local families made more noise, shinning up trees or standing on their hands. Michael took one look at the water and at once swam to a jetty on the far side, emulating (Gill explained) some American uncle in his family legend who'd swam one of the Great Lakes. The farm was even more luckily situated than we'd imagined.

[Artisans were recruited by the agent and came in Deux Chevaux, pulling off their berets to shake hands with everyone. Dan solemnly shook with them, nodding as to the manner born. We walked them from room to room, examining floors, ceilings, windows, shutters and doors. Michael was invaluable, finding the words to discuss our needs with *plombier, maçon, menuisier, vitrier* and *electricien*. In a year we became fluent in this glossary of technical terms, for beams, shutters, granaries, termites, boilers and pumps. In Paris we might have acquired a different, though far less useful, culture. The workers weren't worried by various infestations where their counterparts at home would have shaken heads and tut-tutted. The carpenter would dig a penknife into a beam, gouge it about and nod. '*Très solide.*' The car mechanics were the same, always happy to use a plastic bag to insulate a distributor where an Englishman would have ordered a new part or written off the whole vehicle. This rural economy was frugal. We remembered the wartime slogan: make do and mend.]

Perigueux was the most exciting visit we made, entirely because of a chap called Abadie, architect of Sacre-Coeur and destroyer, in the general view, of many old provincial churches. When you see a couple of cupolas above a village, it's even money old Abadie was there. Perigueux's cathedral is an egg-box of these elongated hemispheres. We'd eaten well, studied Renaissance steps and mediaeval cloisters under the tutelage of tireless Michael, who now insisted we climb to the roof. Vertigo-sufferer Thelma stayed below with the younger children and the rest of us followed him up the spiral stairway, which brought us to a flat roof. Trippers were moving over the domes, with no sign of support. We followed some faint arrows to the belfry and scaled ladders propped against the joists. A rung of the first had broken and been replaced by a metal rod that was part of the chiming mechanism, still attached to it by a wire. *Très solide.* By this means we reached a platform over which hung half-a-dozen massive bells of varied size and pitch.

'Wouldn't it be awful,' Gill began, 'if they all started ringing while we –' and clutched her ears. 'God!'

The peal wasn't as bad as we'd expected but gave the young a chance to reel back crossing their eyes, juddering like cartoons. More climbing brought us to a conical zinc roof sloping down from the centre, above which a stone umbrella was supported by a ring of columns. There'd been no warning at all of what was in store once you started climbing and we now found the descent to be even more dangerous. In fact, the dingy arrows directed us up and down inclines, around turrets, a long walk about the unlikely roofscape of huge stone ovoids high above the city. The hooray-Henry who'd shown us slides in Knightsbridge told us the profession of surveyor doesn't exist in France. The native attitude to termites and bell-towers suggests they wouldn't be welcome. And quite right too.

Our visit over, we divided the hotel bill, Michael and Gill taking into account every drink and tip, going Dutch with a vengeance. They were continuing south, where many more gorges and castles were worth a detour. We drove north and put up for the night at Maintenon, north of Chartres, at L'Hotel de l'Aqueduc, tipped by Michelin, which forgot to mention that goods trains pass all night at intervals, blowing hooters in case you missed their engines and the clank of their couplings. The place had a stuffy air, like faded religion. There was even a list of ten commandments on our bedroom wall. Not *the* commandments but a decalogue of facetious, essentially serious, rules about how to behave in polite hotels.

'Watch your language after midnight – and if possible before!'

Our first course hadn't been served before the lights suddenly went out. At once, as though in a rehearsed routine, the staff brought candles and oil-lamps, the only charming feature of a staid evening. At the next table there were nuns who giggled at the power failure and, after some wine, were nearly hysterical. At another, an English couple, whose conversation was loud and clear in the candlelight.

He: I don't like cold meat. It's no use trying to persuade me I do.

She: And I don't care what you like.

He: Trying to persuade me I like it when you know damned well I don't.

She: It doesn't matter to me one way or another.

He: You've had too much wine. You're drunk.

(*Short pause for eating.*)

He: A crêpe is only a pancake.

She: Well? What of it?

He: I'm only telling you. That's all it is. A bloody pancake.

She: You think I care? I just don't care.

23 September

My aching teeth announce the approach of winter. A cool morning like today's starts that steely tingling that bars me from ice-cream and mousse and whistling in the open air. I took the kids to school in cold sunshine with the first leaves falling. Catherine now goes for mornings, coming home midday. At half-term she'll go full-time and their babyhood will be over.

A little black girl stared at me and said 'Is that your Dad?' Catherine shyly nodded. 'Your mum looks young but your dad looks old.'

After this, I didn't resume a conversation I'd begun days earlier with an attractive au pair girl at the gates. The secret of success with women, Thelma assures me, is arrogant indifference. My few triumphs confirm this, always happening when I was most sure of myself. This will go into the play I'm halfway through.

2 October

The National Health reopens at the Cambridge, joining Maggie in *Hedda* and *The Beaux Stratagem* and *The Merchant* and a Somerset Maugham comedy, in each of which Olivier plays a Jew. On Saturday last the stalls were only two-thirds full for *TNH*, proof that the management has undermined our success. It's played for less than two months in a year (in terms of actual performances) and nothing's been done to help a non-star company (well, except for Jim Dale) to move to the West End.

Michael Blakemore learnt that, during our rehearsals, the composer Marc Wilkinson asked the general manager for more money to engage extra musicians for the recording session.

'But, Marc,' he was told, 'this is a bad play. It's only going to run six weeks. Not worth our while.'

[To deal with this, Michael called regularly on Irving Wardle, critic of *The Times* and a friend of the play, to re-review. After praising it lavishly, his notice ended: 'I can think of no justification for killing this obvious success when two of the theatre's generally acknowledged duds are being held over well into the next booking season.']

11 October

A sustained campaign against the play carried on by enemies *within* the company has at last succeeded and the show's been withdrawn. I've told everyone we can; Tynan's repeated his claims that Olivier's a Stalin and I mine that Tynan's a Beria; Mike naively plots to reveal all in the *Evening Standard*; Peggy counsels caution, as always, except when she's bitching somebody behind their back; formal complaints lead only to formal rebuttals and we're left to hear the news through Jim Dale, after LO announced it to the company, adding that he's too ill to act for a year and will hand over to Scofield.

Incidental pleasures: kinetic art at the Hayward, beautiful toys that you can clap at, whistle to, move in, dodge, alter, operate, contemplate. Before they found that term to describe such stuff, we had mundane examples like the simulated firelight above fake coals on the two-bar electric fire, the Bovril neon-sign in Piccadilly, amusement arcades and the shop-window advert for Silvicreme or whatever the Co-op called their hair-oil, a man's arm activated by an electro-magnet so that he seemed to be endlessly brushing his greasy George Raft head.

Visit to Tower of London: brusque NCO-types bully you round the boring jewels. 'Move along there, don't hover beside the glass!'

'Why don't you get a whip?' asked someone in the crowd.

Reading of my TV play *Hearts and Flowers* with promising cast including Anthony Hopkins, Donald Churchill, Priscilla Morgan, Constance Chapman (as Mum) and (as Uncle Bert) Leon Cortez, whom I saw on the halls with his Coster Pals dressed as a pearly king. He told me, apropos of funerals, that once they get the boilers going at the crematorium, they save money by not turning them out, so that what the bereaved cherish in their urns isn't entirely their loved ones' remains. What's more, the femur and other large bones can't really be reduced in the time so the precipitate is put into a heavy-duty grinder and mashed to a powder. As he put it, 'Fourpenn'orth of mixed.'

28 October

On a quiet road near Amiens, approaching a bend, I braked gently to avoid swinging the car too suddenly for my four passengers – Thelma,

Louise, Dan and Catherine. The engine roared and the car continued on its course, no matter how hard I pressed the clutch and brake pedals. I gripped the wheel and did my best. We skidded helplessly across the road. I can't be sure whether I knew at the time or only in hindsight that this was one of those life-reviewing moments when you feel close to death. But there we were, still upright and unhurt, looking at each other, amazed, though not nearly as much as the occupants of a following car. Passing, they glared at Thelma in the passenger seat, their anger turning to astonishment as they saw that she had no steering-wheel.

I had, of course, accelerated instead of braking. Since this moment, I've never ceased marvelling at how seldom drivers make this simple mistake.

When we got moving again, there was a nasty knock in the motor and at Amiens we called at a Renault garage, where I had to deal with the mechanic and learn that I'd blown a valve by over-revving. While I struggled with the technical vocabulary of *soupapes* and *bougies*, inside the car Thelma was answering another sort of mechanical question.

'Mum,' Dan began, 'under my tail are two little balls. What are they for?'

'That's where the seed is.'

'Seed?'

'That makes babies.'

'How?'

'With the Mummy. The lady you marry. The seed comes out of your tail.'

'Uergghh!' in unison.

'Where does it go?' from Louise.

'Into the lady.'

'What? Her head or what?'

'No. Lower down,' Thelma told her with a gesture.

'Oh-ho,' said Catherine, rolling her eyes, 'so it's bottoms we're talking about!'

'Does it hurt?' asked Dan, with his usual frown of concentration.

'No. It's nice.'

'And have you got to do That Thing if you get married?'

'You'll want to.'

'No, I shan't. I shan't be getting married cos I don't want to do that thing.'

'You will.'
'Shan't!'

[He overcame this in time and our two grandsons George and Robert are the living proof. The girls have done their share too, so far producing Molly, Joe and Vita.]

The car lacked power but couldn't be mended till Monday so we rang Loleh Bellon/Roy and asked her to arrange an unscheduled night in Paris. We chugged down the motorway and had a near-hysterical circuit of the peripherique [or South Circular] a conveyor-belt of vehicles linking the various suburbs. Even after all this, the streets of Montparnasse and St Germain exerted their inextinguishable charm. The children had been good as gold, Louise apologising more than once for vomiting into a lunch-bag as we arrived at Dover. As we hustled them along Rue Dauphine from Quai Voltaire, the nearest parking, Dan emitted one of his terrifying coughs, hawking and gasping for breath, alarming the passing Parisians who heard this old man's agony coming from a small boy and finally saw him throw up on the pavement, saying immediately, 'Sick,' as though to be first at identifying it.

Loleh was acting in a play and Claude was in Geneva but their son Paul received us with Scotch, coffee and a ham supper. As it was now too late to put the car on the southbound train-ferry, Loleh had booked rooms at the Pont-Royal at £26 a night! Thelma stilled my groans by reminding me it was tax-deductible as 'visit to translator'. I slept well, despite Catherine snoring like a brass band in the next bed. Thelma shared mine and we made love, reminding each other of our good fortune: the car hadn't overturned and it was good to be alive.

I lay abed next morning and she finally woke me to say, 'You have a nice shave and bath and I'll order breakfast in the children's room.'

Through the bathroom window came responses from Mass in a nearby church, a meeting of secular and spiritual pleasures and a blissful change from the previous evening's diabolic scene on the ringroad. The splendour of the plumbing was spoilt only by there being no hot water in the washbowl taps. And all this luxury was put in its place by Dan and Catherine coming to call me for breakfast, finding me on the lavatory and running back along the corridors shouting to the English-speaking staff (and even a few guests) 'Daddy's been poohs!'

Long, boring drive in the damaged car. As we arrived at our deserted house after dark, the headlamps started a ghostly barn-owl from one of the attics. We carted furniture between large barn and smaller house. Everything was as we'd left it, though there'd been no locks, no way of securing the doors. By gaz-light, we drew water from the well, collected wood, lay and lit a fire in the huge hearth, made beds on the floor and ate Thelma's magically instant meal. She's an amazing organiser. Setbacks that defeat me only stimulate her. The five of us lay side by side on the stone floors amid new cobwebs and freshly bored sawdust from the burrowing woodworm. What with Cath's snores, Dan's cough and Louise's melancholy sighs, I didn't expect much sleep. Their mother and I agreed it was a far cry from the suite at the Pont-Royal. In no time I was off and dreaming that Olivier was being very nice to me.

Early in the morning, six ragged children passed on foot towards their school in the village of Siorac. Late afternoon they returned. In between there were no pedestrians and only a few vehicles – an old woman on a mobilette, some men in Citroens. After a dry summer, the maize crop was poor and fodder's going to be short all winter.

First we cleared up the three rooms adjoining the barn where we were sleeping and installed what furniture we had; swept away cobwebs and the worst of the owl-pellets on the barn-floor, moved out farm implements from rooms to barn. Walking to the village to ask if our removal van had been seen, I met our neighbour the English surveyor and he took me to meet his wife.

'I was Bromley's only Labour councillor,' he said at one point, surprising me, as he seemed an Identikit Tory, with his military manner and officer-moustache, 'but I overdid it working eighteen hours a day.'

And later: 'I've been working nine or ten hours a day on this place since we moved in. It's certainly the best house we were shown and with the best plot of land by far.'

It stands, prominent and isolated, beside the road in a large open space, the sort of house a surveyor would approve.

'I was promised water by the mayor but, you know, these people's promises are worth nothing. If you're used to English standards, it can get to be infuriating.' One of the artisans stood by, not understanding

English but probably gathering plenty from Belsey's tone of voice. 'They're only just putting the pipes along the road – three months late – and now, would you believe it, we've got to wait for some clown to come and install a meter.'

Told we were waiting for our furniture from London, he said, 'I hope you have better luck than we did. Half our stuff arrived broken and I had to pay them twice to get them to hand over. I'm in the midst of a complicated law-suit to recover the cash.'

Ours came Tuesday, having been held up in Perigueux by the douane. The young mover and I unloaded it in a couple of hours and he drove off back to England, another eccentric. He'd been in the Foreign Service till his wife tired of trekking about the world. Now he satisfies his wanderlust by doing European removals.

On walks to the village I filled my pockets with fallen walnuts and was told this was a mistake. The trees and crop are someone's property and will be collected when they're all down, a right everyone respects.

I sat by the pond a long while staring at three black carp, about nine inches long, lurking beneath the surface. In this silence you can hear leaves fall, trees expand. Hardly any birdsong as there are far fewer birds than in Blackheath, either due to the French killing everything that moves or because there are better pickings on suburban lawns. From the Forêt de Double beyond our land came the whine of tree-saws and an occasional crack of hunting-guns.

I felt happy and content throughout our four days at the farm, though the children were sorry not to go to the lake. Even this late in October, it was warm enough to swim at midday but the Renault was being mended and we depended on John Belsey to drive us to Ribérac to shop for food, which he did with a stiff smile and a shallow pretence that he was happy to help. I felt it was his wife who'd insisted he make us welcome.

At night in bed we read by candlelight, Thelma beginning *Resurrection*, I *Middlemarch*. Orwell said he couldn't read Eliot. Her preacher side can be heavy going but the story's powerful, slow but cumulative and there's a grandly organised moral pattern to it all. Her certainty makes a pleasant change from our purposeless maundering. No poor to be seen, however, except as victims of charity or examples of shady low-life. Perhaps this is what offended Orwell.

Reached Paris again in the evening and had a meal chez Claude. He and his son bickered incessantly over dinner and Claude said, with the sort of shrug only the French can manage, 'He is a savage, but a *nice* savage.'

9 November

Louise's vomiting continued at home and Blakemore, coming to work on the script, diagnosed whooping-cough. As he's ex-medical student as well as ex-actor, we took his advice and called the doctor who agreed and said Catherine may have it too. Lou's in bed for a month, has already missed Guy Fawkes' and her own birthday party will be postponed.

15 November

The four jobs I had to finish were all cleared in a week:

Hearts and Flowers was recorded with the usual control-room brouhaha and nervous collapses, a process that compares with landing a jetliner which is about to catch fire and plummet on to a huge city. Or so it seems and so they all like to think. These shows aren't even going out live, as they used to when I acted on TV. Chris Morahan's production of this small and ordinary play was perfectly fine but suffered from his usual reluctance to condemn any of the dramatis personae. It finally amounted to no more than quiet fun and teacup drama. I'm so tired of the kind of writing I've specialised in and feel ashamed that so much energy, ingenuity and money was spent on my paltry sketch.

[Thirty years later, it's now clearly the best of my plays for television. After its repeat broadcast, the original colour version was wiped by one of the BBC's Beechings (to save money by re-using the videotape), and only in the 80s a Bristol producer sent me a pirated copy in black-and-white, all that survives of exemplary performances by the whole cast and, for me, a family souvenir.]

Joe Egg re-shooting hardly needed me and is a lost cause anyway. *The National Health* film's being revised and wrangled over by Columbia's top brass, who must be having second thoughts about me now the first's a dead duck instead of a goose that will lay them golden eggs.

Back to *Down Memory Lane* with diminishing enthusiasm. Another about the family. But in the next few days, I wrote two good scenes to round it off, two surprises after two quiet acts. Vowed never to write more episodes of my life. Or at least to try something else as well, that won't involve accuracy and checking in Diary and all those finicky habits of the naturalistic manner. Because, no matter how I try to break this down, my plays remain essentially bound by those rules, the people behaving somewhat as they did in life, the events never far-fetched. Vowed to write a far-fetched play before long.

Louise's eighth birthday passed, of course, without a party due to her illness, but she had a cake and presents by post. Being jealous, Dan promised to spoil her celebrations so Thelma wisely invited his friend to tea. They giggled throughout and made rude jokes.

Fatty and Skinny had a bath,
Fatty blew off and Skinny laughed.

[Had the play typed and sent copies to Ewan Hooper, director of GreenwichTheatre, Blakemore, Peggy and Michael Medwin. Ewan and Michael B responded quickly and favourably. Ewan said that, though John Mortimer's isn't very much like mine, he wishes he'd had mine earlier and could have presented them in sequence as contrasting memory-plays about playwrights' fathers. We at once started fantasy-casting, the A-list everyone draws up and rarely achieves. Usually it's a compromise, which no-one can admit for fear of insulting the actors who actually appear.]

Peggy delayed two days before ringing, so I assumed she hadn't liked it and was about to ring Ewan and say this augured a great success when she phoned to say she thought it the best thing I've done. If Harold Hobson also decides to like it, I'm done for. He's lately shown signs of revising his opinion of me by referring to my unblinking truthfulness.

22 November

Death-toll of Pakistan's earthquake and tidal wave may reach a million if the expected epidemics follow. In Hampton's witty play *The Philanthropist*, a cynical novelist says that whenever he receives an appeal leaflet telling him he can save an Indian child for the price of a prawn cocktail, he goes straight out and orders a prawn cocktail. This gets a laugh of guilty recognition. The affluent world sends off its tanner on the collection plate, as it also sent a million sterling to Aberfan. And when this disaster's over, its dead counted and forgotten, the millions of the sub-continent will still be there amid the horrors of Calcutta, messy relic of the East India Company's greed. Plus ça change . . .

In Alec McCowen's dressing-room, I praised the play and asked was it true Hampton's only about thirteen even now.

'You mustn't,' Alec said, 'he hates that. He's twenty-four.'

'Well, we can only hope he burns himself out,' I said.

'What a terrible thing to say!' said an actress who had also 'gone round' to A's dressing-room.

I remember Charles Wood's response to hearing of O'Casey's death: 'One less to worry about.'

25 November

Spent some hours in the office suite occupied by Memorial Enterprises, discussing the new play with Michael Medwin, Albert Finney's business partner, recently deserted by his wife, idle-rich middle-aged Sonnie. He gave Blakemore and me an account of his bachelor life – clubs and starlets and unlimited opportunities for sexual adventure.

'Of course,' Blakemore said, 'being a film producer, they must be throwing themselves –'

'There is a freemasonry, of course. Chums in clubs, a circle, we pass it around when it's available. This was passed to me by Lady Whoever-she-is that I met in Simpson's and she introduced the German as something that wanted to be in films. So I was away to the races. I've got it booked for next Wednesday p.m. The matinée. A crack at the title. It's all very peaches-and-cream but I like that. No bra. Charlie Clore's taken it out but I think he only wants to be seen. I had no idea how many friends I had till I took it into some clubs. People I scarcely knew. "Hallo, Michael, how've you been?", you know, their eyes firmly fixed on it. One had the bloody sauce to say it reminded him of Sonnie when young. I said, "I don't think that's very funny." No, I can arrange it for you. Nothing to pay. Be my guest. There are one or two others on the go au moment . . . one's sixty quid a time, really class trade. Not that I ever pay.'

Albert looked in briefly and joined in the casting fantasy. It can't be much good for him that everyone in the office is so sycophantic.

3 December

Francis Hewlett arrived to stay, first time for a year. His cabaret turn this time was the Fall of John Layard.

[This shamanistic figure is depicted vividly in Humphrey Carpenter's life of W.H. Auden, first as the poet's mentor and (briefly) lover in the Berlin days and later as Loonie Layard, a man whose mind could only (Auden's words) 'see the light once, after which is darkness. To me, illumination is a progressive process.' Spurned by the poet, Layard put a bullet in his head but survived into his eighties, fetching up in Falmouth just as Francis needed some sort of psychotherapy to deal with a crippling onset of Crohn's Disease. Surgery had failed but the old man's quasi-Jungian sessions helped. Layard, Thelma and I met in 1969 at the Hewletts' house, an encounter described at some length in my autobiography.

Francis's new instalment reads (in Diary, at least) like a parody of his attempted suicide in 1928 in Berlin.]

At nearly eighty, John had developed a passion for a local boy who'd become the chief supplier of pot to Falmouth's young set. The old man gave the boy money to buy some stock while in London but never saw him again. Arriving back from an errand, Francis found his wife Elizabeth's note saying Layard had had a serious fall and she'd gone to his house to help. (Francis believes John threw himself down the stairs but this was never proved.) He hurried off and found Liz at the bottom of the stairs with Layard, a dreadful sight, blood everywhere and the old man's always remarkable nose now pointing sideways. They insisted on half-carrying him up to bed, Francis already alarmed at the possibility of Layard's imminent death, as he'd become dependent on him to save him from further intestinal surgery.

In the bedroom, Layard began shivering, saying 'I'm cold, come into bed and keep me warm.'

They did so, cuddling him, though he continued to bleed over them and the pillows. Despite his scorn for conventional medicine, they finally persuaded him that he needed an ambulance and emergency treatment. While Liz went to phone, Francis stayed, keeping the patriarch warm and trying to staunch the flow.

Suddenly Layard looked past him and his face lit up.

'My dear girl, there you are, how nice to see you!'

Francis turned round to find that a nun had entered the room. It so happened that, some years ago, Layard had treated this woman when, as a novice, she was having violent dreams about the Mother Superior. He'd cured her of these ill-feelings but thirty years later they'd begun recurring and she'd sought him out and arranged a consultation, the hour of which had now arrived.

'Do come in. Why don't you get into bed, help keep me warm. Have you met Francis Hewlett? Sister Mary. He insists on calling a wretched quack to look at my nose. Ah, here's his wife Elizabeth. Are they coming, Liz? Get back into bed, there's a good girl. D'you know Sister Mary?'

The GP arrived to find these four in bed together – Loonie Layard, Sister Mary, Liz and Francis – but took it in his stride. Cornwall's an extreme county in more than just location. His examination indicated that the old boy should go to Casualty. This, of course, he refused to do.

'But, John,' Francis told him, 'you look an awful sight.'

'Do I?'

'Your nose is all twisted to one side.'

'Is it? Oh, Lord.'

'Give him a mirror, Sister. Let him see.'

John looked and agreed. 'Ghastly.'

'You'd better let them do some cosmetic surgery.'

The ambulance men treated Layard with the greatest deference, though he made difficulties about everything. At the hospital, it was 'Got a special case here. Doctor Layard. Can't hang about.'

Francis thinks it was as much the toff accent and patrician manner as the medical title and old age that earned him such respect. John noticed that many of the staff were Asian or Caribbean and began expressing racial (not racist) views dating from his days as an anthropologist in Melanesia before the Great War. The doctor who attended him was Indian and John couldn't understand anything he said, so Francis became interpreter. He'd always addressed the stonemen of

[111]

Malekula as though they'd all been together at Cambridge. 'My dear fellow,' to a tribal chieftain, 'how good to see you! Come along and meet my friend Rivers.'

Now he said in a loud aside: 'Seems to be talking Welsh.'

The doctor told him: 'Now, don't you worry, old chap. We'll soon have you looking shipshape.'

'Amazing accent.'

'Now I wonder if you can tell me about this scar in the roof of your mouth?'

The Hewletts (and possibly Sister Mary) knew he'd tried to top himself for the love of Wystan, so couldn't think what to say.

'It was a very long time ago,' murmured the old man. 'Not worth talking about.'

'A war-wound? Is that what you're trying to say? It looks very like a bullet-hole.' He turned to his nursing staff. 'There you are, you see. Everyone, please pay attention to this. When you bring in these old fellows, you must treat them extra carefully because who knows what injuries they may have sustained in the service of their country? And I've found that more often than not, they don't like talking about it, stiff upper lip and all that. Theirs not to reason why. Now, don't jump, old chap, when I take hold of it firmly like so – and –'

He wrenched Layard's nose with an audible click and it was back in place.

'Extraordinary fellow,' Layard said, 'did you see what he did? Deeply impressive. Welsh, you say?'

They got him to stay in hospital for a few days by playing on his vanity, showing him in the glass how badly his face was damaged. He enjoyed himself too, as everyone ran to do the bidding of the gallant veteran.

Francis had brought his latest drawings and water-colours and we bought three, though they weren't really for sale, mere sketches for paintings and inflatable sculptures he means to make. His existing ceramics – breasts in brassières, huge hands and noses, a Max Miller hat, two people screwing under a sheet – are fired in Falmouth Art School's kilns, probably the best use they'll ever be put to.

5 December

Hearts and Flowers droned through on our new colour set. Louise kept asking, 'Is that you? Is that me?' till we told her to shut up and listen. At the closing music, Elgar's *Salut d'Amour* (my choice), Thelma said, 'Nothing wrong with that, my dear.'

'Small stuff,' I said.

As the credits began to wind, she said, 'Charles is late ringing up' and when the first call came it was Gill Frayn's. Several others followed, Geoff the last to get through, full of praise, which was a relief as I feared the family might take against it.

[Especially my brother. The introduction to it in my first volume of plays tries to sort fact from fiction:

'At the time I wrote it, my brother was still a teacher in Bristol and I was a playwright in London. Due to a superficial resemblance between Tony/Bob (in the play) and Geoff and me (in life), relatives and friends may have thought I was debunking my own pretensions as Tony and claiming that my brother envied me as Bob. The truth is that Tony and Bob are two aspects of myself. Like everyone I know, including my brother, I'm a divided character, hoping for an exciting and passionate life but equally enjoying the claims of work and duty. The play is based on that tension and how their father's funeral brings it briefly to the surface.']

Went to bed at last and made love to Thelma, which is what the play had begun and ended with.

Notices next day all good. None in *Guardian*, though one for a play on both Yorkshire and Harlech by Charles, not shown in the London area. The critic complained of obscurity but said it was memorable.

Harold Pinter rang to say *H & F* had hit him north, south, east and west and hoped we would be associated at some time. A few days ago we'd seen his production of *Exiles* at the Mermaid so I was able to return the handshake.

Among many more calls, Michael Hallifax from the National spent some time praising the ironies of the piece, while I tried to remember some and said, 'Absolutely, thank you,' when suddenly, without warning, he told me that *The National Health* would be kept on till February, then scrapped forever. Six more performances at the Vic and that's the lot. This functionary claimed it's not done well at the Cambridge and seems to have exhausted its audience. I said that the production's goodwill had been squandered by perverse programming, lack of a tour and its total absence during the summer season when the best houses could be expected from American and other tourists.

What shits these people are, to ring under cover of praising one play to tell you they're scrapping another!

Cutting sent by Charles of a notice in the *Bristol Evening Post* of both our televisions. His was apparently ten years before its time like *Citizen Kane* but mine was more entertaining. 'About sums it up really,' he writes, adding that Tom S was on BBC2, 'did you know, put on weight he has but still the boy genius ahead of his time too and Rita Hayworth.'

I read this out to Thel who lay laughing in the bath while the kids looked on, wondering why. Got rid of them and climbed in with her. Bath too small but her wet warm body irresistible.

9 December

The lights have just come on after another power cut, resulting from electrical workers striking for a 30 per cent rise, after turning down 10. Rights and wrongs confusing. I don't blame them if they're trying to bring down the Tories but I'm almost certain they aren't. If 'the people' hadn't wanted them, how did they get voted in when a vast majority of the electorate are workers? They either don't care so don't vote or prefer Conservatism, or at any rate a regular swing between two slightly different alternatives, unimportant once in power. Any party has to do as they're told by The City or the Unions

Anyway the power-cuts have brought a return of Dunkirk spirit. Candles change hands at high prices. Long queues at filling-stations for petrol and in Blackheath Village for paraffin. Gill wanted to borrow our Calor stove but we'd left it in France. Our gas boiler's kaput without electricity which controls the thermostat. We have gas hotplates but an electric oven, and an oil-lamp but nothing to burn in it.

To the Cambridge Theatre last night to see *Health*, as some chaps from Théâtre de la Ville, Paris, France, were supposed to be seeing it with a view to doing it in their next season. Terrible technical balls-up when a lot of apparatus slid off its truck and went careering downstage because of the severe rake. An actress rushed from the wings and rescued it, averting disaster as it had nearly reached the stalls. Later two screens got entangled and Anna Carteret and A.N. Other tried to pull them apart, like owners restraining two rabid dogs. Anna finished roaring with laughter and couldn't say her next lines. It's noticeable that two members of this company are most prone to corpsing (a 'professional' word that pretends to exonerate these amateur lapses): Anna and Harry Lomax. When a trolley began rolling downstage, I said, 'Look out!' so loud Anna said she could hear me onstage. I had to go round afterwards and tell them off. Well, not really, just accept their apologies.

On the question of how this show has been treated by the régime, Gerald James said: 'This company's a rhubarb plant. They keep us in the dark and throw shit over us.'

Cleo Sylvestre said that, during the power-cuts, she was in Selfridges with her white friend, who told her:

'Keep your mouth and eyes open so I'll know where you are.'

16 December

Abigail's tenth birthday. Thelma rang Hortham Hospital and was told she's unchanged, except that her bedsores have healed. 'A small miracle,' said the Greek sister. No other miracles to report. They're having a little celebration for her. What, cake? Jelly? Musical chairs? Postman's knock? No crackers, they could start a fit. The only cause for celebration is that she won't know a thing about it.

I was writing a b-&-b to someone who'd given us drinks when the phone rang.

'Hullo, 762 7989.'

'Is that Peeder Nichols?'

An American woman.

'Speaking.'

'Oh, my Guard! D'you realise you've written the greatest play since *Hamlet*?'

'Oh, good. That's good, right.'

It was Mrs Donald Ogden Stewart and she'd just managed to see *TNH*.

[Her husband had been one of the Algonquin Round Table crowd and an intimate of Dorothy Parker. They were now members of the Tynan circle.]

Michael B, when I told him it's coming off in February, said, 'We'll see about that.' There's been an attempt to buy him off by making him a staff director. He reported on his first meeting with Scofield, Tynan, Olivier and – um – Frank Dunlop? He told LO how hard-done-by and resentful I felt over the intended aborting of my play and the cunning old bastard feigned disbelief. Tynan proposed commissioning new plays by current playwrights, including me, and O asked whether I'd still be interested.

'So I'm ringing,' M said, 'to ask if you would.'

'It's not a dazzling prospect for an author, is it? If I ever want to write a large-cast play again, I'll go to the other lot, the RSC. If it's a smaller play, the West End's best, running every night and bringing in a decent wage. Why would one want to leave it to the management to decide how often a play goes on, regardless of its audience?'

'I agree. Both companies must sort out better contracts.'

'Okay. So – first things first. Are you coming out to work on the other play?'

'I'm pretty tied up. Difficult to find two clear days.'

'There's no point in doing less.'

'You could come into the office at Aquinas Street.'

'And have the phone ringing all the time? Here we'll be undisturbed.'

'Well, I don't know what to say.'

'I do. Let's leave it till after Christmas,' and rang off. Or shall we leave it longer? Shall we forget it altogether and ask Chris Morahan to take it on?

[No hint that I saw what now seems obvious: Mike was beginning his directorial career and already sensed that any absence from the nerve-centre, even a mere huddle of prefabs in Waterloo, would be to risk his new foothold. He who leaves Rome loses Rome. His interest had already passed from my play to his future.]

23 December

Frayn had invited us to dinner with S.J. Perelman, but he was in Ireland and called off. Were able to go to the Oliviers' drinks party at a decent hour instead. It really felt we were in the House of Lords at last. Well, *a* lord. Mostly young and middle-aged guests, not L's circle at all but Joan's. To him, always renewing himself, this must be like an injection of monkey-glands.

We arrived with Maggie [Smith] and Bob [Stephens], who were bearing enormous wrapped gifts, which in our case we had not got. I recognised the very modern block John Boorman had used to shoot the tycoon scenes for *Catch Us If You Can*. They've rented the penthouse, now furnished, a few minutes' walk from Buck House, handy for investitures, and with a grand view over the West End, his little fiefdom.

At long last met John Osborne and reminded him of our last contact, fifteen years ago at Frinton-on-Sea, when we played in *See How They Run* and *Ten Little Niggers*. A surprisingly amiable man, almost shy, where I'd expected truculence. I asked him if he was doing anything for 'this lot'.

'They want me to but no. Poor company really. Youth clubby. And too interested in success.'

His wife Jill Bennett told me he'd voted for me on the *Evening Standard* panel. He said he'd enjoyed being on it, especially when the other judges turned up with their charts.

'I kept making silly remarks and they only had to say "piss off" but none of them did. I could only manage it once but, yes, I did enjoy it in a ghoulish sort of way.'

I ate trifle with Tom S and Alan Bennett and talked for a while with T's new girlfriend. His first wife Josie wasn't mentioned, but the day afterwards we received a Christmas card from her, wherever she is, no address, but scribbled under the printed greeting was a note: 'Thelma, I should love to see you again'. Poor soul. We hardly know her.

Sir came late. We felt he might have been resting in the bedroom, perhaps swatting Joan's notes on us. I was talking to the editor of the *Sunday Times* arts page when LO looked about, decided to do a press release and came over. Asked how he was, he told us about the various tubes and treatments and that it had all been a success, as far as he knew. He wasn't drinking and seemed less than his usual over-defined self.

He told the journalist that the film business is so unreliable that, during casting, if one of the company said they had a film in January, he said, 'Fine, we can release you, of course,' and entered the actor's name on the programme anyway. He hardly ever had to rearrange the schedules as the films so rarely happened.

All at once people were beginning to leave. Thelma warned me only hangers-on weren't putting on their coats, so we found hers but couldn't trace mine, hidden beneath a huge heap on the bed. LO thought he knew where it was and said, 'Peter, come here.'

'For God's sake, go with him,' Thelma said.

'But that's not where it is. Bob threw it down the other side.'

'Never mind. He's trying to help.'

'Is this it?' he asked, and it was. How did he know? Had Joan even made notes about our overcoats?

'Does that feel familiar?'

'Very.'

'Good.'

Joan saw us off at the lift. Thelma told her and other guests how Dad had kept saying after she'd visited our house in Bristol, 'This is the chair where Sir Laurence Olivier's good lady sat.'

26 December

Christmas over, thank God.

Mum arrived two days before and crept about myopically, searching for ashtrays, hoping for cups of tea. Complaining of cold, she went out the first morning and bought a hot-water bottle, despite the house being like an oven with solid-fuel central heating I replenish with constant trips to the cellar.

I had a piano lesson that she chattered through with our cleaner. The woman Dad married because he thought she loved music never ceases to complain that my piano-playing spoils her television. We trusted this daft old thing to look after the children for three hours while we joined Tom S for drinks at Claridge's en route to pick up Auntie Millie from the Swansea train: it was nice meeting old friends, the Boormans and the John Woods.

All week carol-singers and a Salvation Army band had been standing under our nearest sodium street-lamp looking pretty but lacking snow. Now suddenly here it was. One looked up, expecting to catch celestial flymen sprinkling boxes of confetti.

Got Millie home for a great meal of goose. The first TV, drinks, gathering winter fuuuuell, putting children to bed, dampening Cath's hopes and cries of 'I'm so excited!', clearing up the evening's debris, filling pillow-cases with oranges and sweets, cursing Dickens.

Thelma's parents with Uncle Frank expected at noon but at ten a ring on the side-bell (why not the front?) and there they were. Reg has just had an operation for hernia but insists on driving 120 miles and laughing at having tricked us, as he does every year, by arriving early. 'Some people want to stir their stumps in the morning', with near-inaudible asides from Frank and Win.

Our street is a very pretty picture, the Queen Anne houses facing us, dark reddish brown, edged with snow, like a negative print.

'The countryside's lovely too,' said Reg, 'if you had the time to look.'

Helping them carry their half-dozen cases up the front path, unloading presents, moving ours from the Christmas tree to the front room, to find more space; the three kids rushing about with them, soon knee-deep in discarded wrapping-paper. Exclamations all round: Cath happy with her toy record-player and 'Bibbetty-bobbetty-boo' record played so often and so loud we have to shout to make our gratitude heard.

Louise: a pogo-stick she practises on the carpet until forcibly prevented.

Dan: a plastic knight to assemble: cuirass, gauntlets, greaves, plastron, pauldron and halberd, supplied by Marx of Swansea.

Thelma: dress from parents, books from me, toilet things from the kids that I bought and packed.

For me: a riding-crop. Had Millie gone mad or been misinformed that I'm an equestrian type or that I keep a horse in the garden shed? Bewildered thank-yous till I looked closer and saw a shoe-horn on the end. Lots of useful stationery from Reg, courtesy the Bristol Aero-Engines office, a source of presents for most of the work-force.

'Did you get my record-token?' called my mother over the uproar.

'Don't think so.'

'Now, everyone,' bawled Thelma, 'Listen! Catherine, turn that record off or Auntie will take it back to Swansea. Somewhere under all this there's an envelope containing a record-token. Sealed or unsealed, Nana?'

'Oh, I can't remember.'

'Will everyone go through their wrapping-paper and make sure it's not there.'

After this, we emptied and examined the contents of the waste-baskets. No sign.

'Perhaps you forgot to bring it down, Vi,' said Millie and, sure enough, she had.

'Thanks, Mum,' I said when she'd at last fetched it from her room, 'very nice.'

I gave her and Reg cheques for £500 each, a gesture that says in effect that I'm absolved from seeing very much of them for the coming year.

From then on it was mostly television. Every few minutes Mum starts patting herself from head to foot, searching for some vital missing element – cigarettes, lighter, Minto, screwed-up paper tissue, which she refolds before dabbing each corner of her mouth. Every so often, Thelma tells me to get the drinks moving and I pour the bizarre concoctions they've learned about since last year: brandy-and-port, advocaat and lemonade, Snowballs, Pina Coladas. Thelma produces tubs of rahat-la-coon, Moroccan dates or minty chocs.

As the last Christmas party or circus or Jesus story draws to its close, Reg says, 'Now you know all about it,' and Win adds, 'All come out right in the end' or 'We may not have much money but we do see life'.

Monday morning, Reg had everyone up good and early for a swift run back to Bristol.

'Hope they haven't got signs out on the M4 keeping us down to flipping thirty,' he said, scanning the snow and ice from our front window. While Frank incompetently struggled to pack their mostly empty cases in the boot, Reg reprised the history of the Cortina, its perished hoses, burst inner tubes and collisions, the cost of servicing, tyres, petrol, road tax, depreciation.

He didn't own it and had never been able to afford a car until Frank bought it with his savings from his long working life as a male nurse.

This obligation always irked Reg and he never acknowledged it. For his part, Frank earned a place in the family and sat in the back seat while Reg drove with Win beside him in front.

This ritual done, the rest of Christmas was predictable but pleasant. We tobogganned on the slopes of Greenwich Park and in old gravel pits on the heath.

This morning's *Times* has the complete text of the Rev. Paul Oest-reicher's address yesterday in the Church of the Ascension a few doors away. He claims Rudi Dutschke's more Christian than the Berliners who spurned him and that it would be England's shame if he's not allowed to stay here. It all makes good sense but only in the context of church sermons where one is surprised to hear anything remotely intelligent or relevant.

1971

[Near the start of this year, I bought my first page-a-day diary and after a month, began handwriting the entries. This became my method until 1993 when I switched to word-processing. The occasional, retrospective notes of the typewritten years at last became a true journal.]

9 January

Down Memory Lane has become *Forget-me-not Lane*, as I'm convinced the first is too much a cliché to have any effect, even as irony. Blakemore and Medwin think the new one's twee.

11 January

To Leicester in Albert's Rolls, the first time I'd been in such a car except at funerals.

'See this lot?' said Terry, ex-stunt man, now Albert's chauffeur, nodding back at the police car behind us, 'they'll be keeping on our tail a good way yet. That's the snag with a Roller.'

They were following, not from any regard for public safety, but an envious vindictiveness, keeping us below the limit as other vehicles streamed past on the fast lane.

Bill Maynard was on our list for the part of Charles, based on Dad. He was appearing at the Civic Ballroom, de Montfort Hall, as Mother Goose. As we sat in the manager's office, he told stories about the last gasp of Music Hall.

'I was depressed by playing Archie Rice in *The Entertainer* because I'd been there, you see, I'm sure I knew the man Osborne based it on. That was all only too familiar to me – the nude Britannia and the old couple in the fourth row eating crisps and the solitary commercial traveller with his hand under his raincoat and the heckling Teddy Boys . . . oh, yes, too sad . . . '

When the manager wanted to entertain friends, we had to move to Maynard's dressing-room, where his beautiful eighteen-year-old son was doodling with an electric guitar. Maynard read some speeches for us and our high hopes sank as he obviously couldn't find the right manner. For courtesy's sake, we saw some of the pantomime, finding a quarter-full house being bombarded by a PA system at maximum volume. We moved seats several times and finally left when we could take no more. The principal boy was Dickie Valentine, who'd topped the bill at the Palladium about ten years ago. It was as sad as Maynard's tales of the halls.

Why must the show go on and why do these gallant performers want to be in at such a death? Because, I suppose, it beats work, they earn more than they could elsewhere and still can't resist showing off. I'd admire them more if they refused. But they've had to grow thick skins and may as well use them. And, for all the talk about bravery, the worst they'll meet is cold indifference. A Monday first-house sitting on its hands may be depressing but isn't dangerous. Teachers face worse for six hours of every working day.

13 January

At a press conference at Greenwich Theatre to puff the new season, which will include my new play. I found myself seated beside Elsie and Doris Waters, Cockney-cameo stars of genteel Variety and radio, who are doing their turn in Ewan Hooper's so-called Music Hall, though it's really nothing of the sort. They reminded me of my Auntie Lil.

Walking back across the park, I read the dates of my play, taking in that it will open on April 1st, Dad's birthday. He'd have added that to his list of Remarkable Coincidences.

18 January

Reading and enjoying (if that's the word) Updike's *Couples*, about the sub-Kennedy stratum of New England, devotees of a religion of hedonism but unable to feel they've any influence over the government of their country. To raise one's eyes from ones own life and narrow field of experience is to feel depressed and impotent.

I raised my eyes this evening to respond to an invitation to appear on the platform of an Anti-Apartheid Society meeting at Central Hall. Thelma and I had both had colds and lain low over the weekend but by Monday I was on the mend and decided to go. A row blew up at children's bath-time, as she was being left to cope alone, there being no mother's help till the next arrives.

'If you don't want me to go, I won't.'

'No, I think you should. You ought to. You've said you would. It's only that I'd like more warning. And why are you wearing that suit? Isn't it a student thing?'

'No. Bishop Huddleston and Lord Ennals.'

I ran through a rainstorm and sat in my car staring out, wondering why on such a night. Locked car again and returned to house. At the sight of me, she was like a dervish. Raved and insisted I go. The children stared.

'By now I'm probably too late. There's only twenty minutes to get to Westminster.' (A forty-minute drive)

'Never mind that. For Christ's sake, get off!'

I drove off through the quiet streets of Deptford and Rotherhithe. Now intent on missing the rally, I realised I had nowhere else to go. If I ever leave home, I'll have to make careful plans. Of the wide acquaintance I now have, there's no-one who'd be glad to see me or that I could bear to spend much time with.

I finished up at Westminster at 7.30, as the meeting was due to start. The celebrity line-up in the first row included Huddleston (The Rev Trev), David Steel, Bernadette Devlin and Susannah York, the only showbiz representative I could see from my place in the raised seats behind which sat a mixed bag of invitees, black, white and cappuccino. We all faced an audience that filled four-fifths of the hall. While they assembled, I spotted several odd types, contemporary Cockney wideboys, well-dressed, expensive haircuts, thick-set, with the sort of figures that come from regular work-outs in gyms.

Huddleston was first to speak, with a mild attack on Heath for supplying arms to South Africa. One or two catcalls came from the gallery, no more than you'd expect.

The chairman said that Miss Devlin would have no trouble controlling 'our friends from the National Front', a rash promise as, in fact, she found it quite impossible even to be heard. The odds were certainly against her, as none of the three table-mikes worked well enough to raise her voice above the rhythmic chanting of 'Trait-or, trait-or!', 'Stand by the whites' and 'Red scum out!' The gymnasium men were obviously a controlling claque and kept moving their hecklers about the hall to outwit the stewards, decent young men who hadn't the authority to evict them, only request them to play the game. Free speech was shown to depend on co-operation. As in any assembly, there had to be rules. Like most freedoms, if carried through it would lead to chaos. Auditorium lights showed that among their numbers were the bearded sort with damp umbrellas who shout at Marble Arch, tough old men knotted with nameless angers, young aggro boys out for a punch-up and scrubbers with dyed hair and PVC raincoats. The brown woman beside me was most astonished by these, having assumed there were no female Fascists. Some black stewards, provoked by the slogans, tried to apply a strong arm or two and fights broke out, at which point the police were called. Judging by their prompt arrival, they'd been waiting outside. An officer, a sergeant and a dozen constables appeared at the back but did nothing, beyond making a show of strength. Heckling subsided briefly. The NF members had been corralled into one part of the gallery where stewards found it easier to localise each shouter. Then they asked him to leave and, if he didn't, police escorted him out. By this tedious democratic means, the hall was at last cleared of troublemakers. Meantime the meeting was in ruins. The diversion had worked, as planned. Little could be heard of complex arguments against Heath's alibi that arms were needed to defend us against the Soviet fleet. Denis Healey, hotfoot from The House, got an ovation by wishing Mr Heath could be here to see the quality of his support. Last came the leader of the Mineworkers' Union to recite some Burns.

With thanks to all who had turned out on such a night to add their voices to a noble cause, etc., that was the end. Police still stood outside, in case of real violence, but the NF members had all gone home or to wherever they usually gather to plan the next example of misrule. As an event, it was a great advance on the pantomime at Leicester and on the few examples I've seen of Theatre of Cruelty or Violence and on all the safe Audience Participation devices built in to such plays as my own. Such excitement, of course, is also meaningless. And the appetite it creates is insatiable.

20 January

The principals are cast: Anton Rodgers as Frank, Michael Bates as his/my father, Priscilla Morgan as his/my wife and Joan Hickson as his/my mother. Bates is nothing like the real man, being small and quick where Dick was large and grandiose. The few grand-manner actors who remain – Peter Bayliss, Alfred Marks, Bill Fraser, Lionel Jeffries, Warren Mitchell – were all unavailable or didn't fancy the part. I suggested Guinness might go for it but he'd already agreed to do Mortimer's when it transfers to the West End.

We auditioned comedians and dancers for the parts of Mister Magic the old conjurer and Miss 1940. The men were down-at-heel middle-aged character actors, from which we chose Eddie Molloy, who (Medwin said) evidently needed the job by the look of his shoes. This told us more about Michael than Molloy. Still, despite all his callous criteria, he's quite a kindly man.

The dancers brought a burst of radiant sunshine onto the Prince of Wales Theatre's stage, all stacked scenery and dim working-lights. Some earlier applicants, told they'd have to remove their bras, went back to their agents and complained. Permissive Society a sell.

But these new ones had been warned. Lovely busty leggy girls without the inhibiting braininess of actresses. Both said they'd take their bras off. Chose Stephanie Lawrence.

'I bet she's a good sort,' said Medwin.

For Young Ursula, we settled on a pretty grey-eyed blonde called Sandra Payne, who's obviously Blakemore's type. 'Such a lovely face,' he kept saying. 'I'm amazed she hasn't become a film-star by now.'

Between sad comics and lovely girls, we discussed 'ancient' v. modern theatre architecture. As in other matters of taste, Blakemore favours Edwardian or Victorian rococo. I said it was all very well if you could afford to sit in the stalls.

Sometimes, when Albert dropped in, he, Medwin and I did Old Mother Riley imitations, mostly with our elbows.

25 January

Evening Standard Awards lunch means meeting a few friends not seen for a year. At our table there were place-cards for Alan and Mrs Bates,

Joan Littlewood and Friend, and two managers Donald Albery and Michael White.

'You can sit here by me,' White told Thelma, 'because there isn't any Mrs Bates.'

'There is,' she said, 'and she's just had twins.'

Albery told her he was proud to be at our table because he'd so enjoyed *Hearts and Flowers*.

'Tell me, has he done anything else?'

She was able to point to the list of my previous winners facing the menu for our meal.

Gielgud and Richardson shared Best Actor for David Storey's play *Home*. This led to a few minutes of wild hilarity. Because they're in New York performing the same piece, a ceremony was mounted there and filmed for us all to watch. The lights of the banqueting hall went down and there on a screen were the two ageing actors standing either side like book-ends flanking an inner trio: the critic Clive Barnes, the producer Alex Cohen and the city's mayor. This was funny enough and far-off tables started a smouldering laugh while these two upright knights stood waiting, in Richardson's case gently nodding, while the three residents spoke at length. I'm sure no-one could repeat a word because the distant giggle soon grew to a roar. On and on went the tedious speeches, on and on stood the two actors, like upended medi-aeval tombs, obviously wishing they hadn't come. Bursts of applause punctuated the laughter. Danny La Rue fell out of his seat. At long last came the handing over of statuettes and speeches of acceptance, the cue for more prolonged howls and appeals for mercy. At last it finished, the lights went on, water was poured and gulped down as everyone recovered from a euphoric interlude of mass hysteria. When some sort of order had been restored, the toastmaster announced: 'And now, my lords, ladies and gentlemen, pray silence for The Best Comedy of the Year!'

'That film!' shouted someone and off we all went again. The toastmaster himself was unable to speak for a full two minutes.

One man sat with head in hands, unable to look up. I asked who he was.

'Sidney Edwards. He's responsible for the film.'

We needed a laugh because Frankie Howerd was busy elsewhere and neither Ingrid Bergman nor Lord Eccles were very funny.

28 January

Olivier attacked Blakemore at the National Theatre board meeting.

'You're a nice one, going to Irving Wardle and sitting with him through the play.'

'No, you're mistaken. He was there because I invited him, yes, but I had no idea which night he'd come.'

The boss went on to justify his neglect of the show and to offer a sop: five more performances. Since Wardle re-re-reviewed it, all three of the season's houses are up near 100 per cent.

Albert took me on a guided tour of the half-built New Winter Gardens theatre. He's considering taking a lease and setting up a rep. company there and would like me to write him a play. Interesting auditorium designed by Sean Kenny and a revolving stage that includes the front five rows of seats.

> [In the late nineties, we took our granddaughters to see *Cats* in its 25th (?) Glorious Year and there was the revolve, still in action, a whole section of the audience being shunted to one side for one of the effects.]

We met the architects who said they'd considered changing the name but decided Winter Gardens had glamorous overtones of Tsarism and St Petersburg. Found my origins showing, as for me it had overtones of Weston-super-Mare or, at best, Bournemouth [the theatre was, in fact, pretty promptly renamed the New London].

3 February

Charles Wood came to lunch, in town to see about a film job. I told him about our dancing girls and their unexpected modesty.

'Oh, Peter, you haven't got bare tits? We're not doing that any more, love, not in the avant-garde. Everyone's fully clothed and it's all true love.'

4 February

A Rolls pulled up outside and Thelma took delivery of a letter it had brought, a fulsome apology from Sir for his treatment of the play. A nice job of crack-papering.

5 February

Watching Apollo 14 moon-landing with Dan, I said he'd be able to tell his grandchildren he was alive for these momentous sights.

'I shan't have any children because I shan't get married,' he said, eyes on the screen.

'Why not?' But I knew at once that this referred to his horror of coition as described by Thelma at the time of our accident on the autoroute.

'Well, I might get married but I shall forget to do that thing you're supposed to do. Are there many people who forget?'

'There's no need to think about that until you're much older. It's like shaving.'

'Well, I think about it now I'm a boy and I don't want to.'

Dinner at Frayns': Shirley Conran, Alan Bennett, Tony and Margo Bailey, S.J. Perelman. Tony's an Englishman and *New Yorker* journalist who knew Updike in Stonington, the actual setting of *Couples*. He thought life there more agreeable than anywhere else on earth but has come home so that Margo can study art.

'Why are you doing that?' someone asked.

She looked astonished and explained, as to a child, 'Because I want to be famous.'

Perelman was courtly and quiet and sparing of speech. Only with difficulty could we persuade him to hold forth in his rounded phrases – 'fumbled in her reticule' and so on, just like his funny pieces. I hoped for more from him but Margo insisted on telling us one of her favourite jokes, that at her girls' school they'd always called the Hitchcock film *The Lady Varnishes*.

'Varnishes?' repeated Perelman, as though this thought had never struck him.

8 February

'Not too bad,' said Thelma's father, arriving from Bristol with birthday gifts for his daughter and grandson, looking at his watch through bi-focals, 'three and a half hours.'

This set the tone for his visit. Tales of his time-keeping triumphs, struggles with the South Circular, plans for French holidays, his good sense in refusing shares in Rolls-Royce which has recently collapsed. There may be three children and several adults to be attended to, but we're supposed to sit still and quiet till he's finished describing his successful negotiations over no-claim bonus and Green Card. If anyone tries to break in, he repeats the word at which he stopped until he's allowed to resume. He drove us down the hill one day in his automatic Cortina which rapidly accelerates to forty. Sitting outside the bank while Thelma was drawing money before they close for a few days to convert to decimal coinage, he deplored the traffic on Lewisham High Street. 'I saw a cartoon in the paper that just summed it up. A lot of drivers with hunting caps on and a lone pedestrian crossing the zebra and he's got a fox's face and the drivers are all shouting 'Tally-ho!' and bearing down on him.'

When Thel rejoined us, he took the car round the block and approached a crossing as an old man limped across with a stick. Reg put his foot down and the car shot forward. He shouted "Tally-ho!" and laughed as the poor sod just jumped clear.

Driving up the hill he said: 'Our next-door neighbour's got a hi-fi system, all tapes, see. He records it off the radio and TV. He can give you quite a performance, entertain you all evening. Got a mike in his parrot's cage and every time the bird squawks or speaks, it goes on the tape. Mind you, with this car radio I can bring it right up to maximum with no distortion at all.'

As soon as the music or speech begins, he looks at his wrist-watch, a reflex action. I begin to work out my traffic play, starting with him and a family who never manage to get a word in. He works on the engines that power Concorde.

'It's all a rat-race,' at one moment and the next, 'Still, people won't face the need for progress.'

[These uncharitable views of my father-in-law can't be left unqualified. He and I never achieved détente. I could do very little to please him and he always struck me as a bully, not only to me but to his wife Win, his daughters Thelma and Valerie, to Uncle Frank and more or less everyone else he met. But we were separated not so much by a generation as by a very different upbringing. His South Wales childhood and the hard years of unemployment during the 1930s probably accounted for a bombastic manner, as he felt the onus of keeping and controlling three females. He was a foreman and shop steward and his bossy style may have suited a workforce but wasn't right for me.

When – in the 1990s – he lay dying in a Swansea hospital bed, I visited with Thelma and Win.

'My Lord,' he said, laughing, 'Peter here? I must be ill!']

The parents of the friends Dan invited to his birthday party were a mosaic of class: Patsy Grigg with her sleepy assurance, lively middles from the architect-and-teacher belt of Blackheath, and the women from the estates with startled faces and sibilant speech, 'Thanks ever so much'. The only black boy, Mark, wasn't picked up by anyone afterwards so I drove him home, following his directions round and round Greenwich in the dark.

'It's got a blue door,' he kept saying but this wasn't much help at seven o'clock of a February evening. We finally found it, next to Ewan Hooper's. A small girl, letting him in, thanked me but didn't apologise or explain. They could be the family Ewan told me about. When he could take no more of their all-night parties, he courteously complained, aware of the danger of the *Kentish Mercury* reporting 'Martin Luther King author smears black neighbours'. One of the men came out shouting 'You hate my people.'

'Don't be silly. My son plays with yours. I just want to get some sleep.'

'Get away from here, man. You hate my people.'

11 February

Lunch with Peter Hall and Dimitri de Grunwald to discuss their plan to form a film circle of writers, directors and a producer. On balance, it seemed the directors had nothing to lose and the writers little to gain. His protestations of Socialist ideals come trippingly off the tongue but I kept thinking of the boy Mark and the hidden millions.

12 February

Pinter's one of those invited to join the film circle and we met him and his wife at the Morahans the next evening. He smiled what Tynan called 'his slightly sinister dentist's smile' and Vivien Merchant reminisced in a demure voice about her Presbyterian upbringing. We talked of old films and I said I'd wasted my youth in cinemas. He rounded on me and said I should not be ashamed of my culture. It was my culture and that was that.

'I wasn't allowed to see any films at all,' she said.

'Oh, well, you!' he said, as though it was all he expected. They spent the evening savaging each other. Was it just in fun or a serious and deadly game? Their rows seemed as implausible as his actor's voice or her leather pants which creaked whenever she moved.

We enthused together about Larkin and Pinter's eyes glowed behind their glasses.

'For my money,' he said with finality, 'he's really – well, he's – *The Man*.'

When I later told Blakemore about P's assertion that my culture shouldn't be questioned, he said he can't stand that refusal to make value judgements.

'You end up thinking Hitler quite a nice man.'

16 February

Fetched Cath home from St Thomas's hospital (designed by David Allford, met when we were both aircraftsmen in Singapore), where she'd had a view across the river to Parliament and Big Ben that would have cost a millionaire fifty quid a night. Only the civil servants of County Hall enjoy such a vista. Even the Primate of All England doesn't, except from the battlements of his palace, as the hospital's in his way.

She'd had swollen adenoids removed and her gums and nose were bloody, her pallor off-white, otherwise unscathed.

To see a play at Hampstead in the evening. Dinner with Frayn and Anton Rodgers afterwards. Browsed in the new public library beside the portakabin theatre. A quiet and unmarried place, cool and restful.

[Two firsts: meeting Anton, who later appeared in three of my stage plays. And Swiss Cottage library (designed by Basil Spence) had just opened and is now, thirty years later, a candidate for demolition. It functions well but has been a victim of Thatcherite anti-social policies. Though I, of course, support the campaign against library closures, there's a demoralised air about it and whenever I go there are few users. The staff look as neglected as the buildings. Sections have headings like Gay Interest, Easy Reading and War.]

18 February

Reading *Couples* on the train. Its deep and affecting emotions contrast with the shallowness of my own work. I must move on from the Phenomenal or Observational style and try to say what I mean, which would entail discovering what that is.

20 February

Went in evening to Old Vic for penultimate performance of *National Health*. Dozens standing, responsive house, lively playing. Felt adequate and recovered some faith in the Phenomenal style.

21 February

Was to have played Diabelli duet with daughter Louise at our piano-teachers' little concert but had to excuse myself at the last moment to entertain Michael Bates and family. Thelma took Louise, who played her piece without too many wrong notes. Michael Frayn, trying to accompany daughter Becky, made three tries at one passage before giving up. Thelma felt for him, the only man in a roomful of women and girls. Becky was the star, pausing for her father, coolly reprimanding her young sister, playing without a slip.

I walked with Bates on heath and in park. Deeply conventional, with a little trilby and neat moustache. His father an Anglo-Indian civil servant. He seems a decent reactionary.

'Is it true Greenwich theatre hasn't got a curtain? I love a curtain down when I go to a play. I like the lights to dim and the curtain to rise and there you are, a nice lounge.'

You can't ever tell how much he's role-playing. He enjoyed my stories of Dad but worries about how to grow old.

'Shall I wear *two* hair-pieces, I wonder?'

23 February

After a stormy interview with Olivier, Michael Blakemore finally said: 'But, Larry, you can't have it both ways.'

The old man looked at him from under those hooded lids. 'I can have it any way I like.'

'God!' Mike told me, 'it was like Richard the Third.'

But O can only have this effect because people are susceptible to that sort of melodrama. Something in Mike wants to sup full with horrors.

25 February

Took children to Warhol show at Tate. Very bland and stylish but unaffecting somehow, more art criticism than art.

Gave them lunch in gallery's cafeteria. While Thelma queued for food for us all, I ogled strapping sixth-form girls with strong legs and breasts bulging beneath their blazers. Soon our young fell upon the food and we helped them cope with Coke and cups of yoghourt. I pointed out the schoolgirls to Thelma and got an irritable reaction.

To Science Museum to join hordes of kids banging away at the do-it-yourself demonstrations, trying to elude the burglar alarm or catch the vanishing metal ball, filling and emptying the bladder in a vacuum jar, pulling a weight various ways. The principles involved seemed to escape them all, as they would have me at their ages. Teachers and parents sat nearby snoozing and glancing at their watches. On the bus home, my wallet was stolen by an old lady sitting beside me as I nursed Dan on my lap.

1 March

First reading of *Forget-me-not Lane* in church hall near Greenwich Theatre. First Mike explained our design from the stage, standing on the set for *Macbeth*. I'd entered the auditorium with Joan Hickson who exclaimed, 'Oh, my God!' and I doubt if Michael Bates was converted to a different architecture by this chilly mid-morning glimpse.

I cried with laughter to hear my own (or my family's) jokes read aloud. Embarrassing and impossible to explain. Joan seems unhappy, as though she can see no way of adding to her version of the same woman in *Joe Egg*.

Young people very good: Ian Gelder as Young Frank (me), Malcolm McFee as his best friend and Sandra Payne as Young Urse (Thelma). She's so pretty that Mike doesn't know how he's going to direct her, especially in the sex scenes.

4 March

Had agreed to share Philip Mackie's box at the Albert Hall for a Film Awards dinner. There was quite a struggle to get in, most doors surrounded by autograph hunters who luckily turned away as our unknown faces appeared, leaving a way through. We downed a bottle of champagne on empty stomachs and I was soon happy-drunk.

Silence was demanded for Princess Anne, who arrived with Attenborough simpering a few paces behind her, making sure his knighthood's safe. We were saved from drinking The Royal Toast as there was no more wine. In corridors behind our box was a sordid struggle for victuals by a churlish band of serving-women.

After the terrible meal, the terrible prize-giving. Best moment came when clips were shown from a documentary called *The Tribe That Hides from Man*. On a vast screen, in a jungle clearing, appeared three Amazonian Indians. They stared at the camera, at us, the half-naked actresses, sycophantic show-offs, bored bandsmen, surly servants, at Jack Hawkins and John Mills, and I doubt I was the only guest reflecting on the nobility we've lost. They seemed to take us in, with one long steady gaze, then refused to stay, retreating into the undergrowth. How wise, but for how much longer can they hide?

7 March

Discussed with Mike the question of dialect in the play. Should middle-aged, sophisticated Frank have a Bristolian accent at all? Should his younger self keep his accent after he comes home from National Service?

'The point is, Mike, that many people keep local brogues all through their lives.'

'But when you're living in Bristol among Bristolians you're not much aware of them. It's only after you leave that you really notice. If *we* did that, emphasising Frank's local twang, we'd be in danger of taking a metropolitan attitude towards the characters, so making it into a regional comedy, which you surely agree it's not.'

I did. Despite his prickly personality, he thinks clearly as a director and editor.

8 March

Mike told Thelma (as an indirect way of telling me) that he had to have time on his own to do *his* creative bit. Of course, but an author who's spent a year on a play has too much at stake to stay away for more than a quarter of rehearsals. It was helpful my being there yesterday as I corrected a few awkward or ambiguous lines and cut a few superfluous words. Better now than after the actors have learnt them, when they'll be more resistant to change.

Useful too to discover where, despite all our preparation, the director hasn't grasped the meaning. It transpired that Mike thought 'Old Butterfingers up there' meant God, not the dead father. Our Father who art in Heaven?

He goes through a similar process to mine during the writing. He's worried that Bates is very funny but can't take that plunge which will show the despairing man behind the public clown.

9 March

The last moments of the play are sad and funny at the same time, even erotic in a pitiful way. Saw two soft-core films at the local Odeon and was mostly unaroused. My taste is for women as furniture rather than rapacious monsters. The slave-girl images in the play are laughable but exciting too, especially as played by Stephanie Lawrence.

Wanted to make love afterwards but Thelma read her French grammar.

10 March

Mike led me aside to ask me not to sit close to him, as it upset the actors.

'You were pissing yourself at Bates. Did you see what it did to the others?'

'Nothing much, that I could see.'

'They laughed at him to show they didn't mind.'

'You exaggerate my importance.'

'You're the ultimate authority. It inhibits me to have you there.'

'I'll certainly sit to one side if you think it helps.'

'I don't want you to feel unwelcome.'

But, of course, I did.

Talked to Robert Bolt in the evening about this thorny problem, how to deal with directors and how often to go to rehearsal. He stays from start to finish and sits in the same misery, wondering whether to explain or wait till he's asked.

This was at a meeting of Peter Hall's film-group in a restaurant called The Belfry, a converted church. Where bell-ropes had swung, we sat at a round table eating borscht and salmon pie. Pinter shouting, John Hopkins speaking with quiet intensity, de Grunwald patiently defending his scheme, Hall flattering everyone. I made jokes and finally said I felt *de trop*, to be loudly reassured by Hall that I was a corner-stone. Bolt left early, after pocketing my five-bob lighter, which I at once reclaimed. After he'd gone, I asked if we really wanted a klepto-maniac as a member.

'An *unsuccessful* kleptomaniac,' said Hopkins.

11 March

To the Tynans for dinner. I sat between Kathleen and Francesca Annis, a beautiful actress I'd seen in her earlier days as a promising child. She gave me, for the first time in some years, the exciting sensation of being desired by a stranger, probably an illusion, but she certainly lingered at the table when the others had mostly retired upstairs, and let her hand rest on my knee. She was so pretty, in a white semi-transparent blouse, the black bra visible beneath. She believed plants respond to vibrations and Thelma thought she meant the washing-machine but no, it was people's auras.

She and I wanted milk in our coffee. I tried the kitchen door but couldn't find the doorknob.

'A friend of mine,' she said, 'was taken home by a sinister man and finally decided she should leave before things turned serious. When she tried, she discovered the doors had no handles on the inside.'

'D'you think we're in for something of that sort tonight?'

'No such luck.'

Later Ken brought out a tape-recorder and asked for silence. My hopes were briefly revived that this was to be one of the kinky games for which the Ts were famous. But it was only guessing famous voices.

Miss Annis left early and Thelma and I soon after.

'I scored with her,' I said.

'I could see that. But I didn't do too badly. Tynan praised my tits and called me the white Cleo Laine.'

16 March

Bates grasps the part with both hands and Joan Hickson's going to be excellent, funny until the moment when she breaks down, then suddenly frightening, even in a daylight rehearsal room on a cold winter's morning.

22 March

Michael Frayn, Tom Stoppard, John Hopkins and Alan Bennett assembled in a BBC viewing theatre to watch *Hearts and Flowers*, which they'd all missed. After ten seconds, the tape broke and the showing was called off.

28 March

The doctor, coughing as he heard me tell of my cough, said it could be psychosomatic and prescribed Librium to ease my anxiety. The pills haven't had their well-known sedative effect but led to an odd, unpleasant disparity between mind and body. In fact, I'm happy with the way the rehearsals are going. Anton's greatly improved now that he knows the lines. Bates has started getting jumpy, questioning every direction, refusing to learn which doors he enters or exits by, fussing about a bowler hat, the precise handling of a bag of eggs.

29 March

The set looks perfect: six doors on three plain walls and, above and behind, filling the great space where in old theatres the proscenium arch would be, there are two suburban bay windows. A single sofa stands facing front, of the same material as the walls, brown hessian. The only colours are brought on by the actors' costumes or revealed when the doors open to admit Frank's past.

While they struggled through a run, I sat near Stephanie and Sandra, as they waited in slave-girl sarong or gym-slip to represent my dream-girls. Gave up, crippled by shyness.

31 March

Public preview to a full house. Friends galore and a good local crowd received the play as we'd hardly dared to hope. Applause on lines and exits, plenty of laughter and a heart-stopping moment right at the end as the actors turned upstage for the last few lines of the song and everyone burst out clapping.

An evening of sheer happiness. Everyone euphoric afterwards. We ate supper with Priscilla Morgan and husband Clive Dunn. Blakemore, cool as ever, warned us it was bound to be worse tomorrow night and of course he was right.

Rex Harrison's Rolls was parked outside the Spreadeagle when we left after midnight and his party remained.

1 April

So here it is. Fools' Day, Dad's birthday and the play's first night.
Telegrams included one from Osborne signed 'All those at Frinton'.

The first-line critics were mostly there and saw a pretty good show, though the first act seemed depressing after last night. In the interval, I wandered alone in the remote art gallery but met a woman who told me that young people might enjoy being reminded of the war but she certainly didn't.

Second act better. Albert kissed me on both cheeks and there were tears in his eyes. It's the ending: Tony Martin sings 'You stepped out of a dream' as Sandra shows Anton her naked body beneath the schoolgirl's gaberdine raincoat. A popular and potent image.

2 April

Thelma brought breakfast to bed, with the papers.
    'What's it like?'
    'Not too good.'
    I'd somehow expected this, though in fact the general tenor of the reviews was favourable, only the *Guardian* hostile and the others, though far from ecstatic, were for us.
    Met my mother at Paddington. I was worried she'd take the play too seriously, as it laid bare a great deal about her marriage and our family life. But she seemed not to have been upset, carrying on the customary stiff-upper-lip reticence that's been her – our! – way of dealing with the slings and arrows and bearing the fardels.

London evening papers fair-to-good, Shulman especially. Felix Barker in the *News* carped, beginning with a grudging apology that after my last two plays, they expect more from me. 'He's in a vulnerable position.'

3 April

Saw Mum off on the coach to Derby, where she's spending some days with a friend. Poor soul, I wonder how she really felt to have her private and tender memories rummaged through for public amusement.
    Good prospects of a transfer. Medwin, Mike and I looked over the Apollo, Shaftesbury Avenue. Terrible sight lines. No complete view from anywhere but the stalls. Afterwards Mike admitted he'd revised his view that rococo theatres are best.

4 April

Brother Geoff and wife Mary, here from Bristol for the weekend, were up reading the Sundays before us. All good, including Hobson, who'd disliked the other two. Mike had predicted he'd change with this one, because it has no illness or handicap. Even now, though, he gave it third place but was deeply moved by Sandra under the raincoat. Bryden was most generous, with more than two columns and shaming comparisons with *The Entertainer*. They all said it was too long.

Peggy thinks it just the right press for a play that's expected to transfer. Medwin says we're away to the races.

Evening: drank at Griggs, Geoff and Mary a big success. The men talked politics, the wives antiques.

6 April

I'm successful again, praised, acclaimed and highly paid. But the anxiety of the last week has settled now to a dull ache and the recognition that nothing's changed. The play describes my feelings exactly. Do I want another family holiday in the Dordogne? Or more money to buy more gadgets? After a year's work on this and its warm reception, what's it doing for us? No, *me!* I want what I've never had. Infatuation. Sex. Adventure. Somehow Thelma's fixed it again so that I shan't take advantage of the play's run, not returning from France till it closes at Greenwich. When it's at the Apollo, I'll still be here, with no excuse to see my dream-girls. Other men leave their wives, take lovers. I'm moral by omission. I found the other day that even Francis has had seven women to my *four*.

9 April

Arrived Chez Magnou in fading daylight. All the work we'd ordered had been done by our troupe of artisans: there's now a bathroom, a kitchen and running water. A dooble-vay-say disgorges into a subterranean septic tank and new windowed doors open on to the orchard. The apple-trees are clouds of white blossom and buttercups shine in the grass. My little cell upstairs has been replastered, the oval window looks on to walnuts and figs.

Unlocking doors with great rusty keys, finding the barn emptied of its sabots, ploughs, harrows, milking-stool, yoke, and – sad to say – the blue cart on which the children loved to play. Evidently our poor

French had failed to make our meaning plain and the men had cleared the place of *all* traces of its former rural life. The rotted hay has gone too, which is some consolation for the missing charrette.

[David and Meg Mendel arrived with their daughters, having started with us but gone a different way. A cardiologist at St Thomas's and neighbour at Blackheath, he was getting used to a long retirement. Their marriage was novel: a Jew and a Quaker. Later he learnt Italian, bought a house near Piacenza and became a translator of Primo Levi. At this time he spoke useful French.

In a quinquallerie, not knowing the word for some tool, he'd always find a way, asking for '*Une chose que fait comme ça – oui, d'accord, un tournevis*'.]

10 April

Modestly accepted the Mendels' admiration for the farm. He at once started organising. We found him wonderfully helpful and tiresomely bullying. He's intelligent and practical though and gets things done, so you have to forgive his tendency to give orders and carp at your efforts to carry them out.

13 April

In the warm afternoon, the wives took the children to the lake.

David and I worked, shifting earth or pruning trees of dead limbs. When the heat became intense, we went inside and he played Mozart on his flute. I shaved, shat and showered and was wiping lather from my ears when our neighbour Mrs Belsey came to say hullo. That morning in Ribérac, the Banque Nationale Populaire had swarmed with English cashing their cheques and complaining about all the English who were spoiling the place. But they only spoil the bank; otherwise one need never meet them.

We'd planned dinner in Brantôme and were about to drive off at dusk, when there was a cry that Peter Foy had pushed Catherine from the granary window, twelve feet from the ground [Mrs Foy was the latest in a line of English mother's helps and foreign au pairs. Her son Peter came with her to share our ménage]. David checked her limbs and she seemed unhurt, though sobbing from shock. Lou and Dan complained about Peter. Thelma told him she hoped he'd learnt his lesson, whereupon his mother shouted back that he wasn't yet three and the others blamed him for every accident. Thelma retorted that ours were covered in scars and he was unscathed. I tried to suggest that this fuss was achieving nothing but they were both roused and beyond reason. I waited in the car with David while they simmered down. She joined us after a while, saying Mrs Foy had given notice – later withdrawn. We drove to our dinner, discussing the servant problem, which in 1971 and for soi-disant Socialists was as much ethical as practical. We ate well and sang all the way home.

15 April

Two of the local gendarmerie called at 9 a.m. and exchanged pleasantries. Dan admired their uniforms. One showed his pistol and let Dan try on his cap. They laughed at Dan's refusal to shake hands and went, giving no explanation for their visit.

[Why did he refuse now after doing so well at first? We probably praised him, always fatal.]

The kids had found the old cart in a steeply sloping field down by the woods and after breakfast we began hauling it back. David had gone to spend the night in Bordeaux and walk some wards in the hospital, partly to justify claiming this trip on St Thomas's, so Meg, Thelma and I did most of the pulling and pushing. We took all morning to drag the cart up the field, with only one coffee-break. Instructed to clear the farm entirely, the men must have had an easy job running it down the slope. On the road it nearly ran away and we broke into a trot to keep abreast. Looking back from where I was trying to hold back this juggernaut, I saw the children's faces bobbing along and laughing. We backed the cars away, opened the huge barn doors and gave one last push and heave. A triumphant chariot restored.

[This incident was a climactic moment in the first drafts of my next play *Chez Nous*. I was always sorry that it had to be dropped in later versions, never reaching the stage of the Globe in 1974.]

David returned with Hobson's rave re-review. I've always said that if I ever found favour with this sentimental eccentric, I'd know my time was up. The excesses that are so sickening in his praise of others were all here but he couldn't resist making the point that my apparent cynicism is a pose that repeatedly gives way to involuntary affirmation.

Still, it's hard to resist flattery, even if you can't respect the flatterer.

16 April

David and Meg have enviable self-assurance. Their view of our species is that most people are fools and we're certainly most people.

'They haven't got it up here,' he'll say of some waiter or neighbour, tapping his temple.

He tried to tell me Thelma had no sense of humour because she hadn't grasped one of his brusque surgeon's quips. When I repeated this to her, she said he'd told her he marvelled that I could write plays when I hardly knew which end to hold a screwdriver.

His approach is always direct and effective. Within a day or so he made friends with the village mayor, M. Dignac, a spherical and unshaven man who occupies the large farm on the farther side and who came to visit us with an enormous quantity of his own rough wine and eggs.

A little eccentric also comes to call, an itinerant fruit and vine labourer who stays in a roadside hut, which we'd taken for an implement store. He speaks in a falsetto gabble, which doesn't make his patois any easier to follow. He asked permission to draw water and salad from a spring on our land and took Thelma to see what he meant: a natural source with watercress growing in profusion where it surfaced. He reports that the land agent Varaillon had fished our pond, which accounts for the absence of all but frogs this spring, after we'd seen so many carp last year.

18 April

I was hacking and sawing wood in the shed this fine evening when Dan came out to complain that he suffered from imagination. If you keep on imagining, he explained, you don't know where you are when you suddenly have to realise this isn't all true.

'But does it matter, Dan?'

'I'm trying to get rid of my imagination,' he said, still frowning. 'I've got it down to about this size now' and he made a circle with both hands.

19 April

The Belseys came with their ill-tempered daughter of twenty-six.

'I'm getting her to take home our income-tax forms,' he boasted. 'Costs a fortune to send them from here.'

By his own admission, he's done everything wrong: bought the wrong stove; their car breaks down; he's slipped a disc ('That cost a fortune') and the house is intolerable in winter.

'We had to live in the kitchen,' said Elizabeth, a very decent woman and a martyr to the whims of her curmudgeonly husband. Yet he was good and gentle with the kids. Catherine took a fancy to him, hugging his legs and continually saying, 'I love you'. He smiled and said it was nice to be liked.

21 April

M. Blanchardie, the plasterer, came with wife to discuss making good the kitchen ceiling. When I spoke in my halting French, he stared blankly as though I was trying Sanskrit and seemed unable to understand even the simplest words. He began shouting pidgin French, infinitives and all.

'*Moi!*' – pointing to his chest – '*faire – le travail – vous comprenez? – moi plâterier!*'

It was a demonstration of the stupidity of raising your voice at foreigners. When he *did* understand, he raised objections – the house was too damp, not très solide enough, etc., finally saying he was too busy anyway. It seemed he didn't want the job and was being obtuse to ease his refusal. Then why come?

22 April

Left early and made Nogent-le-Rotrue by six p.m. The children had been angels, even Peter Foy behaving well for a change. Stayed at Hotel

Dauphine, as before, but it was disquieting to find a tiny envelope by the bed containing two balls of malleable wax. The instructions told me they were earplugs. We remembered some traffic noise before but nothing much, forgetting that this had been Good Friday eve. To bed early, had sex, slept for three hours. I was woken at one by the sound and feel of long-distance lorries shaking the hotel at three-minute intervals. The room was too hot but to open the tightly shut casement windows would have been to let in more din. I tried the balls of wax but they were worse, squelching and self-ejecting. Cath came to our room in the same state and shared our bed. I finally dressed, took a pillow to the car in a garage at the back, arranged the seats as a sofa and cat-napped for a few hours till dawn at five-thirty made more sleep impossible.

We imagined the whole stretch of country road between Chartres and Le Mans subjected to this brutality, to line some bastard's pocket.

24 April

Forget-me-not had been playing to packed houses, not a seat to be had that whole week. We saw the Saturday matinée and they were standing along the back wall.

27 April

Our production 'took over' the Apollo. All the actors happy to be in The West End and in what most of them call 'a real theatre'. How could anyone *want* to be in this gruesome quarter, the end of the pier without the sea? Strip-clubs, dirty-book shops, belching vehicles, piles of rotting food on every pavement, sad casualties pushing buttons in 'amusement' arcades, an air of febrile promise and inevitable despair. This mood can't but affect the work presented in these old theatres that stand like dowagers in a slum.

I went from room to room trying to spread gloom and despondency but they were all happily unpacking their good-luck cards, lucky charms and bottles of wine to entertain their chums when they 'come round'.

28 April

Opening night. Perhaps the worst performance they've given. Usual first-night audience, many queens and weird showbiz fellow-travellers from Golders Green.

'There's Geraldo,' said a woman behind us, 'he's married again. They say he's very happy, got a lovely home in the country. There's Albie Finney, bless him, with his wife Anouk. No tie. You see, Albie can get away with it. They look happy.'

The set, designed for Greenwich, here seemed small and ugly, the action happening through the wrong end of a telescope.

There was warm applause at the final curtain but for me it came too late.

29 April

Thelma passed her driving test after an hour of revision with me that ended with us shouting at one another and the car parked diagonally across the street.

Played tennis with Michael Frayn, taking a set off him at last. Letting me have this may have been his first-night present.

1 May

In the afternoon, in chilly sunlight and sudden cloud, The Blackheath Fayre with a 'y'. The village, as they call it, only goes back to the advent of the railway and never was more than a stop for commuters. Now it's a traffic jam by day, a morgue by night. The tone of idiot nostalgia is carried through by the Romford Drum and Trumpet Corps ('I need this like an 'ole in the 'ead,' said a bystander), a jazz band, a Punch-and-Judy, the Blackheath Male Voice Choir in Victorian top hats and, main attraction, The Sealed Knot.

This has 1,400 members who make their own costumes, though there is a Gentleman Armourer who will provide reproduction breastplates and greaves to order. Dan and I had a position near the ropes for the Mock Battle, re-enactment of a sham fight that the programme says was actually put on during the real Civil War. A space had been cleared and some booths representing houses erected at the base of the triangle. A Ford 1100 saloon was cruising with a loudspeaker on its roof and inside a man in Caroline clothes and horn-rimmed glasses was sitting with a mike and a lapful of notes.

'Please keep the opening clear,' he kept saying, 'this is for the entry of the cavalry. We don't want anyone hurt during the battle.'

For the next chilly quarter of an hour there was only the Lady Mayor's arrival to divert us. Another car joined the first to corral the crowd. A young man lolling in the front seat muttered into his mike: 'How many times must you be told to keep this entrance clear? You, sir, will you please get back!'

At last some troops mustered with pikes, making a good – or goodly – sight. They marched towards the 'houses' and, would you credit it, children from the local dance academy were tripping round a maypole. The other instance of Merrie Englande we could see from our place was a slapstick rape by two Cavaliers of a village maid. Desultory cheers. They did an encore but by this time we were all pressing forward to see some mounted Parliamentarians. This brought the young man in the car tearing up the field shouting about the clear space again. Cut off by the horses, he stopped in front of us, engine running, spoiling the view and fouling the air. He finally got away by a fourteen-point turn, which threatened more damage than all the horses could have done. Cannon went off and the roisterers left the maidens and set about defending their plywood homes. A chorus of Lewisham women were like the crowd at the coronation in Shakespeare's *Henry VIII*.

As the captain of horse urged his men to another charge, one said, 'I'll bet he never gets a word in at home.'

'Look,' said her friend, 'there's another house on fire. Bring it a bit closer, love, we're like brass monkeys here.'

'Hullo. Mrs Mayor's had enough, she's getting in the car. No stamina, some of them.'

But it was all in a good cause – or a variety of causes, ranging from the South Thames Referees to The Sydenham Guild of Handicapped Scouts.

Evening: we saw Act Two of the play, which seemed to be going well, then to the Royal Court for Osborne's party celebrating the fifteenth anniversary of *Look Back in Anger*. We entered the auditorium to see the stage full of guests eating from a square of tables. We joined them, ate and chatted, mostly with Alan Bates, who said the film of *Egg* is being held back till Janet Suzman's second film, *Nicholas and Alexandra*, is released at the end of the year, so that she can be presented as Spiegel's discovery. The tables cleared, the gypsy orchestra gave way to pop records. Dancing followed eating. Someone brought the Sunday papers, all favourable for our show. Bryden wrote that if he sees a better play this year, he'll be lucky.

8 May

Lovely day. Tennis with Frayn at Ranger's House, then with Louise in our garden. A friend came with his son and daughter to watch the Cup Final on our new colour TV. We pulled curtains on the bright afternoon, drank iced Pernod and watched Arsenal win. The boy, a Liverpool supporter, cried with grief. After tea, we were out on the road waving them off when Mrs Foy came to tell me the Bristol hospital was on the line. Not another crisis? It wasn't likely, I thought as I walked up the path to take the call, as they hadn't bothered us with false alarms for some time now. Louise had answered and was handing me the receiver now, looking alarmed and interested.

'Hullo?'

'Are you Mister Nichols, the father of Abigail Nichols?'

The professional voice of death. I knew it at once.

'Yes.'

'Well, I'm sorry to have to inform you that she passed away peacefully at half-past six this evening.'

About an hour ago. We'd been eating.

'Well, in the cirumstances that can only be seen as a good thing.'

We exchanged the obligatory clichés – happy release, blessing all round, end of her suffering, stopping short only at 'good innings'.

'She was seen by Doctor yesterday and there appeared to be nothing unusual. Her chest finally couldn't stand the strain.'

Thelma cried when I told her. For a while I held her in my arms. Louise had already gone to bed complaining that she was ill. I went to see her.

'Abigail's dead,' she said.

'Yes. I'm glad too, aren't you?'

'She might be happier in another life after death. If there is one.'

'She could hardly be less happy, as far as we can see.'

'If I'd been the first, it could have been me.'

She's always been the most conscious of her eldest sister's existence.

We sat in a dazed mood, rang our parents, decided to tell the Frayns and Woods. Thelma suggested putting a notice in *The Times*. I asked whatever for, as no-one knew her, and then only as a disaster. Even *we* knew only what we'd invented, a personality based on accidental gestures and reflexes. We comforted ourselves with the thought that her state had helped us understand each other and strengthened our marriage. Deepened it even. She dies obscurely, this well-known invalid who had smiled a few times, cried a great deal, never learnt to sit up. Her death had been postponed eleven years by drugs, her fits suppressed, those outward signs of her inner chaos.

9 May

Drove to Bourne End for Tom's party, through empty Sunday streets, coming at last to the thronged motorway, then the implausible Georgian-poet countryside of Thames Valley. The Stoppards' place is next to Cliveden.

'In fact,' says Tom, 'Northcliffe's place is on the other side. I'm between him and Astor. Not bad for a provincial reporter.'

He was pouring wine in the marquee. Entertainments laid on included Punch-and-Judy, a Shetland pony, croquet, badminton, helium balloons and the pool. Our girls were soon in the shallow end and the actor John Stride was the only adult to brave the water. I was standing some way from the edge with Tom and Thelma when she suddenly said, 'Is Lou in trouble?' I stared at our daughter's face, submerging and surfacing, and thought she'd find her feet in a moment. But Tom moved at once, lay on the side, reached out and pulled her towards him. Stride swam promptly to her aid. I arrived too late to be of any use. Louise cried as her pride took a bruising but was otherwise unhurt.

Celebrity cars were arriving too often now for the geese to announce them. Tynan took pictures. I was watching the conjuror when a sudden splash made me turn in the slow-motion mode that I'd adopted for the day and saw Thelma comforting Catherine. Stride, now fully dressed and soaked to the skin, had jumped in to save *her*. To lose one daughter may be a misfortune. To stand about while other men save the other two is emblematic of my trance-like incompetence.

10 May

Thelma and I joined Joe Melia at the Embassy, Swiss Cottage, to watch the Central School's production of *Egg*. Those lines about whether the child could outlive 'us' had a new depth and there were moments when I felt like standing and announcing, 'She's dead, everyone. It's over.' The students made a creditable shot at it, considering the age, say, of the young woman playing the grandma [Susan Wooldridge, later so memorable as Daphne Manners in *Jewel in the Crown*].

We took the cast to supper. Joe, of course, knew of Abo's death but we didn't bother telling the others.

11 May

Notice in *The Times*' column of Births, Marriages and Deaths.

'Nichols, Abigail, eldest daughter of Peter and Thelma, at Hortham Hospital, Bristol. Funeral Friday, Canford Cemetery: family flowers only. Donations, if required, to the hospital.'

14 May

An easy train ride to Bristol. The quiet rolling voices reassured us after the nervous and pushing Cockney we've grown used to. Mary, Geoff, our mother, Thelma and I sat in the Co-op limousine staring out at Clifton College, The Zoo, The Downs, Badminton School and at last Canford where the hearse was waiting.

'There she is, Mum,' I said to Thelma, expecting it would be the last time we'd use this manner of speech, invented to give her some character, even to make her falsely articulate. It was a child-size coffin, of course. As we reached the chapel, one of the undertakers whispered, 'Give me a nod when you've stood enough and the coffin will go down.'

What ceremony else? We now doubted whether we'd been right to insist on a non-religious cremation. Should I make a speech? There'd be nothing, no minister or music. We followed the coffin in, borne by four men. Only the box could have weighed much; she had wasted away to nothing with lack of exercise. We were in the front row and behind us Thelma's parents, Mum, Uncle Frank, Mary and two of the nurses who'd cared for her. When the coffin was set in place on the lift, we decided to kneel, a position that at least suggests humility, but to what? To some far-fetched sadist who could have allowed a cruelty like this? I wish now I'd had the guts to stand. But at least it meant that those who were capable of praying were already on their knees. And this occasion wasn't for us but others. I held Thelma's hand very tight as she started giving convulsive sobs. Afterwards she said, 'It was the size of the box.' When she'd spent her tears, I gave a nod and the coffin sank.

I shook hands with the nurses and one said she was lovely and her little heart was strong but she'd at last succumbed when her lung collapsed. She'd even shown signs of knowing them, she said, and I thought 'Not bad for a ten-year-old.' Nothing anyone said made me feel anything but relief that her long-delayed death had at last been allowed by our clumsy ethics.

[During one of our visits to Hortham, I'd asked a nurse if it wouldn't be kinder to let her die.

'But she's a holy innocent,' she replied, with a smile so sancti-monious I could have hit her. Whatever doctors may feel, their actions are circumscribed by these simple priest-ridden women.]

As we drove back, the driver gave a covert wave to a mate of his arriving with the next coffin. We soon passed near the house Dad wouldn't buy because he couldn't bear to watch funerals coming and going all day.

20 May

Blakemore and Tynan have asked me to do an Orwell programme for the National, which could also be a road-show and some sort of answer to the RSC's four-hander on Royals Down the Ages. I'd jump at this invitation but can't see how it can be done. There'd have to be an impersonation, as the work so much depends on his personal 'voice', and here the widow Sonia would be a handicap. Chris Morahan had dealings with her over his TV versions of the novels and found her poisonous.

Heard from Mum on the telephone that Uncle Bert, sole Nichols survivor on my father's side, had been admitted to a geriatric ward after being taken ill in the Ilford house where he'd been living with his niece Dora and her father since Sister Hattie's death.

Drove that afternoon through the Blackwall Tunnel to Chadwell Heath. This was a mental asylum in all but name, much like Hortham, red-brick barracks amid dismal lawns and outbuildings. On the upper of the two floors, a pretty Eurasian nurse directed me to the far table where Bert was slumped, half-asleep, already much altered from my last sight of him at Hattie's funeral. He woke slowly as I touched his arm and spoke his name. Then I had to tell him mine. His eyes flickered into an expression that could have been recognition or merely the attempt at it. I showed him the bunch of rather blighted roses we'd picked from the garden and the get-well cards written by Catherine and Peter Foy, who didn't know him. He tried to answer my banal questions but his tongue couldn't frame the words. I gave up and stared about the ward, a pleasantly modernised interior in pastel shades with bright curtains on alloy runners and newly surfaced vinyl floors for easy cleaning. I guessed the reason for that by the small pool under my uncle. The patients, of various ages but all ageing, all male, stared silently about them or sat huddled in sleep.

'Did he bring his guitar?' said an Asian nurse, as she and another began tidying beds. They moved among the stricken figures, smiling and indifferent, laughing at private jokes.

'How long you staying?' said a patient sitting near me. His head had been shaved, his eyes were red and staring.

'Only a little while. Seeing my uncle.'

'Uncle?' He nodded. 'What car d'you drive?'

'Renault.'

'Good?'

'Yes, fine.'

'Singer me.'

Was I about to hear his life story? Would he give us a song?

'Oh.' I understood. 'You drive a Singer?'

The nod again. He stared about him, suddenly angry.

'Can I go now?'

'You ain't going nowhere,' said another patient some way off. Then to me: 'He don't know where he is.'

After what felt ages, I decided a decent time had passed and told Bert I was off. He tried to hand me back the children's cards and spent a while putting one back in its envelope before I said he must keep them. He shook my hand firmly enough and I waved to the other patients.

'Where's he going?' said the staring man.

'Saying ta-ta to his uncle. Off home.'

I found a large black charge nurse repairing the mechanism of an aquarium, his hands in water that was iridescent with tiny tropical fish.

'I hear you're going away for the weekend so came to see your father first.'

'Uncle.'

'Uncle.'

His accent was posh, his manner effete. 'Where are you going?'

'Oh, to a cottage in Kent.'

'Very nice. I hope the weather keeps for you. I was at the Chelsea Flower Show yesterday and it absolutely poured. Between the tents it was like a pig-sty, well dressed women picking their way through the mud on high-heeled shoes. Dear-oh-dear. But the blooms were beautiful.'

His hands still among the fish, he told me Bert had a large mass in his stomach and the prognosis wasn't hopeful.

Driving home, I thought of Bert's life: his years in the Flanders trenches, about which he would only talk with a gruff dismissal, then his whole working-life in the Co-op factory at Silvertown, pushing barrowloads of pepper about. His hobby was his stocks-and-shares and every day he walked to the public library to check their progress in the *Telegraph*. Yet he was literate enough to read Maugham ('bit smutty, boy') and took me to see *Anna Christie* at the Theatre Royal, Stratford, in the days before Littlewood arrived. He came alone on the 15 bus to the first night of *Egg* and helped us short-list the Koestler Award entries. It's always surprising how little can sustain a life. Perhaps he exhausted his bravery during those years he couldn't bring himself to mention.

[He was one of the funeral chorus in *Hearts and Flowers* and he and his sister Hattie were done in more depth in an unperformed play *The*

Stratford Strangler. Fragments of him and his brother Robb were in *Blue Murder.*

When, some time later, his estate was settled, he'd left thousands to his nephews and nieces – Frank, Dora, Geoffrey and me – all kept in a bank account. The house wasn't theirs. He'd paid rent for it all those years. When he came to stay with us at Blackheath, he'd been riveted by television but never had one at home, only radio brought in on a wire. £2000 could at that time have taken them round the world or – if that was too much for Hattie's digestive system – at least had an inside toilet and television. But she had said, in a line I used in one of the plays about her, 'I've seen it! I hate it! You look in there, all that glamour. You switch it off and what have you got? Stratford!']

Eve: Alan Badel as *Kean* in Sartre's re-hash of Lemaître's play at The Globe. American women stood with sequinned handbags in the bar saying: 'Illusion and reality? I knew about that when I was a kid. There's no insight here.'

'Mamie said we should have gone to *Fiddler.*'

'We'll go tomorrow.'

We look to them to keep our theatres going but the whole business is a sell. For them too. They expect so much of Europe and find only a tired America.

1 June

Made off early to Mendels' cottage in Kent for the Whitsun weekend.

Some rain and cold, much warm spring sunshine. Pheasants and partridges coughing in the woods, a rabbit frozen in fear as we drove up their lane, the hedges sprinkled with cow-parsley and yellow dead-nettles. Duster, their red mongrel terrier, sprang out of a field of barley, like a salmon going upstream, a lively sight. But he was after prey and finally flushed out a hen pheasant that took off clumsily, barking an alarm. A moment later the dog had her chick in his mouth and David tried to rescue it, but too late.

I tried my animal sounds on sheep, horses and cows. The last was the most effective. I'd watched the pedigree black bull swinging his hard-on from cow to cow for some time without coition. David described his leisurely courting when he was seriously looking for a mate.

'Sometimes takes the best part of a day,' he said, 'a far cry from whip-it-in-and-wipe-it.'

When I mooed at the cattle beyond the wood, they stared for several seconds then lolloped off, their udders bouncing. I never did it again but whenever we approached after that, they cantered off to graze elsewhere.

Even the tourists (hey, that's us!) couldn't spoil Canterbury Cathedral's magnificence, its lightness, its dramatic choir and altar, cloisters and chapter house. Dan especially loved the funeral achievements of the Black Prince. While we described Becket's martryrdom, he frowned his visualising frown and evidently saw the knives going in. I hope we can escort him safely into adult life with his spirit intact.

4 June

Last performance this season of *Health*. Only one ticket for sale so Thelma sat while I stood at the back among a good few others. The play was going almost too well, with a too-great readiness to laugh. And at the end cheers. It's become one of their warhorses. We'd meant to leave at the interval to see the second half at the Apollo but couldn't resist wallowing in the Old Vic audience's uncritical approval. Michel Fagadau was there, no doubt noting Michael's moves and business, as he wants to do it in Paris. So also does Jean Mercure of the Théàtre de la Ville, but he's so pompous, so full of reasons why it will fail with the French.

Blakemore brought the designer Jocelyn Herbert, mistress-widow of George Devine, who'd been famously taken ill while in drag for the ball in *A Patriot For Me*. She had to watch him go from paralysis to death and this, she said, made my play too distressing to enjoy.

5 June

Cousin Dora rang to say Bert was dead. I left the car at home and met my mother at Paddington, arriving with another pair of her numerous Canadian cousins. While they went to see the sights, we took the Central Line to Gants Hill. Only six of us came to see off my last surviving uncle: plump, powdery Dora, her father Bert Mott, her brother Frank, his wife Betty and we two.

I was becoming a funeral aficianado, so wasn't at all taken aback by a man who came got up like a shabby Fred Astaire in silk topper, etc., and a smile of complicity for the men, as much as to say 'The women like it, don't they?' After the flower business, we all squeezed into the Rolls for a slow stuffy drive to West Ham. Back in the same chapel where Aunt Hattie had been seen off, we now sat while a poor stricken youth recited some Jewish history in a sing-song voice and added a few cracker mottoes. Prayers done, he pressed a button and Astaire re-appeared, repressing a smile at some joke the undertakers had had over their smokes. Dora and I, senior mourners, walked behind the coffin to the grave.

'They'll have to make this path wider for us fat ones,' said Mum, walking with Betty just behind. Slim as ever, she meant that Betty had let herself go.

'Grass needs cutting,' grumbled Bert Mott.

A sheet of plastic grass was laid around the hole next to Harriet's grave and the coffin got caught on it and had to be raised again so that the minister could pull it clear.

And in their death they were not divided. Two lonely people un-mourned by anyone, I thought as I stood staring around during the last few mumbles. But no, Betty was in tears. On the way home, the chat was jolly and, as we re-entered the house, Frank said he doubted whether we'd done right to have this sort of ritual.

'Uncle told me only lately he'd never believed in an afterlife. And I must say I don't either.'

Mother and I agreed.

'I don't know what to think,' said Betty. 'I cried because I thought of my father's death. I was terribly fond of him and so upset when he went. And it's funny, I was impelled to his bedside moments before he died. I watched him go. I found that very mysterious.'

Dora moved us from tiny room to tiny room while she laid out cheese straws, chicken salad, stuffed tomatoes, trifle, sponge cake and tea, in her best Domestic-Science-Teacher style. Her father, the retired woodwork master, was on my right as we sat facing his beloved garden plot through the French windows. He had by now, I think, got it straight who I was, having first called me 'Geoff'.

'Goodness, what a spread!' my mother exclaimed, stiffly disapproving.

'Well, I thought I'd be catering for eight,' Dora came back, with her malicious laugh, meaning of course that Geoff and Mary should have come. What for? No-one believed in this but herself. The occasion seemed a washed-out parody of long-ago burials when there were still profound economic or superstitious reasons for a proper send-off.

Bert turned his hearing-aid towards me and told me the details of his prostatectomy.

'Usually they put a needle up your penis and cauterise it but this surgeon was of the old school. A stroke of the knife and – ssk! – '

(I thought of the line from *National Health* – 'And there you are – Bob's your auntie.')

'Though,' this awful old man continued, 'later on some pus started oozing from the stitches.'

At five, I told Mum it was time to go and, to my horror, she said she'd stay a little longer.

'I don't want to stand about at Paddington.'

No? Wasn't anywhere better than here? At least a mainline station would have crowds of expectant people actually going somewhere.

At last we were away, walking to the tube, saying we'd done our duty, which was the main thing. I promised myself I'd never see that house or those relatives again, but didn't speak this aloud as that sort of anti-familial resolution scares her.

In bed at night I read Lawrence's poignant short story 'Fanny and Annie', with its description of returning to a deathly scene from one's past life.

'Her heart nearly stopped beating as she trudged up that hideous and interminable hill, beside the laden figure. She knew it all too well. It is easy to bear up against the unusual, but the deadly familiarity of an old stale past!'

9 June

At the Griggs', a lady minister from Mrs Gandhi's government defended her leader's record against attack by relentless, well-informed Mervyn Jones [ex-Communist novelist, journalist and sometime drama critic]. I liked his refusal to be fobbed off with poor arguments but felt sorry for the Indian lady who'd only yesterday arrived from a trade fair in Moscow, to be given this verbal mugging by an intellectual thug.

'I met So-and-so in Delhi,' Mervyn said in his scoffing monotone. 'What a truly awful man!'

'He's a very good minister.'

'Maybe, but a totally discredited character.'

'He's done some wonderful work in his ministry.'

'But he's a crook. Not only that, he was *shown* to be.'

And later he told us: 'I've only once met Indira Gandhi. She struck me as the world's most respectable woman.'

'It all depends what you mean by "respectable".'

'Well, alright, I shan't quibble with words. Say "square".'

'She's very shy in company, due to her secluded upbringing.'

'She's a terrible public speaker. She makes these deadly boring speeches with audiences of thousands all yawning their heads off.'

She remained jolly and bright and changed the subject.

'One of my favourite people,' she said, 'is – who wrote *Howl*?'

'Ginsberg?'

'Allen Ginsberg, yes. I don't know why I forgot his name when I know him so well. Jet-lag, perhaps. He was so funny, coming to India to shock people with nudity and so on and finding a festival with all the gurus and yatris with no clothes and nobody paying him any heed. He said we had the true Beat community already. Then he asked me to find him a gay guru.'

John asked: 'In what sense?'

16 June

With Thelma to George Inn, Southwark, for a lunch of steak-and-kidney pie, cherry pie and beer. Expected hordes of American tourists but found only English, including three young men with posh accents who went through a repertoire of advert slogans, radio catchphrases and anecdotes about cricket, bloodsports and motors, even calling beer 'ale'. We decided they were the urban counterpart of those yokels the National Trust employs to lean over five-bar gates on its rural properties.

Afterwards to Southwark Cathedral crammed between the vegetable market and the overhead railway. Then walked across partly-built

London Bridge (the previous one sold to decorate an American golf-course) and turned down the steps to Lower Thames Street and Magnus Martyr Church. Last time I came here was a Sunday morning on my bicycle in the 50s. A woman was replacing flowers and a church cat ran among the pews. I could see what refreshment Eliot must have found in this place during his lunch-breaks from the City bank.

> Beside a public bar in Lower Thames Street,
> The pleasant whining of a mandoline
> And a clatter and a chatter from within
> Where fishmen lounge at noon; where the walls
> Of Magnus Martyr hold
> Inexplicable splendour of Ionian white and gold.

In Billingsgate a black 'fishman' was hosing down the abandoned stalls, and baskets of lobster and crab awaited despatch.

19 June

Letters are coming in complaining of anti-Semitism in *Forget-me-not Lane*. This play seems to be attracting a less sophisticated customer than the others. Most rabid is one from an American with an address in Mallorca:

'In attacking the stinginess of the father, the mother said "He's as cheap as a Jew with no arms". I am not a thin-skinned Jew and would consider myself sophisticated but cannot help compare the contrast to the reaction which would, without doubt, occur in New York to this slander. I am certain the Anti-defamation League and Jewish Defense Leagues would be protesting outside the theater.'

To make sure she causes the maximum annoyance, she sends copies to the Jewish Women's Club, *Jewish Chronicle*, *Jewish Bride Magazine*, Jewish Vanguard, Jewish Friendships Club and Jewish Board of Deputies. This means I must reply, if only to ensure that all these influential bodies don't advise their members or readers to boycott the show. I've talked it over with David Mendel who advises a letter to the *Chronicle* suggesting an interview with one of his staff to argue my case, though I'd have thought it was too obvious to need it.

[The original line I wrote was one I heard my father use: 'like a man with no arms'. It was Michael Frayn who said he'd always heard the phrase used with 'Jew' in his own South London suburban family. I of course used this instead, making it far more funny and telling. What strikes me now is the bullying tactics adopted by these guardians of decency. I can find no mention of writing to the paper but I remember doing so. The editor wisely ignored all the fuss and we heard no more.]

26 June

Awoken on Sunday morning at seven by Aunt Millie arriving by taxi from the airport.

'Yesterday we were in five countries – Austria, Germany, Liechtenstein, France and Switzerland, because Basle airport is just beyond the Swiss border.'

Thelma had expected her the following night. We missed our Sunday morning read in bed. I'd also wanted a Sunday Reed [Thelma's maiden name].

After giving the girls their dolls and Dan a toy alpenhorn that makes a mournful noise, she began her catalogue of holiday marvels: the 'syupah' prawn cocktails, and pineapple desserts; the 'pukka' courier who was only doing this until he'd got himself 'hitched'; Mozart's house where they made *The Sound of Music*; and the lovely coaches and nice terraces above the lake and she didn't know how Global could do it for the money.

'Mind you,' said her companion Phyllis, 'they've got these package tours down to a tee. Nice cassettes playing Viennese waltzes as you go.'

'You could buy them too. You bought the Boys' Choir, didn't you?'

'No. "Music From Many Lands." And England's was "Greensleeves".'

4 July

I took a rehearsal of some cuts we're making in the play, part of an effort to propitiate the gods of theatrical success, who have taken their favours elsewhere, leaving our show with thin houses. Memorial (Medwin and Finney's production company) will spend more on advertising if I make it shorter. It simply isn't West End meat but will stay there as long as it covers its get-out. I think perhaps all these dusty old buildings should close, like the provincial reps we once worked in. Trying to think of a new use for them, I could only come up with multi-storey car parks or a Wall of Death, which is what it feels like to venture into one of their obsolete galleries, from where all of us watched plays until we could afford to move down.

To the Royal Court Upstairs, not much more than a rehearsal room. They were doing *Skyvers* by Barry Reckord, a revival from 1963, and simply terrific, a frightening and accurate account of life in a London school of the sort I taught in in the late 50s. Ranted that it should be at The National, not hidden away in this fringe place, like a nonconformist chapel for some intellectual Luddites. Bucked nonetheless, some faith restored in our mostly disappointing job.

Took taxi to see our cuts in action. A decent house, but the play could hardly be heard over the singing of drunks just beyond the exit-doors, the revving of motor-bikes and the wailing of police sirens.

Blakemore was a a a bit rude about the way I'd done the cuts, then had the nerve to say his sex-life's in ruins. I gave him short shrift, saying only that chance would be a fine thing. Thelma and I had to walk to Hyde Park before we found a taxi to take us back to Sloane Square where we'd had to leave the car.

6 July

Good instance of female behaviour this afternoon. We were in the garden on our chairs, reading, the children playing happily, the two helping-girls getting tea, Thelma in her beach clothes.

'What about it, Mum?' I said, still using the Abo-speak we always used with our late daughter. She smiled.

'After tea, Dad.'

So, after cucumber sandwiches, raspberries and cream, when she went off to get dressed for the evening, I followed. We were off to see the event of this theatre season, Peter Brook's version of *The Dream*. In the sweltering bedroom, we undressed. She chose evening clothes and started minor repairs. Then began running a bath while I shaved and asked, 'D'you want this?'

'After you.'

'You have it first if you want.'

'It's too hot.'

'I'll have it first then and you can add cold water for yourself.'

No recognition of her promise so I said:

'It's always been like this with women. Always will be, I suppose.'

'Like what?'

'Trying to guess what they mean.'

'I'm trying to guess what *you* mean. D'you want a bath or not?'

Since then, I've jotted this down and now she's shouted 'I've finished!'

Why are they always like this? Does she know what I mean? She's not naturally a cock-teaser so why? Is it really so unimportant to her? Perhaps I should have said 'What about that fuck then?'

To finish that story, I did make clear what I'd wanted, once my bath was over.

'Before tea you promised we could have it.'

She stared critically at her fully-dressed appearance in the long glass.

'I forgot,' she said.

8 July

Blinding heatwave and Greenwich by-election coinciding, the schools used as polling-booths, so our children home, we took off for Brighton. Too long drive – next time by train – but still enjoyable. Only my second visit [the first resulted in the television play *Promenade*]. I'd remembered sand but of course the beach is pebbled.

According to today's *Guardian*, the electoral turn-out was dismal: Labour won in a safe Labour seat. But democracy's seen to be done. One of the few beneficial effects you could directly attribute to politics was our nice day by the sea.

10 July

Day sweltering in the garden – up in the 80s. I pick nearly a pound of raspberries and quite a few strawberries every day. First hollyhocks in bloom.

Postcard from Mum, whom we expect home from Morocco today. On the front a picture of the Arabian Hall of the Rif Hotel; on the reverse her message: 'We've been to the Kasbah this p.m., also to a Sultan's Palace for tea. Seeing belly-dancers this eve. Love to all at 17.'

We found a full house at the Aldwych for Pinter's *Old Times*. This elegant puzzle, as unaffecting and unhelpful as a crossword, held them rapt and respectful. At the end they clapped the solemn actors, whose demeanour implied that this applause was as *de trop* as whistling at Holy Communion.

When we got home, Mum, her cousin Al and his wife Jess were drinking tea, as they had in the Sultan's Palace.

'The king was nearly assassinated,' Al said, 'and boy, were we lucky! The last party to be let outa there.'

The women told their stories of fierce heat, bone-aching cold, tummy upset, Mistral, alarming lavatories, beggars in the Kasbah, nice people on the coach. It was all one: either slightly disconcerting or mildly pleasurable. Mum belched resonantly in her mezzo-soprano range.

'Oh, pardon. Spanish tummy.'

Like Millie and Phyllis, they're full of the couriers. Is that all they really take in? Of course, they're entirely dependent on these guides, hobbling about, holding on to each other as the beggars advance for bakshish.

Mum had brought us souvenirs of a place we've never seen: a leather magazine-cover for Thelma and a scaled-down scimitar for opening letters. We imagined the scene: Omar Sharif-looking men rushing in and out, disembowelling each other with large-scale letter-openers while, oblivious, these three sit looking for a waiter to bring more hot water to top up the teapot. Souvenir du Maroc.

Little bald cheery Al has kept the frontier myth alive.

'You want a play, Pete? You should write the story of my uncles Mick, Dick and Jack. When things got tough in Bristol, they got outa there and headed for Australia to join the gold rush. But they needed an outfit to be a part of it – you know, horses, a wagon, all the tools and gear. They met a feller in a pub and he agreed to go in with them. Well, they give him their savings and never saw hair nor hide of him again, no siree.'

And so on, through opal-mining, attacks by bushwhackers, murder, disease, betrayal, infatuation with dockside molls, diamond rings, hairbreadth 'scapes. I have a vivid memory of Uncle Mick, a midget perched beside his immense wife Annie on two similar upright chairs at some point in my adolescence. When she tried to stand, the chair fell apart and Mick failed to save her from falling to the floor. Did these Robert Service adventures really happen to him and his brothers? Probably. And afterwards they crumbled into suburban henpecks.

17 July

Party next door. Alan Norton, host and psychiatrist, fussed over the canapés and punch. The treacherous English summer had suddenly cooled from heatwave to chilly evening and we stood in the garden making middle-aged middle-class conversation. Women acted like Edith Evans and historians sneered at television drama.

[Memory fills a gap in this entry. Another guest was a member of The Great and Good called Burke Trend who, we were told later, seeks out likely candidates for honours. Perhaps he wasn't on duty tonight but if he was I failed to join his group and sometimes wonder if this accounts for the Palace's mysterious oversight of never awarding me a K or peerage.]

John Grigg praised Churchill and Nixon. The first conducted the war in a way that saved British lives.

'He wanted above everything to avoid the kind of carnage he'd seen in the First. He couldn't stand the thought of some senseless slaughter.'

The difficulty in refuting John is his insider's knowledge.

'As a matter of fact,' he'll say, 'he was in my father's company in Flanders. Some of my father's letters home describing him are extremely amusing.'

And Nixon? The liberals all screamed blue murder when he extended the war to Cambodia (despite the fact that no-one seriously believed in the neutrality of that nation or Laos) but now that this policy has proved successful, all criticism has suddenly died. Whereas poor misunderstood Bomber Harris, committed to civilian bombing, couldn't make it work and has been discredited by hindsight.

I pointed out that Bishop Bell of Chichester, humane opponent of this policy, had been overlooked for preferment. And that was about the only point I scored.

19 July

Dropped in to the last few scenes of the play. Terrible performance, terrible audience, actors depressed. But business last week was up £800 to nearly £4,000.

20 July

First night of Blakemore's co-production (with Dexter) of *Tyger*, a celebration of Blake by Adrian Mitchell. Intermittently enjoyable, with music in a half-jazz half-rock idiom that kept promising without ever quite delivering. But it had more fun and more of a vision of life (how could it not?) than many an alleged entertainment.

'I can't tell you the scenes we've had over this,' Mike said. 'Grown men in tears.'

'Which grown men?' asked Thelma.

'Well, Tynan for one.'

'I suppose he is, yes.'

'Olivier shouting at us to cut scenes attacking Enoch Powell. We may have to resign if the notices aren't good.'

21 July

Hope-Wallace in the *Guardian* gave it a bitter review in his flippant style, but was, I thought, more fair than he'd been to mine. He had, though, assumed Isabelle Lucas to be Cleo Laine, because they're both black singers. Cleo's off-white and Isabelle's much darker. Their voices and styles are quite different. Sent Isabelle a telegram saying 'They all look the same to Philip Hope-Wallace.'

23 July

To the farm, this time with Thelma sharing the driving.

Called for the keys at M. Simeon's (the *sous-maire* and stoneworker), to be told my *beau-père* had them still. We'd thought Thelma's parents would have gone back to England but might have known they'd wait over to meet us. The children asked, as is now traditional, to be let out at the top and race down the incline to Chez Magnou. Dan came last, having made a bad start due to his shorts being undone and falling round his knees. The Reeds were laughing and shouting as we drove in and Frank gave me one of his bone-crushing handshakes.

Later Reg drove me to Mussidan station in the Cortina to meet the mother's helps, Charlotte and Emma, who were staying for the summer. A hair-raising, stomach-clenching drive down, with Reg complaining that the only snag with the Dordogne was the twisting roads.

The train from Bordeaux (whence the girls had flown from London) drew into the Will Hay station soon after we arrived. As it came in sight, the stationmaster shouted into the waiting-room: 'Traversez, m'sieurs 'dames!' and we were expected to get across the line before the engine reached the platform.

We sat this manoeuvre out, staying on the home platform and saw through the carriage windows our girls climbing down. The train moved on and arriving passengers crowded across the track.

On the way home, Reg demonstrated the wonders of automatic transmission, all but turning the car over at a sharp bend.

24 July

Our guests and artisans have looked after the place with care and skill. Two new doors protect the pump and well-shaft; M. Simeon had restored the fallen stone gatepost and connected it to the barn by a sturdy wall; new shutters are hinged beside the front windows and the living-room chimney's been made good. M. Maze has scythed the gardens, field and orchard, propped up the peach-tree and trained the decorative vine. The cherries are gone, eaten by birds as soon as they ripened; the peaches are small but red and sweet; the figs swelling, apples ripening; clusters of grapes hanging over the kitchen door. Reg has cleared trees from around the pond and made steps to the water. He'd seen half a dozen carp.

25 July

When our mayor M. Dignac first saw the sea, he thought it was a vast field. He puts this in between stories of the war and how the Nazis took over many neighbouring farms, including ours. We thought he said ours was used as an SS post but couldn't be quite sure.

As I transcribe this some months later, I have in mind Marcel Ophuls' film *Le Chagrin et La Pitié* that we've seen since coming home, a story set in Clermont-Ferrand during the Vichy regime and subsequent German occupation. The spa's only 150 miles south of here and I believe the border between Vichy and 'occupied' France fell not far north of here. After the film's various episodes of collaboration and over-zealous Jew-hunting, we'll have to take a pinch more salt with the oral history the locals give us over their *petits gouts*.

31 July

[No mention of my 44th birthday. Surely we must have marked it somehow? The family usually forgot to buy presents before we left and went shopping in the local Maison de la Presse for pencil-sharpeners and ball-point pens.]

A back-and-forth of telegrams (and anger) before we met the Blakemores at Mussidan station. They brought the familiar tensions, Mike frowning and fretting like a dowager over tickets and suitcases and seating arrangements in the car. Arrived at the farm, Conrad said, 'Is that the barn? I thought it was going to be *much* larger than that.'

They calmed gradually, Michael unburdening his bad and good news. The box-office figures are holding but Michael Bates is seriously ill. He's suffered an intense depression and lost a stone in weight. Often he has no idea how the play begins. Meeting Joan Hickson in the wings before one of his entrances, he asked 'Where are we, dear? What are we doing?'

'You remember, Michael? The play about Peter Nichols's family. You're the father and I'm the mother and –'

'No idea at all. No memory of –'

At that moment he heard his cue, opened the right door and walked on speaking his first line.

His Gurkha-officer sense of duty makes him doubly anxious he's letting the team down and might crack in a crisis. We discussed replacements.

1 August

Patrick and Mary Bennett and kids, our Blackheath neighbours, came for Sunday lunch, just passing through. This made eight adults and seven children, the incredible Thelma coping and managing not to seem too pressed.

2 August

After long sleeps and longer sleeps to recover from the long sleeps, Shirley and Mike looked stronger. He'd been exhausted by *Tyger*, for which the Sunday notices had all been bad. Dexter had been im-possible and Mike vowed he'd never again co-direct. Now he recovered his fighting spirit and found there was no-one to fight except me. This awful competitiveness, discussions always becoming arguments, every chore and diversion a test of strength – woodchopping, swimming, chatting up Charlotte and Emma, games of Scrabble. Mike's a roman-tic. I should have seen this long ago but his superficial puritanism misled me. He craves the intense experience that I run from but crave.

3 August

After supper, mellowed by the Mayor's rough wine, Mike asked the girls about pot and they told us all the young use it. He was explaining the difference between hash and grass when Charlotte broke in to say this was too elementary and I should know it.

'Well, I don't,' I said, 'I've never tried but if you've any stuff here, I'd like to.'

They hadn't, for fear of Customs at Heathrow and Bordeaux, but last year the bouncing-hockeysticks Emma had smuggled pounds of the stuff from Israel sewn into her clothes, meant for a dealer in London, who took the dope and disappeared without paying. To think of this school girl risking jail for nothing! She seems excited and frightened and ashamed to confess that she's *not* taken LSD. When asked if she'd used it, Charlotte said 'Oh, yes,' as though she was telling us she was a regular reader of *The Beano*.

'I've dropped acid, of course, but I'm not an acid-head.'

Mike elicited this through his fascination with the young, his belief that they're privy to some revelatory secret we've never had and that it's wonderful to learn about their sub-culture. No wonder his favourite author's Scott Fitzgerald.

4 *August*

A bad morning, failing to write, after some awkward talk with Mike about his interference in the US production of *Health*, which now seems to be cancelled because he couldn't make *his* production work in the proposed theatre.

P.m. I tried again, wrote a poor scene, with southern sunshine beating down outside my upper window. Gave up and went to join the family, to be told by Charlotte that the adults had gone for a walk and she and Emma were off to the lake with the children. I took Mike's letters and mine and walked to Siorac-de-Ribérac to hand them to Madame in the post office facing the fortified church tower. Walking home, I noticed local washerwomen under the shelter where a spring supplies the trough with fresh water. Also alarmed an old rooster on the road by crowing at him. Some people were laying plastic flowers at the tree-shaded shrine, a monument to someone '*Assassiné par les Allemands*'. Reaching the crossroads beside the small holding of the fighting couple, I saw Thelma, Mike and Shirley ahead and whistled. Thelma came back, unusually affectionate, and I showed them cards I'd bought with views of the village and told them I'd had a rotten day's work but the walk had slightly cheered me.

And had *they* had a good time?

'Absolutely marvellous. A long walk through the woods. Goes on for miles, that forest, you don't see another soul.'

But why were they were gabbling so excitedly about a stroll in the woods?

We walked back to the house, Thelma's arm round my waist. Had Emma supplied some pot after all? On the doorstep she said: 'Shall we tell him what we really did?'

'Yes,' said the other two, as one.

'Swam in the nude. We found a private pool with a boat moored at the side and these two brave ones walked right in and we stood discussing it for a while then Shirley threw her clothes off and ran in and Mike and I did the same.'

He was watching my reaction, eyes wide, smile exultant.

'Well, that's the story of my life,' I moaned, 'always somewhere else when the fun happens. Always missing the event and writing it down later.'

'Oh, come on, Pete,' he said. 'That's all in your mind. This was very innocent.'

Crap, I thought, we aren't innocent. Nothing we do is innocent.

'It was very spontaneous,' Shirley said. But even Mike saw this wouldn't exactly console me for a lousy day at the desk and a missed swim in the buff.

'No, it wasn't, Shirley. We discussed it. It was very middle-aged and middle-class.'

So not innocent after all?

'Thelma felt she had to tell you or it would have become a secret, something furtive.'

If they'd judged my mood better, they'd have seen that the last news I wanted at that moment was that my wife had been nude bathing with a notorious voyeur.

That night Thelma insistently made love but without success and I lay in the dark, wide awake, till four a.m., seeing myself as a figure of fun, coming down the road to show them some bloody silly picture postcards. What's more, I own the farm that provides the scenery for his little stripshow with my plump wife. I spent hours working out practical ways of leaving her. Next day Mike told me he too had lain awake till four.

5 August

Thelma took me, Lou and Cath on the same walk to their pagan pool, where today a French family were fishing and swimming. Our girls

[171]

paddled and we walked back. It wasn't at all a pretty pool, all slippery clay at the bank.

When we told Mike, he said, 'Just think . . . yesterday was probably the one day of the year no-one else was there', meaning 'you will never experience the pleasure I shared with your wife'.

Every time she betrays me, however slightly, I feel a little more free. When, if ever, the break comes, it will be complete and guiltless. Innocent. [This episode became a crucial scene in the play I'd been unhappily working on that day, *Chez Nous*.]

A telegram from Medwin had arrived while we were in the woods, asking us to ring him back at a time which had already passed. Michael at once was in a state. He craves the telephone. It was too late that night but he fretted all the same and perhaps it's as well for me he does, as he's in my corner, fighting to give the plays a fair chance in the dogfight that is showbiz.

6 August

Early at Siorac post-office urging our shy but willing postmistress into putting through a call to London. Mike hasn't a single word of French, despite years at the most expensive Australian public school, so Charlotte came to help me cope. It took an hour to get through, what with the operator at Ribérac not answering, lines to Angleterre being engaged, our postmistress having to see to her dinner, no reply at Medwin's number, and finally a slow gathering of leeks from the garden beside her shop to add to the meal she was cooking. The outcome was that we had to wait another twenty minutes before a new line would be free.

'In that case,' Michael suggested, 'will we use the time to ring Mussidan Station and find the times of trains to Bordeaux tomorrow morning?'

This was done, the first of a full day's anxious preparation for their journey to Biarritz, where they were to spend two weeks more.

During one wait, Charlotte and I explored the church, finding the key where the mayor had told us, tucked under the door.

'Don't go out of earshot!' called Mike from his position beside the post-office.

Finally there was Medwin's voice, incongruous in the wholesome summer of Siorac, telling us that Michael Bates's doctor has given him permission to remain in the play till October 2nd. Nothing very urgent after all, nothing that a letter couldn't have conveyed in more detail and at leisure.

7 August

Mike kept asking if there was enough petrol in the car for the journey to Mussidan. Once there, an hour early, he had me asking the booking-clerk about connections at Bordeaux with Biarritz, arrivals there, distances from station to waterfront, availability of taxis, likelihood of crowded carriages and whether it was worth going First. Shirley watched this exhibition and murmured: 'Conrad and I have been half way across Europe on our own carrying our cases.'

It was good to have them here and good when they left.

Conrad had removed the old timber his-and-hers outside lavatories beside the woodshed, to show the skills learnt from his latest hobby, Demolition.

10 August

We rested from company for a day, until the Morahans arrived.

[Christopher and Joan Morahan, with their younger son Andy and daughter Lucy. An eminent and excellent director (especially of television), he did six of mine from '63 to '84.]

Few birds, much gunfire. The French kill everything that moves, except bats, rats and insects, the real pests. Horse-flies are the worst, their bites on ankles and arms often swelling into pustules of subcutaneous fluid that burst and form again at once. Mosquitoes fill the house at night and there's no Keatsian lying in bed listening to the night sounds. The panes are firmly shut to keep out flying things and the night air of our rooms is scented with super-actif non-toxique Kapo.

All this is the price we pay for the sight of so many species of glamorous moths and butterflies, from black velvety ones to small, citrus-coloured creatures dancing among the grass. Electric-blue dragonflies hover above the pond, some four-winged and fluttery, tame enough to alight on our hands.

14 August

Finished first act of a new play that I might call *Chez Nous*, a pun that will only be understood by those who know the name of our real holiday home. It's been written quickly and is, I'm afraid, slick and trivial, the second act a closed book at the moment. All I know is what happens during the interval, while the audience is knocking back their gins and Scotches.

> [This had the longest and most tortuous growths of all my plays for the stage, finally appearing in London two and a half years later.]

The families went to the lake, leaving Chris and me at the farm, where I worked and he coped with an upset stomach. Thelma fetched me after he and I had had lunch together, watching our half-dozen carp lying below the surface of our pond. At the lake I swam to and from the jetty then read more of Connolly's *Enemies of Promise*.

Eve: We four parents drove to Brantôme to see and hear Claude Luter, the only contemporary French jazzman whose name I know. At Bourdeilles, an encampment of filthy nomads under the cliffs beside the Dronne. In these parts, there are *real* gypsies, not the pale clean kind aristocrats can feel sentimental about at home, but Egyptian-skinned tinkers shifting their wild broods and mounds of junk from place to place, always unwelcome, kept on the move by permanent signs: 'Interdit de stationnement des nomades'.

Arriving at Brantôme, we tried to buy tickets for the concert but there was no sign of life at all. Later, after we'd eaten in a crowded restaurant, the scene had changed entirely. The French are profoundly conventional. As gregarious as Italians, they do everything together. How do their solitary eccentrics survive? Now the streets were thronged with noisy car-parkers and door-slammers, all shouting with excitement, forming a long queue for tickets, in which we too waited and paid for entrance. It was dark, not long after dusk, when we followed others across the elegant courtyard, closed on one side by the sheer cliff which dominates the small town, and on the other three by the ancient buildings of the former abbey, now the *mairie*. Under the projecting limestone cliff-face, the monks had found a natural chamber, the size and shape of a large, low-ceiled hall, and on the rock-face the artists among them had carved reliefs and against this background, raised above the smooth floor, a group of kids were making the usual electronic din through colossal amplifiers and an audience of shortish young people listened rapt. Occasional outcrops of greying heads and vaguely smiling faces belonged to visiting English dads. We climbed on and up to approach the music. Their set over, the band left the stage. A hectic man gabbled into a mike. Under the overhanging cliff an amazing spectacle: hundreds of standing and, behind them, seated people in evening dress at the far side of the natural chapel. Lamps on their tables bounced light off the napery on to the carved Christs and crucifixions behind. These posing people seemed like extras from a Fellini film, so obviously modern and secular against the devout background.

Luter is a living extension of his mentor Sidney Bechet, with whom he'd played a lot during the old man's last years in Paris. Here was a direct link with the origins of jazz. His soprano sax whinnied for all the world as Bechet's did on any of my beloved discs, first collected on 78 ten-inch singles during the war, now packed on to LPs, fifteen at a time and free of surface hiss. It was the young Bechet who struck Ansermet between the ears in 1919, when the conductor wrote with amazing prescience: 'this young man's way is probably the way the whole world will swing along in future.'

The acoustics were appalling and amplification never helps, but we forced our way through the dense crowd till we were near enough to catch some real sounds, standing among the cognoscenti who listened critically and scorned the inevitable rabble-rousing drum solo.

Drove home past the inhabited cave-dwellings along the winding road through the Dronne valley, while lightning flashed silently ahead. Standing at the roadside for a pee, I looked above at a black sky with incredibly bright stars and not a cloud to hide them.

17 August

The scream of the jet-engine is nothing to the thud of the sonic boom, probably from Concorde, testing north of Toulouse. I was writing an angry reference to it into my play later, trying to recall its exact effect, and had reached the 'p' of explosion when it came again, more than just a bang. You hear it before it arrives. Birds and animals are all disturbed and fly or career about.

> [Thelma's father tested its engines both in Bristol and Toulouse. Nothing would have given him greater joy than to be given a flight in a plane he'd helped make safe. But that was for journalists and those owed favours. This always struck me as a perfect example of how the dice are loaded in favour of parasites and against anyone who does anything useful.]

Orwell failed to guess that technology would go so fast and be so much more important than politics. Air-travel's barely mentioned in *1984*. Of course, the book's not prophecy but a distorting-mirror image of 1948, with all the shortages, war-weariness and ever-present fear of atomic warfare that plagued us all after '45 and still does. I've re-read the book during our holiday and come to a decision about the Orwell evening for the National. It should be set in a sound studio of the kind he knew, with a cast of radio actors doing a reappraisal programme.

Tynan's written to remind me of this subject and that he and Olivier would also like to commission a play for the new South Bank building, opening in 1973. Too tasty a chance to miss.

18 August

Peggy keeps me in touch with events at home. *Forget-me-not*'s not only survived the dog days but business has reached its highest figure yet, £4500 last week. Not good for the peak period of American tourism but about the best that can be hoped for an ambitious quirky play with an unknown cast. No such risk of that with Mortimer's *Father* piece with Alec Guinness replacing Mark Dignam.

19 August

Chris's elder son Ben was brought from Royan, where he's been staying a few weeks with a French family. Only fifteen, he's already a mature young man, drinks easily and speaks French well. He took to the prettier, younger but less interesting of the two girls and the other could hardly attach herself to thirteen-year-old Andy. Caught between childhood and manhood, he ate continually to cope with his sudden physical growth, already taller than his brother and sister, sitting in on both children's tea and adults' supper.

Chris, neither a good swimmer nor a French speaker, unable to deal with his sons' abrupt burgeoning, tried to rule them like an old-style father. We could see rebellion brewing as the boys tried not to demean their dad by making fun of his pomp.

'Andy, don't sit there with your mouth open, okay?' Chris would say and, not content with that, press on with 'Alright, Andy? . . . Fine, okay.'

Or: 'Ben, could I have a word with you?' and off they'd go into another room, returning minutes later with a false smile from Chris and an assumed tolerance from Ben.

Thelma was driven to simmering anger by Chris, Joan and Lucy, all in their various ways difficult guests. He stirs up trouble, as in rehearsal, scratching some minor irritation till it bleeds, then quickly takes the role of peacemaking mediator, smiling his false smile, with eyes shut and cheek muscles contracted, saying from his six-foot-two eminence, 'Don't worry, Thelma, it's perfectly alright, . . . alright? Fine', till you feel like hitting him. No wonder Tony Hopkins said he'd never work for him again and had that set-to during *Hearts and Flowers*.

I was reading *Huckleberry Finn* to our children in the other house at bedtime when I heard either Charlotte or Emma run sobbing into their room next door. Thelma followed, shouting about the girl's laziness and depressions and that she must get hold of herself and do the job she was being paid for. The kids and I sat agog and I paused till Thelma went, slamming the door, to be at once replaced by Joan bringing Lucy and muttering bitterly, 'Bloody woman! Well, dear, we must all buckle under and conform.'

During the next pause, I picked up the wonderful adventures of Huck and the nigger Jim on the Mississippi. And when our three were quiet and able to sleep, I went, finding Charlotte still sobbing in the room beside theirs. She told me she felt aggrieved and upset by Thelma's outburst, and I assured her she was only being used as a scapegoat because Thelma didn't dare turn on the Morahans.

[177]

Back in the main house, Chris was doing his false smile business, like a priest called in to pacify a brawl.

'It's quite alright, nothing at all. Best forgotten, alright? . . . Okay. Fine.'

But in bed before we too dropped off, Thelma said he'd fanned the flames and swiftly turned to throwing on water, an arsonist posing as a fireman.

This was the necessary crisis, and after the boil was lanced we all got on better. The last few days were very enjoyable – bathing at the lake, L'Etang de la Jemaie, lively sessions of The Game at night, walking in the woods on misty days, climbing M. Abadie's cathedral cupolas, eating and drinking, buying three ducklings in the market.

22 August

Again, great relief when the Morahans went. Twelve at every meal was a few too many and we found our lazy days more pleasant than the coach-party routines required by two families.

Wild life: a snake swimming with its head above the surface of the lake and the French shouting at one another and seizing sticks, though freshwater reptiles aren't venomous; a glow-worm moving through the long grass at night, like a fragment of glass reflecting light from a lamp; a huge frog stranded in the barn after dark; the lizard's tail that went on twitching for minutes as we passed it from hand to hand; the orchard floor strewn with russets and cookers, the fall of an apple a resounding boom in the otherwise unbroken silence.

25 August

Reading: Naipaul, Connolly, Orwell, Lawrence stories, Paustovsky's five-volume *Story of a Life*.

Writing: b-and-b letters, these notes and a hundred pages of *Chez Nous*, which has gone from triviality to pseudo-profundity in two acts.

Playing: Scrabble, jokari, boules, skittles.

Speaking French with the artisans, making slow and slight improvement in our guesswork, which is a big part of grasping any lingo. Glad of Charlotte's help. But we were both beaten by a coarse dark man with bleary eyes who reeked of wine and garlic and appeared without warning one evening and stayed, talking unintelligibly in patois while we tried in vain to find out what he wanted. By the way he kept dropping the cigarette I gave him, we saw that he was pissed. M. Maze later told me he's an alcoholic and was probably looking for casual work of some kind, though he owns a farm on the road to La Jemaie.

28 August

Anton Rodgers's son Adam turned up at the lake and we surmised that Anton himself was skulking somewhere among the pine-trees because, in fact, the play had been taken off and no-one wanted to let us know. Dan made friends with Adam's gang and these four used to go off in their sailing dinghy and inflatable boat, returning after hours for a quick report to us before beating out again to some remote shore or the wooden jetty with its fishermen, swimmers and sunbathers.

Far from having come off, the play was doing its best business to date, partly due to a rave from Clive Barnes in the *New York Times*, says a cable from Peggy. But when a copy of the notice came, it seemed – like many of his reviews – favourable but unconvincing, as though he's cowed by his own fortuitous power and doesn't dare be positive in case he gets it wrong. A two-steps-forward one-step-back. He manages to make four mistakes in as many paragraphs, saying:

that the 'hero' is a Cockney when he's Bristolian;

that he went to university when it was only a training college;

that he's left his wife when he's only considering it, as he will forever;

that I'm the author of *A Day in the* Life *of Joe Egg.*

29 August

Chez Nous is the most moral and thoughtful thing I've done and actually has a story that embodies its ideas. Nobody talks to the audience and formally the play is absolutely naturalistic, though there is a short passage where two men look over the expensive part of the audience and talk about the former occupants, how rotten the 'stalls' are and how they'll have to be pulled down before another year is up. This will almost certainly be cut from the second draft.

2 September

Busy last days, depositing money in French account at BNP, buying pâté de foie gras for the specialist who operated on Cath's tonsils, long overdue Grateful Patient bribe for a private consultation at his home. [Also bought car!]

The local garagiste, M. Moreau, had a Deux Chevaux we assume was assembled from cannibalised parts rescued from his field-full of old Simcas, Renaults and Peugeots. When we went with him to try it up an incline, four adults and one boy, he had to change down through the gears to bottom to keep it going at 15 m.p.h.

'As you see,' he said, 'a very nice car for touring. You have plenty of time to look at the scenery.'

Dan was with us because we had, on the way, left the ducklings bought at Perigueux market to be looked after by M. Maze. When he first saw them, Maze estimated they'd be ready for eating in about three months, good time for *Nöel*. We told him they were for the children to play with, not to be eaten, and he laughed and shrugged and said alright but it would be far better to – and he made the gesture of throat-slitting. Couldn't M. Belsey have them, he asked, still unable to believe our sentimental wishes. He assumed this was a pretext for not giving three free meals to a French family and that we'd happily let a fellow-countryman have them for Christmas. We told him Belsey didn't eat meat.

'Pourquoi?' At this point he frowned, upset and confused.

'Parce qu'il n'aime pas tuer ou manger les animaux.' When it finally sank in, Maze roared with laughter, shaking his head, punching the air, as much as to say there was no limit to English eccentricity.

No sooner were the ducklings in the pen with his black ducks, suddenly in the real world, being pursued by them and trying to escape under the chicken-wire, than Dan came running up the road from Chez Magnou, wanting to ensure they weren't about to be guillotined or whatever they did to murder living things in France. The French attitude lacks the Disney-ish anthropomorphism of English city-dwellers. Just the same, there's a certain gloating greediness about them. The adverts in *Sud-Ouest* for Samaritain, the chain-store, show an idealised huntsman dressed in every available item sold in their sportswear department, from rifle to boots and with a ravenous hound at his heels.

And a favourite French poster shows a wounded gamebird plummeting earthwards through a blue sky with, beside it, a blow-up of their most reliable cartridge. We're told that, in Bordeaux, where birds of passage meet for southerly migration, the natives snare them in huge nets and pick them off one by one. We see few birds in this remote part, either due to mass extermination or because they keep well clear of humans. Still, there must be plenty, as they denude our trees of all their cherries.

4 September

Brand-new British ferry from Boulogne: no waiter-service, only a cafeteria serving tepid fry-ups with steam-baked bread and St Ivel yoghourt. But most passengers spent the crossing in a queue for cut-price drugs and intoxicants, which would have been even cheaper in France. We were back in the world of fair play.

In the women's toilet, Thelma reported, an English woman was trying to change the nappy of a handicapped black baby. She asked for help from a chic Frenchwoman who was making up her face with almost insane concentration. After several failures to get a response, she at last elicited a brief, 'I'm sorry, really,' before madame went back to her face. Thelma helped the Englishwoman and when they left the other had done her foundation and was beginning on her eyes.

6 September

Into the clamour of London to a reading of *Ben Spray*, a ten-year-old television comedy of mine that already sounds quaint, a period piece full of words like 'jive' and 'cool' and such expressions as 'do me a favour'. John Alderton, current favourite on the box, read the part as a gormless prole and I had to indicate as tactfully as I could afterwards that the eponymous anti-hero is more intelligent than any other character and went to a decent grammar-school.

Bad lunch in expensive café. Sour Vichysoisse and Alderton complained about the cloudy sherry.

[In 1960, this had been my first success, slight but perceptible. *Ben Spray* was named as one of the plays of that year, a list that shows how far television writing has declined since then. The roll-call included

Ronald Harwood, Jack Pulman, Harold Pinter, Peter Draper, Rhys Adrian, David Mercer and Henry Livings, about par-for-the-course at that time. It also marked the advent of *Coronation Street*.]

9 *September*

Paris was very warm in brilliant sunshine. Having guessed wrong in London, I was wearing a raincoat and carrying a briefcase. I wanted a word with Claude Roy before meeting Jean Mercure. Kept to shady side, walking through the back streets of St Germain, coming on to the Seine near Ses Pères and climbing Claude's stairs, arriving breathless at the door of his flat. An unknown servant nursing a baby told me the Roys were in Mexico till the 20th.

Now with time to spare, I took it easy, pausing on a bridge to watch the smart, almost empty river-buses passing beneath. It's still a pretty place, though the roaring traffic on the bankside death-traps comes close to spoiling the river scene as it has London's squares. To Place du Châtelet past the animal and bookstalls (with cages for some of the few surviving birds, all endangered species), admiring the elegant women and feeling almost euphoric to be free of family and Michael Blakemore, whom I'd left conferring with a bank official. Such an excursion's an insult to so beautiful a city. That evening we'd be home again, the reason for coming mostly so that Mike could finagle a deposit on the house he's buying in Biarritz.

After a pastis in a bar beside the theatre, I met Mike in the foyer. In his office, Mercure waved his arms and shouted, thrusting a signed contract for *The National Health* into my hands. Soon after, still shouting, he led us through the streets to a restaurant where we ate lunch at pavement tables, with two of his assistant directors.

I raised the question of local accents in a play that has English variants of London, Bristolian, Welsh, Scottish and West Indian. Now we saw how sealed-off Parisian theatre is from ordinary life.

'Oh, it's impossible, we don't allow accents on our stage,' said Mercure, 'and no French actors speak with local dialects.'

'What about Raimu, Gabin, Fernandel, et cetera?' one of us asked.

'Oh, these people are monsters, they won't do what you tell them.'

'I'm not suggesting you should cast them – even if you could – only that they surely speak in local accents, a patois, argot?'

He gestured the idea out of court.

I nagged on: 'Michael's speaking with an Australian and I with a Bristolian accent.' They looked at one another, shocked and embarrassed.

'Are you saying you're all Parisians?' asked Mike.

'Of course not. I'm from Bordeaux, he's from Lyons, he's from Dijon.'

'So you're not all speaking the same French?'

'Of course! At this table, only the very best high-class French.'

'So if a young actor joins your company from, say, Marseilles, can't he revert to his native way of talking if he's playing a provincial character?'

'He wouldn't, no.'

We mentioned the peasants in Chekhov or Brecht, the modern proles in Edward Bond, the plays of De Filippo, Tennessee Williams, Molière . . .

Non, absoluement pas. Metropolitan snobbery had triumphed here, as in many other sides of French life. Parisians aren't interested in France, and provincials still deeply resent this self-interest and influence.

They later introduced us to some company members and showed us round the fine theatre. Formerly the Châtelet, it's now Théâtre de la Ville. Only four years ago, it was rebuilt within the old walls, a handsome auditorium on the Greenwich lines but twice as large, one enormous raked bank of seats. By retaining the old shell, costs were halved. It's backed, not by the ministry of culture but the municipality.

I tried to interest Mike in some sightseeing. Nôtre-Dame's towers were shut so we had to be content with a few ground-level imitations of Charles Laughton as Quasimodo. Mike noted that they'd cleared away the boiling oil very well. Walking from Île de la Cité towards Invalides, his arm was jerking up every now and then to check our plane's departure time. We finished at Orly two hours early and ate in a horrible airport café.

He'd hated working with Dexter and resented the man's sexual bragging, which turned out (he said) to be the vainglory of an impotent man.

'It's like a limp chipolata, dear,' said an informant.

'I mean, Pete,' insisted Mike, 'I didn't establish an intimacy with John, but working with him I made every effort to be candid and friendly and told him about one or two of my affairs and got all this in return about bi-sexual orgies, which I suppose may have been the sort of thing he imagined would interest me . . . all the same . . . '

16 September

Ben Spray run in afternoon. Actors seldom understand their function. They all behave as though they're required to make a silk purse out of a sow's ear, when perhaps the playwright only meant it to be a sow's ear.

Eve: Frayn's new play *The Sandboy* opened the Greenwich season. An ambitious, witty, disconcerting comedy with Joe Melia cleverly miscast as Michael's self-portrait, a man who always lands on his feet. Guiltily he declares: 'Honestly, I was happier when I wasn't so happy.' The second half fell away a bit and Michael lacked the coarseness to exaggerate the action into a crisis or climax, but it was so subtle and entertaining that I felt sure it would be another success for him.

At the party at the Frayns' place, Patrick Allen explained why he'd taken the smallest part.

'I represent God, you see, just sitting there playing chess, controlling the other people.'

Or was he meant to be a sow's ear?

Andrew Sinclair, well-known novelist, buttonholed me.

'I'm tone-deaf, absolutely. When people know about music, I grovel.'

Joe mentioned performing a narration at the Proms and how Boulez had read the enormous modern score and pointed out a D-flat to someone who'd played a D-natural.

'Oh, that sort of thing,' said Sinclair, 'I simply grovel.'

He's made a film of *Under Milk Wood*, just praised at Venice, and claimed he'd solved the problem of distribution. He tapped the side of his nose, the gesture of conspiracy.

'But, Andrew,' said his agent, 'you're still more Candide than anything else.'

Meeting me later at the pudding table, he confided: 'My agent may call me Candide but I'm also The Fox.'

Michael tells how he lost his temper one day after Sinclair had been boring everyone with how he was about to write The Great English Novel.

'But, Andrew, you couldn't possibly *ever* write the Great Novel of any kind because you never, *ever*, even for a single moment, take the least notice of what anyone else does or says.'

Polite as ever, in remembering this, Michael says 'It was a stupidly rude thing to say and I was covered in confusion as soon as I'd blurted it out. But to my surprise, Andrew accepted it with a good grace and quietly told me, "You're absolutely right, I never do. But as soon as I've finished this present series of essays, I'm going to start noticing other people, you see if I don't".'

18 September

Due to a union dispute, the only paper to come out was *The Times*, with a bilious dismissal by Irving Wardle based on a scrappy impression of what Michael's play had been about. Feeling I must try to take his mind off this rotten luck, I asked him to play tennis. He beat me, as usual, 3–2 this time, despite his best efforts. In the play, Joe wins a chess game he's trying to lose, even cheating to give himself a handicap. But Michael's charmed life seems to have faltered lately and the prize he most wants to win – the theatre – eludes him.

Heard by phone from Mum that, being driven back from Southampton with Aunt Maud by brother Geoff, they'd had a collision and the car's a write-off. If they'd not been wearing belts, they'd probably all have been killed. As it was, Geoff's legs were injured and he's off work for some time. When I rang him, he said that, as he crawled towards a nearby garage on damaged knees, he'd seen that the sign above it said 'Marks Brothers'.

23 September

I turn with relief from the landscape of modern London to the solace of pre-revolutionary Russia in Paustovsky's *Life*. He claims that nothing of Chekhov's birthplace, Taganrog, appears anywhere in the author's work. He writes: 'Most writers keep notebooks or diaries but rarely make use of them for their novels.'

This certainly isn't true for me. One of my recurrent anxieties is losing mine. Sometimes it strikes me I might do better without them, stretch my imagination, stop depending on what's happened. Then I recognise that this is, after all, my method and must be accepted. My deficient memory means I need to record what people say.

[Thirty years after writing this, the British Library has agreed to accept my papers for its archive, joining those of Peggy Ramsay, Pinter, Rattigan, Tynan, Wertenbaker and, if they can afford them, Olivier. Mine will include two filing-cabinets full of playscripts, a drawer of correspondence and over thirty volumes of journal. The absence of these books from my shelves will be a weight off my mind. I may even have to start imagining and inventing.
Or be struck dumb.]

24 September

Turned up at Town Hall to hear the last day of Greenwich Society's objections to the Greater London Development Scheme, a bureaucratic name for a ruinous network of ringroads. The participants included the GLC party, local witnesses, the panel of inspectors with their chairman, a suave QC, and Colin Buchanan with two hats on – one of a witness for the local interests and the other as advisory planning expert for the council. They all muttered into microphones which only just broadcast their proceedings to 'the floor', an audience of about twenty-five sitting on tubular steel chairs. I hadn't read Buchanan's report and had a hard time grasping the planning jargon of 'hierarchies of roads' or 'coarsening the secondary network'. Some startling figures still emerged from this ritual contest, such as that 40,000 vehicles a day pass through Greenwich between Inigo Jones's Queen's House and Wren's Naval College. This massive problem is dealt with, as always, in the common-sensible way of all government inquiries. Nobody cares or believes. They have their briefs and strategies and steer a course between various partial interests.

[Revising this diary in 1999, I understand more. A recent TV programme told the brief history of the motorways' golden age. Had this scheme gone through the process and the network been built, much that we now prize and enjoy in London would have vanished under roads on stilts, as in Birmingham, Newcastle and other ravaged cities. This was the moment when people with clout saw the dangers and started shouting back. Nothing's good about London's traffic but at least there's the remote hope of finding a solution. Had this lunacy gone through, we'd have been living in one enormous Westway and nothing much would have survived.]

After lunch, an audience of three came back to hear some residential group's objections. Boring beyond belief, mostly because of the way it was read. I watched a local pressman bending over repeatedly behind his table. At last he showed a fellow reporter the result – a blown-up brown paper bag, which he offered in mime to smash between his hands. Fair comment, I thought, and wished he'd done it.

I didn't speak, though I felt like shouting. I left and walked about the small square of streets that people think of as Greenwich. The appalling din and stench made those figures seem conservative. I saw too the smug bastard who had read out a local woman's letter in a facetious voice, discrediting all she said by his manner. He looked content with his day's work. We're wrong to leave our lives to men of affairs.

Blackheath too is crossed by a cobweb of roads that are never quiet. We're having double-glazing fitted to our bedroom. So everyone who can afford it has to go into retreat against the horrors of modern life. While I've been writing the last paragraph, four jet-liners have gone over, their noise easily penetrating my study's double-windows. As one makes its approach to Heathrow over one of Europe's most densely peopled areas, another queues up behind.

Hardy wrote in 1922 that civilisation seemed to be in for another Dark Age. Some of the old problems have been solved, poverty relieved, disease reduced, but the new ones make life nasty in a egalitarian spirit, not just for the poor but everyone. The worst air-traffic is over Windsor.

30 September

For Catherine's sixth birthday, we gave her a bike. She drove it around the dining-room much of the morning, getting off now and then to assemble a jigsaw or exclaim with joy at the arrival of cards. Lou and Dan controlled their envy, which in future years is bound to cause them suffering. We've done nothing to discourage it.

[This was the start of a cycling career for our youngest daughter that included marathon rides such as an 'end-to-end' – Scotland to Cornwall – on the front saddle of a tandem with a blind person behind. In his youth, my father was a racing cyclist. Cath was born the year he died. A cycling gene?]

6 October

Thelma's Dad's movies of the various holidays he's taken them on in the Cortina. Silent, but with his commentary from behind the projector.

'This must be Aberabagow. Tell that from the German writing on the signs, see? . . . now that's Cannes . . . or could be Nice . . . Nice, yes . . . *now* where've we flipping got to? North Wales? No, the Black Forest.'

Shaky pans across mountains or seascapes and occasional zooms in on Win or Frank standing as ordered against an Alpine chalet, cottage, Niagara Falls, dolphinarium, Win always with her handbag as though she'd just forked out to buy this beauty spot or celebrated monument. Loading more footage, he'd give me a lecture on film editing and how one shot must relate to another.

Thelma went walking on her own while I mowed the front lawn. When she came back, I was clipping the hedges.

'Where did you go?'
'Greenwich Park. I got picked up by the usual sexual maniac.'
'Good. Who's he?'
'What d'you mean?'
'The usual sexual maniac.'
'I don't mean always the same one. I mean there always *is* one.'

He'd told her about the Argentine ship moored at Greenwich Reach and the sailors looking for girls, but he wasn't interested in that for its own sake, only taking pictures of them. He'd been busy at The Mall too, taking photos of the state visit of Emperor Hirohito, but no, he wasn't interested in him as such, more the Girls – what d'you call them? He forgot but they did things for men. Geisha Girls, that's it, yes. He enjoyed photographing girls.

Hirohito's visit has aroused some dormant jingoism. The tree he planted in Kew was torn up by next day and a note left: 'They did not die in vain'. Our neighbour heard a man on a train: 'I reckon there's them that died is turning in their flipping graves.'

Flipping and perishing are substitutes for *language*, as Dad used 'blooming' and 'dashed', putting as much vehemence into them as though they'd been the words he wanted to say but couldn't. Mr Reed will on occasion use 'something', as in 'This *something* radio's on the blink again'.

8 October

Saw the first of six final performances of *The National Health*, better than ever and with one great casting improvement: Bill Fraser takes over the surgeon, doing a lovely Dr Cameron skit and getting his lines over far more clearly in the ward.

High spirits in the pub afterwards, and a man from South Africa tried to get me to allow my plays to be done there. Not that I needed much persuading, as I'd already written to the *Spectator* supporting Wesker's change of heart about the play boycott.

[This meant that, if anyone wanted to, and given some assurances, our agents would license productions there. I was not a signatory of the original anti-Apartheid manifesto anyway, as my first stage play had come on too late. Also I could see too many anomalies for this boycott to be a tenable position. E.M. Forster had pointed out that, if authors sold their screen rights, they had no choice about where the resulting films would be shown. Like all other lefties and liberals, I always excluded companies that played to white-only audiences but it didn't seem likely that great numbers of black Africans would be clamouring to see my comedies about life in Bristol or in some London hospital. My guess was they wanted their own stories and white theatregoers in Africa wanted Ayckbourn.]

Supper with Nick Amer and Monty Haltrecht, who've been in the republic for the last year, Nick acting in a tour of *Sleuth*, Monty reporting for a liberal magazine. They said it was all very Bing Crosby and 1940s. Apartheid is expressed especially in terms of avoidance of genital contact. Seats are segregated. One of the reasons blacks aren't allowed to see a show in the same hall as whites, *even at a different time*, is because their buttocks and privates must not rest on the same chairs. A fresh nuance to 'bums on seats'.

Nick argued that, in this mental climate, the sort of laughter my plays try to evoke can only do good, however slight or indirect. Of course, *TNH* is proscribed anyway, even by an all-white company blacked up (as Olivier wanted), because it features miscegenation and ends with a mixed marriage. It wouldn't even be noticed that the happy ending is a parody of 'liberal' TV; more likely seen as enviable liberty. And irony of any kind would certainly not be on the agenda of an Afrikaaner regime that had, after all, banned *Black Beauty*.

10 October

Two days at the Mendels' cottage. Mist cleared to sunshine as we left the motorway to wind through country roads then lanes cut deep between hedges by centuries of cartwheels, beside stately parks and hop-fields where the crop hung drying after harvest, finally into David's track, scaring rabbits and flushing out pheasants that flew up with metallic barks of alarm. We walked in the woods with Duster the terrier bounding after the frightened birds. Thelma kept looking for a clearing where we could make love but my libido was low so we only embraced and caressed, what she called 'a lick and a promise'.

Picked a bagful of blackberries.

That evening, back in Blackheath, we watched a film about Edward Lear by Bernie Cooper and Francis MeGahy.

> [Bernie, whom I'd met at Trent Park teachers' training college, had been the basis for my two TV plays about Ben Spray. He and Francis served as models for characters in my second TV play *Promenade*. It was due to them that I'd got a small and undeserved reputation as a spokesman for The Young.]

Thelma sat beside me in an orange velvet dressing-gown and nothing else. We eventually went to bed, where – as Tolstoy put it – I failed to control myself.

Life's very good for us. We're overprivileged, with far too large a slice of the available cake. I quench my uneasiness a bit by remembering how long I had to wait and with the thought that I've never sought material wealth and might prefer to have less. Reminded of Frayn's line, 'I was happier when I wasn't so happy.' Our real good fortune is in our varying feelings for each other, an affection that's precious enough not to be jeopardised by chasing other people. Also in my interesting work, which she makes possible, though I'm guilty to be paid so well for doing what I've always done for fun.

13 October

Ewan Hooper rang to say he can fit in a revival of *Joe Egg* in the three weeks before Christmas, to be directed by me. Alec McCowen wants the weekend to read the play. Until he decides, I couldn't do much more than make long lists of likely actors for each part.

16 October

Alan Bennett's new play *Getting On*. Too genial. Not enough action or theatricality. But, of course, the playing and production distorted it in the interest of West End success. Kenneth More lovable in the lead, Mona Washbourne the ideal middle-class theatregoers' Mum, all smiles and slightly risqué remarks about getting off with young men. Alan should have played this part himself. Is anyone's Mum like this? Mine's nervous, vain, slow, enervating, always reproachful of all you've failed to do. So I passed her the cheque for £1,600, my quarter-share of Uncle Bert's estate.

Before taking her to catch her train at Paddington, walked for a while in Hyde Park, joining the promenade at the Serpentine. Horses on Rotten Row, colourful sailing dinghies, anglers casting lines, Dan inevitably falling in. Mum complained of a light breeze that ruffled her perm.

18 October

Alec thinks he's too old for the part at forty-six, not physically but in his ability to understand or convey the way the man thinks. Rang Glenda Jackson to know if she'd like to try Sheila. Predictably, she goes to Spain to do a film next month.

Spent rest of day on phone. Cast Ray Brooks, who'd turned it down at Glasgow before Joe said yes. He now atoned by accepting at once.

Told me he's not a good judge and had once declined a part in *Uncle Vanya* because he didn't care for the play.

20 *October*

Saw *West of Suez*, Osborne's latest, a drink in the desert after the incompetence and cynicism of most other plays seen lately. He's made it known he wants to write like Chekhov and is photographed these days with beard and pince-nez but his great strength remains that of writing monologues, while other characters sit around listening, which isn't how I think of Chekhov. He once thought of a new way of doing this (in *The Entertainer*), by addressing his tirades to the audience, but he hasn't followed that up and now brings on lots of plaster gnomes to listen in uncritical silence to his current spokesman, in this case an elderly writer played by Ralph Richardson, a great part superbly played. Why wouldn't Michael ask him to do my Dad? There's no lack of vigour there. Would he perhaps consider doing it for America?

22 *October*

Wesker was attacked in the *Spectator* for changing his mind about S. Africa. It was suggested that this was because he couldn't get his plays staged anywhere else. I wrote a heavily ironic letter ostensibly agreeing with this, while actually defending the right of any author to think twice or however often he wanted to.

> [The last paragraph of mine ran:
> 'Now all these playwriting fellows are changing their minds. The least they could do is keep their opinions to themselves. Sensible chaps never make their views known in case they afterwards have to admit they've changed them. In fact, sensible chaps are better off not having views at all, just helping Mr Vorster to run the diamond mines and enforce the pass-laws. Anything else is pie in the sky . . . ']

Arnold wrote privately, thanking me but saying he had got half way through before he realised whose side I was on.

Took Monty Haltrecht to a meeting of the anti-Apartheid Movement to discuss reaffirmation of the boycott. Arrived after some difficulty at David Mercer's house in St John's Wood to find Penelope Mortimer,

Clive Exton, John Bowen, Harold Pinter, Hugh Whitemore, Ted Whitehead and some unknown others, including an Indian and several Africans.

Mercer read Arnold's letter and asked if anyone else had had similar thoughts. I owned up and Mrs Mortimer said she'd defend to the death my right to say so. The arguments were gone over: was the ban working or would it be more sensible to put our faith in the civilising power of art? But hadn't the Nazis enjoyed the world's highest culture, getting Jewish musicians to play Bach even as they pushed their families into the gas-chambers? One of the Africans said plays by any of the authors present were irrelevant to the situation in the townships. Only LeRoi Jones would have any meaning when he said, 'Get off your mother-fucking knees'.

Pinter, loud-voiced and assertive even when asking a question, got us all on his side when he said, 'Let me get this straight. We're all irrelevant and what we say has no effect whatsoever?'

'That's right.'

'That's what I understood you to say. And I agree!'

Mercer tried to get everyone to sign a draft resolution, though there was still a lot of quibbling.

'This is a foocking thankless task,' he said.

A formerly amiable African suddenly blew his top and shouted, 'Why don't you declare your hatred for white Africans? Isn't this the only useful thing you *can* do? Say you hate them and align yourself with the blacks who have clearly stated that they wish to kill them.'

I understood how feeble we must all have seemed to him but the prospect of a black overthrow didn't seem much of a solution, put like that. After all, blacks with guns wouldn't wait to ask which white playwrights had been on their side or insisted on mixed audiences. The whole occasion was a social comedy on the lines of the Leonard Bernsteins entertaining the Black Panthers. But would it play well to an unsegregated audience?

Ethel de Keyser afterwards told me she'd seen my interview in the *Rand Daily Mail*.

'But I gave no interview.'

'I've had the cutting. I'll send you a copy.'

Next morning one arrived anyway, sent by a friend who was out there: 'Boycott Playwright Rethinks.' The fact that I never have been one of those was the most distorted (or just misunderstood) point the journalist made. It was evidence that the ban's effective, if only with liberal newspapers, and gave me a rare taste of the spurious authority of fame.

26 October

Have cast *Joe Egg*: Ray Brooks, Caroline Mortimer as his wife, Hilda Braid and Anthony Newlands as the guests, Constance Chapman in the part played before by Joan Hickson, and 18-year-old Maxine Holt as 10-year-old Abigail.

28 October

We arrived before noon at Sawcombe Farm on a beautiful morning. Michael Frayn came bounding up the track exclaiming at our brilliance in finding the way without a guide. The Plowdens, that's Bamber Gascoigne's sister Caroline and husband William, were just leaving.

The house stands on the steep side of a valley, probably nineteenth century, but it's never easy to tell in the Cotswolds, where building styles seem not to have changed much since the seventeenth. By climbing a few steps to the field above, where grain's stored under shelter beside a strawstack, you can see the telecommunications tower half a mile away, a tapering concrete cylinder with an assortment of saucers, shields and rings painted green or naked steel. Lose one or two of its more mechanical protrusions and it could be Visitor IV or some other exhibit in a sculpture show. It rises above the woods, as though asking to be taken to our leader. On Sunday morning bellringers seemed to be practising peals inside its body. An electronic mock-up or synthesiser imitation? A new GPO service to reconcile the locals to this alien presence – Dial-a-Chime? Alexander Graham Bell?

Next day we undertook a long-standing plan to show Bristol to the Frayns. Parked near the cathedral and toured its curiosities. Pevsner says it's clear a genius worked on its design, one of the great anonymous mediaeval architects, but I must say it strikes a chill whenever I go. The Norman chapter-house is very fine and solid and there are some wonderful windows celebrating Bristol's war effort, showing wardens with stirrup-pumps, Home Guards and WVS ladies. After this we traipsed with the kids through the ugly and deteriorating city centre.

Anything good has gone to Clifton. Abandoning the lower level, we ate fish and chips on Brandon Hill and went on to the Georgian 'suburb' that most visitors, students, academics and actors think of as Bristol proper. These squares and terraces have been raised still further as the centre has declined.

Returning from a look at Royal York Crescent, we noticed a policeman and a small crowd peering over the downstream wall of the Suspension Bridge. Three long-haired climbers were on a ledge half way down the gorge's cliff-face, one having fallen and broken his/her ankle. We joined the crowd and watched the rescue. A breakdown lorry was brought on to the green at the highest point beside the camera obscura. Two men in helmets and carrying a stretcher were winched down. They first gave the injured climber first aid then were hauled back up, keeping the stretcher clear of the cliff by using their legs as props, as bargees did in tunnels, 'walking' the wall. As all this was being done a few yards from the busy bridge, a huge audience soon gathered. Down below, a traffic jam of cars and lorries waited to cross the fly-over at Hotwells; from up the Avon came a sand-barge; out from the Somerset-side tunnel came the Portishead train; overhead flew an Auster light aircraft. The Gorge always has a touch of the Boy's Own Paper Album showing Many Forms of Transport but this was ridiculous.

Charles and Valerie Wood now live in Leigh Woods, not far from the bridge, a pretty grand open-plan place, with fine views across to Clifton but a continuous hum of motors.

'It's still there at 4 a.m.,' Charles said. 'Where's anybody going in Bristol at that time of night?'

1 November

Discovered more about the Frayns by living with them for a few days.

He's all ebullience and amiability, unfailingly courteous, opening doors and providing drinks and praising your clothes and always turning the conversation away from himself and towards others. Gill's the wet blanket to this lively blaze. Thrift, unpunctuality and pessimism about anything Michael's writing are all signs of her efforts to bring him down or slow him up. This time we saw why she's always late. If everyone's been painfully assembled, ready to go out, children pacified, baby-sitter installed, car-engine running ready for the off, she'll say 'I'll just put a few things in the washing-machine'.

3 November

Medwin says *Forget-me-Not*'s returns have dropped too far and it will come off in three weeks to make way for *Charley's Aunt*. I'll just miss having all my three stage plays on in London at the same time.

6 November

Francis Hewlett stayed a day or two. At the Tate Gallery, the children were most interested in the chest full of notes and coins, put in to aid the purchase of artworks.

'Yes,' he said, 'it's the one object on display that appeals to all tastes. The perfect solution to the artist's problem of finding something everyone enjoys looking at.'

8 November

Direction (of *Egg* at Greenwich) has proved very taxing and am writing this exactly two weeks late, having found no time or inclination to keep a log of rehearsals. I've walked every day to and from the theatre, seeing an Indian summer turn to winter. From the summit of Point Hill, you look over the East End where the river takes its northern twist around Millwall. At the bottom on the south side are the pretty terraced cottages of Greenwich. Thelma established a routine of bringing cakes to the rehearsal hall for tea.

10 November

Spoke to the Lit. Soc at Eton, as guest of a boy who looked like a rich man's Bernard Levin. Amazing to turn off the motorway and find boys walking the streets in those ludicrous togs, like apprentice waiters (or undertakers?). Gave a boring and ill-conceived talk to twenty or so volunteers (you, you and you), ate and drank with the housemaster and drove home.

[In 1948, reviewing a history of the school, Orwell wrote, 'Whatever happens to the great public schools when our educational system is reorganised, it is almost impossible that Eton should survive in anything like its present form because the training it offers was originally intended for a landowning aristocracy and had become an anachronism long before 1939. The top hats and tail coats, the pack of beagles, the many-coloured blazers, the desks still notched with the names of Prime Ministers had charm as long as they represented the kind of elegance that everyone looked up to. In a shabby and democratic country, they are merely rather a nuisance, like Napoleon's baggage wagons, full of chefs and hairdressers, blocking up the roads in the disaster of Sedan.']

13 November

Up the stairs comes the chaotic din of Louise, who's nine today, with Dan, Cath and their friends from next door pounding on the piano keys.

The Woods came, stayed a day, lunched with Gielgud and left soon after. As we came into the house, after seeing them off, the phone was ringing. Bill Stair from Bristol.

[Bill had been a neighbour and close friend during our years in Bristol in the sixties. He and his wife Tina (who ran the local Montessori) were the models for the parents in *Joe Egg*. He worked as a designer and ideas-man on John Boorman's *Point Blank*, going with him to Hollywood. It was about this time that I asked for his help with the Orwell programme and his illuminating letters and designs outline a solution that would have been far more striking than the one I finally wrote. He was an exploited, unrecognised original.]

Whilst I talked to him, Thelma worked herself into a righteous rage and decided we must give Louise more attention on her birthday. And what could be more pleasant than to drive into the thick of Lewisham's shopping centre on a Saturday afternoon to buy rubbish in Boots? We were soon in the car queuing to pass the Odeon, queuing to turn off to the car park, queuing to *get into* the car park and finally giving up. She got out with the children saying she'd see me at the bottom of the hill after she'd exchanged Lou's tokens for goods. I then queued to get back into the High Street and to get past the Odeon and found by sheer good fortune a few feet of empty kerb to leave the car against. I walked back to meet them through crowds of slave-class people, Irish drunks, slovenly women, fat black mothers and men trapped in stationary cars.

15 November

Hundredth performance of *Health* (in two years). Congratulatory telegram from Olivier, ho-ho, ha-ha.

17 November

The actor playing Freddie in *Egg* came in tears to tell me his mother's dying and refusing to eat unless he feeds her.

'I'm not a mother's boy but this is all too much. I've no time to study.'

I sympathised but didn't argue. It had been obvious he wasn't working hard and I hadn't relished the prospect of pushing him. Easier to release him. Took a chance and rang Michael Wynne, who'd been excellent in my TV play *The Hooded Terror*. He said yes at once (always a pleasant surprise, when most actors are so snooty).

18 November

Rehearsed hard all day with the new actor and felt we'd gained by the apparent disaster. He has plenty of time to find his feet and luckily doesn't appear till Act Two.

24 November

'How a man laid his spastic son to rest' is today's headline in the *Mirror*.

'Price, 35, of Birmingham, denies murdering his son Gordon on the grounds of diminished responsibility. The boy was found in the River

Stour near Kidderminster. Price decided to drive the boy back to the hospital where he was a resident patient, but when he saw the other patients there, realised his son was "twenty times worse than they could ever be". It was then that he decided to find a way to end the boy's suffering, the statement said. The magistrate said the bench felt they could not grant bail and remanded Price for a further week.'

25 November

Thelma came to our second run and thought it very good. One of my problems has been not knowing whom to trust for a second opinion. When Mike Blakemore complains of my not allowing him enough freedom, he should imagine doing it alone, without any guidance at all.

[Startling innocence. I hadn't even now grasped that what attracts so many directors to plays by the glorious dead is the freedom to take what liberties they like. But by 1995 I had learnt this lesson and could write the following speech into *Blue Murder*, a director speaking to his author:
'You need us more than we need you. We've got two thousand years of dead playwrights to choose from. And those buggers don't come to rehearsal.']

Eve: to Louise's and Dan's primary school to look at their work and meet their teachers. Their behaviour there appears to be averagely naughty and their workbooks show no signs of the interesting and amusing personalities we know at home. I buttoned my lip to hear the pettish complaints of teachers who don't look old enough to be out of school themselves, mostly fresh from training college and assuming airs of an experience they don't yet have, using current educational catch phrases.

[One only has to think how Divinity became Scripture became Religious Instruction (RI), then Religious Knowledge (RK), Religious Studies (RS), finally becoming a branch of Sociology, so that now the Church is suggesting the addition of a little Awe And Wonder, or as we know it in our family, Bringing Back the Magic.]

Arithmetic is now Number Work and whole groups of activity are classed as Creative. As distinct from what – Destructive?

Louise's book didn't have a word of praise or encouragement and the word 'mountainous' was corrected in the teacher's hand to include an 'e'. On the way home, I advised Thelma that we shouldn't worry if either child was described by these chits as disobedient. The school takes care of them for some hours every day and instructs them in rudimentary reading and writing; more important, it gives them a child's society to mingle with.

We reported back to them, telling Lou how to spell 'mountainous' and asking Dan to be quieter in class, then read them to sleep and climbed the stairs.

There was a theatre staff party at the Apollo so she had a bath and lay leering at me, her breasts glistening.

'I'm going to have half an hour in bed,' she told me, as she climbed out and left me her water. I followed and we enjoyed each other for some time, ending with an orgasm that exhausted us so that we had to sleep for twenty minutes before bathing again and dressing for the do.

27 November

Due to Saturday traffic, half an hour late for the last performance of *Lane*. Full house and good show, though Michael Bates was dashing through faster than he needed, as though he couldn't wait to see the back of this one. At the curtain, there were management flowers and high kicks from Bates, who had survived the run, despite his mental disturbance. The women left their bouquets on the sofa so that they could dance the title song and, as the six doors closed behind them all, it was Magritte again, the name we'd always thrown around when trying to define the show's visual style: beige walls, doors, floor, sofa, all reminding one of pebble-dash, and on that sofa, glistening packages of dead blooms.

No-one there we knew but John Osborne, whom I stopped at the exit to thank for *West of Suez*.

'I had to come and see this again,' he said. 'By the way who was it used to say "I'll give you a kick in the pants – boom!"?'

[One from Dad's repertoire, repeated often by him in life and quite often in the play, and ending by suiting the action to the word. But which old comedian had said it first?

'Was it Stanelli? D'you know, I'm not sure.'
'I'll find out.']

Clive Dunn in Priscilla's dressing-room didn't know but Eddie Molloy did.

Next day I wrote John a card saying only: 'George Doonan.'

28 November

Gave dinner party for Constance Chapman and her son Mark and daughter-in-law Jane, with Nick Amer making up the six.

[Connie had spent much of her life in provincial rep, mostly in Bristol. In her fifties and sixties, she enjoyed a late afternoon of far more interesting work, becoming a Royal Court regular. One of the few actresses of her quality to have an authentic Bristol accent, she was in three TV plays of mine, the film of *Joe Egg* and this stage revival. Nearing her ninetieth year, she has just broadcast in my recent comedy, *So Long Life*.]

The young gave us a stiff dose of leftist moralising. Jane's one of Wilson's personal staff and Mark works at the Warburg Institute, where he says you can study such subjects as thirteenth-century beekeeping. They're both very forward with their correct humanitarian views, ready to put you down for your callous indifference. You begin to feel that wit and humour are indecent and finish trying to prove your heart's in the right place.

Nick had at least *been* to China and told us about it with some spirit.

'I was very keen to get in with our courier, who was somewhat to the left of Mao but spoke excellent English. I kept saying, "I *am* a Socialist, I vote Labour." He finally turned to a peasant woman in a quilted coat and said to me, "You would give *her* the vote? You would vote for the party that gave her the most eggs." '

Whenever Mark told a story, it sounded uncharitable and patronising and Jane's harking on underprivilege verged on ill-temper. They both scoffed at Connie who told me funny stories in an undertone for fear they should rebuke her lack of solemnity.

Next day Connie asked Thelma what she thought of Jane and nodded when Thelma ventured a few critical words about her puritanical piety.

'Yet she won't have anything to do with her parents. I heard Mark saying she should visit her father who was very ill and she absolutely refused and was terribly unkind about him.'

[Jane was beautiful, though I'd never have dared say so anywhere near her presence, and later became famous in the tabloids for going barefoot and short-skirted to the Labour Party Conference.]

1 December

The preview [of *Egg* at Greenwich] was all we'd hoped. Of course, it's always the best night. After it, the soufflé never quite rises again. The audience knows they're the first, in on a secret and getting it half-price. No technical flaws. Full and mostly local house, responding with the right mixture of laughter and attentive silence, and we all felt our time had been well spent.

Card from Osborne, crossing mine to him: 'Give yourself a kick in the pants. Boom! It was George Doonan.'

2 December

Press night. Of course the audience refused to come up from the bars until after the play was due to start at seven (for the sake of critics and their supposed deadlines). So suddenly the taped carols gave out when they'd all been played and a chilling silence fell on the house. The last song was supposed to be interrupted by the entrance of Ray Brooks shouting, 'That's enough!' Everyone looked about, embarrassed by the sudden lull. 'Rewind and play it again!' I implored the young goofs in the sound-booth, but only inside my head, from my impotent position in Row N. But the sound that broke the silence was the recorded school bell that should have been the first effect, minutes hence. Nobody'd noticed that this was on the same tape. Now the audience shifted about, wondering if this was an alarm and they should be making for the exits. Then poor Ray at last came on from one of the audience doors and shouted 'That's enough!'

I sat with knotted stomach through Act One, which only by slow degrees recovered from this unforeseeable disaster.

[No. It should have been foreseen. Directing plays is partly learning to predict avoidable accidents and human error. As a result of this incident, I now try to close every loophole. The willing and underpaid volunteers of Greenwich must never be allowed to exercise their hippie goodwill, any more than you'd welcome them as air-traffic controllers. Someone had blundered. The light brigade's charge failed.]

There was little laughter but by the end I felt they'd been won over. Touch-and-go though and it never looked anything like as good as the previous night's.

At the party afterwards, the Frayns were powerfully reassuring.

'I thought during the first few minutes ,' Michael said, 'that this was going to be an occasion for polite compliments but once that was over it was absolutely gripping. I really think it was the best production I've seen of one of your plays.'

3 December

Times and *Guardian* polite, *Financial Times* a denigrating reappraisal, *Evening News* a rave. Local rags either thought it a searing masterpiece or too much like GBS. Another was headlined 'First-rate first act, second-rate second act,' and told me how I should have wound up the play. 'To give it unity, it should have finished with the parents crooning over Jo, and rapturously praising the hospital staff who had saved her life.'

Thelma suggested, 'Where the blue of the night meets the gold of the day.'

Hilda Braid said of this critic, 'I don't think he'll ever make the nationals', though I wasn't so sure.

In general, I was told to stick to writing and leave direction to others. One or two noticed that the play, for the first time, had been done in the accent of its native city.

To the BBC to record an interview with Billington. I grumbled about the ready-made scoops we all try to provide for journalists, these contrived first-night events and the fact that he and his mates always see the worst performances.

9 December

Awoke remembering a dream. Mike and Shirley Blakemore, Thelma and I were in a posh brothel, an interior mostly of lobbies and vestibules like cinema foyers. Thelma made off at once into a spiralling complex of corridors and soon lost me. Groups of men with brief-cases were entering or leaving. Exploring the corridors, I began to worry about the cost of what was going on behind these plain walls.

('You would,' said Thelma when I told her.)

I checked my wallet to find a single note for 106 of some unknown currency. Mike approached in one of his indignant, self-righteous moods.

'Peter, I really don't think we should hang about here any longer.'

'Alright, no. Where are the girls? Are they fixed up?'

'They're fixed up, yes, but it's going to cost a fortune. And that's not the only thing I'm unhappy about. For instance, look over there!'

He pointed to where John Hale, the very proper ex-petty officer and authoritarian theatre director, was struggling on the carpet with a naked member of staff, watched by passers-by and a small group of onlookers.

This slapstick scenario had a charge of danger though, probably because I've still never set foot in a whorehouse and never touched a tart.

[The 1990s film *Boogie Nights* has a similar incident beside a pool, so this is probably an erotic archetype. An onlooker's indifference is a crucial element of any scene of sexual arousal.]

10 December

Lunched at Café Royal with John Schlesinger and his producer Jo Janni, who want me to write an original film for them. John told me he liked the ward scenes in *National Health* but not the interpolated fantasies. Quite right too.

Like man-and-wife they enjoy a riotous relationship. At one point, when Jo was saying something in his Chico Marx English that John disagreed with, John snapped at him, 'Oh, shut up, you fucking old organ-grinder!'

Another dream: Nibs Dalwood and Thelma were playing a lewd-looking game with a yard-long pole placed between their legs, grunting and gasping.

> [Hubert 'Nibs' Dalwood came from my part of Bristol, had been expel-led from Cotham Grammar School, was briefly at the West of England College of Art with Thelma, and became a well-known sculptor, with work in the Tate, V & A, Guggenheim and MOMA. He had a low boredom-threshold and a playful way of pulling rugs from under solemn occasions. I was too prim to take much of him, but in small doses he was wonderful fun. We'd shared good times with him and his family in Yugoslavia (1962) and Wisconsin (1968), where he was visiting professor. His lectures often began with him entering the hall on a pogo-stick.]

I was arranging some tiny glass boxes full of coloured sand on a man-telshelf while this filthy scene was acted out behind me. Finally they took a break from their energetic jerking and started referring to me as Paddy.

'Look at old Paddy. He's not enjoying it.'

'Can you wonder?'

'Cheer up, Paddy!'

'D'you mind?' I said, still busy with my boxes. 'If you can't think of anything else but Paddy to call me, don't say anything at all.'

'Oh, lordie-lordie!' one of them said and they returned to their pole-game with new zest.

Cut to Thelma alone on a sofa, my POV, approaching her as she raises her arms, allowing her clothes to fall open.

'You must keep an eye on me,' she says, 'and stop me playing games like that. If you don't, I shall be getting up to all kinds of tricks.'

When, as always, I told this dream to her, she said, 'A likely story.'

Last at night, after the games of whist and 'Shop' and 'Pit' and story-reading and final packing off to bed, we subsided into the couch, staring like fish at the TV screen. I asked why she didn't go upstairs and change into something more comfortable like her velvet gown.

'Because I'm more comfortable the way I am,' she said.

So we watched the war news from India and Ulster, Princess Anne being horse-of-the-year, a nice film about one of Brighton's piers,

Hans-Werner Henze agonising about being a successful and wealthy Marxist composer, and a straightforward report on the daily life of people in the refugee camps of East Bengal. This is the nature of TV: a collage. Often it's the way the disparate items succeed each other that gives them a depth they wouldn't have in isolation. Henze makes a decent impression of a sensitive artist with a conscience that tells him not to settle for money and fame, so he sees his music as having social significance. But he was at once followed by shots of people in the most hellish situation on earth. Refugees from war, flood and famine are being given so much aid in the camps that the slum-dwellers of Calcutta envy and resent them.

'Of eight million people living here,' said an organiser of their development scheme, 'six million are without ordinary amenities.' By which he probably meant sanitation, water and enough food to sustain life. The expense of helping the refugees means that the redevelopment's been suspended.

'Some solution's got to be found to rescue its own population from the demands of the refugees.'

This hard-headed commentary went with scenes of everyday life at the lowest level such as I saw during my year near the city in 1946. A middle-class babu-type with glasses and a cherubic face denied that the poor suffered more than he, 'because – well, I'm used to certain standards, you see, it's harder for me.' The old caste attitudes intact.

Henze's pieces for solo percussion, though he explained their Marxist context, didn't say much to me about this. Hard luck on him because, of course, he knows as well as the rest of us that some sort of *real*, not alleged, Communism is the only answer.

14 December

Evening drinks at John and Patsy Grigg's. A.J.P. Taylor, young Runciman, son of Stephen, and Fred Gollings from Santa Barbara. Taylor told Thelma most men care only for rank and status but he's quite indifferent to all that. A few sentences later, he called himself the best historian in the country.

16 December

With Louise and Dan to a carol concert in St Alfege's Church beside the main traffic-circuit of Greenwich. Their music-master, Turner, is an enterprising teacher. At their last prize-giving his choir gave Britten's *Golden Vanitie*. Now he directed the older children in a Jazz Chorale with bits of contemporary reportage stuck in – comparing the fortunes of babies born in Lewisham and an African township, UFOs sighted over Salisbury Plain, the inevitable starving Indians. Vague assurances of goodwill and some magic for good measure. Piano, choir, percussion, recorders, a parade of huge masks made and worn by the children. But the interior of this Hawksmoor church, with its Gibbons carvings and Thornhill murals, has the worst sight-lines and some of the hollowest acoustics of any I've known. We had to sit on the pew-backs to see anything. These buildings were for the congregation to see *each other*.

17 December

A good Friday night house with quite a few friends too. A member of a party of Norwegian students asked me, 'Was I supposed to *like* this play? I hated it. I thought it was very good but I hated it.'

Ewan told me a West End manager had offered to transfer the production to the West End. I was at first pleased for the actors – and myself – to have this short run extended. Later I began to hope it wouldn't happen, as it would take time and effort I should be devoting to new work.

20 December

Began a new play for TV, perhaps to be called *The Common* (to follow *The Gorge*). Good subject but I can't see how to develop it. My idea is to link modern Blackheath with Wat Tyler's Revolt, which camped here on its way to sack John of Gaunt's palace of Savoy.

21 December

Saw half of *Health*, even in this worst week of the theatre year drawing good houses at the Old Vic. Gerald James, so strong and authentic as the Welsh doctor, says he's staying with the company till this play finishes in March. He was alone in his dressing-room reading a work of religious philosophy.

'Have you read this chap? Terrific. Makes me think about the meaning of my life, what I'm here for, you know. Here I am, about to be unemployed after six years. And I feel I'm just beginning to live.'

23 December

Puddings, birds and cakes all cooking from morn till night. Thelma making predatory swoops on Blackheath Village, coming back laden with trees, parcels, bags of fruit and nuts, cases of bottles.

The children have broken up, bringing their festive emblems – cardboard crowns, Wise Men's lamps made of polythene egg-boxes, paper-chains. Dan's King of Orient is larger than himself. One foot fell off as he struggled with it up Morden Hill, 'but you can see what it was like by the one that's still there.'

28 December

First mid-winter stay at the French farm. Drove through morning mist, slowed by poor visibility, but still made good speed on almost empty French roads. Reached Ribérac by early nightfall.

A few sizeable changes at the house since autumn: new unplastered walls to form new rooms are in red breezeblock, not at all pleasing. The kitchen, though, is finished, solid-fuel stove and sinks installed, looking habitable. The furniture had been left piled in the middle of the sitting-room and our first task was to move it back to where it belongs.

Thelma's extraordinary Girl-Guide skills and unstoppable energy soon had a hot meal on the table, heaters and fires in every room we'll be using, and a semblance of comfort spreading through the chilly house.

Mice have eaten into packeted food and opened a pillow filled with foam-rubber pellets. Tame and bewildered by our arrival, they run about the kitchen floor, up and down walls, and stare from shelves as we open cupboard doors.

29 December

The morning brought falling temperatures and the sight of bare trees and dead ground. It was hard to remember this place as so hot that we sought the shade of cherry and apple leaves or emerged from cool kitchen to stunning midday heat, making lizards scatter on the stones.

Routines of hewing and humping wood, lighting and feeding fires. Gradually putting on more and more clothes to cope with the cold. I've settled for long underpants and sleeved vests, cord trousers, polo-neck sweater and pullover. Odd that Thelma complains of cold at home in our centrally-heated house but seems to keep warm without difficulty here. Is it that she can't live without a challenge? Is that why we're all here, to share her struggle with the elements and watch her successfully overcome them?

30 December

The water heater didn't function till the second evening so we boiled kettles to wash and shave. It's perhaps useful to know the place in winter as one of the families in *Chez Nous* lives here all the year. But this play is a worry too, as I can't see the way to save it.

A steady procession of artisans and halting conversations in schoolboy French. Gifts given and returned. Walks in drizzle and drives to the deserted lake, where in summer the locals flocked to see fireworks and water sports. The children, losing themselves for hours in fields or barns, came back with stories of hunters and their dogs. Now and then men got out from Citroens and skulked past carrying huge cannons and anti-tank guns – to shoot what? – wagtails, finches, owls, crows, field-mice? We thought of inviting them in to rid us of our vermin. A trap I bought in the *quincaillerie*, a vicious pairing of gibbet and guillotine, involving lengths of thread and twin garottes, succeeded only in feeding the mice, not killing them. Strangers called to offer their cottages for sale to any of our English friends who might be interested and advised us to use a poison called Rouge Blé. This we did

and within hours found three rigid corpses among their black drop-
pings on the shelves lined with copies of *Sud-Ouest*.

The children held a circus in the barn, lit by bright sun through
the roof-holes. Most of the action was changing clothes and getting
trousers stuck over shoes. At one point Catherine advanced on the
audience (we two and Mrs Faircloth) and shouted a riddle:

'What did the big pillar-box say to the little pillar-box?'

'Don't know.'

'Bang!' came the answer. Perhaps we were wrong to take them to the
Magritte exhibition.

31 December

In bed last thing and shivering, we remembered it would be 1972 in an
hour. She said we should stop quarrelling because whatever you were
doing on New Year's Eve you'd be doing the rest of the year. Following
this principle, we made love.

1972

2 January

Explored the derelict house amid the trees, a hundred yards down the road. Roof and walls had collapsed in places – *les termites*, we suppose (a diagnosis often arrived at by the carpenters and joiners who come to discuss our woodwork) – but obviously it had been a good house in its day, *trés solide* and far grander than ours, built on two storeys, with wide corridors and a sweeping staircase. Quite a few domestic articles left lying about, as after the final curtain of a Chekhov, including a calendar for 1952. So it could be that a mere twenty years have done that damage. Small wonder there was so little left of Ozymandias's place.

Reading Solzhenitsyn's *A Day in the Life of Ivan Denisovitch* and Updike's *Rabbit Redux*.

And worrying about *Chez Nous*. What happens in their winter? Doesn't Dick go nearly mad, as I would, realising he's not a natural hermit after all? Doesn't he change himself or learn to know himself? And isn't that expressed in a change of partner? The play's structure is an hour-glass: (Dick – Liz) + (Phil – Diana) becomes (Liz – Phil) + (Dick – Diana), with the interesting catalyst Phil + Jane = Phil's baby son who is also Dick – Liz's grandson. And what's it all about? People fighting despair, changing their natures (or trying to) late in life, or realising what their natures are after so long spent living out a mistake.

3 January

Most famous Frenchman died this week: Maurice Chevalier. His brand of ooh-la-la never much appealed to me but he was an original and confirmed the idea of the saucy Gallic shrugging lovaire for Anglo-Saxons, especially in the States. Claude Roy told us he was sent to escort Chevalier home to face trial as a Nazi collaborator, and he was shaking like a leaf.

4 January

A reporter for *Stern* magazine and his English wife are buying properties in the area. At the last count, they had two. It may be a new Hundred Years' War, meaning the English, but there are almost as many Dutch, Swedes, Germans and Yanks. They were knowledgeable about the area and its natives, not only about who delivers the best bread but who controls the society and has the 'old' money (still literally reckoned by them in *anciens francs*), meaning land and property. They say the old landowners drive around in the tattiest of Deux Chevaux. Land, they say, is valuable, which I can't believe, as ours is infertile and mostly clay, so quickly floods. Why would we have been given so much with our house? And why is so much let run to seed, not even fenced, though strictly allocated on all the cadastral surveys? Why are the farms derelict?

I risked a joke. Showing him the barn and our new car still on its cardboard underlay and with a flat rear tyre, still waiting to be used.

'Our Deux Chevaux,' I said, then pointed at the bullock-cart we'd hauled back from the woods. 'And our Deux Vaches.'

He didn't even smile. Proof they have a sense of humour after all?

5 January

Paid and said goodbye to our artisans – Jouvent the joiner, Moreau the motorman (offering his wrist to shake as his hand's oily), Simeon the stonemason. This alliteration only works in English: in French they're *menuisier*, *garagiste* and *maçon*.

Packed and moved furniture into centre of rooms, to protect against ravages (between now and our return in spring) by damp, vermin, termites and the painter, a clownish little chap with a strawberry mark, who comes often to discuss the work but never actually begins.

7 January

At the Boulogne car-ferry, there were perhaps six cars to be carried across to England. We sat for ages while various crew-members and dockers chatted, laughed, enjoyed a few mock-battles and finally, ungraciously, pulled themselves together. We were told to take passports to the office so the dozen of us obediently left our cars and queued at a desk where an officer glared at us and gave us each a pink card. Back in our cars, we waited for their next move. We were allowed at last to draw forward to the gangplank where the same officer who'd given us the cards now walked the row of vehicles taking them back.

Jacques Tati lives!

8 January

Glad to be back in our warm house, though it wasn't to be for long as next day we booked air passages to Brussels for the opening of *Health*. Travel agency crammed with people staring hopefully at poster girls on empty beaches, white liners steaming through Reckitt's-blue oceans, Spanish balconies and palm-trees. Summer-holiday-booking time was here.

Among my mail an invitation to join the Arts Council Drama Panel. Felt flattered, I admit, though sensed that such an offer can also be a kiss of death. Wrote, accepting.

11 January

In Brussels, they put us up at the Plaza, very posh and only a few hundred yards from the Théâtre National. Twin beds reflected in four adjustable full-length mirrors.

Afterwards we bathed, dressed and went to meet Claude Roy in the theatre's great marble lobby. The cloakroom girls and ushers were dressed as nurses and Jacques Huisman, the director, was all in white as a doctor. I laughed politely but it signified a trivial approach to the play. In fact, the show was a clumsy version of Mike's original. Several actors were very good and Olivier would have been pleased to see that the West Indian nurses were played by blacked-up whites. In the interval, sophisticated Claude summed it up: 'None of these people have ever been in a hospital, only private clinics. For them this is all as *exotique* as Mexico.'

There was a suffocating crowd of Amis du Théâtre and I had to stand with my back to a wall shaking hands till I was fit to drop. No wonder the Prince of Wales had a broken wrist and learnt to divide the shaking between left and right. The guest of honour was the British Ambassador, who told us of the procurement of a new tank for NATO, how it had become quite a favourite toy of his and how he'd tried to get the manufacturers to run off a scale prototype to decorate his desk, until they told him it would cost £1,600. Claude stared at me with a stunned half-smile, as though expecting me to explain or apologise. The ambassador's wife sat facing me, was extremely tall and had lost much of her voice, but by no means all, wheezing and piping.

'We hardly ever get to the theatre. Last thing we saw was the one about Elizabeth and Mary. That was actually rather good.'

No wonder the Belgians want us kept out. Surely there are more representative people looking for a sinecure, certainly someone with better French. HE's didn't sound much better than Heath's.

The day finished in Huisman's office. Now the conversation was all in French. Claude was attacked for the patronising air of Parisian theatre and deserved to be because he was putting it on terribly, his raincoat draped over his shoulders in a way he'd never dare in Paris. They see Belgians as provincials.

12 January

Claude took us to the Musée des Beaux Arts where we learned to tell Brueghel *fils* from *père*. Walked through the older part of the city and found it to be a capital of some scale and maturity. Steep cobbled streets, palatial banks holding all that colonial loot from the Congo. Many dog-turds. No parks or trees, very much a stone place. Magritte's no accident. The Grand Place a car-park with a difference, surrounded on four sides by old Guildhalls.

Lunched with Huisman at Comme Chez Soi, where glass windows gave a clear view of the hectic kitchen and where framed notes of approval on the walls were from Cocteau, Michel Simon and Princess Paola. Thelma declared it the best meal she'd ever eaten. Jacques preened and glanced at Claude, who shrugged off her opinion as laughable. An Englishwoman approving food?

[The son of our village mayor in Siorac-de-Ribérac had actually passed through England en route to New York.

'Did you manage to eat well?' we asked.

[214]

'Oh, yes. In a French restaurant.'
Yet in Paris Claude could hardly find anywhere to drink coffee.]

The patron attended us assiduously and shouted at his waiters in a way only possible in a country that still enjoys – or suffers – a residual feudalism. Is good food dependent on this? Produced on this level, at this price, it must be an endangered species.

Over coffee, Jacques called for the papers and we read the first two reviews, one good, one bad. The second said that Huisman's production was so good the critic had felt he deserved better material to work on.

'It's not true,' he said, trying to be fair to his guests.

Later Thelma and I shopped in a chic boutique and walked back through twenty minutes of side and main streets; glimpses of men peeing in cobbled alleys, and of steamy bars full of Brueghelesque faces. Not many long-haired youths but a feeling of *déjà vu*, like Isherwood's pre-war Berlin without the excesses. Georg Grosz perhaps. Shops for cigars, coffees, candied fruits, hot confectionery, lace. Stalls boiling escargots. No erotica to speak of but perhaps we didn't stumble on their Soho.

[That took another ten years or so, 1982, when we went for our next première, this time of *Passion Play*. Walking from one theatre where it was being performed in Walloon to the National where it was in French, we found the shop-windows with their tableaux of suburban living-rooms, women doing crosswords, knitting or thumbing through magazines by the light of satin-shaded standard-lamps. And all for hire.]

Incredibly ornate hotel lobbies, bière cafés jutting on to pavements, cheerful and welcoming, the massive Bourse, like St Paul's, guarded by stone lions. It's the right place for a Common Market HQ.

At the Plaza, rested and again observed our four reflections.

15 January

To see Ed Berman's outfit at the Almost Free Theatre, who've decided to do my sketch rejected for *Oh! Calcutta*, which I've called *Neither Up Nor Down* and reinforced with some obscenities at the end. We tramped through muddy building-sites from Inter-Action's HQ (a room beside a shop in a mean terrace) to a private house with hardly any furniture. The actress was in court for a speeding offence and the actor had gastric 'flu. After we'd read the sketch and talked it over, we returned to HQ and met Berman, the CO, an ageing maverick with beard, a soothing American voice and an elaborate sense of fun. There was a half-seen staff of gentle-looking people and a dog asleep on a bed. In the kitchen a schedule of dietary do's and don'ts:

Penny – no meat or fish.

Jim – plenty of dates but nuts and dried fruit come top.

Ed asked me to write a play for the double-decker he's bought from London Transport.

At Greenwich Board meeting, discovered that our theatre won't earn a penny out of the tour of *Lane*, and didn't from the West End run either, because the contract they made only allowed a percentage of producer's profits, not the gross BO. Christ, what incompetence!

18 January

Company, a New York musical. Unusually good of its kind, but the kind doesn't appeal much any more. A few years ago I'd have been cheering with the rest of the sweeties invited to this matinée preview. Well, I grow old. This seemed a waste of everyone's talent and hard work, only adding to the world's stock of harmless pleasure. One number was sheer joy – a vaudeville show-stopper with straw hats, flags, tailgate trombones and crashing cymbals. This indulged in, and at the same time parodied, the best of their native tradition, unequalled anywhere in the world.

[So much for one of the most exciting and original achievements of my future friends Hal Prince and Stephen Sondheim. That day I wasn't in the best of moods, as the matinée followed hard on the *Evening Standard* lunch where I hadn't won an award. *Lane* had been short-listed for both Best Play and Best Comedy, but they'd gone to Simon Gray and Alan Bennett. Maggie Smith, at the sight of my face, said, 'Well, you can't win them every year, dear.']

To meet Sonia Orwell at the Tynans' place. The proposed anthology or 'evening' has come up again because she's interested in the National Theatre doing it.

Kathleen T was outside their house in Thurloe Square, unloading baskets of cats from her car. 'They've been to the vet. The fleas are bad this year and when you find them all over the children's beds, it's time to worry.'

Orwell was one of the most admirable personalities in literature. I see him as both an old-fashioned middle-class public-school boy and an old-fashioned English socialist, certainly not a philistine, as Mary McCarthy thought, unless she was using the word in a special sense known only to graduates of Vassar.

I tried to convey my enthusiasm and ideas in an opening statement but Mrs O seemed set on putting the worst construction on all I said. When I tried, for example, to say that the decay of language in *1984* was one of his lifelong concerns, she insisted – tangentially, I thought – that it was a purely intellectual book. Certainly, if you compare him with another writer of that time, J.B. Priestley, with whom he had a good deal in common, it's easy to see that Jolly Jack was a sentimental Englishman, where Orwell was outside the national pale. His sympathies lay more with Koestler, Joyce, Henry Miller.

'I wouldn't like to see him sentimentalised,' she said, and at this I very nearly asked if she'd heard what I was saying. But the meeting was meant to be reassuring and pacific so I bit my tongue.

'There'd be no attempt to psychoanalyse him,' Tynan said, 'would there, Peter?'

'Oh,' Sonia said, 'I couldn't bear that.'

'No, I want to describe him through his work, as revealed only in his work, perhaps try a reappraisal.'

It was a sticky encounter, with Ken playing Mountbatten to our Nehru and Jinnah. In the end I agreed to do a draft for her approval, which she had no trouble agreeing to as, after all, a 20-page synopsis is the hard grind done. And I'd be held to the outline rigidly by this classic literary widow who controls the estate by having married him only three months before his death.

'Oh, Kathleen, please don't go,' she interrupted at one point, when I was trying to convince her of my credentials for the job, 'do tell me where I can get one of those Victorian cameo brooches you showed me.'

She seemed to be quite out of sympathy with that part of Orwell's work that most appeals to people like me. Certainly I'm surprised to find her so snobbish, dropping French phrases and wincing visibly when I claimed not to be an intellectual.

'That was your major tactical error,' said Ken after she'd gone, 'otherwise you were smashing, love.'

I can live without these manoeuvres. If she doesn't want me to do the thing, fine, though this would be a pity, as I relish the prospect of doing him justice on the stage.

21 January

To Paris to discuss the production of *Santé Publique* (or *Health*) with Jean Mercure and to see Dress and Opening of *Ne M'Oubliez Pas* (*Forget-me-not Lane*).

At Théâtre de la Ville, Mike Blakemore and I sat through Dario Fo's play about Columbus: lively to look at, well staged and far less boring than we'd expected. The full house tittered here and there but never really let go.

'French audiences don't laugh,' Mike whispered to me, 'they kind of rustle.'

22 January

To the Right Bank ('I am hardly ever here,' said Claude, a Left-Bank habitué and snob) to the dusty, Cupid-and-Psyche, four-tiered old Théâtre de la Renaissance, which has been closed for two years. My play will mark its reopening but, judging by today, may never happen. We met the actors, including Daniel Gélin, but the inertia of bricks and plaster had settled on the company and we left again before any work was done. Took the Métro home and even here Claude bought 1st class tickets. A city with that revolutionary history having two classes on its underground!

Abigail, Thelma, Dan, Peter, Louise. (Bristol, 1968).

*Albert Finney, Susan Alpern, Zena Walker (*Joe Egg, *New York 1968).*

Taking Abigail 'home'.

Blackheath on screen. The Common, 1974. Inc. Peter Jeffrey, Denis Waterman, Vivien Merchant, Gwen Taylor.

Blackheath reality: Thelma, her parents and daughters.

The front garden: Dan and Louise.

Back garden: Catherine and Louise.

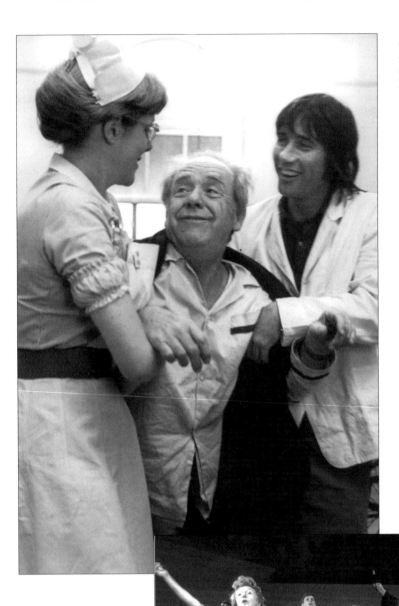

Lynn Redgrave, Mervyn Johns, Jim Dale. (The National Health *film, 1973).*

Joan Hickson sings 'There'll always be an England', (Forget-me-not-Lane, *1971).*

Chez Magnou, Dordogne.

Thelma, Christopher Morahan, Anna Carteret.

Thelma and M. Maze, the gardener and gardien.

Francis Hewlett painting the house.

The family, Old Rectory, Shropshire, 1980s.

Geoffrey Nichols, Antoni Gaudi, Peter, El Capricho, Spain.

Saw Mercure's production of *The Possessed*, adapted by Camus. Faced it with heavy heart, agreeing with Mike that Dostoevski's one of the acknowledged Great Writers who makes no appeal. I simply don't recognise his view of life as in any way matching my own. But the production was fine, with only one typically Parisian moment when a stage carpenter crawled on on all fours into a doorway to oil a sticky hinge. Understanding none of the dialogue and never having got through the novel, I at first assumed this was part of the action, an assassin coming to plant a bomb under the Tsarist tyrants.

In his dressing-room afterwards, Mercure was as impossible as ever, rejecting all our casting ideas, so that we wondered why we'd sat through either of these plays, when the idea was to scan the company for likely actors.

23 January

I asked Claude if French boys really are initiated by their fathers into sex via the local brothel. He said this may have been the custom once but not nowadays and never for him. And, from what he remembers of the sad whores in his birthplace, Angoulême, he isn't sorry.

24 January

After Mike had gone home, so as not to see how carefully the Roumanian director Fagadu had cribbed his original, we were allowed to see a rehearsal at La Renaissance. The Roys kept insisting he's only an imitator and had carefully noted down and repeated Mike's production of *Egg* and was trying it again with *Lane*. This time he hadn't been careful enough. Gélin's notorious offstage life is the opposite of the character's and various kinds of self-abuse have left their mark. The few lines he can remember are gabbled incoherently. The father, Guy Tréjan, is in some ways better casting than Bates and has the right grandeur. The adolescent boys are appalling.

25 January

At Tuesday night's opening, we sat with Israel Horowitz, author of *The Indian Wants the Bronx*, a friendly American, with a track record of success at home and flops here, except for one which runs and runs. The audience reaction was as dusty as the building, but Israel bet me a good dinner we'd run for three months.

Writing this a week later, I know from the press that he'll lose the bet, as the play will probably close in a fortnight. Parisian critics simply don't want to know about the problems of an ordinary Englishman during WW2, wondering what's made him the mess he is, especially as they believe we betrayed them in 1940.

29 January

Squash with Frayn in his club, which he's pushed me into joining. He kindly showed me the only review so far of the sketch at The Almost Free. De Jongh in the *Guardian* describes me as a reactionary taste, the play as awful and finishes, 'What a triumph of technique to get three titters in thirteen minutes!'

Cheered by an afternoon at Goldsmith's College, Deptford: about fifty mostly middle-aged adults, asking intelligent questions for two hours. What's more, they seemed to enjoy it as much as I did. Far better than the similar event at Eton.

2 February

Notices of *Ne M'Oubliez Pas* sent by Claude, almost all bad. The *International Herald Tribune* begins:

'Parisian impresarios do not realise that what was twaddle in English is twaddle in French, so that we have *Saved, Plaza Suite* and now this one all running here.'

3 February

After Carl Foreman, Ned Sherrin's the latest producer to dip a toe into the possibility of filming *Health*. At a meeting in his Chelsea artisan's cottage, costing no doubt an arm and a leg, he put up Jack Gold as director. Good news, as his latest TV films were a bit more than alright.

Afterwards a ride in Ned's huge chauffeur-driven Mercedes through the hateful streets of the rich. The driver did his best to kill off a few, particularly a party of girls in straw hats coming from a school, but they've all become very agile at dodging the fast cars, drunks and junkies of the district so he didn't score even one.

[In the mid-fifties I'd been sharing a flat on Chelsea Embankment when Ned came down from Oxford and occupied the front room with a river view. One evening he was spruced up for a meeting, 'With someone I've always admired,' he told me, 'the comic novelist Caryl Brahms.' The start of a long partnership. They both later joined the board of Greenwich.]

5 February

Dan's eighth birthday party, a United Nations of boys from his junior school, stuffing cake and jelly with the host asking questions like 'Which white boy likes sausages?' or 'Hands up all the black boys who like milk.'

At Greenwich Theatre a real treat: *Never the Twain*, a recital of Kipling and Brecht songs about the Raj. The balance well kept by John Willett's selection, Kipling's emotionalism illuminated by Brecht's intelligence. The Marxist hugely admired the Imperialist. 'Mandalay', 'Surabaya Johnny', 'Recessional', etc, beautifully sung and 'Gunga Din' stirringly rendered by that neglected actor Jerome Willis.

6 February

Lay late in bed reading the raves for Tom's play *Jumpers* at the Old Vic. Whereas for *R and G*, Hobson only compared him favourably with Beckett, Pirandello and Shakespeare, this time he puts him in the scales with God and finds the older man a bit lightweight.

7 February

Work on *The Common* entails reading the history of Blackheath and the various rebellions that have mustered their forces on what was a handy open space with good views towards London. There have been three main events of this sort: Wat Tyler's Peasants' Revolt, Jack Cade's rebellion against Henry VI and that of the Cornishmen against Henry VII. I'm using Tyler's, the best known, most successful and probably most justified, but only in a comic way in the comedy, as rehashed in our day by a sort of Sealed Knot outfit as seen at the last *Fayre*.

8 February

Opening of a mixed show of Francis Hewlett ceramics and the paintings of a man named Mycock. F wanted to call it 'Don't look at Mycock' – but they did and so did we: mildly pornographic pictures of a faceless blonde (or parts of her) on crazy paving or in front of joints of meat, with perky tits and fuzzy minges. They were selling well. We bought two Hewlett ceramics, a glazed sphere with a hand and breast drawn on in blue and a solid rexine armchair with a man's vest thrown over its back. F was pleased to find he'd sold two but disappointed that we were his only buyers.

Claude rang: the weekly reviews in Paris are better and the weekend business much improved.

9 February

Dan's eighth on the seventh, Thelma's fortieth today. Among my presents to him was an Illustrated Bible, as I'd been suddenly aware that they're all growing up without any scriptural knowledge. At nine, Louise doesn't even know about Moses and the bulrushes. Why aren't their teachers at least telling them the *stories*?

I also gave him (to give to his mother) *The Young Visiters* by Daisy Ashford, which I first heard of when going with Thelma before our marriage and had slightly resented, as she and her teacher friends kept repeating its jokes as catchphrases (like Goons buffs), so I refused to look at it. Since Monday I've read it aloud to her and find I agree with James Barrie that it's a minor masterpiece. The snobbery of the nine-year-old author is an unwitting parody of Edwardian society. If it's a fraud (by Barrie?), it's brilliant and deserves success, but I hope not. Ashford died last year and, if there was any funny business, she never told. Never repeated the trick either. I'd have thought there was an adult future ahead of someone whose opening sentence is: 'Mr Salteena was an elderly man of 42 and was fond of asking peaple to stay with him.'

We took train from Lewisham and wished we were going like Salteena for a stay 'in the Gaierty Hotel' and 'a very fine compartment with a large douny bed and white doors with glass handles.' But 'arrived in the gay city, I hailed a cab to the manner born'.

After haircuts, we saw a show of British sculpture at The RA. One of the best and certainly the largest was by Nibs Dalwood. Back for the children coming from school and read them the Creation from Genesis. Their minds worked, as mine always did, on a banal rational level. If Eve was made in Chapter One, why did God have to do it again in Eden? If Cain and Abel married, it would have to have been to their sisters, so small wonder we've all been such crackpots for 2,000 years.

[This was the time of national power-cuts brought on by a deadlock between Heath's government and the unions. Diary doesn't reveal much political passion or even conviction, my stage plays could be taken as left or right wing and Sonia Orwell told me she thought *Health* reactionary.

Though never joining any party, I'd always voted Labour, without any illusions that Harold Wilson would bring us an inch nearer the Socialist nirvana. Trades-unions, far from champions of the oppressed, were now as conservative as the House of Lords. I couldn't – and still can't – fathom how anyone with Socialist ideals could want to keep men underground hacking coal and developing silicosis when they could be working in a pleasant factory estate. Meantime milk-snatcher Thatcher was watching and learning, and Heath kept turning our lights out.]

12 February

Chris and Joan Morahan rang from Dulwich. Could they come to tea to escape their latest power-cut? They came at five and at six *our* lights went too. They stayed to dinner by lamplight and candles, and Chris lectured me on his plans for the autumn when he takes over as Head of BBC Plays.

Harold Pinter told him how, one evening, he and Vivien were at home in their flat in the Nash Terrace when the doorbell rang. There followed a characteristic pause as they considered their course of action. At last Vivien advised him to answer through the entryphone.

[223]

'Yes? Who's that?'

'Oh,' (an unknown male voice), 'I am a stranger.'

Pause.

'Yes?'

'I wonder if you could let me have a glass of water?'

Pause.

Harold: 'No.'

Hangs up receiver.

Chris told it to illustrate his premise that writers only notice events that confirm their view of the world. He thought the negro charge-nurse in Uncle Bert's hospital ward was as right for me as The Stranger was for Harold.

13 February

Power went off as thirty million families tried to cook their Sunday roasts.

15 February

One of a pop-group called the Monkees was touring in a version of *Lane* that had reached Eastbourne. The theatre manager rang the London producer, refusing to let it play for more than one night.

'You told me it was a family show and it's hardly started when there's this teenage idol talking about "tools" and tossing-off and a man whips a naked girl. I was so ashamed I wanted to jump off the pier. I've got school parties booked for the whole week and it's sheer filth!'

18 February

Claude Roy arrived to stay the weekend and work on the text of *Santé Publique* and see the play in English. We went to visit Dan in St Thomas's, where he's been since yesterday having adenoids removed to help repair his speech impediment. He was lying asleep in the noisy children's ward, a little blood at his lips and nostrils. Across the river Big Ben's face was blacked out and Parliament very dim.

At the Old Vic, they almost got through the first act of *Health* before the lights went as a warning. We made for the bar and drank coffee by candlelight. We've forgotten how pretty this can be. The second half was done by follow-spot.

20 February

Finished our two full days' work after dark and went walking in the blacked-out streets. The public lighting's haywire since the cuts, whole areas suddenly plunged into darkness as time-switches work automatically at the wrong hours. Collisions everywhere as all the traffic-lights are defunct.

Claude was interested to see a blue plaque showing that Gounod had bolted to this house during the Paris Commune of 1871.

'Naughty, naughty!' he said, wagging his finger at the composer's ghost.

23 February

Jumpers at the Vic. I enjoyed it more than anything else he's done but Michael Frayn, who read philosophy at Cambridge, thought it shallow. This was unusually positive from him as he always leans over backwards to see the other point of view. His answer to the dilemma of how to be a good citizen and at the same time show solidarity with the miners is to economise on power while sending a cheque to the NUM.

Tom was there and wanted to bring Hordern to eat with us. I tried to find a restaurant but we finally gave up in deepest Clapham and I found myself apologising. This chase was mostly due to the Frayns' baby-sitter having to be relieved. So we drove back to Blackheath, passing two accidents, and ate takeaway curry after M had run the sitter home.

24 February

Morning: my first attendance as member of Arts Council Drama Panel. Other members were three critics, one playwright and one or two others I couldn't put names to. I told them Ed Berman doesn't pay royalties to authors at his Almost Free, giving instead a performance fee of something like 50p. They made a memorandum to change the conditions of his grant. Dare say now no-one will get anything at all.

Afternoon: Mrs Faircloth took care of the children while I rang the local garage to have the car's starter-mechanism checked. Had hardly begun filling the vacant pages of this journal before I heard Thelma calling in her come-and-answer-the-phone voice and went promptly to the bedroom to find her resting under the blankets.

'What are you doing?' she asked.

'Writing my diary.'

'Well, come and do something that's worth writing about.'

'I thought I was wanted on the phone.'

'Not on the phone, no.'

Later, while we were discussing post-coital feelings, there was a ring at the front doorbell.

'Can that be the girl who's coming about the mother's help job?' she said.

I ran to my study for a view of the street and saw a man in dungarees moving down the front path towards my car, as though he was about to drive away again. I ran back to put some clothes on, by which time Thelma had already dressed and now helped me with mine, like a rehearsal of the old scene in farce where hubby's caught with his pants down. Mrs Faircloth, passing me on the stairs, must have wondered how I'd disarranged my hair by writing my diary.

26 February

Our next-door neighbours are anaesthetist Patrick Bennett and his Roman Catholic family. His younger son, Everard, is Dan's age and they've made friends. He's staying in our house for a day or two but nipped off briefly to Confession. He seems such an irreproachable boy, Thelma was curious about what sort of sins he owned up to.

'Well, you see,' he said, 'I jump out at people.'

Griggs for drinks. John advocated the continued wearing of antique drag by members of the judiciary, on the grounds that this invested them with authority. Like the Black and White Minstrels?

28 February

Genet's *The Balcony*, an intermittently powerful play preaching that everything's an illusion. Tonight, by accident, a fat actor really-and-truly broke a real dressing-stool, thus effectively disproving the hypothesis. ('I refute it thus!' said Johnson, kicking the stone.)

Power-cut in second half.

2 March

At Lewisham a black man and I got into a compartment of the London train already occupied by three adolescent boys. On a closer look, I saw they were yobs, their faces glazed by violence and stupidity. Their leader moved from window to window throwing stones at passing buildings. The black man got out at the next station and I should have done the same. Having missed my chance, I was stuck. One of the seated boys was the comic, dressed in garish plaid trousers and a silly hat. They had a repertoire of private jokes, as we did at their age.

'Al Capone!' the comic shouted at an ordinary-looking man on the platform at London Bridge.

'Al Capone!' they shouted in unison.

'Don't argue with my guns,' he went on, in passable American.

'Paddies! Paddies!' they chanted together at a gang of Irish labourers. All the time the nervy yob moved to and fro, trying to throw his pocketful of stones through somebody's window. Luckily he was a rotten shot and much of their behaviour was bravado.

'Don't throw at the cars,' the comic said as we crossed a roundabout. Then as the active one took to spitting out of the window, 'Disgusting!' he chanted, dwelling long on the first syllable, 'di-i-i-sgusting!'

Who was he expecting to hit but himself? Perhaps the game was to dodge the gob on the way back.

I was scared, wondering what I could do or avoid doing. My chances weren't good if they took it badly. When the monstrous Early Stalin Shell Building loomed up, I thought that if the boy hit that, I'd have to thank him. But now he'd stopped. I thought he might do some damage to my beloved Festival Hall's plate-glass.

'What's that?' the comic asked, 'The Albert Hall or summink, innit?'

The train halted on Hungerford Bridge. Beyond the steel girders and protective mesh, pedestrians walked the footpath.

'Big prick!' shouted the thrower, as a bowler hat moved by.

'Di-i-i-sgusting!'

'Big prick!' and he threw a stone, missing the hat.

'Terrific,' I said.

'What?'

'Your dialogue. Witty.'

'My what?'

'Your jokes. Terrific.'

This feeble response was enough to stall them till we'd pulled into Charing Cross and they were released into London, full of the sort of energy and aggression I'd felt at their age. I thought of the teachers whose job it is to force them to sit still at the very stage when their bodies and minds are most restless.

At the Arts Council Drama Panel's meeting, some discussion about middle-class and working-class audiences was brought alive by the chairman quoting Jack Dash, the union leader: 'Look at the Festival Hall. That was built by our lot and none of our lot have ever been in it.'

Or did he mean The *Albert* Hall?

6 March

A day with Ned Sherrin who sat with scissors and paste sticking together a collage of my script, to be presented to Columbia. Jack Gold's non-committal in Ned's company. Saving his energy for the actual shooting? Let's hope.

Ned's driver gave me a lift home and his secretary, a long-haired and presumptuous youth, rode as far as Dulwich. Smart Cockneys on the fringe of showbiz.

'Don't talk to me about Spain. The fuzz there – well, they un*nerve* me. I'm totally un*nerved* by them. They asked me what was in the can I was carrying.'

'Carrying the can, were you?'

'Right. Well, it was this home-movie I'd made, you know, about Jesus and that. And they asked to see it through and I said "sure", figuring they might enjoy it. Then I remembered there was a scene

with my girlfriend half-starkers eating an apple and carrying this balsa-
wood cross, that kind of rubbish, Anyway . . . '

16 March

Letter from someone in Perth, Scotland, about last week's repeat of
Hearts and Flowers, which looked good, with more coming over than
was directly said.

'This was a sick play, starting in bed and ending there. Even the sex
acts under the covers were limited to the sudden passion of the animal
in man and a reflection of your own inability to understand a woman's
needs.'

(Quick look at the signature, Iain somebody.)

Etc., etc., finishing in verse:

> It's not for me because I'm free
> To criticise another
> But listen please to what I say
> As you would to your mother.

At night in bed, I put that bone out in my neck again, but it was worth
it. She found a new excuse for having the lights out: being visually
sensitive, she's always being struck and surprised by phenomena
of light and shade on my body and around the room. Too distracting
for her to concentrate on what we're doing. It's as though, she said,
there was print all over her skin and 'You'd be too busy reading to do
anything.'

Wrong. I'm more responsive to bodies than books.

18 March

Positively the last night of *Health*, a self-indulgent performance,
especially by Paul Curran who acted like he was in *Mother Goose*.

A party afterwards in the rehearsal room upstairs where it had
begun over two and a half years ago in the sweltering summer of '69.
Yet in all that time, only 129 shows. In seven months *Forget-me-not Lane*
had 250.

[But at the Vic, most houses were full and there was the sort of loyal following only a 'company' attracts, not the casual passing trade of the West End. The company's a marriage, the commercial theatre more like whoring. How far can that simile be sustained? Both have their points, like Socialism and Free Marketing. In the end, I suppose I plump for the marriage bed, the quiet life, but always with one greedy eye on the tart in the doorway.]

24 *March*

I'd finished a first draft of *The Common* and was doing the title page, wondering whether to call it play, film or comedy, when Chris Morahan rang. Thinking it was to ask if the script was on the way, I started gaily but he cut me off, saying he had bad news.

'Joan's seriously ill, I'm afraid. In King's College Hospital. I wonder if you'd write to her, cheer her up.'

'Of course. But what's wrong?'

'Put euphemistically, she's making too many white blood-corpuscles.'

Leukaemia! Christ!

'So what are her chances?'

'Nil, I'm afraid.'

He described the likely course of her condition, its periods of recession, the inexorable end.

'Does she know?'

'No.'

'And have the children been –'

'Just a minute! . . . Lucy, go and find the boys, will you? . . . No, they haven't.'

'If there's any way we can help –'

'No, thank you, everything's settled, thank you very much.'

His terrible independence and pride. Even as I listened, my sympathy was mixed with sorrow that he hadn't found some new resource of behaviour to cope with this crisis. She's so young! I spoke to her some days ago and heard how she'd been up five nights in acute pain, crawling about the room. The GP had diagnosed rheumatism or pulled muscles.

I wrote a cheery letter all about future plans, which Thelma said was a masterpiece, as she has to about everything I write.

Saturday 25 March

Saw Charles [Wood]'s play *Veterans*, his first success, a starring vehicle for John Gielgud, the only actor to make his lines sound easy. This could, of course, be because he insists on the hard ones being cut. The play, based on Charles's experience as screenwriter of *The Charge of the Light Brigade* in Turkey, has had a traumatic tour, with seat-backs going up like machine-gun-fire in Brighton because it starts with their beloved John Mills exposing himself (albeit upstage) and swearing like a trooper, which is what he is, after all, though a high-ranking one. It's a wonderful study of Gielgud himself, graceful, vague, selfish, sly, superficially considerate, spinsterish, scared of horses, the great Hamlet of our time stuck up on a wooden prop like a clothes-horse while a Cockney technician blows smoke all over him from a box. There's also resonant imagery about Aeschylus being killed by a falling tortoise – 'What a fate for a tragic writer, how unfair!' The tortoises have the names of film location departments written on their shells, adopted by the various trades.

'They live for years, you know. Just imagine them years from now, roaming the hills, still marked "Sparks", "Props", "Wardrobe", all over them in white paint.'

Monday 27 March

Sunday evening party at Blackheath home of the *Daily Mail* drama critic.

John Mortimer brought his latest Penelope, 20 to his 50, bright as a new penny, which is what she is. He was fresh from defending a murderer. How does he keep all these careers going?

'D'you know a policeman called Palfrey?' our hostess suddenly asked him.

'Yes,' John said, 'Chief Constable of Yorkshire. He's turned out to be a Fascist pig but when I met him he was rather nice. I thought he was One Of Us, you know, a Socialist like the rest of us.'

'Could a Chief Constable,' spluttered the actor John Wood, through one of his instant rages, 'ever be One Of Us? I mean, not that *I* am, but could *he* be?'

Tuesday 28 March

Le Havre loomed grey and gradually acquired colour. An industrial flame burnt horizontally, blown by an offshore wind. We lost our way at once then never again all the way down, arriving same day 6 p.m. Chez Magnou.

Thelma soon prepares a meal while I scrabble for wood in the almost empty shed. M. Maze the gardener hadn't planted any new trees or fruit. It was wintry still, though both houses are smarter now, with white plastered walls and electric lights. Only the traditional turd-brown woodwork is a shock.

The Deux Chevaux we'd bought last summer was supposed to be ready so we took it for a test run, three adults and three kids. Like driving a dodgem car, and bristling with hazards for hands and feet. We got down the hill well enough but coming back the brakes seized up altogether and we couldn't even push the thing. We left it standing there and I went back an hour later when it had cooled enough to be rolled home.

Wednesday 29 March

By next evening, things were running well. Scrabble with Sylvia, the latest in our sequence of mother's helps. She's of mixed Austrian and Polish parentage but speaks with a Cheshire accent. She peeps from between two slabs of brown hair that hang either side like a horse's blinkers, and is further protected by grannie glasses perched on the end of her nose. Her feet point inwards, all overt symptoms of her intense shyness. Thelma says she's willing and good with the children. She sits for hours playing folk-songs on the upright piano or recorder duets with Louise. She arrived with a glockenspiel she'd made herself.

Sat writing journal in orchard with bees buzzing amongst the cherry blossom and once or twice the scream of a jet fighter or heart-stopping boom of some supersonic flying machine. Lizards emerge to rustle among the dried ivy on our walls, still stained blue from copper sulphate they used to spray on the vines. The kids collected tadpoles in yoghourt cups. Wood was delivered.

Thursday 30 March

Just before we left home, Tynan rang to say I should send a note stating my intentions for the Orwell evening and on the strength of that, the dread Sonia would give written permission. So I'm working on that now and reading the only novel of his that I so far haven't, *Burmese Days*.

Ken said this in no way affects his wanting an original play from me. He'd been over the half-finished National Theatre buildings and 'Honestly, love, it'll send you running to your tah-typewriter.'

The bikes arrived from Mussidan, and the Mendels soon after. David's intolerant and boorish, in a medical-student, callous-surgical way.

'Tell you what, master, what you want to do *trés bientôt*, as we say in the trade, is to get rid of those graffiti the kids have done on the barn walls and stop them doing any more.'

'Oh? Why?'

'Cause they look bloody awful, don't you think so?'

'No, I like them a good deal.'

'Oh, well, *chacun à son goût*.'

Saturday 1 April

Apart from the car, which started belching smoke yesterday when Dan and I were having a run, things are going well. Bousquet the nursery-man says he thought the trees we ordered were to be collected so didn't deliver them to Maze. Now it's too late for planting and they'll wait for next spring. We walked to Maze's to explain. His house was full of family and all four of us had to shake hands with every one of them. This took some time and even they began to laugh, but the ritual's sacrosanct and compulsive, as you can see any day on a beach or camp-site, as huge families stand making the pacific gesture. Maze had promised a chicken as return for last summer's ducks and he came at me with a plump white hen, alive but sedated, with feet tied, which he laid in the hall ready for us to take. We had to explain that we couldn't kill it and would he be so kind? I thought the gift of a live chicken to the incompetent townees would be a good scene for *Chez Nous*.

Monday 3 April

Eve: David and I visited the Mayor's house to buy wine and eggs. Mme Dignac was at first irked to be *dérangée* while watching *The Count of Monte Cristo* but warmed later. She'd seen the TV version of *Santé Publique*, with a mug-shot of me. Though I thought this might have put up my stock with her, we were still only allowed into the kitchen, along with the labourers, not admitted to the inner living-quarters as we knew their friends were. David said he thinks thespians and the like are still looked on as gippoes in this part of rural France. I suppose the coupling of a gippo and a Jew was just too dangerous, even if he was redeemed somewhat by being M. le Docteur.

Thursday 6 April

How has the idea grown up that England has a difficult or unreliable climate? It must be that we can't do without the dream that elsewhere the skies are blue, seas warm, every day without fail. Thelma told us one morning that the porridgy sky was only a heat-haze and would soon clear. I've never let her forget it, staring out at the teeming rain saying it's only a tropical heatwave, warning everyone to get out their bikinis. This morning she awoke late but immediately eager to use 'the lovely drying day', meaning the gale-force wind that was keeping the hammock at forty-five degrees. This soon brought a fresh heat-haze bucketing down and the children came back drenched from a bike-ride saying, 'What's this, a hurricane?'

Tuesday 11 April

We put wildflowers in pots for the Woods' supposed arrival from a week spent on the Riviera with some showbiz chums – Markie, Dickie, Tony? – and I was painting our staircase wall when a telegram came: 'Exhausted, burnt, bitten, going straight home, love Woods.'

I'd expected this, they'd done it so often, but perhaps because this time I was so looking forward to seeing them I almost began to believe they'd come. You have this image of Val at her most Miss Havisham, pining for Ashton Court and the shops of Clifton, and Charles saying,

'Let's get home.' Why do they say they'll visit when they've no intention of coming?

But the word 'burnt' left me feeling envious.

Wednesday 12 April

Thelma and children raided the empty house a few hundred metres down the road, bringing back a prayer-book with some handwriting in Latin and the date 1789. Also an elaborate papier-mâché corset, hard as wood, an exact delineation of the ideal female form of the Belle Epoque.

Thursday 13 April

David's friends the Brays came to lunch and talked our heads off. On our third meeting we realise they're a pair of middle-aged lovers. John's fifty, looking barely thirty-five; Sally's perhaps fifteen years younger. He knew her parents before they married, before she was born. Despite this, they were opposed to their daughter's being hitched to John, so that in them one sees what Romeo and Juliet might have come to if they hadn't made such a cock-up of the potions.

Sunday 16 April

Southampton in the sunshine after so much French rain was incredibly beautiful, the avenues of mature trees, the well-heeled suburbs, then the burgeoning fields and woods. After this, Deptford High Street could only make you angry.

Hardly home when Joe Melia rang to ask our opinion of Olivier's dismissal. Had to tell him we knew nothing.

Wednesday 19 April

Michael Blakemore reported on the crises at the National, being cool and courteous, accepting that Hall's appointment and Olivier's dismissal are *faits accomplis*. He, Jonathan Miller and one or two others had backed the wrong horse, the less crafty politician.

He'd like to direct The Orwell Show, if it ever gets that far.

[235]

Friday 21 April

John Mortimer, 48 today, married Penny Gollop this afternoon. We were at the evening party in his maisonette on Regent's Canal with all the motor launches moored outside. Where do they *go* in them – to the zoo?

It was one of those standing-up-juggling-curry-and-a-glass-and-shouting-over-loud-pop-music affairs. Struck by the height of almost everyone present – Peter Cook, Tony Richardson, James Villiers, Diana Rigg, and, towering over all, Germaine Greer in four-inch red wooden heels. Why does a feminist want to be the tallest in the room?

Poor Thelma spent the whole thing staring at stomachs.

Monday 24 April

Wrote letter of intent to Tynan outlining plans for the Orwell, which I first wanted to call *The Lion and the Unicorn* but second thoughts have thrown up *Beasts of England*, the revolutionary song in *Animal Farm*.

Sunday 30 April

Our cleaner Mrs Taylor brought a cutting from the *People*:

'I predict that *Joe Egg*, the British film about a spastic child, will rock the nation this year.'

As much as it rocked the author?

Monday 1 May

Train and taxi to British Museum to join the queue for Tutankhamen's Treasures. Beyond the great black railings, a holiday atmosphere with men selling souvenir newspapers and drinks, coaches picking up school parties clutching their I've-seen-King-Tut plastic bags. After fifteen minutes we were let into the forecourt and filed obediently around an obstacle course of barriers, then shuffled forward while British Legion NCOs half-humorously bullied us into ranks of four. The largely British crowd did as they were told and stood facing front under the lofty portico. In about two hours, we were past the ticket kiosk. Blow-up pictures reminded us that the profits would go to saving the antiquities of Phylae from submergence by a new dam and that the main building to be rescued was a kiosk. The word is Turkish and means an Eastern garden pavilion. Was its new use as a ticket-office or sweet-shop to do with the Egyptian craze in pre-war cinemas, which itself came from Carter's discovery of the tomb? We climbed to the first floor, crossing other visitors to the permanent exhibits, like a confluence of rivers, and upstairs joined another queue in a Roman Britain room. In another half hour, we were at the inner turnstile. Now there were temporary cubicles and displays of the discovery with captions of the dialogue between Carter and Carnaervon. 'Can you see anything?' 'Yes, wonderful things.' No such luck for us as yet, and it was hotter by the minute. If the idea was to recreate the arduous archaeological donkey-work in a closed space and suffocating heat, it was well done. The first statue came after more twists and turns and was of gilded wood and something of a let-down, not as sleek and glittering as the colour photographs and not nearly as large. Badgered continually to keep moving on, it was impossible to read the catalogue in pitch darkness by light reflected off the artefacts. You couldn't really look without blocking the line and letting the huddled masses pass by. An ugly mood grew among us and people began asking their companions to skip the next exhibits: the young king's game to distract him on his journey to the next world (an ancient Travel Scrabble), the model boat of acacia, the alabaster unguent vase in the form of a Disney lion poking out his tongue.

'Mum,' a boy said, 'I've been chewing this bit of bubble-gum for an hour and the flavour's all gone.'

By the time we reached the fabled jewellery, we were past caring and the room with the golden mask was almost empty. But in the room beyond the exit, postcards and souvenirs were selling well.

Monday 8 May

Eduardo de Filippo's company in the World Theatre Season, a decent slice of life from thirty years ago, quietly and truthfully performed, but an interesting measure of how theatre's moved on since.

Grand party afterwards at the Kensington palace of Laura del Bono, the agent who represents my stuff in Italy. Didn't meet the playwright, who was next to Vanessa Redgrave.

[One of Diary's amazing lapses. I sat between Sean O'Casey's widow and Moura Budberg, mistress of Gorky and Wells, widely known as The Bedbug after Mayakovsky's play of that name. I wonder what I found to say to them, if anything.]

Tuesday 9 May

Agreed to do an interview on TV with Janet Suzman, to avoid having to sit through the film of *Joe Egg* at this afternoon's press-show. Eventually a mournful gang of pressmen filed into the upper foyer of the Columbia and fell upon the sherry and cakes (funeral bake-meats?). I was forced on to a lady from the *Glasgow Herald* and a man from *South Hants Gazette* who, after a sticky silence, told me I simply must see *The Hospital* which made illness hilarious. Peter Medak shook hands with me, a showbiz version of the Judas Kiss. Even now he was acting as though the film would be a great hit.

At home, after watching Janet and myself on the screen, a terrible sight, we caught Bryan Forbes dropping a superb clanger.

'How long did it take you to write this novel?'

'Oh, I've been carrying it around in my head for about ten years. You know – thinking it was time I wrote The Great British Novel. Somehow I never found the time until this last year. And then suddenly I did.'

Thursday 11 May

Notices piling up, mostly saying the film's a hopeless mish-mash of documentary and West End play. Some tried to like it; none really succeeded. I found myself depressed and hurt, in spite of having hoped that Medak would be brought down. The trouble is, you all go down together.

Wednesday 17 May

Dinner with Alan and Vicky Bates in their tiny house in St John's Wood. The twin boys were just in bed and stared at us without a sound. Alan had cooked most of the health-giving supper, though fish was offered as a concession to us omnivores. Alan was piqued that

Janet had walked off with the acting notices for the film and realised too late that Peter had put it over on him too. That old Hungarian revolving door.

Friday 19 May

To Mervyn and Jean Jones's place for dinner. A letter-box outside at shoulder-level had a note, 'Mail, please', which made me uneasy before we even rang the bell. Sure enough, as soon as we did, there came sounds of growling and gnashing and a bumping as of someone dragging a dead body down some stairs. Jean opened the door, flushed and fearful, and led us upstairs apologising for the noise, saying they'd just taken on a new puppy. As Thelma went ahead to greet Mervyn, she was nearly savaged by a beast half the size of a pony that shot forward to the full extent of a leash little Mervyn was holding on to for grim death. I saw two sets of canine teeth snap together inches from her outstretched hand. The other guest, Fay Weldon, was sitting with her legs retracted under her. She said later that my face on the stairs wore a mixed expression of courtesy and terror.

All evening, Jean and Mervyn took it in turn to be jerked out of their chairs as this hound bounded across to the window when anyone passed on the Regent's Canal towpath. In these conditions, conversation took second place. I made a snide remark about psycho-analysis and Mervyn took me up on it, though more politely than he'd done with Mrs Gandhi's minister at the Griggs' place.

Only now I learnt he's the son of Ernest Jones, pioneer analyst and Freud's biographer and friend. He showed me a framed telegram on the wall sent on the day of his birth. 'Welcome Mervyn, Freud.'

'Right now I'm sitting on my father's consulting chair.'

'Where's the couch?'

'That was so moth-eaten it had to be thrown out.'

He said he'd met an American at a party who asked if it was a hellish handicap to be Jones's son.

'Not really,' he'd said. 'He's well-known in the States but over here hardly anyone's heard of him because till lately analysis has never caught on. There wasn't a single psychotherapist practising outside London until after the Second War.'

'But it must be hell when you go to America. Surely?'

'Different certainly. I'm sorry, I didn't catch your name?'
'Linus Pauling Junior.'

Wednesday 25 May

Second meeting with the widow Orwell, this time at her house in Gloucester Road, bijou and tasteful.

'Be an angel,' she implored, as I set down my whisky glass on the floor, 'and use the table for your drink. I've just had the parquet polished.'

Tynan was late so I had to manage the early part of the discussion alone. The agent for the estate was there to support her and said at once that they felt my selection was more biographical than they'd been given to expect. I said this hadn't been the idea from the start but turned out to be the best way. When Ken arrived, he said at once that my programme wasn't to be seen as definitive but mine own, a personal view of a writer I admired. She said she was worried by the thought of seeing her husband impersonated.

'Well, given that,' said Ken, 'who would you least object to in the part?'

'Paul Scofield?' she said, which hadn't occurred to either of us but seemed good casting. For her sort and age of woman, he has the sex-appeal the young Olivier had but isn't nearly so flashy. This possibility of seeing him embody her husband seemed to wash away most of her objections and she agreed not to interfere any more.

The business over, we were all making hopeful noises when the doorbell rang and she let in two surprise visitors, Stephen and Natasha Spender. They came on like Burton and Taylor, a couple of copper-bottomed literary prima donnas, quickly sizing up the company and deciding Ken was the star. They by-passed me and the agent and we stood nodding and smiling as S.S. told the other two how he was lining up successors for the Poet Laureateship (is that right? Is it a ship?), now that our Blackheath neighbour Cecil Day-Lewis has died. The obvious contestants are Betjeman, Auden and Fuller; more eccentric names were Larkin and Hughes. Apparently Larkin would like it. Why? The arteries must be hardening.

Saturday 27 May

The forecasters told us wind and rain would continue through the Spring Holiday weekend but we'd booked hotel rooms to meet and stay with our parents in Swansea. Drove down the new motorway to Bristol, taking half the time we had on the old A roads. At Severn Bridge service café, coachloads of excited Welsh clung to each other or queued for breakfast. We were quarter of an hour late, giving my father-in-law his cue for jokes about some people needing to get up in the morning.

Lunched at Millie's place in Black Pill halfway round Swansea Bay where Thelma spent much of her childhood. I like the way her original accent returns when she's with all these natives, her acquired Bristolian dropping away in minutes. Even hearing her speak to them on the phone, it's obvious who's on the other end.

Took Mum to register at The Osborne Hotel, right above Langland beach, a shit-hot situation. We later walked to the head, with her worrying continually about her hair being blown by wind.

Thelma's Dad had retired the day before and brought us his testimonials of long service and his photo album of previous departures, short-haired men shaking hands. Reg is there, evidently older in every one, watching others go and now gone himself. Other pictures show their life-achievements – monstrous aeroplanes, many of which never even went into service, barely flew, follies of industry, obsolete before they even left the ground but tokens of vestigial British technocracy.

On our frequent car-trips, Millie's monologues kept us happy.

'Wonderful in Milan, our party saw everything, the cathedral, La Scala, Leonora's Last Supper . . . In Cumberland we stayed at this bee-you-tifull farm. He'd just built a new barn, £70,000, and they say farmers are poor, there he was in his shirt-sleeves, mind you he'd been to a public school.'

Monday 29 May

We enjoyed the bracing breezes and occasional sunny breaks in the rain, the rock-pool hunts for crab, winkles and shrimps; Thelma and Reg bought and ate cockles and laverbread in the market; evening hotel meals with picture windows crammed with sea and sky, swifts careering for prey, and Lynmouth lighthouse flashing at dusk across the Channel. [Laverbread: the fronds of Porphyra boiled, dipped in oatmeal and fried.]

Tuesday 30 May

Left children for a week by the sea with their grandparents, dropped my mother at Bristol and drove on to Tormarton. Lady Altrincham was charm itself and in the afternoon we played tennis on a hard court slippery with moss and John accommodated his game to our incompetence. He showed us a pets' cemetery in the wood, including a grave for a parrot who'd lived to a very great age.

Over tea, they discussed the Windsors, as Edward had just died. John had an interesting hypothesis in which he became a commoner, (as John himself had and as HRH apparently wished) and the next Labour Prime Minister. I found the topic a dull one and it struck me that the Griggs' interest in this pair put them on a level with our parents, except of course that they'd known them both and Lady A called the Duchess 'Wally'.

[By the 1990s I'd forgotten all this and myself became intrigued by the Windsor story, especially his flirtation with Nazism at the outbreak of war. I made a little pilgrimage to the house near Lisbon where they'd stayed for a month while he negotiated with Churchill for a job. During this month also, Ribbentrop planned to seduce or (if that failed) abduct them and keep them on ice till Britain had been invaded, then set them up as puppet rulers. I wrote a play on the subject for the Royal Shakespeare Company but my timing was all wrong, as a musical and then a play about them came on at the same time and both failed. Mine was turned down by everyone who read it and its chances of production are pretty slim, as it needs a cast of twenty-five and a swimming-pool. Finding this diary entry, I wish I hadn't forgotten John's fantasy about the abdicated king as Labour PM. It would have made a better play than the one I wrote, somewhat on the lines of Shaw's *The Apple Cart*.]

Wednesday 31 May

First visit to location shooting of *The National Health* in an old military barracks at Woolwich, due to be demolished but given a stay to earn the Min of Defence a chance to add to its procurement budget by letting us make our film. All seemed to be going well in the partially-dressed billet block that will serve as the Sherpa Tensing Ward.

[Watching Potter's *The Singing Detective* many years later, I caught a glimpse of a sign which used the same name. Was this hommage, a designer's slip-up or a deliberate piss-take?]

Watched rehearsals by a good cast: Colin Blakely, Clive Swift, Lynn Redgrave, Donald Sinden, Eleanor Bron, Mervyn Johns, Bob Hoskins, and from the original cast Jim Dale, George Brown and Gillian Barge.

Jack Gold quiet and receptive. Lunched in canteen with cast and crew. One of the dinner-girls had an accent that gave the word 'soup' several syllables. She told Lynn she didn't enjoy the work at all.

'But you might be discovered for the films,' said the actress, like some princess patronising a roadsweeper.

'Fuck that!' said the girl.

Jim had heard that two sets of plans had been confused when the place was built. One for a Woolwich hospital had been sent out and constructed in India, one for a cantonment barracks put up here. Hardly likely, but I liked his image of huge ceiling fans turning relentlessly in the depth of a Woolwich winter.

Monday 5 June

All week I looked at rushes and first assemblies to try and judge if and when to interfere. The film's turning out well, though so far is nearly all in close-up or two-shot. There's a strong case here for getting the camera back further, taking in the whole ward. On the stage the constant presence of six patients meant the viewer never knew which would die next and that became the style and meant suspense. If the camera stays close for a while on any one character, it's a sign they'll be next to go. When Michael B was spoken of to direct, we discussed this point at length. but Jack's been with it so briefly that I wrongly assumed the point had been made with him as well.

Directors can only do so much, often leaving heads of department to please themselves about make-up, costumes, props, and the overall style. And *their* only concern is that everything should look *nice*, never mind the social status or location. Lynn has been fighting off make-up girls wanting to powder her nose or lacquer her hair. A Nigerian actress playing a hard-pressed NHS staff-nurse appeared in a shot wearing false lashes!

Tuesday 6 June

Actors mostly work from one point of view – the psychology of the character. Discussed this with Joe Melia, one of the few who act for effect, not getting bogged down in some compost of biography and background, which seldom shows in the finished performance.

'It's the Bradleyan heresy,' he told me, 'an interpretation of Shakespeare in terms of individual psychology. A solipsism long ago discredited by scholars but still followed by actors and since given extra mileage by the Actors' Studio.'

There's of course a case for Stanislavskian analysis when the part has enough depth: in the present instance, Ash the teacher and unwitting paedophile. Or Loach, the alcoholic drifter. Even Mackie, the quasi-Fascistic engineer. But my method as a playwright with all these was to see them as phenomena, figures glimpsed in passing. With the lesser functionaries, there's even less room for delving deep.

One of these is The Old Woman who passes through giving out religious tracts, reciting the same Biblical text in turn to each patient. The essence of the joke is that she doesn't register the different people she'd talking to. Patience Collier began at once to differentiate. There was no 'image' or caricature. The rushes were unfunny and Jack partly blamed himself for allowing the actress her head. He called her back for a re-shoot.

Now she came armed with an entire life-story. I put it to her that this was merely an episode I'd observed in hospital, at which she larded me with the sort of flattery that means she's not going to listen.

'My dear, when I was in *A Delicate Balance*, I told Edward Albee everything that had happened to this woman before she even appeared. He said to me, "Why don't you go and write a book about it?"'

The rebuff escaped her: she took it as a compliment. As my mother-in-law often says, 'There's none so deaf as those who won't hear'.

Wednesday 14 June

Dinner party for film people: Jack, Lynn, Colin Blakely, the Boormans and Gill Frayn. Margaret Whiting (Mrs Blakely) was the only disappointment, an actressy woman who'd been at school with Thelma and kept trying to 'place' her.

'You always had a hockey-stick in your hand,' she said.

'I wouldn't even know which end to hold it by,' Thelma said.

John and Crystel B now live in Ireland. He's bored with being a film director and wants only to sit about playing ping-pong and tennis and riding ponies.

Thursday 15 June

David Mendel, tiring of cardiology and feeling he could do nothing more in this field, took up a scholarship or exhibition or something, to read Pharmacology at Oxford and now invited me to be his guest for a night.

After a two-hour train journey which stopped at every halt in the Thames Valley, I was still early so sauntered around, seeing the Sheldonian, Radcliffe Camera, Bridge of Sighs and Bodleian Library before meeting him at the gate of Balliol. Very pretty quadrangle, with vast chestnuts shading the Victorian Gothic Hall of this traditionally left-wing college. A few gowned dons arrived while we sat talking and joined us for some traditional anti-American jokes before we followed the others upstairs to the hall, a varnished place hung with portraits of past masters. On the transverse dais at the end, we chose chairs and stood till everyone had done the same. The Senior Fellow muttered a phrase in Latin and there was a contest to see who could be seated before his last words had died away. In the main body of the hall, three long tables were set for the students who came in soon after and left not long after that, getting away in a fraction of the time it took us to wade through the poor English meal served by Spanish waiters.

David confided his sadness. He'd hoped something of this late sojourn at Oxford, perhaps a rebirth of the male friendships he remembers from his young days at Cambridge.

'I see now we're past all that.'

The worse for college claret, we sympathised with each other over what our wives see fit to offer as erotic excitement.

'Truth is,' he said, 'they don't care for it all that much. The answer is to do what most men do, look for it elsewhere.'

'I'd like the chance,' I said, 'but I don't get out much. Hardly liable to meet available women at our own dinner-parties. Also I'm a bit afraid that once I start I shan't be able to stop. The truth is that sex is just as good with a stranger as with someone you love.'

'I feel the opposite. Can't get going unless I have a high regard for the person.'

As we finished, he whispered 'Keep your napkin,' and we trooped downstairs, guests and hosts, entering another large dining-room where a servant had prepared fruit, nuts and port. Most moved on to coffee but we sat making male chat with an unprepossessing man who turned conversation into a monologue entirely unconcerned with what was going on beyond the walls of the furthest flung colleges. Now and then there was a flicker of spite against someone at Cambridge. After listening to this for a while, we moved on without our napkins to coffee in yet another venue, where the tirade continued. Any political activist was called a trendy-wendy, women students an abomination to be resisted to the death. Did Worcester College being near the station make up for its being beyond the academic pale? I think in some strange way it was an intentionally crappy display, an Oxonian version of get-the-guest. A couple of young sycophants put on a fair imitation of middle age, one with hair smoothed flat down on each side of his head and both wore similar glasses with circular green lenses. The historian, David told me later, was a famous wag, one of Oxford's characters. Also a Marxist. I asked how that could be when he was hostile to any hint of social change and only in favour of those loyal to The Queen, especially if they wore kilts.

[The late Richard Cobb, Fellow and Tutor in Modern History, author of many works on the French Revolution.

I used the mumbo-jumbo with the napkins in an episode of *Inspector Morse* I wrote in the 90s.]

I slept the night in a guest room at Worcester, eating breakfast alone at the head of a long table. The windows overlooked a green where one of the mulberries had been planted by Charles I. The college's being near the station *was* a real advantage and I caught the train after we'd walked beside the lake. It was as ravishing as Cambridge.

Saturday 24 June

Dan and Cath ran in shouting, 'There are hundreds of bees and Lou's been stung.' Checking first that it wasn't April 1st but Midsummer Day, I went with them to see Thelma remove the little barb. By our back gate to the Grove, two men in veils over broad-brimmed hats were clipping branches from a birch to bring down a swarm that had somehow settled separately on two branches. Weird, these great bags of living creatures, intent on their rituals of survival, driven by lust for the queen.

At the same time, Buttons, a black-and-white buck rabbit, a weekend guest from Lou's school, had escaped into the Norton's garden and three of us tried to recapture it, without success.

The apiarists got half the bees into a cardboard box on the ground and left for a conference, saying they didn't suppose anyone would steal or disturb it. They reckoned wihout a strange and mischievous neighbouring boy, with white-blonde hair and black eye-patch, who came and kicked the box, at which the bees all swarmed to a garage door.

Lucy, our seven-year-old cat, can't make head or tail of Buttons, thinking him perhaps to be a mutant puss. The rabbit runs right up to her, innocent and friendly, but with a herbivorous and trusting nature. Lucy cowers behind the shrubs.

Buttons was returned to us by a nun who'd been to tea next door and finally caught the animal in her full skirt.

Sunday 2 July

Dinner at Frayns': Harold Evans, editor of the *Sunday Times*, had sponsored Francis Chichester's latest ocean voyage. He's stolen all the headlines by cracking up on the first lap and having to be rescued by his son.

'Giles wasn't at all keen to go out searching in the RAF helicopter, he was so looking forward to Henley Regatta.'

'The old man must have a death wish,' someone said.

'Oh, he goes to get away from Lady Chichester. You could say he's sailed round the world because She Is There.'

Wednesday 5 July

Preview of Michael B's production of *The Front Page* at The Vic. Amazing it's never been done here before, it's so tough and lively. I suppose Theatre was limping a long way behind Cinema then (1928) as now. Where millions of filmgoers were attuned in the thirties to Cagney, Tracy, Roz Russell, Hepburn and Grant, our stalls customers were still becalmed in Laburnum Grove. By the time they'd matured enough to take this sort of play, Ben Hecht had become so virulently anti-British that his name over here was mud. Mike's production is even better than the play itself, which becomes mechanical in its last lap. A terrific show.

Wednesday 12 July

There's no doubt the final assembly of the *Health* film is disappointing and even producer Van Eyssen said, with no prompting from me, 'I wish we had an earlier long shot taking in the whole ward.'

The marvellous hospital location had been largely wasted. About 95 per cent of the footage could have been done in studios. The film, for all its decent acting, lacks the lively sense of place so evident in Lumet's *The Hospital*. The grammar of British Film, after a brief explosion of life in the 60s, is primitive and plodding.

Van Eyssen says there are no plans to give *Joe Egg* a real release, as it's so far broken all records for bad business.

Friday 14 July

Last day's shooting. A party in the grounds of the Red Barracks. We posed before a great fibreglass cast of Victoria, which Ned Sherrin has promised to pass to me, as I expressed a wish.

[Six foot six, a hollow shell of fibreglass, cast from the nineteenth-century original that stands in so many public places. It was delivered to our Blackheath house, with a lot of bawdy business from the carriers, hands up her skirt, she is not amused, etc., and afterwards went with us to other homes in Highbury, Camden and Shropshire, before being lodged in Charles Wood's garden when we moved back into a London flat which had no space for it. Overgrown with ivy, greened with moss, sunk in the soft earth, her sceptre broken, she stands looking out over the hills near Banbury.]

Left after one champagne to attend Dan's school prizegiving. He was receiving a book for 'Behaving Better Than He Did Last Year'.

The choir sang Britten, and Mrs Richard Marsh, the rail minister's wife, made a speech. I wish the peaceful and creative mood of primary school could continue into their teens. It's the ambition of parents that makes division inevitable. No amount of egalitarian hypocrisy can hide the fact that left-wing intelligentsia and well-educated socialists will fight to get their kids into the best schools. The only remedy's to abolish all private and fee-paying education, as with bought health-care, doctors and hospitals. Fat chance. As Grigg always says to rebuke my fond hopes, the British are a deeply conservative nation and, even when they're underlings, like to see the hierarchy prevail.

Saturday 15 July

Sat in the garden after finishing a second draft of *Chez Nous*. It's convinced me never again to attempt naturalism for the live theatre. An absurd stylistic contradiction.

Thelma says I've made her look more boring than ever before.

Friday 21 July

Collected traveller's cheques, the serviced typewriter and six weeks' supply of dried fish food. As I left the stall in Lewisham market with my cartons of daphnia, shrimp and worm, a mynah-bird said 'Bye-bye, ducks'. When we have kids, we take on the young of other species too – puppies, bunnies, kittens, goldfish And the creatures they eat. And their parasites. And so on ad infinitum.

Saturday 22 July

Joan and Lucy Morahan for tea. J's looking better and claims the leukaemia treatment's successful. But how much does she know? Her illness has made her take a grip on herself. Her conversation is more controlled; she's altogether less wittery than when she felt she had time to spare.

Early to bed to read Proust and Dickens. Thelma's been on a strict diet and all her clothes hang loose on her, all except her pink and blue gingham underwear, which she wore to bed tonight, so Proust didn't stand a chance.

Tuesday 25 July

At Chez Magnou, evidence of drought in the brown grass, shrivelled cherries, clusters of parched grapes the size and colour of dried peas, and a lack of apples, peaches and walnuts. Good holiday weather though. No skin off our noses: if nothing's growing, we drive to the supermart and buy food grown elsewhere. Thelma did just that in the morning while Sylvia washed and prepared rooms for brother Geoff and Mary, with nephew Tom, expected to arrive later. I fixed plugs for tape-player, hung new electric clock, darts board, hammock, wash-line, pitched kids' tent and cleared cobwebs. All games and toys. Nothing serious. That's an important part of *Chez Nous* – every scene is based on some sort of pastime, yet set against the hard background of a peasant farm.

In afternoon, I lay in the hammock reading about the *real* country in *Akenfield*, Ronald Blythe's impressive study of an East Anglian village in the days before rural communities became weekend holiday camps. Lives of agricultural workers before the First War and even in the Thirties were no joke. Boys were told to drink all the water they could before leaving school at the end of the day because there'd be none at home, neither well nor mains, only perhaps in a butt under the roof, as long as there'd been recent rain. One boy walked his five miles home on a sweltering day, took two cups from the butt and got his ears boxed.

Here we're living in such a house. The well wasn't a cute relic for the people who lived here but a source you had to depend on whenever the rains failed, one that soon dries up. Try telling city kids not to waste water by using the flush to wash away a few drops of piss. The little man who comes to tend the vines draws his from a spring in the field he says is rightly ours but which was stolen from us by the local agent.

The children had gone off on bikes with Sylvia, so Thelma in her gingham again, took my hand, saying, 'Let's go and survey our estate.' We passed the pond where the inflated dinghy was floating and crawled into the tent.

Not much later we heard Louise's voice ask, 'Anybody there?' Hastily pulling on clothes, Thel called, 'Hullo, Lou? Daddy and I have been sunbathing in your tent.'

'I knew you were there,' came the answer from the dinghy, 'when I heard Daddy yawn.'

Wednesday 26 July

Another glorious day. Dry, with a cool breeze against the sun. But no use for the drought which will spoil the grapes in autumn.

Nicholses didn't come yesterday and this afternoon, when we'd come home from a swim in the lake, a car-horn announced them. Some time since we saw them *en famille* and first impressions were good: Geoff smiled more than he sneered, Mary had her Woman's Page romancing under strict control and even Tom appeared to have become quite civilised.

Thursday 27 July

Geoff succumbed to his old private darkness and, to counteract this, Mary began pretending the present's better, more exciting, more brilliant, the future fuller of riches, than we know either of them really are. All her friends are rich, clever, beautiful people with dashing roles in exclusive places she's never even visited. Geoff suffers this, often drumming on the table to cut himself off. When we tell stories in reply, he sneers, making us seem name-droppers because in our business some of our friends are unavoidably well-known.

Sunday 30 July

Catherine fell from the hammock and a piece of wood was imbedded in the soft flesh around her knee. Neither Thel nor I could bear to wrench it free but Geoff did at once. The Proper Man.

[As I explained in my memoir *Feeling You're Behind*, these were my mother's words for anyone who came to repair the damage done by my father's attempts to be useful about the house. It's become shorthand in our circle for anyone who can manage anything.

I heard another version one day on Parliament Hill where mothers were helping their young to toboggan down a snowy slope. A boy moaned that his sledge wasn't nearly good enough and asked why his absent father couldn't make a better one.

'Because,' she said, 'he's a thinking daddy, not a doing daddy.']

After lunch, we four parents went for a Wild Life Walk in the woods for Mary to show Geoff how wonderful nature is. By the time we'd reached the pond where the Blakemores and Thelma once bathed naked, we'd seen a couple of dead mice, a withered snake and an owl's wing.

'This is more like a Wild *Death* walk,' she said.

I asked why we'd chosen to sit on the only part of the bank where our view of the water was spoilt by a large black turd. This led Mary into her best vein, not romance but obscenity. She told us about her sister's cat.

'He's incredible. He looks you straight in the eye and has a very disdainful manner. Kate reckons he's a prince who's been turned into a cat by a witch and one day when someone's kissing him he'll turn back into a prince and discover his balls have been cut off.'

[This was at once added to the text of *Chez Nous* and, delivered in Geraldine McEwan's grandest manner, never failed to earn a laugh.]

Monday 31 July

My forty-fifth. Worked.

Friday 4 August

Sitting in the sun on a wicker rocking-chair in the orchard, everyone else at the lake while I'm on duty awaiting the plumber. Our pump has packed up, either an air-lock or a sharp drop in the well's water-level. One can see a circle of reflected light at the bottom of this deep shaft, but that could be beyond reach of the plastic pipe which brings it to the surface.

Absolute quiet, but for a slight rustle of wind in leaves of cherry tree above my head. Buzz of flying insects. Occasional distant traffic, now and then a car passing on our *chemin vicinal*, then I listen for it to turn into our yard or zoom past. So far, all zooms. On the wall, brown lizards dart across in the shadows of vine-leaves. Butterflies zigzag over the stony ground in amazing profusion, one delta-winged beauty almost the size of a wren.

Finished *Akenfield*. You come away feeling that this way of life passed away none too soon and that the middle-class illusion of rural harmony, celebrated by all those Georgian poets, was based on cruel exploitation of working people. Here we're only taking properties that would otherwise be derelict. We make no pretence at belonging to this world, as those retired officers and alleged artists did, living on dividends in East Anglia and hated by the natives with impressive unanimity. We're here by default, because of the failure of French agriculture, the fact (quoted by Blythe) that in this country there are *two million* smallholdings. All we're doing is avoiding the noise and filth of city life. We drive by car 500 miles to get away from traffic. It's turning out that cars are used mostly to escape cars, a typical two-edged sword of technology.

M. Borde, the *plombier*, says the water level has indeed fallen below the level necessary to be pumped up. Use of lavatory at once limited to big jobs, all else in fields.

Saturday 5 August

Another, more idyllic side of country life was seen when we drove to Saint Pardou where Madame put on a nice meal for just us four. Villages en route were thronged with life – men playing boules under great oaks, women gossiping. Why do some thrive and others die? Why is ours among the dead?

Sunday 6 August

The drought's been relieved, though not enough, by a couple of rainstorms. Then the temperature rose again (according to the *Sud-Ouest*) to equal that of Tel Aviv, Nicosia and Beirut.

Morning: finished *Chez* again.

Afternoon: retreated from heat of orchard to living room where we listened to our jazz tapes and discussed old musicians. Geoff's played gigs with a few and says they're surprisingly staid. Earl Hines smokes a pipe and says 'I beg your pardon' all the time.

Geoff had driven into a village and asked '*Excusez moi, messieurs, où est le boulanger, s'il vous plaît?*' of some people drinking at a table.

'Sorry, Geoff, we've no idea,' one of them said.

Turned out to be a painter who'd taught both Thelma (in art school) and Geoff (in training college). Now we were invited to eat at their place outside a nearby village. Searching for the house on foot, I was molested by two rabid Alsatians. Seeing the state of the dogs round here, you can't help feeling our quarantine laws are much-maligned.

Finally found the cottage, where Geoff's old teacher introduced us to his friend George and their three butch women guests. We all sat drinking under a Campari umbrella and admiring the fine view. We were later allowed to tour the cottage, very tarted-up and tasteful, but too perfect, as queers' places often are. They've never had to surrender to children's chaos and expect everything to be in its place. He asked the women if their bedroom was tidy enough to be walked through and one ran ahead to check but left a counterpane creased and, as we passed through, he snapped, 'No prizes for guessing whose bed wasn't made.'

His friend's an accountant but 'by preference a weaver'. Everyone round here's arty in some way – restorers, collectors, potters and furniture makers. What a picture the French must have of England from this fringy crew, forever doing up places the natives wouldn't take for a gift!

Thursday 10 August

Sent off the finished play to Blakemore in Biarritz and eagerly awaited his opinion. When you've worked on anything this long, you want to be told you haven't wasted your time.

Sunday 13 August

Started packing at eight in pouring rain, running through torrents spilt from the picturesque eaves, loading sodden luggage on the roof-rack.

Thelma declared this a heat-haze, saying it would soon burn off, and indeed, as we made westward, it did.

Biarritz, crowded and cramped like Torquay, cars, people, hotels. Mike's house is at the far end of Rue Gambetta, tall and three-storeyed, with facades on two converging streets. He's made it the sort of place he prefers – scraped wood, white walls, brass ornaments and electric bulbs in ornate Victorian lamp-fittings, a mere hundred yards from the Plage des Basques, a magnet for surfers who come to shoot and tube the Atlantic breakers on all the beaches from here down to the Spanish frontier, where the first Pyrenees were visible, merging with a cloudbank.

Mike, Shirley, their son Conrad and guest Nicola Pagett. During lunch, the sky darkened and opened, to let fall a continuous rain. Mike had tickets for a *corrida* later that day in Bayonne, but the only spare one was Con's, which I graciously passed to Thelma. Sylvia supervised the children's games, in which there was a lot of naughtiness being punished by caning and bum-smacking.

The bullfight party returned, Nicola and Thelma chastened as much by the downpour as the killing of six bulls and the crowd's anger at the poor quality of the matadors. Thelma said I'd have enjoyed its theatricalism. She'd had to keep reassessing her attitude. Beautiful and ugly, brutal and graceful, very involving, beginning with splendour and show and only when the horses were soaked with blood did you realise why everyone was there – to watch animals being slaughtered. Weird it's being in the rain too, hundreds of umbrellas, covers coming off the arena as at Wimbledon, pools of water running from pac-a-macs or trickling down their necks.

Tuesday 15 August

I waited impatiently and in vain for the main event, not bullfights or bathes but Mike's opinion of the play. He said he wouldn't discuss it till we had a proper opportunity but proper opportunities came and went with still no word. He seemed more interested in showing me the sights – varnished Yanks and Aussies with scuba-boards and minibuses, shuffling tourists, the old Charles Addams villa on the headland, aquarium, casino, floodlit figure of The Virgin on a rock.

We sauntered in our rainwear through the two hotels on the Grand Plage, one Astaire-Rogers deco, the other reeking of Edward VII and the *entente cordiale*. A poster advertised the opening night 70 years ago, with electric light and an orchestra conducted by M. Waldteufel. This had been the Empress Eugénie's mansion till it burnt down. Faded grandeur in almost empty halls, with a few angry Americans complaining about the service. A biplane flew over the beach advertising Martini.

In the evening, while the women saw to children's tea, he at last got round to my play. Or hovered above it, as though afraid of settling. The gist was that we should think about working apart for a while. In other words, he couldn't have been that keen. I found myself defending a play I'd hated till the week before. Without his showing some interest or attraction, how could I decide whether we should work together again?

It was left in this limbo. He agreed to deliver the script to Peggy Ramsay next Monday to be copy-typed. She'd then send one to Albert Finney to know if he was interested in playing Phil (and producing?). We thought of the perfect casting of the other three leads: John Wood (Dick), Joan Plowright (Liz) and Geraldine McEwan (Diana).

He was enormously relieved to have got this unpleasantness over and cheered up in a seafront restaurant over *soupe de poisson* and *coquilles*.

Wednesday 16 August

Returned from Biarritz to the farm.

Thursday 17 August

Frayns arrived by evening to stay for a week. I was in my upstairs hideaway and could hear Michael exclaiming 'Fantastic! Incredible transformation!', reminding me that they hadn't seen the place since our first visits before any work had been done. When I came down to join them all, he went on, 'I can never imagine anywhere changing. Simply can't see a ramshackle ruin made into a smashing house.' This not only flattered our skill and good taste but deprecated his own. We got used to these social strategies during their stay. Looking back, it seems a social whirl: a coming-and-going of English residents and passers-through and of French artisans and locals. Gill and Michael's

French was often invaluable. Until Thelma told me, days later, I had no idea they were going through some sort of marital crisis.

This is the season for hunting ceps, the large fruity mushrooms found beneath oaks and chestnuts. M. Simeon, our *sous-maire* and *maçon*, turned up with great baskets as goodwill gifts and everywhere we saw people single-mindedly showing others their little harvests in car-boots or unloading them to a chorus of admiration from their families, who then sorted the spoils with scrupulous care as one of the recognised ways of repaying favours or treating friends.

These fungi take pride of place over any other business. Calling Paris from the village post office became even more difficult while Madame first pulled her vegetables then welcomed the arrival of a gift of ceps that had to be praised and allotted before she'd deign to get a line to Ribérac, thence to Paris, only to get no answer from Claude Roy who said he'd wanted to come and stay.

I enjoyed our ceps in an omelette but felt a little went a long way.

[Like them or not, a discussion about the various fungi provided me with a page of dialogue for *CN*.]

Monday 21 August

I found a duckling's corpse in the vegetable garden. Maze says they're being taken and sucked dry by weasels or polecats. Michael suggested that perhaps the children would care to give it a proper burial – 'as a lesson in mortality' – but when we showed them, they turned up their noses and were glad when Maze picked up the dead bird impatiently and pitched it into the hedge.

Tuesday 22 August

Water crisis continues. The Frayn kids won't stop flushing the lav after every leak, though there's a chemical one, not to mention several handy fields. We check pressure and tank level regularly and let off the air, drawn up by the electric pump when the level's dropped below the supply pipe. We take turns filling plastic vessels at the village fountain and Thelma, Gill and Sylvia use the awning over the citterne there to launder the families' linen. Once when they were busy at this, a tourist's car pulled up, a woman got out and took a photo of this idyllic rural custom.

The Blackheath Bennetts arrived to leave their son Everard to stay with Dan, who's been oppressed by being the only boy among six girls. For this one night there were sixteen people sleeping here.

Wednesday 23 August

Michael and I stayed home while the rest went swimming. I'd asked him if he would read my play and he sat in the orchard over it while I wrote Diary, then got us lunch and called him in.

'Peter, fantastic! Made lunch already? How terrible of me, I never even noticed you doing it. How very nice!'

We ate for quite a while chatting of other matters, then he said, 'I really don't know what to say about your play.'

He couldn't find anything in it to admire, thought it badly constructed, the characters superficial, the dialogue stagey and the whole tone a faint echo of Chekhov and Osborne. The central episode of the child's seduction was too startling for the preceding act and he thought on the whole there was terrible danger in trying to write about the middle classes.

Monday 28 August

Geoff's auntieish friend had told us how to use our bread-oven. It's disused and dusty but in good repair so Michael determined to try. We watched three faggots of birch-twigs after he threw them into the shallow space beneath the domed roof. They burned furiously, the flames curling as they licked the stone above. He followed them with a handful of hay and we saw that slowly smoulder, where it should have been instantly consumed. We waited longer, in fact until the kindling had almost turned to ash before testing with another handful of grass, which this time burnt in seconds. With a quantity of clay scraped up from around the pond, we blocked the flue to prevent heat escaping. Meanwhile Thelma had been making and proving the dough in her warm kitchen. We pushed the two loaves on a long worm-eaten but serviceable palette into the hot oven, yanking it back and leaving the dough inside, like a waiter whipping a cloth from under the condiments.

The result was more like cake than bread but particularly nice when warm.

After eating it for supper with soup, pasta and all the usual cheeses, fruits and wine, we tried to play Scrabble in French. Heavy-going but gave Michael a chance to win again, which he did with his invariable modesty.

Tuesday 29 August

M. Simeon came on some errand about his work as a mason and was given a sample of our home-baking. He munched politely and gulped it down then said they'd have been glad of that in the war.

He asked about stone and was given bread.

Wednesday 30 August

Home late after a day in Bergerac to find a note from an Englishwoman who's buying the empty house facing ours across the 'road', owned by an absentee in Mussidan who uses it to hunt, but only rarely. She'd like to talk about renting ours this winter while hers is being renovated. We'd seen English viewing the derelict place and suddenly knew we'd been ostriches to assume we were safe from intrusion. Every French property-owner now saw his number coming up in the new Bingo of selling off to the northern hordes. I was saddened by this, as the idea of having English people right on our doorstep made that long journey seem ludicrous. The woman said she was staying at the Hotel France in Ribérac.

Thursday 31 August

Mrs Joanna Bullock was middle-aged, blonded, gushing. She greeted us with, 'Well, isn't this fun? We're going to be neighbours!'

I was as guarded as I could be but Thelma responded to her garrulous excitement with similar gushing. You'd have thought they were lifelong friends. I grew chillier and chillier. We left it that she'd come and look at our place the following day.

In the car, I asked, 'Whatever happened to our agreement to keep her at arm's length?'

Thelma lost her rag and said she wasn't like me, she was Welsh and I was English, she couldn't be cold with people. I said it was time she learnt. We drove on to the Brays for dinner without saying another word.

[Editing this nearly thirty years later, I want to shout a warning: 'Look out, she's behind you!' Probably nothing would have stopped this female juggernaut, but we shouldn't have made the invasion easier for her. If she couldn't be sent packing and defeat was inevitable, we could at least have shown her a cold front. I now know these two days of friendliness to have been a fatal mistake. She was the worm in the apple of our holiday Eden.]

Friday 1 September

She came at 10.30 with her quieter friends, a builder and his wife. He'll be her partner and renovate the house. These two soon drove off back to England in a Sunbeam Rapier leaving Mrs B with us for the day. I tried to cool Thelma's enthusiasm, raising my eyes at the Sussex snobberies scattered through her monologue, such as a daughter called Samantha who adores ponies. She offered to do the washing after we'd left, and Thelma agreed. We later went to give the children a last swim at the lake and Mrs B came along. The whistle had blown, as we always put it, a sound inaudible to all but the French, and they'd gone back to work or eat, leaving only a few English and other foreigners. She showed a good command of French, saying she'd learnt it from a *Daily Express* record. If true, she must have a natural gift. She took the kids for ices, taught them useful French words and hired pedalos for F5 a time, a treat I've been promising them for two years.

While she paddled past, waving gaily, we agreed she was trying too hard and her arrival was almost certainly a shame, but also a fact of life and had to be faced and there was no harm in letting her look after Chez Magnou during the chilly months for fifteen quid a week.

At the Mazes, she chattered away, fast and fluent, making them laugh, creating a gaiety none of our French-speaking friends had achieved.

Understanding more than usual, via her translation, I saw that Maze is something of an old bore, grumbling constantly about the ingratitude of the young. His son and daughter-in-law came for a pastis and left soon after. Evidently the English view of harmonious French family life is another case of wishful thinking.

Monday 4 September

Home again: Malcolm Muggeridge says he never enjoyed orgasm; Longford is about to publish his findings on pornography; the West End theatre offers R.C. Sherriff and promises Noël Coward; there are more homeless and jobless than ever; Smithfield porters march in protest at the admission of 50,000 Asians from Uganda.

The wealthy stick together and the poor are divided against each other. Would-be reformers are bought off or made to look like lovable idiots.

Tuesday 5 September

To Borehamwood for screening of *Health*.

Jewish hostages had been taken by Arab terrorists at Munich's Olympic Games. Jack Gold had had a bad morning, as his brother-in-law is the team doctor and he'd spent two hours trying to phone Germany to discover finally that he wasn't among the dead.

As we now know, reprisals by the Jews followed as the night the day and just as predictable was all the breast-beating about the international spirit of The Games. In reading Kingsley's *The Heroes* to put the children to sleep at night, I'd learnt that the sacrifices sent to Crete by Aegeus were reprisals demanded for his murder of an athlete who'd beaten him in the games. Clearly the flame burns on.

The virtually completed film looks quite good, but Jack wouldn't accept my suggestions for the final cut.

Saturday 9 September

Amusing and tricky local situation.

Our neighbours the Nortons have set up posts and chains to prevent people parking under the tall planes in Dartmouth Grove, a street about a hundred yards long that joins ours to the open space of Black-heath. In summer, families en route to Channel ferries picnic there in minibuses and throughout the year snogging couples park, leaving all manner of muck, from crisps packets to used condoms. It's left to the Nortons to clear this rubbish, so their fencing-off is reasonable, a public-spirited act that also serves their own interests. No public authority accepts responsibility for this space, which is about the area of our house and its front and rear gardens. The Parks Department prunes the trees, the only duty they acknowledge.

Just before the little posts were put in, a white minibus was driven on to the site. Soon after that, tree-surgery chanced to begin. They saw a black man climbing from the bus and went to warn him that boughs might start falling on his roof, but he ran off as they approached. They left a note about the trees and the imminent fencing-off. No answer came from him, but a white man in the nearby block of flats arrived at the Nortons' door in a towering rage, threatening to call in the Race Relations Board if they continued their campaign of persecution. Soon after, the Nortons went on holiday, so there it rests: the man in the bus, middle-aged, dressed always in the same dark suit and black homburg, leaves his bus every morning, checking that every window and door is secured. With him goes the white woman who shares his mobile home. At six or so they return and are seldom seen at any other time. What do they do? Where are they from? Why did his arrival coincide with the closing-off of this space against other vehicles? Is he a crafty customer or merely a pawn in a ludicrous liberal game? Whatever it is, he's got us over a barrel.

[Cannibalistic as always, I used this story in *The Common*, my next for television. Because of this and the fact that the bus-man was still there in July 1973 when outside scenes were being filmed, I asked Christopher Morahan not to choose Blackheath for the location; there were other suburban commons that would do just as well. Still, he did, and I was there one day watching the shoot of a scene when a black actor, wearing the black suit and hat I'd asked for, was tearing up the letter posted to him by the white residents. Further off, out of the camera's view, I saw the 'real' man, dark-suited, black-hatted, crossing the heath on foot. Seeing the unit's vans drawn up and the action being filmed, he paused for quite some time to watch a fictional reprise of his arrival near our house. I waited for the incident to ring a bell with him, perhaps even an interference and representations from Race Relations. Either he decided not to notice or was too obtuse to make the connection and just passed on to the 'village'.]

Monday 11 September

Gorky's *The Lower Depths* was one of the plays that I read at twenty in that Modern Library anthology of European landmark dramas. What strikes me seeing it (at the RSC) is how much *Health* owes to it. A drunk who's promised a cure becomes in mine one who's *threatened* with a cure; in Gorky, a tart reads popular romances, in mine they're acted out; and the cruel oppressions of Tsarist Russia have become in mine the feeble benedictions of the Welfare State.

A terrific work but the acting last night at the Aldwych was in the shouting-and-reeling style, with jumps on to tables. What table in a dosshouse could bear the weight of a man? Also there needs to be an embargo on actors laughing in classics.

Before the play I'd parked the car in Kemble Street or one of the others named after actors, opposite the dosshouse where various vagrants were claiming their beds for the night. I gave a tramp two bob, the same as I'd spent on a programme. Thelma had gone in first and bought me a Scotch and herself a gin in the theatre bar.

'Enjoy it,' she said, 'it cost a pound.'

As we sat afterwards putting on our seat-belts, a tramp on the pavement asked me for a hand-out.

'Drive on,' said Thelma, always afraid of drunks. But I couldn't and rummaged in my pockets for change. Finding none, I turned to her.

'I haven't any either,' she said.

'I'm sorry,' I mimed to the man through the closed window, 'we've nothing to give you. Well, only these few pence.'

Sitting there in an automatic Renault and a Simpson's blazer.

'Thanks very much,' he said and made off.

'I only had a fiver,' she said, 'I knew you wouldn't want to give him that.'

She was right. But why? Our deposit account stands at £20,000. I wasn't *meant* to be rich. Was anyone?

Wednesday 13 September

Michael B thinks *Chez* needs more work.

'You're in a very vulnerable position. After three successes, they're going to come down on you like a ton of bricks.'

He's also said this about the other two since *Egg*. Even if it were likely, one flop doesn't mean you're finished. And is success the only criterion?

Not to judge by most of the plays we see. Four this week, ranging from Gorky to Ayckbourn. Going to bed, I said I'd rather see a chase film than any of them.

'Yes,' she said, 'you prefer films. I like live theatre.'

'No, I want theatre to be better than this, that's all. I'm not going to praise theatre just because it's live.'

She took this personally and we read ourselves to sleep in silence, which at least meant there was no travesty of a sex act to end the day. Since arriving home almost a fortnight ago, she hasn't found even half an hour of daylight for us to enjoy ourselves. It's all over and who can wonder? During our twelve years' marriage, we've had each other about two thousand times. I drift towards old age thinking of all the women I'll never touch. Our species isn't naturally monogamous but polygamous and polyandrous. Only a kind of character castration in adolescence maims us for life. Should that be the real and so far unidentified theme of *Chez Nous*?

Sunday 17 September

Drove to Fairlight Cove near Hastings to see how Mrs Bullock lives at home. After beautiful coastal scenes east of Battle, we wound off and around through council estates and bijou villas to an unmade road where bungalows scattered in remnant woods were named after their owners' dreams or memories – Sea Winds, Pangkor, Merrie Days, Denorel (Denis-Norah-Ellen?), Bishopsgarth and Haddock's Gap.

Beside a woven-wood garden fence, we found Dove Cottage, and soon the familiar whooping welcome was frightening the doves and squirrels. We were introduced to the equestrian daughter, then the white clapboard cottage and tidy garden.

'There used to be a good few apple-trees but I cut them down. And the garden went right down to the road but I built that bungalow next door, which I rent out.'

Her house's interior was bleak, expensive and too large for her and Samantha, the walls hung with ugly paintings, some of herself. The worst I can say of it is that our parents would think it paradise.

Before lunch, we walked to the beach through a colony of houses all built by her (meaning by her friend and business partner whom we met in Siorac): Sea Rising, Channel View, Two Bays . . . One lawn like a nylon carpet ended abruptly at the cliff's edge where a Union flag fluttered on a pole. We clambered down to the shingle beach and Thelma stripped to bra and pants and went paddling. She looked strong and suntanned and very haveable.

After a tasty roast, Mrs B served coffee on the lawn, where we were joined by the builder and his wife. There was some smelly talk about Africans, as Tanzania had just invaded Uganda. Another walk took us the other way though Idealhomeland, all their creations proudly pointed out, the picture confirmed of a woman with a lot of energy and know-how and nothing better to do with her life than cover the coast with eyesores and, when the available land ran out, move to the Dordogne and start all over again.

'This is all National Trust,' she said bitterly, as we skirted a cornfield that was ripe for development and made towards the cliffs. 'Operation Neptune, they call it.'

Bullockland had given way to a white terrace of coastguards' housing.

After tea, we left, dropping her at another bungalow that she was about to let.

Tuesday 19 September

Next morning Thelma woke me saying she wasn't going to let Mrs B rent our farm, it was too depressing to think of Chez Magnou becoming Mon Repos.

I said 'Fine' and carressed her buttocks.

'I'm getting up,' she said, so I threw off the bedclothes and was up first. It's too late in life to go begging.

Wednesday 20 September

Contrite reply from Mrs B. She realised she'd given the wrong impression, of a pushy businesswoman, but too late now and she wouldn't think of trying to persuade us.

[In time, Mrs B and Prime Minister Thatcher (or PMT) coalesced in my mind. I never met Thatcher but the other was her personal surrogate in our life, spreading disaster like pollution.]

At Willie Mostyn-Owen's invitation, I lunched at Christie's. Another first for me. I was expectant that a posh saleroom would be a knock-out setting for a play. Or anyway one scene.

The porter gave me sherry and, as I was the first to arrive (plebeian punctuality?), chatted in his retainer's brogue, so beloved of visiting Americans.

'You're in the theatre, sir? Oh, I used to go all the time. I saw them all, the old ones. Godfrey Tearle, Henry Ainley, Flora Robson, Rose Marie, Maid of the Mountains. I used to bring sandwiches and stay in town. Then I started going to the pictures, you know, sir, the local cinema? I haven't been to the theatre for twenty years.'

The directors drifted in, bloated men with dead eyes and an air of evil about them such as you'd expect from a gang of thugs. No difference between them and skinheads but their genteel education and membership of the ruling caste. They included a banker, a wine merchant and an MP. Nothing came in the way of drama, only there was an air of cynical commerce sanctified by posh courtesy.

Then Willie walked me round for my maiden visit to the London Library, a lovely reading-room to sit in when I have time to waste in town. John Grigg was there, researching his biography of Lloyd George. And Willie had been John's fag at Eton. It's a small circle, the top people. No wonder *Time Out* sounds so shrill. The high caste is so pervasive.

Saturday 30 September

Awoken in the sunny bedroom by Catherine in a Victorian Miss costume, my mother's thoughtful birthday present.

'Look at me!'

'Very nice.' Groped for watch: quarter to nine. The usual stiff numbness in arms, shoulders and hands that lasts every morning till about ten. 'And many happy returns.' She's seven. What's happening to the years?

Staggered downstairs in dressing-gown, said 'Lovely!' to all her other presents, yawned my way to breakfast, taking for granted it would have been laid by Thelma, Sylvia, Olive Taylor, someone.

In the paper, the usual atrocities and Edna O'Brien wondering what the writer can do about the usual atrocities. I'd already endorsed a donation to Shelter, to atone for not giving that dosser a fiver, so what else? O'Brien echoes a homily by Solzhenitsyn which calls on us to create works 'that alter the perceptions of mankind'. She adds: 'Only by being true to such a big thing will we make any fist at all of our art or our life or our eventual unforeseen death.' [Yes, but there's always what Henry James called 'The dear little question of how to do it'.]

I later played the records for Pass the Parcel and Musical Statues and felt profoundly unhappy. In the evening, Robertson's Victorian comedy *Caste* did a fair bit to lift my spirits. A lively play, slightly altering the artistic and social conventions. Not by any means a fist but good enough.

Friday 6 October

Eve: Willie Mostyn-Owen's and Gaia Servadio's for dinner.

Just before leaving home, we'd seen a summary of Edward Heath's pretty decent life but with a photo of him at the barricades in Spain and the voice-over saying he'd fought on the Loyalist side.

At the party, a classy gathering – Robert Lowell, Alistair Burnett, Sonia Orwell. I stood at the edge of this circle for awhile, like some rugby-player waiting at a scrum for the ball to emerge. Finally thought I heard a hostile remark about Heath and tried to get a foothold.

'I was surprised to find he was on the Loyalist side,' I said.

'What?' snapped Sonia, turning to look at me.

'Well, I mean, fighting for Franco.'

'No, dear,' she explained, 'the Loyalists were against Franco.'

[This is one of those moments when it's hard to save this selection from being *The Diary of a Nobody* with myself cast as Pooter. Honesty compels the inclusion of this awful scene. But even 27 years later the memory makes my flesh creep.]

Having revealed my confused grasp of the Civil War (and after reading *Homage to Catalonia*!) I should have retired from the field without digging an even deeper hole. Instead I tried to explain that I thought it meant they were loyal to the throne, not Caballero's government. Really that war *is* a maze, especially to someone who was eight at the time, but it's no excuse when I'm writing an Orwell play.

I was about to creep away when Thelma shouted, 'So whose side was Orwell on?', not having caught Sonia's name or having a clue who she was.

I later heard Lowell asking Sonia, 'Who is that guy?'

'Believe it or not, he's one of our best-known playwrights.'

My flushed face had hardly cooled when Gaia passed round her visitors' book, wanting us all to sign. As I was doing so, Sonia reeled into view, somewhat the worse for wine.

'You've got a huge signature,' she said. 'Just look at mine.'

Hers could have gone on the head of a pin with room to spare. Mine isn't any larger than most. Is it her intention to wrong-foot me or does this happen because I'm afraid to upset her? Thelma's view is more kindly – that she wants to be thought of and considered in her own right, not as the woman who married a famous author on his death-bed and has since spent her life protecting his name. Her second marriage was to a Pitt-Rivers who was involved in the Montague scandal and went to jail for Boys.

Tuesday 10 October

Viewed a sale of stuffed animals in Hampstead Town Hall. An odd sight, this immobile menagerie, the dogs especially looking as though they were only bluffing, like the attendants at Madame Tussauds, and would any moment bound off their stands and create havoc. The range was from assassin bugs to elephant heads by way of pangolins, a duck-billed platypus and what the auctioneer called in error 'a stimulated dodo'.

Next day I bought a case of storks and egrets (too much at £45), a swan and a brace of cock pheasants. The bidders were as funny as the lots, fringey dealers, half-and-half arty and downmarket commercial, with long hair, outdated clothes and greedy expressions. One man, in green trousers and a yellow sombrero, was as colourful as the bird of paradise he bought. The keenest bidders were a Highlander in kilt and the rest of that hideous rig, and a lepidopterist who wore two pairs of glasses at a time.

Outside, as they loaded their lots into vans and cars, boys gathered shouting and photographers jostled for snaps of a man stowing his donkey into a Transit Van and a couple carrying their zebra across the zebra crossing.

[The case of waders decorated our next three houses. Thelma painted a large portrait of me posing against them and that's all that now remains. They met a bizarre end when we stowed them on the roof-rack of a little Renault 5 to transport to the Shropshire rectory we moved to in the late eighties. Our daughter Louise drove this, with us behind in a saloon, keeping an eye on the outsize load, carefully wrapped in a bright blue tarpaulin in case of rain. This parcel began to let in wind at speed and we watched as it was inflated, rather like the balloons of gas-driven cars of 1940. There wasn't much we could do but blow the horn to warn Louise, who was unaware until suddenly the whole thing exploded, the roof-rack flying off, scattering the case all over the busy road. Feathers, wings, various bits of bird, stuffing, glass and wood were strewn in the way of swerving cars.

A detail of Thelma's painting is on the back cover of Methuen's second volume of my collected plays.]

Tuesday 17 October

Tonight at the Griggs' we were thrown at 'Diana and John Collins' and I assumed at once he was of the publishing house. Thelma soon asked where they lived, always a fruitful topic in this sort of society.

'Oh, Saint Paul's.'

'In Bristol?' she said, naming the only district of that name she knew, though wondering how these two got along in a notorious black ghetto.

'No, London.'

And there it was left. Only later that evening, catching a reference to CND, did I realise this was Canon Collins, Dean of the Cathedral.

I made him laugh with my account of the party of delinquents I took to his church from the secondary school in Notting Hill. He was funny about the budgeting of divine services, saying the choristers are MU members and get proper minimum rates.

John G put the case that the existence of nuclear weapons has been a greater deterrent than any amount of wishy-washy moral persuasion. So far he's right and not only Collins but Bertrand Russell, Robert Bolt, Francis Hewlett and Albert Einstein were all wrong. It's also true that moral persuasion played a part.

Friday 20 October

Finished the Orwell script and am now free to read the views of others on him and his work. My play has taken him at his word, neither criticising nor implying. This may have been a mistake but was partly a strategy to deal with the widow. In one of the books about him, there's a photograph of her in 1949 in the office of *Horizon* just after their marriage, a beautiful woman or, as Muggeridge put it, a catch.

The story of O's life is to become a plain man with a plain name. His glamour was to be unglamorous. He belonged to the circle of upper-middle-class of writers that included Anthony Powell and Evelyn Waugh, though neither of them would have had much time for Henry Miller, so O was also something of a Bohemian. Sonia's at pains to deny the persona he tried so hard to assume.

Saturday 21 October

Half-term week and we were to have flown to Ireland to stay with the Boormans, but they've blocked the calls we made to fix the details so we've booked instead to stay at a farm in the Lake District. Drove up M1 in bright sunshine, arriving at Kendal by afternoon, skirting Windermere, finding the water hidden by the walls of villas. Pausing here to clean up Catherine's car-sickness, we found all Wordsworthian sounds of lake and hill were drowned by a high-pitched rasping, like a consort of chain-saws. Only when we later met police and a lot of reversing cars did we know it to be a speed-boat rally.

The further we went, the better. Quiet and unspoilt, the farm we'd booked had a plaque over its front door, 'Henry and Easter Troughton,

1791'. The present owners, the Robinsons, farm on these fells and provide bed and board to the likes of us. An old woman lurks, teenage sons mumble shyly and the mother provides good plain food. Mr R apologised for having had a few whiskies to celebrate buying the top-price bull for 350 guineas. This beast made a fine sight, being driven across to the facing field.

That night the silence was broken only by the moans of cattle, like someone farting into a bucket. Was he already at work?

Sunday 22 October

Drove in drizzle to Wast Water, which our landlady warned us was thought by some to be sinister. From the road, the lake lies in front of steep fells with banks of scree on the far side. This early on Sunday, we had the place to ourselves. The rain had stopped and we left the car at the head of the water and began climbing towards Elsdale Fell, crossing the becks by stones, bleating back at mountain sheep with red brands on their fleeces. Hot and thirsty, we drank from the clear streams. Near the top the wind was so strong I had to go on all fours. This was above Burnmoor Tarn, a grim lake eight hundred feet up, another world from suburban Windermere.

Mrs R talked a good deal about the problems of sheep-farming. They have nearly seven hundred grazing the hills, recognised as theirs by being ear-marked, a previously meaningless word explained. The Robinsons dosed their flocks against disease and lost very few. Ticks are a problem, especially if the animals' tails are docked, which they did during their first year here. In the south, docking's habitual and carries risks. Their elder son, who farms nearby, had caught brucillosis from his cows. And so on. So much so that, in three years, they're giving up farming entirely, in favour of paying guests. The life's too hard and they can't ever own the land, only rent from some big landlord, in their case an executive of Granada Television. And *his* future plans are to turn much of it into a golf-course.

Other walks beside other lakes: Ellerdale, Bassenthwaite, Grasmere, Thurlmere, a good climb up from Crummock to a high ridge with views of three. Drove down the coast road too, near Ravenglass, originally a Roman mine, with the Irish Sea gleaming behind the nuclear factories of Sellafield.

[271]

Tuesday 24 October

As we were leaving, a man brought the morning paper. Mr R turned to an end page and, cheered by what he saw, told me he'd bought some Hawker shares and they were going up like a lark. Political change in England is so unlikely and so slow. These people looked to me among the worthiest you could find, yet the land they work goes to a wide-boy mucking about with money in Manchester. They feel this injustice acutely but their anger's soothed by a small share in the money racket, a few wins on the exchange.

North through the alarming Hardknott and Wrynose passes, 3 in 1, no sign of humanity but the single road, the most stark and beautiful landscape we'd so far seen.

Arrived Edinburgh by afternoon and at the George Hotel were given three suites with baths and a TV set in each room, one of which worked perfectly.

Wednesday 25 October

Call from Patsy Grigg to say her younger son Edward had suspected appendicitis and they wouldn't be able to meet us in the Highlands after all. We decided it would be dreary to change our plans, having come so far.

So we did the castle, some military museums with their roll-calls of the slaughtered, the superb National Gallery, walked the Royal Mile to Holyrood past shops selling tweed, tartan, bagpipes, rock and haggis. When I was last here, in 1955, it was all more slummy and lively. But that could have been because this new visit was some weeks after the Festival finished. Then I was an actor at the embryonic Traverse Theatre, with a part that kept me on stage only ten minutes before I was shot dead and released to see the operas, concerts and ballets in other theatres.

[I'd stayed behind for this gig after playing seasons with a company that toured three of the best theatres – Her Majesty's, Aberdeen; The Royal, Glasgow and The Lyceum, Edinburgh. My parts had included being James Mason in *The Seventh Veil* and the bloodthirsty count in *Dracula*.]

Now even the gloomy closes are getting a face-lift for the Yanks and twee boutiques show the shape of things to come.

Took everyone to the ballet. Heaviest moment was a dance to Sartre's play *Huis Clos*, bad enough with dialogue, even worse without.

'That was all about standing up and sitting down on chairs,' said Dan, learning how to talk knowledgeably about the theatre.

Thursday 26 October

To Inverness and along the loch, hardly anyone on the road, and castles appearing now and then across the water. I'd been here when I was six or so, with my parents and their closest friends, Lil and Bert, touring in the bullnose Morris Cowley. There are family snaps of us all with tam-o'-shanters, linking arms among the heather. What possessed them to drive so far in 1934, the attraction of the modish monster? Mum says we stayed in a lochside cottage and I seem to remember looking from the window to see the creature floating by. This time we were at the Glen Affric Hotel at Cannick, a bleak greystone building but, judging by its style, dating from the 1930s. One other guest, a genteel Edinburgh woman smiling from a corner table at meals and afterwards, over coffee, gave us our first taste of Scottish nationalism.

'Terrible things were done after the '45 during the clearances. All the best people were deported, only collaborators and traitors allowed to stay on the land. We can't forget that, you see, it's too recent. Not that I've anything against The Queen, she does her job very well. But she *is* German. England hasn't had an English monarch since Harold.'

Back in Blackheath I mentioned this to John, who said it was a xenophobic myth that the British did this damage. In fact, it was the lowland farmers who came up with their expertise in sheep-farming. They were the nearest our islands have ever got to producing a master race. Before this, the chiefs were regarded as Mau-Mau.

We saw the extent of his mother's land the next morning when we visited Tomich to collect our rail tickets at the post office. This was even more primitive than Siorac's and seemed to be kept up for Lady Altrincham's convenience. On the walls were wartime posters – 'Careless Talk Costs Lives' – and adverts for the women's services. We got no response at all till a local came and rang a long peal with the handbell. The subpostmistress arrived without apology, and the customer said, 'Give me change of that,' throwing down a fivepence piece. She gave us our tickets after submitting us to a harsh interrogation.

The village was depressed, dependent, a relic of nineteenth-century servitude. We drove on to Hilton Cottage, a large house standing beside a lily pond, we left the car here and went to peer through windows into rooms seemingly set for a country-house thriller. For readers and audiences who first patronised this sort of thing, it was probably a home from home. Only the murders were fantasies: in fact, all that's killed there are birds and animals and the only bloodstains are in the game larder where the carcasses had hung.

Walked, returned, ate our lunch on the terrace by the house listening on the portable to my only radio play, a version of the TV *When the Wind Blows*, which came over loud and clear and had always been one of my better scripts. Hallam Tennyson had refused a repeat of the TV on the grounds that it was 'essentially cliché-ridden'. Or so Peggy told me. I answered that we must accept his view. As long-time producer of 'Saturday Night Theatre', he'd certainly know.

The Edinburgh lady told us of the excitement when she first arrived because one of the guests, a young man just of age, had inherited fourteen million pounds. He was the next Duke of Westminster, heir to Vancouver Island and The Strand among other bonbons. But it hadn't made him happy, she thought. Very quiet and very naice but sad-looking, whereas the young man with him was bright and forthcoming and the older man escorting them both was charm itself.

Thelma and I went early to share the ducal bed. Why would a future Duke stay here in the ugly bedroom of a bleak hotel? We soon lost interest in this subject.

Friday 27 October

Next day we drove up Glen Farrah, having the road opened by a woman from a bungalow raising a barrier. Lord Lovat resents paying upkeep for the road if the public uses it. We went as far as possible, which was to yet another hydro-electric dam. Many valleys have been flooded and I thought these man-made lakes about the best things to be seen here. Not only are the dams almost beyond belief, their slim walls holding back this immense volume of water, but they tame the wasteful wildness and bring people light and heat, even news of a world where we have some choice in whom we serve, a world beyond Lovat's 200,000 acres. But not, of course, beyond Westminster's £14m.

Wednesday 2 November

Our ten-year-old daughter Louise has begun asking about 'Doctor White's', which were Tampax in my day. One job I can duck: over to Thelma to explain what they're for.

Gill Frayn tried to explain it all to Becky and Susanna. Susanna seemed more worried than Becky, who looked rather dreamy. She wondered whether they were taking it in.

'Anything else you want to know?' she asked, hoping there wasn't.

'Yes,' Becky said without hesitation, 'when are we going to have a dog?'

Sunday 5 November

Fireworks party at a neighbour's house in one of the long gardens like the Griggs' that end at the point where the hill begins its sweep down to Lewisham. Slight mist, though no rain. Figures with wineglasses silhouetted against a bonfire floating on their swimming pool. Behind it, the male host, John Grigg and other pyromaniacs plunging about lighting rockets, wheels and golden-rain-makers. I stood aside for a passing guest and felt my leg sink in water up to the knee; had to go home, empty the squelching shoe and change trousers, then cross the road and join the fun again.

Afterwards there was mulled wine and a buffet and everyone apologised. Thelma said John G's nearly demented, trying to finish his Lloyd George book on time.

'He apologised to me and three other people in my hearing alone.'

'What for?'

'Oh, he hoped the fireworks hadn't made too much smoke, he was afraid the bangers had frightened the younger children, he knew he'd hurt one of the other fireworkers by treading on his toe in the dark.'

'What did they say?'

'They all apologised back.'

'They do it all the time. I come away from every evening with them feeling I haven't apologised nearly enough.'

Tuesday 7 November

Arrived Paris 5 p.m., to be met by Claude. After dinner, we saw Mercure's production of *Santé Publique*, a paraphrase of Michael B's in another language and on a wider stage. Despite using the same music and virtually the same set, it's altogether different. I began making notes about the glittering hospital equipment and spotless uniforms, comic walks of dying men who should hardly be able to stand, etc., but gave up when I heard the grossest mistakes being applauded. Tynan was right to say, when we met him in this city last year, that the French are deaf and blind to reality – in the theatre, that is. The realist tradition of Zola, Flaubert, Maupassant and Antoine has passed to the cinema, where it's easier to be true to life.

Anyway at the end there was a standing ovation as the silly buggers danced about in a finale that had lost all the ironic effect it had in London, becoming instead a way of finishing on a jolly note.

I argued with Mercure afterwards about the single point I'd fixed on to contend, that the mentally retarded youth should *not* join in the slapstick. Even so, it took all my – and Claude's – efforts to convince him and even then he was perhaps only agreeing to shut our mouths. He said he knew the French audience, with the result we now have un *succès fou*.

Late at night, the cars that crammed the elegant streets were mostly as still as their owners. The city became beautiful again and it was clear that Le Car, though making city life almost intolerable during the last part of this century and almost certainly beyond, hasn't yet done irreparable damage. Remove the vehicles and it would again be a pleasure to live here.

[In his text to accompany *Cartier-Bresson's France*, François Nourissier wrote: 'It is pointless to mince words: any talk about Paris in this moon-walking age is, first and foremost, talk about the motor-car. Anything else is just literary froth, a privileged bird's eye view . . . What is the point of writing about the pleasures of walking in the city when they're attended by nothing but risk and nasty smells? Or waxing eloquent over the radiance of Paris when the city's chief activity is reducing its unfortunate victims to nervous wrecks and exhausting its last gallant defenders?']

Wednesday 8 November

Next morning, though, as I walked along the left bank, I twice had to dodge motor-bikes being driven at speed *along the pavements*, to dodge traffic that was at a standstill in the narrow streets.

In the airport bus, weary Americans talked behind me.

Woman (*reading guide-book*): The first thing we're gonna do in Amsterdam is tour the canals, looking at the lovely old houses along the waterfronts.

Man: Uh-huh.

(*At this point, we were passing Les Invalides, its topiary, its cannon, its impressive façade.*)

Woman: And Rembrandt's house with its display of master-drawings.

Man: You're the boss.

Woman: And see the place Anne Frank hid out through the war.

Man: Can we change our francs at the Paris airport into pounds?

Woman: Guilders.

Man: Whatever.

Woman: I guess so.

(*As we passed La Coupole and Le Dôme:*)

'Rightly regarded as a modern classic, this young girl's diary is held to be one of the enduring human epics of our century, especially by people of the Jewish faith.'

Man: That right?

Woman: You remember they read pieces from it at Gary Burke's confirmation party?

As we circled over London, we saw the cars in long lines waiting at crossings and I imagined an immense traffic-jam on the stage. I knew the title too: *The Freeway*.

[277]

Saturday 11 November

Mike rang in the evening to discuss our work-in-hand.

Hasn't read the Orwell yet but will next week.

Won't direct *Forget-me-not Lane* in America because for him it would be warming up cold soup.

Doesn't really like *Chez Nous*.

In other words, he feels no obligation to go on with our partnership or, as I'd put it, to help me when I need it, whereas he was happy to do my stuff when it was confident and popular. He claims rightly to have been more than a director of those plays, so if the result is a joint effort, and I acknowledge that, why quit when I'm going through these doldrums?

Well, though painful, perhaps it's no bad thing.

Monday 13 November

Trying to settle the plot of *The Common*, I tired of walking 3 paces up, 3 paces down my room and stepped into the bright cold morning. Walked to Deptford and St Paul's Church, beautiful baroque building among the ruins of this derelict borough. Once John Evelyn lived in Sayes Court and Peter the Great stayed with him to study shipbuilding, as it was here that England's maritime supremacy was created. Those who know find the interior disappointing but I thought it warm and comfortable and sat for twenty minutes in silence, but for the twittering of two sparrows about the moulded ceiling.

On across Creek Road and towards the river, the only way between two great wharves and a flight of mossy steps where, looking east, you see Greenwich and upstream Rotherhithe. On, past a massive power station and some 30s flats dwarfed by its chimneys, coming at last upon St Nicholas, a plain church with old tower and modern nave. Locked. Discovered later that Marlowe's murdered body lies in the graveyard. And Evelyn's 5-year-old son. 'Here ends the joy of my life, for which I go mourning unto the grave.'

Tuesday 14 November

Claude rang: the Paris notices were all bad but the audience over 100 per cent, which means standing and sitting in the aisles, and cheering at the end. The critics are loyal to Mercure, praising his production of a pointless script.

Tuesday 21 November

Drove to Dulwich to see Joan Morahan, first time for months. Her early response to the chemotherapy was good but slowed, as is often the case, and now seems to be nearing death. We were ready for the change in her appearance but it was still shocking to find the bright, athletic girl looking fifty, yellow skin stretched on the bones, teeth too prominent, hair dry and flat on her scalp. Obviously in pain, the drugs making her forgetful.

Christopher is coping with being Head of BBC Plays and managing this awful domestic scene at night, three bewildered children. He can't share her bed any more and has never been able to sleep without her.

We stayed till she tired of the effort and downstairs met Ben, Andy and Lucy arriving to see her. Ben understands her condition and the others surely guess. They were bright and lively company though and made us look forward to our own children's adolescence.

Friday 24 November

A small dinner-party to reciprocate evenings at the Tynans and Sampsons had grown to a great sit-down do for 25. We felt we'd over-reached ourselves but needn't have worried, as it started with a quick fuse – the Mostyn-Owens – and was soon a merry blaze with Blake-mores, Tomalins and Millers from Hampstead. We're thinking of asking Jonathan to direct my next. He calls himself a director these days but doesn't get that many offers. Other failures present, apart from me, were Mervyn Jones with a rejected novel, John Grigg who's been scooped on his Lloyd George, and Claire Tomalin, similarly stymied. She provided the only drama tonight as her daughter rang to say she'd been trying a bolt on her finger as a ring and it had got stuck. Nicholas drove home – to Regent's Park! – and later rang to say he'd taken the girl to hospital where they didn't have the right equipment, so he himself had removed it with a hacksaw. He then drove back here to fetch Claire.

The Mostyn-Owens, first to come, were almost the last to go. Gaia had brought her knitting, which people tell us is quite usual.

Tuesday 28 November

Struggled all day with *The Common*, while Thelma began Russian lessons in Oxford Street. She feels uneducated compared to Gill Frayn and Gill feels cold and inhibited compared to Thelma. Where do we learn to compare ourselves? In the school of life?

Thursday 30 November

Walking the girls home from dancing-class (in which Lou is learning 'I'm late, I'm late, for a very important date'), I felt a sudden bruised pain in one foot. Given that I already have the current 'flu virus too, I gave up and went to bed.

Rose like Lazarus to go and meet Lou's and Dan's teachers. His classroom's cheerful, despite being a tatty prefabricated annexe, and his teacher's a pretty girl who likes him. Lou's room's dull and her new teacher's only a slight improvement on the last.

'What can I say about Louise?' she asked me, scanning her books. 'She's not very bright.'

When I blame audiences who don't respond to my plays, at least I'm not writing off their futures, it's no more than a jaundiced opinion. But some training-college graduate, who's not all that bright herself assumes the right to sort the sheep from the goats in this cocky way. We can't expect a better world – or call ourselves Socialists – till we pay for better-educated teachers.

Saturday 2 December

At a dinner, Margaret Drabble had been to the same children's concert that we had and hadn't noticed that the conductor had only one arm. She'd been much offended by Mrs Whitehouse because 'she seems to be giving masturbation a bad name.'

Sunday 10 December

Front page picture in our Sunday paper of a happily smiling married couple – Caroline Seymour and Peter Medak. I suppose it's long enough since Cathy threw herself from their top floor flat. The funeral baked meats didn't quite coldly furnish forth the marriage-tables.

Tuesday 12 December

Had my only conversation with the black man in the white minibus parked under the plane-trees of Dartmouth Grove.

Returning from a walk, I saw him talking to two young men holding clip-boards and attaché cases. On the trees nearby he's pinned little cards with the same message on each: Ordinary people stay away from this bus and do not interfere. It could be dangerous.

I loitered, listening to the chaps from Lewisham Social Services trying to discover his name or occupation.

'Your government,' he told them, in a very dense African accent, 'turn people out of their houses and keep all them office-blocks empty.'

'Yes,' I said, joining the group, 'but how's your bus being here going to help put that right? I'm one of your neighbours, that's why I'm butting in. We don't want you to go if yours is a genuine case of hardship –'

'Genuine, yes! Oh, is genuine alright!'

And, in a garbled, fragmentary way, he implied all sorts of injustice – eviction, prosecution, victimisation and claimed this bus on this patch of unclaimed ground to be the only place he could find to live.

'Well, if that's true, I'm sure I speak for the others when I say we certainly don't want to have you moved off or –'

'Ah,' he said, pointing his finger at my face, 'that's the point, you can't!'

'Well, I don't know about that –'

'No, you can't move me.'

'The neighbours here are going about this very decently,' said the first young man, 'all we want is to find out something about you so that we can decide how best to help. So please tell us your name.'

Though the squatter seemed about to help, he never quite did, and gave nothing away. And wasn't this sensible, even if he was genuine?

The social worker's case that we were being decent only described our method and behaviour, not our intention, which was to get him and his bus moved out of there. Of course, his case is altogether fishy, and he's either a crank or a criminal. If a criminal, he can't be doing very well, to be living in a bus. If a crank, perhaps he deserves to stay, like the old woman outside Alan Bennett's house. He's a strong man in the prime of life and ought to be able to find work. He's more likely a lucky parasite, or – as we suspect – one who was tipped off to the unclaimed space by the sympathetic spy in the nearby flats who accused the Nortons of racism. He pays no rent or rates, dresses well, supports the white woman he lives with. They spend their days collecting empties from local bins and returning them to the shops in Lewisham for the deposit money. They get turned out of supermarts amid shouting-matches with the staff. During our long conversation, he kept lapsing into an African language or at least an English so heavily accented as to sound like one.

Thursday 21 December

Delivering our Christmas gifts for Peggy, Tom and the girls in the office, we had our first chat for a long time. She told me Charles is in bed with a suspected ulcer after collapsing and passing blood.

Rang Val to be told he's better.

'I knew he would be,' Thelma said.

Also heard he's got the *Evening Standard* Best Comedy Award for *Veterans*. We remembered how we were all living in Bristol when he got it the first time for being Most Promising. Of course, no-one outside the London area had ever heard of the award and we were all very excited, thinking it was a cheque for £500. They had to ring from the Savoy, where they were staying on the strength of it, to tell us it was only a statuette.

Saturday 23 December

Jonathan Miller's production of *Noyes Fludde* at the Roundhouse. By the time we got into the arena, every place had gone or was being held by gloves and scarves. I complained to anyone who'd listen about the custom of 'bagging'. In a so-called free-for-all, with nothing reserved, bullies are always going to come out best. One of the paradoxes of democracy. The ushers apologised and admitted it was chaos. People shushed my lack of Christmas cheer. It was silly of me and had no effect anyway.

I finally squeezed in and sat cross-legged among my family on the floor.

We all enjoyed ourselves, particularly the community singalongs of hymns like 'For those in peril' and 'Soon as the evening shades prevail'. What with children's choir, orchestra, recorder group, organ, bell-ringers and trumpet quartet, we made a rousing din. And the entrance of great bands of T-shirted kids singing as groups of animals, had (as Wodehouse said of a speech in *Macbeth*) some spin on the ball. Yet it was fey of Britten to use the text of the Chester Miracle Play, further confusing the usual problem of understanding sung words. Why not modern, intelligible English? It's another example of that middle-class snobbery he never quite threw off.

[Among my first experiences of his music was in a post-war propaganda short, drumming up support for the Arts Council. I watched it in a Bristol cinema with a fullish house of my fellow-citizens who sat silently through ballet, painting, sculpture and Shakespeare, giving it the sort of respect they did to anything posh, when suddenly there was Peter Pears singing in that emasculated falsetto an aria that began with the word 'Nancy!' Audience participation's rare in cinemas, almost an oxymoron, but this was an example, as the whole place broke into a concerted howl of laughter which lasted till the film ended and was given a round of applause.]

Sunday 24 December

The Reeds arrived from Bristol after lunch with my mother. Reg lectured me and Patrick Bennett on the marvels of Chicago, saying, 'They've got so-and-so over there', till I eventually asked Patrick how long he'd lived there.

'About a year,' he said, but nothing penetrates Reg's yurrs. He's only ever waiting for others to stop so that he can carry on with his monologue.

The Griggs and Nortons came and I passed the evening in a daze, mixing the new concoctions our parents and aunt had learnt this year – brandy and American Dry, whisky and Tia Maria – and trying to evade Reg's voice. In the end, John took him on and I was coward enough not to rescue him.

Reg was thrilled later when we told him John had been a lord before disclaiming.

'And I was giving him a real yurrful about the industrial sitooation and the Common Market. Well, he seemed interested in my views.'

Monday 25 December

The children came early to our bedroom with their guitar from Red China, their globe of the world from Bolivia, puppets from Poland, oranges from Spain, nuts from Brazil. The poor are always with us but now a bit further off.

Later to Griggs for champagne, and Reg gave his view of the Queen's shortcomings. We remembered John having eggs thrown at him in 1955 for calling her a priggish captain of the school hockey team. I'm afraid John's conservative convictions will only have been fortified by meeting so reactionary a member of the Labour movement. Status quo safe as houses.

In the middle of the night I was woken by the sound of Thelma sobbing. Took her in my arms and asked the matter. She said my mother and I spoil Christmas. She loves giving and receiving presents but we're so inflexible we appear to be going through some pointless ritual. Mum had given her a silver cruet but with so many pieces missing it was almost useless.

'Oh, but that was such a valiant effort on her part, you shouldn't complain that it wasn't complete.'

Far from it. She wasn't complaining, only wishing that having made such an effort Mum couldn't enjoy it more.

Wednesday 27 December

The parents left early. Mum had been ill and Millie dosed her with Lem-Sips, one of the new elixirs that went with their eerie cocktails.

Reg herded them like cattle into the automatic Cortina and off they went.

A pleasant lunch with friends, so enjoyable that I'd forgotten that the manic-depressive solicitor Nigel Simons had invited himself for the afternoon. Madder than ever, shouting with laughter, insulting everyone, hell-bent on shocking us all. He told Michael Frayn that novels were easier to write than plays. When Monty Haltrecht tried to argue that Isherwood was not a shallow writer Nigel said oh yes, he had to be because he was homosexual. He used the word 'fuck' to Gill's mother and, in case I should think he was on my side, told me my book reviews proved I couldn't write prose. He roared with laughter when Gill tried to make him apologise and snorted and spluttered with mocking laughter all through the children's conjuring show and carol-singing.

Thursday 28 December

Next day he rang to thank us and say how much he'd enjoyed himself. And was Monty a Jew? Was Arnold Cawthrow homosexual? Surely Gill's mother must have blue blood, she seemed such a liberated woman beside her toffee-nosed daughter. He loved the elegant way she drank her tea. Was our son Dan frustrated by having a quick mind which wasn't being nourished either at school or home?

There must be room in a play somewhere for such a Widmerpool.

I tried to get back to my TV play, a relief after the enforced holiday. To me, they're the *real* hard work, the labour to be endured for the sake of being free to do what I enjoy. The end of *The Common* was in sight. High time too, as this supposed television script now runs to almost ninety pages and will play for about three hours.

John Grigg fetched more champagne as soon as we remembered – at the end of the day – that it was our thirteenth anniversary. Another year without other women – or other men for Thelma. And really my grumbles can't mean that much or I'd make a real effort, which would mean changing my life to bring me into the company of likely partners. My resolution for this year was 'to take hold of life before it's too late, not to die with all those unsatisfied desires on my head.'

Well, I'm off to America in the spring so fingers crossed.

[A timely entry to be copying this week, in September 1999, as we just happened to look at our marriage certificate and found that for nearly forty years we've been celebrating the wrong day. Not the day after Boxing Day (which was a Sunday in 1959) but the day after that.

Our Ruby Wedding will coincide with celebrations of the new millennium.]

Sunday 31 December

Took first draft of the play by hand to Chris Morahan. Joan's in hospital again but a little better. He says he feels oddly insulated and tries to bury himself in work to escape the temptation to relapse into apathy.

Geoff and Mary came to stay. Enjoyable chats, broken by jealous children, showing off because their cousins Tess and Tom had chosen not to come after all.

Geoff went early to the 100 Club where his band was playing the New Year gig. I drove the wives in later through unexpectedly quiet streets.

They talked about sex much of the way, Mary's ever-interesting topic. Tired of my brother's continual complaints, she began keeping a record and found they were having it an average of five times a week. I think Liz in *Chez Nous* should produce such evidence when Dick complains.

[She did and said, 'I collated the figures and went to him and showed him and I said, "Now just you look at that!" We were well above the national average published in the *Guardian*.']

At the door of the 100, in deserted Oxford Street, when Mary said we were with Geoff, the manager looked at me. 'Yes, you're his father, aren't you?'

This amused everyone, especially the wives and my college friend Bernie Cooper and his Nigerian wife, who showed up briefly before going on to celebrate midnight mass.

We danced the year in to the Avon Cities, forming a long line that climbed over chairs and tables and across the bandstand and I shouted to Thelma that there was one sure consolation for living in this century and that was jazz.

1973

Monday 1 January

Began well with beer and dancing, good company and my brother's jazz band.

Evening of New Year's Day, saw John Osborne's *A Sense of Detachment*. Many good jokes and fierce feelings. Only a footnote to more serious stuff but I'd rather see his notes than most people's masterpieces.

Quite early on, a boozy Tunbridge-Wells type man in the stage box shouts, 'That's not funny, old man, I'll give you a kick in the pants. Boom!'

The 'Osborne' spokesman says, 'He cribbed that from Peter Nichols.'

And someone else says, 'Well? He cribbed it from George Doonan.' (See pp 211–12.)

Elsewhere: Howard Hughes fled the Nicaraguan earthquake, was let into England without a passport and put up in a penthouse suite on Park Lane. If he exists, he's an insane miser and a good example of why capitalism's rotten. At least we could save such people from themselves by the painful but beneficial surgery of cutting off their dividends.

Britain went into Europe. Nixon stepped up the bombing. Distillers Company fought hard not to pay compensation to the children crippled by thalidomide. Greenwich Park is open to cars again.

Tuesday 2 January

Chris rang: he likes *The Common*. He'd read it aloud, he said, to Joan in hospital.

'Oh, Christ,' I said, trying for a modest disclaimer, 'did she survive?'

And at once noticed his embarrassed silence and could have bitten my tongue off.

He said yes.

No resolutions, as last year's now look so sad, brave hopes that came to nothing because of my cowardice. Shall we move into London? Shall I get a workroom somewhere else, an alibi to get away, in case of miracles? The writer's abiding problem is that he gets so sick of his own company but daren't take too long away from it.

Saturday 6 January

School holidays seem to have lasted months. I'm not a good father to them. They spend too much time watching TV. To think that our two or three visits per week to the pictures were seen as decadent or lazy . . .

My guess about their futures:

Louise will be a good middle-class wife and mother, fond of sport and getting her own way.

Dan will be seriously involved in some dreamy solitary pleasure like drawing or writing or (less likely) scholarship.

Catherine will be a political activist, always first at the barricades, guitar in hand, flaunting her bastards.

[In 2000:

Louise is herself a teacher, after abandoned careers as a stage manager and film director.

Dan is a resettlement officer for Cardiff Council, leads a skiffle group and writes songs and screenplays.

Catherine is a solicitor in the legal deparrtment of Darlington Town Hall, dealing especially with child custody.]

Saturday 13 January

We lay awake, as usual, till nearly midnight, reading: for me André Gide, for her Albert Speer's memoirs. Turned off light and tried to warm each other. Woken by her voice.

'Did you hear that?'

'What?'

'A terrific noise of banging on the door of the black man's bus. And cars pulling up.'

She went to the windows, slid back the double-glazing, then opened the original casement, letting in the incessant night-and-day sounds of the Dover Road.

'One of the police has just fetched a paper from his car. A warrant probably.'

Together we watched the half-dozen uniformed men in a group beside the minibus. There was no sign of the occupant and by their patient attitude we guessed he was getting dressed. Thelma went back to bed and I reported from the window.

'Two more police cars arriving. Pausing. No. Going on. Black man getting out, fully dressed as always wearing his suit and black trilby hat. He's smoking. Now he's going round the bus checking the windows while the police stand watching. He's cool, I'll grant him that.'

Patsy Grigg had told me the postman delivers letters addressed to The White Bus, Dartmouth Grove. He knocks on the door and eventually a hand comes out, sometimes black, sometimes white, and takes the mail.

'Now they're urging him towards the police van (the Black Maria?) and he's getting in. They're driving off.'

Didn't go to sleep for a long time, wondering what to gather from this new episode. Whatever they're about – harassment, holding on suspicion, helping with enquiries, genuine involvement in a crime, eviction? – they'll have to tread very warily to catch him. He seems to know all the loopholes.

The sub-plot of *The Common* simplifies the situation and has his woman as black, not white as in life. And finally the residents succeed in having him removed and the bus towed away. In fact, his bus is still there and there's every likelihood he'll be back.

Tuesday 16 January

Saw two Beckett plays – *Krapp's Last Tape* and *Not I*, which being only ten minutes long, was given twice. The first had Albert made up like Scrooge again, the second Billie Whitelaw's lips, isolated in a spotlight.

We applauded again and filed out. I almost expected a collection plate to be passed round. Beckett's now the great cult-figure of Western letters (I nearly wrote 'French'). Honours are heaped on his uncaring head. He continues regardless to write beautiful prose and to pursue his doomed campaign of purifying the theatre. Which is like being vegetarian in an abattoir.

Wednesday 17 January

Began third draft of *Chez Nous*.

Blakemore rang to tell me Patrick Garland doesn't want to do the Orwell.

'The trouble is, Pete, there's not a lot of glory in this for a director.'

'There's not much for me either and I've just spent a year on it.'

Sick of directors and their arrogance, I wondered whether to direct the new one myself at Greenwich.

Thursday 18 January

A 'surprise' arranged by our mother's helps for us and the Griggs to turn up for adjacent seats the Coliseum for *Die Fledermaus*. Delightful. Good tunes, well sung in English. Oddly old-fashioned audience, people out for an inoffensive evening of waltz, czardas, comic-drunk acts and gallons of fizzy water in plastic glasses. They applauded loudly as the curtain rose on a ballroom in pink light with filigree bandstands and lighted chandeliers.

The show confirmed specific fantasies, as do Tretchikoff's Burmese Girl or Shepherd's Rogue Elephant. A mindless euphoria such as you never find at The Royal Court.

Tuesday 23 January

Too early arriving at the *Evening Standard* Awards lunch and ran the gauntlet at the hotel entrance – of weird fans, some with books, some cameras, and of staff reporters for the paper that hosts the affair. No rival periodical will pay any attention, obviously, and it's halfway between a ready-made scoop and a works outing. A good half of the guests at any table are *Standard* employees.

Charles and Val Wood had driven through the fog from Bristol to receive Best Comedy for *Veterans*.

'I had a letter from New York today,' Charles said, 'from Gielgud, telling me he'd got the gong for Best Actor and thanking me for writing such a lovely vehicle. I suppose it was natural for him to assume the play wouldn't get it. Won't his face be green when he hears Larry's getting the acting one again?'

'Why don't you tell us that in your speech?'

'Oh, I couldn't. Shall I?'

'Why not? Those bloody old men are so vain and puffed-up. They get it all their own way and take it for granted everyone loves them.'

'And who's presenting my award? Ralph Richardson, who so hated the play that he advised Gielgud not to go with it to the West End.'

I think Charles may still have played the game and shrugged off these insults if Richardson hadn't given such a boorish introduction. The assembled sycophants laughed so heartily that it stung Charles into hitting back. Richardson didn't mention the play's title at all and at the last moment forgot (or affected to) Charles's name and fumbled in his pocket for a crib before saying it.

'I knew he wouldn't mention the play,' Charles said when he got up there, 'because he sat two rows in front of me and slept all through.'

Then he read the gist of Gielgud's letter. I cheered but most sat on their hands. You mustn't knock the knights. And these sweeties are still thought of by some innocents as gypsies and vagabonds.

Tom took Best Play again, Olivier was cataleptic with humility and Lauren Bacall was respectful beyond the call of duty and, thank Christ, at last Frankie Howerd came on with licence to mock the whole proceedings.

'What I always feel on these auspicious occasions, as I stand here in this distinguished company, watching the winners receive their honours and all that, is the almost tangible quality that pervades the day, that special and intangible *dreariness*.'

And the very same people who'd cheered the knights now cheered him.

Wednesday 24 January

To Gloucester Crescent, dinner with Claire and Nicholas Tomalin.

The news today was of a cease-fire in Vietnam; Kissinger and U Doc Tho grinning and waving for the cameras. Casualty figures for the whole war are still provisional, as the coming of peace prompted last-minute Vietcong land-grabbing attacks to gain ground before the treaties could draw a line.

Connie Chapman's doctrinaire son, Mark Cousins, saturation-bombed us woolly liberals with his merciless views, defoliating us of our half-baked sympathies. He even seemed sorry the war was ending, it had all been such bad PR for the US and capitalism.

Another guest, a young man whose name I never caught, had been in Malaysia. Nick and I had both served there when it was called Malaya, Nick in 1948-50. I told him I'd come home in the year he arrived, when the serious so-called 'emergency' had barely begun, with a few tentative bombings in Singapore. Nick left the table and returned with a metal disc showing a relief head of George VI, with a few inches of green and purple ribbon and across the top the word Malaya. He pinned this medal to my shirt and said I deserved it more than he. And, when I protested, he said, 'It wasn't for gallantry or anything. I was only in the band.'

'Well, I was only in an entertainments unit.'

He wouldn't hear of my giving it back.

[And, twenty-six years after he was killed in Israel, I still have this undeserved award, the only one I got for my Far East national service.]

Claire and I talked of our children. She's had four, of whom one's dead and another has spina bifida. The young man said that fatherhood was an experience that would always be denied him. So he was – what do we call them these days? 'Queer' seems prejudiced and spoils the original use but that goes for 'gay' too, which is what they're calling themselves. I learnt that word, oddly enough, in Malaya in '47.

[And used it in *Privates on Parade*, set in that period, which caused several people to doubt my accuracy. I was able to point to the supplement to Partridge's *Slang*, in which 'gay' for 'homosexual' is given as 'since 1930 or much before'. It was, of course, a word from parleyaree, the secret argot they had to use with each other during those dark days, so it was never seen in print.]

He told of hitching a lift in America and taking the chance to use the comfort station when the driver stopped to refill his truck with gas. Returning, he found the man standing by the vehicle, gesturing to him to keep away. He did so, standing back, looking about uncertainly till the driver turned and threw a wad of Kleenex into the ditch and waved him back to the cab.

'I'm going to the whorehouse when we get to town,' he explained, 'so I was jacking off.'

'For fear of coming too soon?'

'Right.'

'Jees, I'd never risk that.'

The trucker looked at him sideways. 'Well, twice ain't so much, is it?'

At my age, I reflected, once is all, at least with my familiar partner. But with someone else . . . ?

Mark's wife Jane arrived after dinner while he was lecturing me on Chekhov. Together, they sprayed napalm over our nuances and jokes. Finally it transpired that we were expected to drive them home. They disapprove of cars and only use other people's.

All the way to SE10 they gleefully listed those not yet exposed in the Poulson corruption case. Their inside information was totally plausible; only their vindictive relish was a turn-off. The Poulson scandal's pretty rotten but Jane and Mark's puritanical *in*corruptibility is worse. And these people are on our side!

Friday 26 January

Joan Morahan looked old and wasted. She told us, almost in tears, that the drugs are making her hair fall out, which we could see for ourselves. More in control though, chatting coherently, with no sign of dozing.

Brian Phelan also came visiting, a quiet Irish playwright and a very different sort of Socialist. He'd had miners staying with his family during their strike. After watching Brian's domestic life for a few days, one old Scottish Communist asked, 'Why does a Conservative like you want to help our cause?'

'He couldn't grasp the niceties at all, you see. We were pretty well off, we live in a decent district, so how could we possibly be anything *but* Tories? Wealthy Socialists weren't just an anomaly but an impossibility.'

Eve: *Three Sisters* at Greenwich. Full house to see the film star Mia Farrow. But what could husband André Previn find to say to her afterwards – 'You were beautiful'?

John Grigg's view of Chekhov: a writer of fine social comedy, like Austen. She lacked the prophetic dimension, granted, and looked backwards but perhaps it would have been better for Russia if they'd looked forward less. I asked if he thought the Stalin era inevitable; surely he was a terrible accident?

'But it happened in Germany too. Remember that, as soon as he got in, Lenin suspended the constituent assembly.'

'In that chaos, he probably had to. Wasn't it better than remaining in that sloth described by Chekhov, Gogol and Gorky?'

'But Russia was in every way progressing towards a liberal modern state. The Kerensky government would have been superseded without a revolution, which the majority didn't favour anyway.'

Friday 2 February

Our cleaner from Belfast, Olive Taylor, also chars a few hours a week for the Nortons next door. One day, after her stint for them while they were out, she came back asking for Thelma, who'd gone shopping. She'd answered when the phone rang and a male caller asked her to leave a message for Dr Norton.

'Wouldn't you like to ring back later and speak to the doctor himself?'

'No, you just write down what I say and pass it on.'

She was embarrassed about her spelling, she said, and gave me the message to correct and copy out in neat.

'From Dr Carmichael regarding Mrs Johns. This patient likes to put on leather underwear and masturbate with a rubber penis.'

I've forgotten the rest now but copied it all faithfully while Mrs Taylor giggled in the background. I asked if she thought this a bit un-professional, giving all this private stuff to a stranger?

'Not only that. He asked me to read it back to him afterwards.'

That evening Alan Norton called me to the fence between our gardens.

'There's no Dr Carmichael. It was a dirty phone-call. Common occurrence. Receptionists have to put up with a fair bit of that.'

Wednesday 7 February

Peggy rang: she's heard from Sonia Orwell who doesn't like *Beasts of England*. She wouldn't say exactly why because the letter was confidential.

'She simply says she doesn't like the way it's been adapted and asks me to tell her what she should do.'

'Oh, well, let's drop it. I can't bother with it any more.'

After Olivier, Blakemore and Peggy had all disliked it, I'd more or less put it from my mind. Only Tynan had kept the project going. I'm relieved not to have to pander any more to the widow's whims.

'I just don't know, dear,' Peggy went on, 'I'm more worried by the fact that you're breaking off from Blakemore. We *do* need a friend at court.'

'Do I owe Michael all that much after the way he's behaved over the Orwell? He started me on it in the first place, you know.'

[I should have paid more attention to this sound advice from a woman who knew her way around. Never having much relish or talent for what Kenneth Williams always called 'the business end' or 'the suck-off antics', I needed someone in my corner who enjoyed pacing the corridors of power. Anyone who lacks this aptitude should find a partner who has it, a lesson painfully learnt by me over the last fifteen years. The work itself comes at best a poor second to strategy. The wastage of gifted people in various trades is due more to this than any falling-off in achievement.]

Friday 9 February

Thelma's forty-first hard on Dan's tenth. I gave her a silver coaster and together we went shopping for a new stereo unit for the kids. The mono player we bought to cheer ourselves on the day Abigail's condition was confirmed has done ten years of sterling service. No planned obsolescence there, except that such machines are outdated by improvements. We tried this one in Chiesman's department store with a sound effects disc and all the casual browsers were transfixed by jet-planes taking off, a storm thundering behind the pianos and a steam-engine shunting through the paperback department.

Eve: took her for a meal in the Spreadeagle and, as we were finished and about to go, Joan Littlewood and Gerry Raffles came in after rehearsals at Stratford. They live in a grand white house on Blackheath so it's strange that in our five years here we've never seen or met her. We passed a message through the waiters and then she asked us to join them. Far less hectoring than I expected and more willing to listen. She's one important person I was hesitant to meet for fear she turned out intolerable. The most influential English theatre director since the war and creator of the best show, *Oh What a Lovely War*. There's a certain heartiness about her that explains her blind spots. Some words recur like mental crutches – 'clowns' (for artists and entertainers of all sorts from Homer to Barbara Windsor) and 'mafia' (for all crooks, from Harry Hyams to the councillors of Stratford East or Tunisia). But she's no fool, angel or ingénue, just has a strong sense of justice, and her spirited sympathy for the local people is heart-warming and shaming.

'You talk about undeveloped countries. Well, when we came back from two years in Tunisia, we realised that the poor sods in East London are the *real* underprivileged.'

Raffles is a large sweaty Bohemian with a Scouse accent, more moderate than her but with the same period flavour. They both recall the comparative innocence of the 1950s. Now we know they were fighting a losing battle, but they've had some stirring victories.

Monday 12 February

Everyone up early. Olive Taylor, arriving at eight to do her two hours' dusting. A great deal of tidying and generally improving the look of the place. I came upstairs to write the entry for yesterday and kept an occasional eye on the road. At quarter past ten, a mere fifteen minutes late, a dark blue Volvo saloon drew up and first out was a dark girl, presumably the features editress of *Vogue*. A young man with long Tudor locks was next. Finally Milord Snowdon.

He's short and neat, with expensively tailored Levi jacket and trousers to offset any suggestion of belonging to anything as naff as the Royal Family. When I hesitated over what to call him, he jumped in at once with 'Tony'. Thelma offered coffee but he asked to see my workplace first. Before coffee? Yes, please. I climbed the stairs at my usual pace, remembering too late that he limped from infant polio. I saw this was true, though it appeared not to trouble him. He looked doubtful at the sight of my banal, orderly room. Whatever he'd expected or hoped for, this wasn't it. He asked where I went when I left the house. The heath, Greenwich Park, Blackheath Village. None of these thrilled him. He looked out at the flat expanse of heath from my window and asked if we could go to the film location at the barracks. He meant the place they'd used for the film of *Health*, the imminent premiere of which was the reason for this session. I should have seen the red light then but didn't. While he drove us all, including Thelma, to Woolwich, we pointed out the local sights through pouring rain. Tony didn't care for the Frayns' house and at one point talked about Hansard roofs and I heard myself saying 'Mansard' and again could have bitten my tongue. Still a long way off a gentleman.

The stay of demolition had been lifted when the shooting was over and now the barracks were coming down. Tony got out, took off his dark glasses, which was a relief even to me, and told us to stay put. We could see him pulling rank with the Securicor man on the gate and they went off together. After a long cold wait, with stilted conversation and only the oxyacetylene cutters to divert us, he reappeared and went off with his team. Another wait and at last the editress came back and asked me to go in. Feeling a total clown, I posed on the corner of a stairwell, a pretty unnatural position to anyone not being photo-graphed for a fashion mag. Then he did me leaning on a barred door, which can only give me the look of a chronic inmate of Broadmoor.

Had he *seen* any of my plays? We went to another floor and in a damp little room, with paint and plaster peeling and lying in flakes, I sat on an upturned fire-bucket, chilled to the bone, in a half-demolished army barracks, being photographed by the husband of a princess. The chic of squalor! All those Balenciaga models draped over dustbins. And to compound the dishonesty, he and his assistant placed more flaking paint around me, as delicately as though it were French lace.

He drove us home but wouldn't come back into our warm, comfortable house. Thelma made hot soup while I ranted about the silliness of it all and my feeble submission. While they'd waited in the car for us to finish, the American girl had told her that Snowdon hadn't wanted to do me in my house because it was too tidy. He didn't see that as my image, despite its being the house I choose to live in, the real location of my plays.

Poor Olive. Not what *she* had hoped for either.

Friday 16 February

Little change in Joan Morahan, now back in hospital. This time we were the only visitors and could see how the need to conserve her energy to fight the illness has made her more interesting, more reticent. Though we talked still of trivial matters, she seems to have enlarged her sympathies and interests in the light of her own inevitable death.

Her supper was brought but she had no appetite and left it. One visitor who comes, she said, a writer, always gratefully eats up the food she doesn't touch.

After the meal, a morphia injection.

As we were preparing to leave, 'Don't try to kiss me,' she said, 'it's an awful long way down.'

She was probably thinking of our last visit when I tried to and slipped, almost falling on her frail, wasted, painful form.

Friday 23 February

Finished yet another version of *Chez Nous*, the third and, God willing, the last. Bored and fed up to the teeth with this pointless comedy.

Saturday 24 February

After a children's concert in the dear old Festival Hall (Walton, Debussy, Vaughan Williams's *Job*, a harmonica concerto), we ate in the cafeteria. There was a sexist division of labour here: I sat bagging a table, with Dan and Everard who busied themselves making Hadrian's Wall out of wrapped sugar cubes, while Thelma queued with the three girls – Louise, Cath and Everard's sister Faith. When she reached the cash desk with four trays of food and drink, the woman at the till said, 'You'll want some help. Here, you – Abdul – and what's-your-name – Mustapha? Take this lady's tray.'

The Iraqis or Pakistanis or whatever-they-were brought them to our table, giggling and muttering because the woman had evidently only approximated and was in effect calling them Sambo and Rastus. The other waiters, all dignified black men, were noticeably more intelligent than white natives who do such menial jobs.

This was an anomaly in such an egalitarian building. But that idealist age is gone, the hall one of its few monuments. Evelyn Waugh hated the Festival of Britain and all it stood for ('Monstrous constructions appeared on the south bank'). Then what would he have made of later additions like the Hayward, which also express their times – brutal and windowless, standing among bleak and windswept piazzas, their concrete stairways leading nowhere, epitomising our return to barbarism?

Monday 26 February

A real treat on TV: Betjeman in Metroland, retracing the grandiose scheme of the railway north of Baker Street, which was to have linked Manchester with Paris but managed only to stretch from New Cross to Aylesbury, Bucks. En route, he found houses by Norman Shaw and Voysey, the pond where W.S. Gilbert drowned, the crowning of Chorley Wood's Carnival Queen, an intrepid walker of Neasden's nature-trail and another who had bought the mighty Wurlitzer from the Empire, Leicester Square, and had it reassembled in his Harrow living-room. He played steam-train noises and 'Varsity Drag'. Cut to Betjeman's uncertain face suddenly breaking into a smile of joy and admiration.

['Thank God for the telly!' as he himself said, years later, when he was allowed to escape a dinner-table to watch *Coronation Street* in the next room.]

Wednesday 28 February

Gill Frayn and Thelma shopped and Olive Taylor walked two miles from her home, all the buses being full, to clean our house.

Peter Hall rang: he wants me to continue with the Orwell script, as he thinks it could work in another form that Sonia would approve. Doubtful.

Over lunch, Thel reported Gill's account of sitting by Harold Evans at a party [then Editor of *Sunday Times*, later moving to New York with his next wife Tina Brown. I borrowed bits of him for Agnes's dead husband in *Passion Play*]. He told her he'd wasted his youth as a virgin and envied the freedom of modern 16-year-olds. He'd been excited by erotic temple sculpture in India and, since coming home, had been going through all the positions, one by one, with his wife.

Thelma said we must go to the village to post my mother's birthday present and my niece Tessa's and buy cards to them both from us all. I said I'd hoped we could pass the afternoon more pleasantly than that and she said that if we hurried we'd have time for that too.

Hardly home again when Albert Finney rang to bend our ears for an hour about the bad notices for his opening last night.

Finally the day did turn out pleasant and I was resting in the bedroom, when Catherine arrived home from school and Thelma went down to see her. She soon came back to change out of her housecoat, saying, 'Poor Cath had to bring all that metal back up the hill from school, all alone. She agreed to because she thought Alexander Grigg was going to help but Patsy picked him up in the car to go somewhere else.'

'All what metal?'

'The metal she and Alex have been collecting for the Blue Peter Old People appeal.'

I lay watching in a post-coital doze as she got out of her housecoat and pulled on her pants and dropped her breasts into the bra.

'I thought they'd already achieved their meals van at Christmas,' I said, 'wasn't that their target?'

'Well, they're going on with it now to buy them some meals as well.'

'Not much point in a meals van without, I suppose.'

'She and Alex have been collecting metal ever since. They've got the address and want to send it off but by post it'll cost far more than they've got. I'm very cross at the way these telly people have got the poor kids traipsing back and forth with this load of scrap. Yet I don't want to pour cold water on her enthusiasm. Perhaps we can take the metal out tomorrow in the car and dump it somewhere and tell her you've sent it off.'

'Why not?'

These schemes are a sell. They only work if you pay colossal sums to *send* this stuff they collect. The cost is not in the collecting, that's the fun part, but in the *getting it there*, which the parents have to in the end.

I went to my study to write the day so far – calls from the famous, shopping, sex, metal collection – but hadn't got far when Lou called me for tea. Downstairs more turmoil, the girls dressing for ballet-class and being badgered by Thelma to sign Nana's birthday cards, which we'd chosen and bought. She appeared with tea and crumpets. How does she *do* it all – and why can't she forget to once in a while? I told her it had been a funny day and she was soon howling at me for taking all this for granted.

'Finished?' she snapped, taking the tray.

'Yes, thanks.'

'That was a waste of time then.'

'What? It was terrific, very nice.'

'Oh, wonderful, he's said something at last. Hooray!'

After that, the usual row and the usual patching-up. Her guilt's so strong she can't luxuriate. Though God only knows what she's got to be guilty about. She's lived an exemplary life.

Thursday 8 March

The end of the latest wage-freeze, that right-wing remedy for every social disorder, has brought a relapse into strikes of all kinds. Hospital porters and orderlies are out, leaving piles of soiled laundry to be destroyed for fear of infection. Maternity, child and geriatric services are the worst affected. Patsy asked Thelma if she'd mind doing some bed-linen for Lewisham hospital. My dear wife said staunchly that of course she wouldn't touch it, and not out of fastidiousness. Here were some of the worst-paid groups of people doing filthy work on which the nation's health depends, using their only weapon (with-holding labour) to draw attention to themselves. She, a shop-steward's daughter, was being asked to break their strike?

Other trades are out too – gas-workers, teachers and train-drivers. Are they too to be morally blackmailed because they do essential jobs? The Christian ethic that consoled the oppressed and enabled oppression to continue has at last been shown the door. It's a good time to be rewriting *The Common*, my most didactic play so far.

Wednesday 14 March

We were at breakfast when the telephone showed itself to be a satanic tool, violating our lives in ways no human can manage.

First Peggy rang, having read *CN*, raving that it's not only my best so far but – 'I mean this in the least offensive sense, dear, your most commercial'.

We discussed how and where to get it done and the matter of Michael B directing, and decided to wait for Albert's reaction to playing the part of Phil.

I put the phone down and began again on the bacon-and-egg that Thelma had kept warm, when it rang again. She answered brightly.

'Hullo? . . . Yes, Chris? How are you? . . . '

By her side of the duologue, I knew he was telling her Joan was dead.

Two calls with hardly a break, one full of future, the other a cold finality. Thelma recited the correct clichés – a blessing, given the circumstances a blessed release . . . let us know about the funeral . . . we're so sorry.

I finished my breakfast.

Friday 16 March

To Dulwich School to see the boys (and girls of Mary Datchelor) do *Troilus and Cressida*. Andy Morahan had sprained his wrist and wouldn't be appearing but Ben was on the lighting.

This was the first time I'd seen it acted. Full of interesting lines, scenes and ideas, with sudden startling glimpses of the author's burgess capitalism, a tradesman currying favour at court. And elsewhere savage rancour and lyrical romantic passion. Made me want to see it in modern dress, without all those skirts and swords. Or do it.

Saturday 17 March

First cold of the year and a right bastard that makes up for all those I avoided. Tried walking as a change from sneezing, sniffing and profuse sweating, and was going along Dartmouth Grove beside the black man's bus when a couple approached from the heath, obviously American by their honey-colours and too-clean garments. Some odour of sanctity about them suggested that they were guests at the ecumenical diocesan house beside our church, where zealots of the world gather in swarms.

'Where the hell does that leave me?' I was surprised to hear the man angrily demand of his morose woman companion. Then he saw me coming, flashed me a radiant smile and said, 'Greetings!'

Tuesday 20 March

Back to Dulwich, along the toll-road where you pay two shillings (or 10p) to drive through a bit of south London. The interior of St Stephen's seems to have been done over, all Tyrolean beams and brightly coloured woodwork, very fresh looking. High Anglican, someone said, but Joan's service was low enough – a few Victorian hymns, Nimrod variation (more or less) on the organ, an emotional rendering of something from the prophets by Mrs Brian Phelan. Brian was in a pew, along with a posse of playwrights – David Mercer (on sticks), Pinter, Stuart Douglass and John Hopkins in tears.

For the committal to the ovens, we drove to the crematorium at Norwood and the very chapel where Christopher filmed a similar scene for *Hearts and Flowers*. Leon Cortez, who played Uncle Bert, is dead too. I began counting while Joan slid out of sight – as well as these, Dad, Abigail, Mrs Medak, Hattie and Bert, Uncle Frank, Mary's mother have all shuffled off, though it was a relief to realise that only two were roughly from our generation and one of those a suicide.

Sunday 25 March

I'd decided earlier not to take Thelma to America this time, as she's not directly concerned with *Forget-me-not Lane* and it could be, in Peggy's famous words, 'like taking a ham sandwich to a banquet, dear' – but, as the time drew near, I began regretting. We reckon we've only been apart about two weeks in thirteen years. Kept making love but without real sensuality. Her insistence on lying down tends to make it – well, a ham sandwich that might have been a banquet.

Memorial Enterprises (Medwin and Finney) will option *CN* and we'll get Albert committed eventually. His only misgiving is that the part won't stretch him at all, won't be any challenge, though he also feels attracted to a commercial venture after months of Beckett and Storey. Everyone now sees my play – a box-office draw. Peggy's overjoyed that at last I've given her a boulevard piece without a nasty side that could put off the carriage trade.

Monday 26 March

Monday midday, stomach churning at the prospect of adventure, I drove with Thelma to the terminal and sadly kissed goodbye.

Air India piped sitar music (a musical anomaly) as a few hundred of us went aboard their 707. A soiled plastic bag handed to us by a sari'd stewardess contained a pair of eye-shields, slip-ons for the feet, a ball-point pen, a badge of a bowing Sikh on a card with the words 'with my salaams' and other pictures of bazaars, temples and polo at the Calcutta Club. Formica murals on the walls of the aircraft were of discreetly erotic temple sculpture. A suggestion from Harold Evans?

Arvin was at Kennedy and drove me to New Haven, Connecticut along a freeway jammed with huge cars.

[Arvin Brown was at this time and for twenty years to come, artistic director of the Long Wharf Theatre, a toehold in America for English writers, presenting premières of Storey, Frayn, Bernice Rubens and me, casting them with both good regional-theatre actors and sometimes bigger names like Richard Dreyfuss, Jim Dale, Chita Rivera and Stockard Channing. His productions of native plays attracted the likes of Pacino, Robards and Woodward.]

Scenes of appalling ugliness in the industrial hinterland of New York and chock-a-block urban freeways showing that the jeremiads are right about roads only creating the traffic to fill them. Six times or so Arvin took small change from a stock all drivers keep on their dashboards, hurling nickels, dimes and quarters into a metal basket at the turnpike. By nine p.m. (the early hours of morning for me), we reached his wooden house across the road from Long Island Sound, over which of course the Old Sport himself gazed at the winking green light of his lost love. Inside, through the usual American gloom relieved only by Tiffany-lamp-shaded low wattage lighting, I just about made out his wife Joyce in a safari-suit. She used the phrase 'fine human being' several times in the first few minutes but was very nice all the same.

They mixed Martinis, chargrilled some sizeable steaks and followed with fresh strawberries.

When they saw my jet-lag was making me nod off, Arvin drove me to the Plaza-Sheraton in New Haven itself. Crossing the strip of false grass before the revolving doors, we heard swing music and a sign in the lobby told us Woody Herman's band was doing a one-night stand in the Top of the Park restaurant. He's one of the leaders quoted in the play I'm here to see – *The Woodchoppers' Ball* preferred to *Peer Gynt* by the wartime juveniles. And still doing gigs!

I learnt later that the nylon grass bit is called a Leisure Lawn, and that rhymes with seizure.

[Of course, it would have cost a packet to sit and listen to that band without eating but now how stingy that seems. I should have responded to the happy omen by paying up, even if I'd only heard one number before falling off my chair with fatigue. Hearing the latest Herman herd would have been the perfect welcome to America.]

Tuesday 27 March

I breakfasted on tasteless scrambled egg (you're expected to add taste yourself from various bottles), real orange juice and excellent coffee, at once replenished, as was my glass of icy water. Hot, not lukewarm, toast and preserves in foil sachets: 'With a name like Smuckers it has to be good'. The waitress made me feel, by her upward inflections, that nothing would give her greater pleasure.

'How are you today? . . . . *Al*righty . . . Surely . . . More cawfee? . . . You're welcome . . . Have a nice day.'

And I did, walking out to find old New Haven a beautiful town. On the green, three of those attractive chapels that come to mind at the words New England – dazzling white with a façade of wooden Doric columns, relieved by the red brick of the body of the kirk.

'But they were locked,' I told Arvin later.

'Oh, well if you're going to be *pushing*, Peter.'

He has a loud and encouraging laugh and a nifty sense of humour, characteristics that make his company enjoyable.

I soon sensed the curious emptiness that we'd known on our stay in Wisconsin. So few humans on the streets. Perhaps it's after south-east

England, but outside New York America feels deserted. Are the people all in cars?

On the Yale campus: more quiet streets. At the entrance to a quad, a donnish figure emerged with gossiping youths, so I went in there and explored the courts and squares of the university. I was the only living creature. Of course the colleges are down at the moment, so the place is quieter than usual. These Victorian halls are of stone, but the predominant and charming feature of the town's everyday buildings is that they're mostly of wood. Americans I've so far met have little feeling for the porched houses, often painted dark green, brown, grey or purple, with turned columns or intricate carved frames for the doors, roofs steeply pitched to cope with their severe winters, the whole thing standing not in a walled or tended garden but an open plot of unfenced grass with the box on a post at the roadside for the mailman. It may be the echoes of Andy Hardy or Norman Rockwell that make them unable to enjoy that part of their native scene.

Arvin fetched me at eleven and drove me to a desolate area where the Long Wharf company has been donated a rehearsal room. A nasty moment came when he told me they couldn't use the six-door setting as in England because their theatre has a three-sides thrust stage, with a wrap-around auditorium. They had instead an elaborate lot of levels and stairs and rostra, which it had been our particular pride to have avoided. Why not *less* doors? One or two? That wouldn't do here, as less is worse, waste is virtuous, frugality equates with poverty. This goes not only for goods of all kinds but words too. On TV, in studio discussions, logorrhoea is king. There are no barbs, no knives, just padded gloves and a lot of dreary feinting and now and then slugging. 'At this present moment in time . . . thank you indeed, sir . . . in your estimation . . . that would not be a correct evaluation . . . ' A solemn people, despite their great humorists and habitual wisecracking.

The rehearsals were a pleasant surprise, the English accents far better than a company of ours doing American. Everyone trying hard, *too* hard when it came to the emotional scenes. But to advise them to do no more than is set down for them is to question their *raison d'être*, which is for each one to display and explore his parent-problem.

In the evening, some guests came over to watch the Oscars. Though Arvin and one or two others made fun of this, it's obviously their royalty-substitute. Brando refusing his award is like Edward VIII's abdication. It was the lead item in the news bulletin that followed.

Friday 30 March

Rang home once so far. Thelma was out so Sylvia put the children on. Cath and Dan tended to shout and he eventually said 'bye-bye' and rang off. Within ten minutes, Thelma called back and we swore how much we're missing each other and I said I wish she *had* come. After all, theatre companies are hopeless places to find available women. Actresses are rarely pretty. There *is* a beautiful blonde of Norwegian stock who usually does props but in this show is playing Miss 1940, the roller-skating fantasy figure. At the Oscars party, she told me about her visits home to Norway to see aunts and uncles in villages where everyone's over seventy. I was wondering about my next move when Joyce brought up some admirers to meet me. Somehow I fumbled the chance and let the girl drop out of the circle. When I finally got back to her, Astrid was saying goodnight and going home.

> [Years later, I was in New Haven again for rehearsals of *Privates on Parade*. With me this time came Denis King, who had set my words to music. He and Astrid met, and she later divorced her husband and came to London, became Mrs King and she and Denis still live a mile or so away from us.]

I talked to the company in terms of Noël Coward to describe the English style. He died the day I arrived here, only a week after Binkie Beaumont, so they'll be able to camp all over God's heaven, arm-in-arm.

Saturday 31 March

The eating and drinking: a single portion of beef would feed our family of six. Doggy-bags are provided and most of the meat is taken home for Henry, a terrier about eighteen inches long. On TV militant consumers complain about food prices and Nixon tries – and fails – to freeze them. It never occurs to anyone to provide or consume less. The

Sunday Times is as heavy as a family Bible and nine-tenths adverts. Everywhere's over-heated. The cars are immense. Like Gulliver in Brobdingnag, I somehow force my way through the fruits of freedom.

A fat man interviewed me for the *New Haven Register* and on Saturday took me touring the local scenes. A fag, clearly, but I kept mentioning my family and he never so much as touched my knee. The first stop was Essex, which he told me his father had worked hard to preserve, as he virtually owns the en*tire* town. One of his parents' homes was a white palace on the waterfront in the midst of an elegant garden.

'I'd ask you in for a drink but we'd best get on.'

He himself has a 76-acre farm on a mountain. He dropped out of Harvard because it was too embarrassing being upper-class in the egalitarian climate of the time. He's a spoilt rich boy, a snobbish queen, his uncle Henry Cabot-Lodge, but not flashy, gentle in manner and good company.

We'd just finished our tour of a preserved nineteenth-century theatre when a swing bridge opened to let through an enormous oil-barge, towed by a little tug.

Next: East London, where Eugene O'Neill had grown up.

'No wonder he hated it,' he said, driving through streets of attractive white, green and maroon wooden villas. 'It's truly *aw*ful.'

'I'll have to take your word for that,' I said, 'to a visitor's eye these are charming.'

'Hey! So close together?'

This was the nub of the matter. What denotes *class* is how far you are from your neighbours. I asked what he thought of (old) London's terraces and he admitted he found them horrible. 'Row houses,' he said, with a camp shudder. Our own street is Dartmouth Row and I'm sure it would cut no ice with him that many of the houses are Queen Anne. They're just too close together.

We looked over the Harkness House, the real setting for *Mourning Becomes Electra*, now the O'Neill Foundation and smelling of gravy.

On to Stonington, an isolated and intact wooden town about which Tony Bailey wrote his amiable book *In The Village*. An atmosphere of bucolic fantasy, supported by hard cash – oil-lamps, ship's chandlers, old nautical charts, Baptist chapels converted into houses, and a board denoting the premises of The Portuguese Holy Ghost Society, Inc.

At one of these well-heeled homes, a child admitted us and a Latin servant asked us to sit and wait. The workers here are all dagoes, descendants of the original Portuguese fishermen. We waited among the Windsor chairs till an uptight middle-aged couple appeared, gave us Martinis and told us Tony shouldn't have used real names, he'd rubbed a lot of important people up the wrong way. They were just off to cocktails at the house he'd lived in, now rented by someone else. Why didn't we go round there?

Darkness had fallen and the streets were empty for Happy Hour. School Street is in the poorer part of town, easy to see by the closeness of the houses. The present tenant was at once welcoming, threw our coats on the bed and took us to meet another group of commuting out-of-towners.

When I was introduced as having a play at Long Wharf, a small man with a small beard shot questions at me as if to blow my cover.

'How many characters? One set or two? How many acts?'

They groped to recognise me and, when *Joe Egg* was mentioned, looked even more suspicious, darting looks between them, and the hostess said she thought that was by an American.

The couple from the first house drifted in on the tidal swell that carried people up and down the street. After their brief stay, they floated off, followed by us. As we passed their house on the way to the car, they were coming out again, freshened up for the next flow and ebb.

I was enjoying the rich boy's company by now, especially the vulgarity that lay not far beneath his *class* act. Arriving for dinner at a huge restaurant – they call them 'inns' – he peed profusely on the manicured turf.

'Dying to do that in Stonington,' he said, zipping up his flies, 'but I daren't ask in case she showed me something truly awful like the only bi*day* in town.'

During more aperitifs he left the table and didn't return for fifteen minutes. I was wondering whether he'd seen there was no joy with me and decided against paying the check. Was he even now speeding away fast up the freeway? If so, how was I to get back to New Haven? But he came at last, saying he'd had some intestinal problems.

Thursday 5 April

The next week was dress rehearsals, previews and the opening. Technical runs seem to stimulate rather than confuse them. Even the actress playing Joan Hickson's part managed to learn a few of her lines. Everyone kept telling me she was a genius and in a week or so would have 'become' Amy. This isn't what one asks of an actress, of course, only that at given times, on cue, she can *pretend* to be Amy, who isn't a real person anyway but an invented character.

They rehearse from noon till four. Far more crucial, in the Browns' scheme of things, is when and where we eat. Arvin will say to me while driving us to work in his custom-built Mercedes, 'Peter, we have a real prahblem. Joe's eating with us tonight and can't take seafood. But Mary's joining us and eats nothing but. Now the best seafood restaurant' . . . etc.

In a sequence of enormous eating halls we picked, slurped and hacked our way through vats of clam chowder, prostrations of lobster and crayfish, and whole scenarios of Peking Duck. No wonder my fairy friend of the weekend had his prahblems.

Arvin's parents arrived from California, far further than Europe, a buoyant pair, touchingly proud of their son.

'Isn't it wonderful watching Arvin direct?' the father would whisper.

'This is going to be a terrific hit in Los Angeles,' they told anyone who'd listen.

'I'm in hardware but customers coming for bathroom fittings get a lecture on Thee-ayderr. We'd be so happy, Peeder, if you made it to California, be our guests.'

I'm in the ideal position for an affaire. Room 923 in my standard, anonymous, no-questions-asked hotel, heated to suffocation, with an en-suite bathroom and efficient room service. There are pretty girls in the cast. But, after so long, what few seductive techniques I ever had have atrophied.

The average age of the preview audience was twelve-plus. They identified only with Young Frank and hissed Mister Magic, the ageing conjurer, when he made a pass at him. He was played by an amusing queen called Henry.

'Thank God my mother's dead. I could never take these parts till she'd passed on.'

In the 'pub', late at night, Jasper the house manager told us of a two-headed goose he'd shown at the World's Fair.

'I won't allow geese onstage with me,' Henry said, 'or dogs or children or undressed girls.'

When Astrid appeared as the fantasy slave, 'Look at her,' he said, 'she's beautiful. I hate her.'

They didn't laugh enough but cheered at the end and the company seemed happy. Next day, after notes and tightening some loose bits, Arvin's secretary said she'd drive me to Kennedy. As I left, the company applauded and I remembered just in time to applaud back.

Friday 6 April

Thelma met me at Victoria looking marvellous. I drove us home and soon after that we went to bed, desperately, as though for the first time.

The kids had come home and opened my presents before I came down. They were watching a TV cartoon and scarcely noticed my arrival.

News: Chris Morahan grudgingly accepted *The Common Mk II*, saying its politics were too overt.

Peter Hall reported a depressing meeting with Sonia. He thinks we should forget the whole business and I agree.

In the night I rang New Haven and Arvin reported that Clive Barnes said he'd liked it, which was all that mattered. I was finding the adjustment hard and felt myself still in America.

[But had no time to be accustomed to home, as next day we drove down through France for two unrecorded weeks at Chez Magnou. There's no reason for the lapse of diary, except fatigue. I did manage to mention the improvements: a new tiled floor in the living-room, the old mangers and rotting granary floor removed from the barn; undergrowth and saplings cut back around the pond; new fruit-trees in the orchard – peach, plum, pear and apple; mains water has arrived at the front gate. The cherry-trees in blossom and water high in the well. But how we passed the time is lost.]

Tuesday 24 April

Long phone call with Peggy, who's off to stay at an oasis in Tunisia. I had cartoonish visions of a tiny pond in a vast desert, palm trees and camels watering. Then she tells me John Mortimer will be at the same *hotel*.

Vogue's piece on me came out. Monty Haltrecht's text too sycophantic. 'His eyes strike through', etc. One serious mistake: Abigail described as mongol.

Two of Snowdon's portraits, one impressive straight close-up, though grim and glaring, the other sitting on the upturned fire-bucket with peeled ceiling paint tastefully arranged about the floor.

'Bloody cheek honestly,' said Patsy Grigg, 'it looks as though you're on the loo being sick.'

I think he was wrong to come with a closed mind and not to change it when he saw my tidy suburban household. As the stuff I write is mostly domestic comedy, why show me as a character from Beckett?

To discuss *Chez Nous* with Albert F. That done, he talked about money and how, if he sold his house in Brompton Square, he could live at the Savoy on the interest for the rest of his life.

'I'd take the book I was reading at the time, leave all the others on the shelves. Apart from a dictionary, what d'you want with more than one book? Why own pictures, carpets and curtains?'

Perhaps he is, after all, closer to the old acting tradition of gypsies and vagabonds, though was never in fact working-class, his father a bookie, comfortably off. He paid Albert's fees to RADA and sent him five pounds a week, in those days more than many men were supporting families on.

'I got a cheque for a million dollars when they reckoned up the percentages of *Tom Jones*. I bought that Rolls but hardly used it. It was an embarrassment, especially in daylight.'

Thelma joined us from the salon and, when she told him her grocery bill was £20 a week for a family of six, he couldn't believe it.

Thursday 26 April

Nibs Dalwood's new studio is in a former Jewish school on Stepney Green. We reached it through Rotherhithe Tunnel and rang a bell or intercom at the playground gates. After quite some time, he appeared and let us in. While he was fiddling with padlocks, his new girl Rosalind Archer arrived on a bike. Large-boned, young and slavishly in love with him, not a dental assistant as we'd been told but a sculpt-ress as well. No, sculp*tor*. They led us past a yard full of that sort of modern sculpture that's all sheets of steel welded in various com-binations, then up white-tiled stairways smelling of turps and along passages to the assembly-hall that's now his workroom. Nibs is a crafty operator, using whatever mechanisms the system allows to further his own ends. This huge studio was wangled through Space, which is a sort of Shelter for artists lacking it. But he's left Carol, his second wife and their sons, installed in an equally large one in Maida Vale and, as far as I know, the most she can paint are her fingernails. He pays £8 a week here and has a free hoist for his larger pieces. He's never been far to the Left, more anarchist, but in middle age he's turning to Rightish or at least male Chauvinist. His charge against Carol is that she started dabbling in Women's Lib. Not a very admirable character, he's still good company in small doses. He showed us a huge thing in wood he's making for the Walker in Liverpool.

There was no sign of a dinner-table or bedroom, only a tiny door up a steep stairway leading to the attic room they seem to share, illegally as well as illicitly, as none of the tenants is supposed to live here. Later we went to the Good Friends' Cantonese restaurant. No Chinese cus-tomers, though, only braying middle-class and media people scooping rice into their mouths from little bowls.

After a final drink back in the school, we left. I envied his energy and youth, though he's several years my senior, and the night he'd be spending with his Ros.

Friday 27 April

At Greenwich, Tom Stoppard's production of *Born Yesterday* (in which play I'd acted the William Holden part in Edinburgh, Glasgow and Aberdeen). Tom was there entertaining O'Toole and Sian Phillips.

We felt the charm was wearing thin but that could be because I'm annoyed he's moved in on *our* theatre, translating Lorca and directing this marvellous Garson Kanin comedy.

Lynn Redgrave good as Billie Dawn and Dave King passable as Brock, certainly better than he'd been in *Lane* on tour.

'I loved that play,' he told me afterwards, 'though we made a few additions here and there 'cos some of our friends and family said they couldn't understand it. Like, when Davy Jones came on, I used to say – out-front! – "I was a good-looking kid in those days". That used to put them straight . . . ' When I mentioned the reviews, 'I don't take no notice of those bastards. Long as the arses are on the seats, that's all that matters.'

Monday 30 April

Making notes for *The Freeway*. Best to get on quickly, as P. Hall wants one from me for the new National.

To Goldsmiths College in New Cross for an intensive course in French speaking, three days each week of the summer term. Our group of about fifteen, all with little French but eager to improve. Our teacher is Jean-Jacques, a bright young man from Jersey with frizzy hair and steel-framed glasses. For the first hour we talked in a mixture of shy English and halting French about our clothes, jobs, families, visits to France and reasons for coming here. So few sounded happy in their work.

'Depuis quand êtes vous ingénieur de la poste?'

'Oh, beaucoup d'années. Malheureusement.'

After coffee, equipment was dragged in – film projector and tape-recorder – and we were all disappointed. We want conversation.

Tuesday 1 May

Reading Nigel Gosling's study of Leningrad and learning about the six-foot-seven horror-comic figure of Peter the Great. I knew nothing much beyond his Deptford episode, when he ruined Evelyn's hawthorn hedge. This was him on his best behaviour for the English.

Nothing like the way he carried on at home, cutting off the heads of two hundred insurrectionists in one day with his own hands; crippling the poor till they starved, to pay for his pretty palaces; torturing his own son to death, impaling his mother's lover. The empresses who followed were well up to scratch, especially Catherine, who had to have sex every day and her numerous lovers were auditioned by her friend, Countess Bruce. As Kenneth Williams would say, 'Can you handle the business end? Whoops, you're engaged.' Over twenty are known by name and the last was performing on the empress only an hour before she died of a stroke at sixty-seven.

And who's this, from somewhat later? 'He set up a vast and powerful network of secret police and a rigid system of thought-control. Education, literature, philosophy, science, history and art were strictly circumscribed and censored. Foreign travel was forbidden.'

When we consider Stalin, we should not forget Tsar Nicholas I.

Sunday 6 May

The latest Sunday newspaper extracts from Waugh's diaries included a visit to Combe Flory by a party of boys from Bristol Grammar 'led by an old queer called Garrett'. Great to read that, after having put up with that same Garrett's plummy snobberies for much of my adolescence. He was concerned only with his coterie of Sixth Formers and with luring celebrities down to impress them – Auden, Guthrie, Gielgud, the Spenders, the Astronomer Royal. But I'd have expected Waugh to like him, except for his well-known antipathy to 'buggers'.

[Mark Gerson, the well-known photographer of writers, took the iconic one of Waugh swaggering between the garden sphinxes. The novelist had agreed to his publisher's request for a new portrait only if a family group was done at the same time. Mark was met by the author with 'Are you a bugger?'

'No,' Mark said, without being quite clear exactly what he meant.

'Oh? I thought all photographers were buggers.'

He forced a cigar and half a pint of brandy on his abstemious guest and, only after he'd been violently sick, did Waugh show some of the charm he'd had when young.]

Tuesday 8 May

Greenwich Board: Mr Turk, the pedantic secretary, broke in at one point:

'You're suggesting we co-opt on to the Woolwich Young People's board from between three to five members. D'you think you could be more precise? Could we say, for example, four?'

Saturday 12 May

Sat next to Alan Bennett and Ronald Eyre at matinée of Hampton's *Savages*. Promised to see Alan's new play and meet for a drink afterwards but when we tried to book there were no seats left. He always has a star – Gielgud, More, Guinness (twice). How clever he is, despite his vague and homespun manner. He's very happy with Eyre's direction of the new one, *Habeas Corpus*.

Sunday 13 May

Last Waugh extract. I wonder if it might one day transpire that he was an atheist radical who thought deeply on the besetting problem of the fiction writer – i.e. how to exert a political or moral influence through one's work – and came to the conclusion we mostly do, that advocacy cuts no ice. So adopted this wonderful parody of a choleric toff to discredit the aristocracy. In which case he's done far better than all the earnest left-wing sniping.

Nibs and his girl Ros came for Sunday roast and we later played ping-pong in the garden. Can't make out why he has taken us up so busily but decided she might be dull to spend much time with. She's taken on all his characteristics, even the Bristolian accent.

Saturday 19 May

'Blackheath Fayre this afternoon,' said Thelma.

'How can it be? The sun's shining.'

But by two p.m. when it started, the drizzle was gently falling. We trudged about in our anoraks.

'Get your tickets,' said a tannoy voice, 'for Eltham Light Opera's *Pirates of Penzance* in aid of South London League of Limbless ex-Servicemen.'

The drizzle became a downpour and we came home for tea with the Frayns, John Hopkins and Shirley Knight.

Sunday 20 May

The Tynans' party for Ken's daughter Tracey's twenty-first was held in the auditorium of the Young Vic Theatre, formerly an Express Dairies cafeteria. It began quietly, though flashing and wheeling spot-lights were an omen of worse. Kathleen had sworn in advance there wouldn't be anything to frighten those of us who'd survived a world war.

'Who d'you think will tire first?' I asked Kenneth Haigh (the original Jimmy Porter), 'the spot operators or us?'

'They can go on for days,' he said, then told us about Tracey's life, a pig-in-the-middle modern girl caught between divorced parents living in two continents. She'd just dropped out of Sussex University.

Ken himself, in a pale safari suit, led us to Max Wall, hard of hearing and tired of his own act. 'I've been doing it for nearly fifty years.'

Kathleen, in silk trousers, introduced Eric and Joan Morecambe. Joan and Thelma took to each other and he was as funny in life as on camera, though the wrong-footing and compulsive joking could soon pall.

The noise was getting nasty by now. Famous faces flickered in the disco-lighting – Sellers, Minnelli, Bacall – posing on rostra or sitting out on leather cushions marked 'Watford Town, not to be removed from the ground'.

As we'd feared, records gave way to a live rock group, which drove everyone over thirty to the foyer.

'That was worse than the blitz,' said Eric.

We sat eating curry from paper plates and watching the showbiz Debrett arriving – Dudley Moore, the Mostyn-Owens, Tony Garnett. We were lucky to be among comedians – Peter Cook, John Wells and Frankie Howerd who was very serious: 'I don't care for these *big* do's. I prefer a small dinner-party where you can talk business.'

Kathleen dragooned us back inside to see a cabaret: John Wells with jokes about Nixon and Heath, Moore playing funny piano and finally Max as Professor Wallofski, an eerie invention, like a grafting of Dr Caligari's creature on to a hydrocephalic Hamlet. It was an act I'd been watching since the 1950s, first of all in the Chelsea Empire before that became a Reject Shop. The turn is as sad as it's funny. 'How desperate can a comedian get?' he suddenly asks after delivering some ripe old gag. He could have asked the same of his clownish rig – the Henry Irving wig, black jacket, white vest, ballet-tights and large boots. He'll sometimes stand staring out over the stalls, letting the laughter die, till the hiatus becomes too sticky for comfort. A truly misanthropic comic. When someone heckles, he admits he's rather deaf. One's always hearing of comedians 'dying' but I'd never seen it. Wall may have been self-critical but that only worked when he'd won approval. He had nothing to say to A.J. Ayer, trendy Tracey or her gang of cool mates from Sussex. I noticed that Morecambe and Howerd had left early on. Max felt the chill, cut his act short and went off with his eccentric dance.

Kathleen knew they'd made the wrong choice. Had it in fact been Ken's? Both Tynans seemed maladroit, considering what celebrated hosts they are. We saw them swooping about like flamingoes, avid for success, even at an age when they might have been looking for a quiet life.

Max passed me in the gloom and I said he'd been brilliant. He didn't meet my eye, just clutched my arm in passing. The image of his sad face was the end for me. We left with Michael Blakemore, who came late from a rehearsal of *The Cherry Orchard*, drank one glass, heard the noise, said 'The decay of the West' and turned to go.

Tuesday 22 May

French class. Much admire Jean-Jacques, who teaches in an East End comprehensive by day, then takes our evening class.

Took Albert and Anouk to dinner in the Café Royal's Grill Room. Arbroath Smokies, Boeuf Marco Polo, and strawberries, washed down with a Lynch-Bages 62. I signed a credit card for £40. I didn't 'pay' in any way that makes sense. The well-off don't 'pay', just sign a chitty.

Drove them home to Brompton Square, drank tea and admired their house, three dogs and six cats.

Wednesday 23 May

In the morning paper I read of the migrant workers from Spain, Portugal and North Africa on whose backs France's prosperity rests. The Paris *bidonvilles* or tin-can towns are among the world's most repellent slums. And last Sunday the colour supplements featured the new Elysée Palace interiors – silver swans on gilded tables.

I wish the antique glass of the Café Royal could shatter for ever and the carved cherubs go up in flames and the Lynch-Bages pour into the sewers.

Thursday 24 May

Paid for Greenwich's Bowsprit company to do their Wat Tyler play at our children's primary school. Invited Chris Morahan and designer Natasha Kroll, because a similar event is a recurring sequence of *The Common*. In the morning session four teacher/actors work with four groups. Chris paid very little attention to what was going on and they soon left, implying it had all been a waste of their time.

I returned in the afternoon to see the play, a nice bit of pop history, with the kids as knights, grooms and revolting peasants.

Afterwards a child called for three cheers for Mr Nichols.

'You shouldn't have looked so shy,' Louise complained on the way home, 'anyone who comes to the school gets three cheers.'

Anyway the whole event cost me less than half our meal in the Grill Room.

Saturday 26 May

Early start for a weekend at the Frayns' shared cottage in Gloucestershire. Motorway, country road and burgeoning lanes, all before sighting the Wootton-under-Edge radio tower like an interplanetary advance-guard waiting for instructions among the fields and cottages. Harold Evans's *Sunday Times* reckons they're almost as sinister. There's a grid of such towers all over Britain and the Regional Seats of Government (or funkholes) are all along their beams.

Spring in full cry; on sheltered banks the pungent scent of wild garlic, in hedges clusters of wild-flowers – forget-me-not, violet, vetch, red campion, herb robert; in the fields buttercups, daisies, clover, thistle, primroses and even, here and there, cowslips. Gill named those I couldn't.

We walked in sultry sunshine through the valley to fetch home a horse they'd arranged for the kids to ride. Jenny fell into a stream and Michael walked her back, as he not only has no interest in horses but actively dislikes them.

We found the unbridled pony in a field with two others of the equine persuasion and the girls tried to attach his/her/its bit. But in the end a youth in cut-off jeans did it for them. A proper man. Michael rejoined us, having driven over. He insisted that we take it back to the cottage rather than leave it there another day. Gill proposed the opposite motion, so once more we were caught in the crossfire of their polite marital skirmishing. Things were settled, as usual, in his favour. Though we all gave in, for the sake of a quiet life, yet we'd have to somehow get the beast home as he couldn't bear being anywhere near it. Thelma heaved and pushed and encouraged it along most of the muddy track, just managing not to be pushed headlong down the bank and into a bed of nettles. Once in the open again, it bucked and let fly with its hind legs. Children were no sooner mounted than they sobbed and had to be taken off. Thelma at last gave up, hot and tired, as we approached the last lap, a steep hill which there seemed no hope of coercing it to climb. I grabbed the bridle and slapped its haunches and tried to guide it up the incline, pushing hard on its downhill side and keeping up a stream of idiotic patter like 'clever boy!' and 'that's the style'. It could smell fear and knew I wasn't proper, kept pausing to graze, waiting with a horsy grin for my next effort. I managed to keep my feet from under the flailing hooves while it went galumphing upwards. We at last reached the summit, to Michael's unbounded admiration.

That night the poor thing spent in a nearby meadow and next day refused the saddle, so none of us ever rode it. Finally we did the return journey, much easier. Seeing the home field, he bounded to the others and they to him, fondly licking necks and frisking about, all as relieved as an Irish bomber's family reunited after one was taken in for questioning.

The excursion had been as miserable for the pony as for us but Michael's sense of duty had been appeased, for a while at any rate.

Eager only to work, I found a disappointment in my engagement book – lunch with Ned Sherrin, to meet Stephen Sondheim.

Worked till noon, finishing a first act of *The Freeway*: two to go, as I see it in the old length. Driving through Peckham, approached an articulated lorry on the offside on a one-way street and waited beside it for the lights to change. When they did, he began to swing round and across my lane and I saw that he'd be slicing the top off my car and, if I didn't look sharp, decapitating me as well. Luckily he too noticed and stopped in time, waving me on from his cab some yards above. We had to stop again at more lights after a hundred yards and I turned to find him on the road, banging on my door. I wound down the window. A small gingerish man, red in the face.

'You blind?' he bawled over the busy traffic's boom.

'Sorry?'

'You blind or what?'

'Was there something I should have –'

'My indicator, saying I'd be turning right. And you come up and park in my road. You could have been crushed to death.'

Before I could think how to answer, the lights changed and the other drivers were blowing horns.

'Bleeding car drivers!' he shouted, climbing back to his cab.

Once clear, heart beating fast, I thanked my stars I hadn't had time to reply. He was obviously in no mood to consider arguments against vehicles like his being on the roads at all. And very likely he'd been as much frightened as angry.

The meal in Ned's Chelsea home was provided by his Miss Godfrey: salmon, strawberries, Rhine wine.

Sondheim wasn't as benign as I'd expected, considering that his show *Gypsy* had opened last night to a standing ovation and rave reviews. He appeared not to like anything he'd seen for ages – Anderson's film *If...*, Max Wall, the new Ayckbourn, Mike's Chekhov – only his own musicals and *Forget-me-not Lane*. I coined a new phrase (new to me anyway) to describe the Chekhovian sort of comedy that I emulate – Funny Boo-Hoo – but he didn't respond to that either.

Monday 4 June

Catherine to St Thomas's to have grummets put into her ears. Small burrowing insects? Mediaeval woodworking tools? Churls? Fifteenth-century French for the curb of a bridle? No, a short plastic tube to drain exudation.

Reg and Win arrived from Bristol ('Not bad, eighty, eighty-five all up the M4'), en route to Amsterdam, Brussels, Paris and Chez Magnou.

He drove us to Lewisham to collect our tickets for a flight to Moscow. He toured the High Street for twenty minutes to find a parking place in which to wait for us, gave up and drove home, leaving us in capitalist chaos to deal with Soviet incompetence. Due to Intourist allocations, we'll be spending one less day in Leningrad, one more in Moscow, more hours at the Palace of Economic Achievement and miss Tsarkoe Selo (Pushkin) and Kateriniski Palace.

Walked back through appalling Lewisham. Surely somewhere between these extremes there could be a lively but serene habitat?

Monday 4 June

Travel agent rang: the embassy hasn't processed our visas so we can't go to Russia after all. He'd been there in person this morning to be met with shrugs and *niets*. We suspected it was the agent's fault for not allowing enough time for the wheels of Socialism to grind, slowly but exceeding small.

Tuesday 5 June

Cath was comatose after her operation. One of London's greatest outlooks was at the end of Seymour Ward but has been obstructed by a nurses' room being stuck between ward and window. They've shown their contempt for a view of river, Westminster Bridge and Houses of Parliament by painting funny bunnies on the glass.

I doubt if David Allford, my national service friend and senior partner of the architects who designed the building, would have made that decision though he might have defended to the death the nurses' right to put them there.

Wednesday 6 June

A proper man rotivated our front lawn, and took up the stepping-stone path which required a hop-skip-and-jump from everyone who came to our door, uprooted the roses and shrubs, laid new turves and planted laburnum, hydrangea, azalea and rhododendron. To help the new lawn survive the drought, I spend hours with hoses and sprinklers.

Friday 8 June

In our French class, a film-strip story of Pierre and Mireille describes a child saying to its parents, '*Ah, vous êtes gentils. Je vous embrasse.*'

After a shocked silence, Jean-Jacques explained that it's more common in France for a child to embrace its parents.

'They do in England too, when they're young,' said a middle-aged woman defensively.

'But we soon knock that out of them,' added a businessman I'd always thought rather stuffy. Shows how wrong you can be.

Saturday 9 June

Invited ourselves to David and Meg Mendel's cottage for the day.

Held up by a nose-to-tail traffic jam but enjoyed a *fête champêtre* sort of afternoon while their children and ours splashed in the pool. We ate the picnic Thelma had brought, drank sparkling wine, another young man from Israel strummed his guitar, David practised his flute and I picked out jazz and minuets on the harmonium.

Returned before dark, heard on news that the contents of a truck had fallen on a car killing three soldiers home on leave. The Belgian driver, needless to say, escaped unharmed. This accident had caused a six-hour jam. My play is set in the future but perhaps, by the time it's on, its central episode – a gridlocked motorway – will have come to pass.

Monday 11 June

My mother came to stay, with her brother Uncle Harold and his wife Doris from Vancouver. After a few minutes, helped by the one-by-one arrival home of the kids from school, we'd exhausted all our conversational topics.

Harold stared around the floor, like a schizoid subject trying to find his bearings. Suddenly he'd tune in, focus on one of our faces and deliver some truism or a gibe at Doris, often followed by his alarming sudden laugh. He must have had more at one time? To have joined the elite Royal Flying Corps in the Great War? Was he damaged by action, like Uncle Bert? Or did he never see any? Ground-crew perhaps? Of course. Family myth implies sorties over no-man's-land, silk scarves and jolly waves at Von Richthofen.

Whatever life he had Doris may have snuffed out. Fat, childish, child-*less*, semi-crippled, taking a regular Worthington to soothe her nerves.

'The doctor 'e gimme pills, ya know like for my nerves? But oo wants pills? I like a glass o'beer.'

They discussed their London itinerary.

'We could go to St Paul's Cathedral,' my mother said.

'Oooh,' whined Doris in her 'nervous' voice, 'I ain't never bin there.'

'Sure you did,' said Harold.

'I don't remember.'

'Sure you do. You had gas in the Whispering Gallery.'

Tuesday 12 June

Took them to see a West End musical. There was no question of car, bus or train so we went all the way from Blackheath to Piccadilly by cab, Doris oohing with fear, Harold saying 'They got all that over there'. What they have over there (in British Columbia) includes Old Kent Road, Waterloo Bridge and Lower Regent Street. He never says, '*We* got all that', always including himself *out* of any share in his adoptive country.

Wednesday 13 June

First reading of *The Common* at the BBC Acton rehearsal rooms. Good cast. Chris told me apart that Vivien Merchant had been terrified that everyone will see she's not a London bourgeoise but a Lancashire girl from a convent.

After French class, we found Harold and Doris watching a Bernard Shaw play on TV and Mum in the kitchen making yet more tea. She told us they'd been to Westminster on a pleasure-boat, preferring to see the Abbey to St Paul's.

'Don't say anything, will you?' she asked us in an undertone, 'only we thought it funny when they searched us at the door but I said it was because of terrorists. And when we got inside, they only let us sit in a sort of gallery, very small. And I was surprised to see that it wasn't a bishop speaking but the Prime Minister. And there was all the government behind him and the others facing.'

All the same, they'd been quite happy, especially when the MP for Bristol North got up to urge the building of a third London airport. But she wasn't sure they quite grasped that they hadn't seen the Abbey.

Thursday 14 June

Doris chats away, a running tap, while Vi and Harold smoke and sleep.

'That's nice. I like ut. S'nice. I sez t'arold, s'nice.'

And suddenly, prompted by Catherine's chatter, from a childless woman: 'I like t' 'ear the children talk. I 'ear 'em at 'ome, on teevee. They come on that show, with that guy – whatsisname, 'arold? Uh like 'im. He gets 'em talkin'. Uh like their answers. S'cute. They get five dollars.'

Saturday 16 June

Took them to sweltering Greenwich Park, where they sat in the sun as though having treatment while I helped Dan break in his new cricket bat and stumps. Tried to create an air-conditioned bench for them, with not too much wind or too much sun, not too shady and not too still.

Sunday 17 June

David Allford had noticed some weeks ago a small notice advertising a one-night stand by Jack Benny and at once booked four stalls. Since then there'd been no further mention of the show and all through a pre-show dinner in Charlotte Street we made nervous jokes about what we might find – Jack Bennett direct from Vegas, Jacques Benet from Moulin Rouge . . . But the Palladium was full and the band onstage, as always for American acts. After ten terrible minutes by a singing trio, the band went into the soupy strains of 'Love in Bloom' and almost before anyone knew it, there he was, not a day older than when we last saw him on that stage in 1952, sober-suited like any Coca-Cola executive, a Jewish wedding fiddler playing Carnegie Hall. We clapped our hands till they were sore. He let it die.

'I can't be *that* good.'

But he was. Twenty years vanished as he reprised the old routines, with some variations: the painfully recited joke ('I don't tell jokes') interrupted by the brash trio doing an encore – so that's what they were for! – the fiddle thrown across the floor at him by a churlish stagehand, the child who asks for his autograph and holds his violin and bow while he signs, then begins playing a showy virtuoso cadenza. His expression then isn't deadpan but frozen fury and fear.

The timing's masterly:

'This was in Waukeegan, Illinois (his birthplace, established by this time as a running gag that gets a little laugh at every repetition) – so long ago (pause) that our rabbi was an Indian (laugh, longer pause). He used a tomahawk (bigger laugh, longer pause). I want to meet that guy again one day (laugh, quickly topping it). And so does Mary!' (his wife, already shown, sitting among us).

There was one sticky moment when it seemed that after all geriatric sentimentality had got him. The child prodigy had left the stage after sharing a duet with him. 'What a beautiful child. Fourteen years old. I met her in Dublin when I was playing there. She'd never before been on any stage.' His affectionate look after the retreating girl and – fondly, in the approved manner of American showbiz – 'Fourteen years of age.' Then, as someone clapped, the sudden flash of anger: 'She's twenty-nine if she's a day!'

The Pinter of comedians, a unique master, born Jacob Bugelski, in 1894. So he's seventy-nine if he's a day.

My mother, uncle and aunt had watched Bogart on television.

''E sez, "Come on, baby". I seen 'um. Guy in Vancouver imitates 'um. E says, "C'mon, baby".'

Monday 18 June

We watched and waved them out of sight in the car we'd hired to take them safe to Paddington.

I adjusted the water sprinkler, hoping to keep the new lawn from drying into oblong turves like stale sandwiches.

Thursday 21 June

After lunch, Thelma put on her orange velvet kaftan over a blouse and skirt and I my black velvet suit and frilly-fronted shirt. Left the house at three of a warm afternoon. The Nortons saw us on the pavement packing our car-boot with hampers, one of which had just been aired of cat's smells from our last trip to the vet.

'Glyndebourne?' asked Alan. Right first time. John Cox, director of productions there, who's also on the Greenwich board and lives a hundred yards across the heath, had invited us to see his production of *The Visit*, Van Einem's opera from Dürrenmatt's play. He brought along the Chablis and a girl called Elizabeth.

Drove through the middle-class green belt between here and Brighton, one vast suburbia, at last joining a line of cars all driven by men in black jackets and ties.

'Isn't it nice seeing the cows and sheep?' bleated a matron, as if relieved to be among friends.

After leaving our food and drink in John's office, we looked at the organ room and made our way down through various gardens across a croquet-lawn to the artificial lake, where bottles of white and sparkling wine floated on lines, cooling for the interval. Another obstacle race for the Great and Good to show they can carry off any absurd forfeit imposed on them by the club committee. Most, in fact, didn't, for my money anyway. A dowdy Moss-Bros–looking scene, the women in curtain materials, the sartorial counterpart of the Morris Oxfords they arrived in. Two Indian women and our party brought some dash but otherwise . . .

The opera that began at 5.30 was a marginal event, a pretext. First act terrific, a strong production of a subversive story. The richest woman in the world returns to her native village with an offer of untold wealth if they will kill the man who jilted her, the real story, of course, their moral adaptation to the necessity of his murder. I looked about, wondering how long it would take this crowd to do the same?

During the hour-and-a-half break we ate asparagus soup, pigeon-pie, smoked fish pâté and a fruit-salad from our garden of mixed berries, red currants and rose petals. From nearby dressing-rooms came voices raised in scales and high notes as singers cleared their throats of wine. It was seductive, obviously. We returned to our seats.

'In the usual way,' said a horsy girl beside me to her friend, 'I see six or seven chums in any audience that I personally know but here I can't see *anyone*. What extraordinary people!'

After all the food and drink, I dozed through the second act. Shaw thought opera was an entertainment for audiences who hate music but they must hate drama almost as much. Who'd tolerate a new play done by a polyglot company, all speaking broken English, yet all meant to be from the same village? Applying those conventions to the picnic, we'd have had our strawberries floating in the soup.

[This outing was at once included in *The Freeway*, the posh couple caught in the enormous traffic jam in their evening dress while everyone else is dressed for a camp-site.]

Wednesday 4 July

Run-through of *The Common*. I made the mistake of going in by car, from Blackheath to Acton, across most of central London. Hundreds becalmed in the Marylebone underpass, appalling heat and noxious gas. Every time I leave the house while writing my traffic play, I feel how strongly it bears on all our lives. Nothing's of such pressing importance as the unreason of the private car and city streets used for heavy freight. Tanks in a living-room, because the streets *are* a sort of living-room, or were, and should be again, not car parks and rivers of hurtling metal.

My play came over as amusing and passably intelligent. Vivien isn't right but she does what she can, elocuting her words and pursing her lips.

In the canteen during break, at one table, three actors who'd all played various versions of Dad – Roger Livesey, Bill Fraser and Michael Bates.

Thursday 5 July

Polite letter from Ronald Eyre, the director, turning down *Chez Nous*.

Later an American rang to say he was an associate of the producer who's supposed to be moving (or redoing) *Forget-me-not Lane* in NYC. Was surprised to hear I haven't seen Walter Kerr's notice of the Long Wharf show in the *Sunday Times*, which he called 'devastating'.

What a filthy cheek these people have got! How do they get my number? Decided to change it and not tell anyone, but friends, not even Peggy. Anything they want to say can be written. The phone's another double-edged sword, like the car.

Friday 6 July

Last French class. We gave a farewell party at our place. They all turned up with surprising partners. The post office clerk didn't bring his wife but a girl. Was there a wife at home? They held hands all evening and when he left he gave Jean-Jacques a visiting card with, under his name, the slogan 'Deception With A Difference'.

Monday 16 July

At the BBC-TV Centre they were giving *The Common* a sumptuous production. Things have changed since I acted in a few serials and plays in the 50s, when they went out live and a repeat meant going in and doing the whole thing again. Or even since *Ben Spray* (1960) when actors still ran from set to set, changing costumes as they went, just off-camera. Today they recorded one sequence only, the dinner-party, as in a low-budget movie.

Thelma drove into the forecourt, the roof stacked with luggage for the summer in France, Sylvia and the three kids squeezed into the back of our inadequate car.

Tuesday 17 July

Down through sun and rain, several octaves of French weather.

Playing word games, using puzzle books. One page asked what various tradesmen and professionals do. They couldn't answer Choreographer so Thelma said, 'What they do particularly concerns you girls. Of the people in this car, you two would need it most. I mean, be most glad of it.'

'Sick-tablets!' said Louise.

They weren't sure of Upholsterer either but Cath suggested a man who climbed up poles.

Thursday 19 July

Nearly seven of an overcast evening, I'm sitting in Chez Magnou before a wood fire, listening to a baroque trumpet concerto. Hard to believe it was so hot at home. This part of France is often cool, despite Thelma's insistence that it's an inland Riviera. For people wanting sun this year, better rent a villa in Lewisham than Dordogne.

John and Sally Bray delivered the Deux Chevaux and updated us on the gossip.

'We've left the kids in England for the summer,' John said, 'bloody glad to get rid of them too, in many ways.'

The Salukis, of course, had stayed with them here and were at that moment scratching the insides of their car windows, aided by Polly Fisher, the boxer pup. Saluki-breeding is another of their get-rich-quick schemes that's so far come to nothing.

'The French won't bloody buy them. Let them off the lead for a second, they're liable to run for fifteen miles without drawing breath. Coursing hounds, you see. Bugger-all use to a Frog farmer.'

Monday 30 July

Monsieur Maze, scything grass outside Joanna Bullock's cottage, found an enormous toad but told us not to go near.

'*C'est une sale bête,*' he said. '*Un jour j'en ai trouvé et il fait pipi dans mon visage. On dit: villein comme un crapeau.*'

Tuesday 31 July

My forty-sixth. At breakfast they gave me old picture postcards bought by Thelma from a junk-shop and signed by the children, glimpses of life sixty, seventy years ago, now mass-produced as a half-joke. We trivialise the past. Why not? They're none of them alive to be insulted and better that than treating it too solemnly. Probably.

Louise gave me ping-pong balls, shuttlecocks and a badminton net. The barn's on its way to being a play-room, with tennis-table, dartboards and skittles, serving too as a cycle track on wet days. Every scene in *Chez Nous* is based on some sort of pastime, taking place in a building where hard labour was the way they passed time not that long ago.

Thelma gave me a Nikkormat single-lens-reflex camera, which at once scared me with its battery of metres, gauges and cranks. Whenever the subject had been raised, I'd said an ordinary Brownie was enough for me. But, of course, they're now valuable antiques and in any case nobody can process the films any more. The only complex camera I've ever owned, the Voigtlander, was stolen in Calcutta (possibly by my best friend, for money to bet on horses).

'The few minutes you spend familiarising yourself with the apparatus will increase your picture-taking pleasure many times over,' began the manual. We two spent most of the afternoon on pages 1 and 2, 'loading and unloading the film'. As Sylvia brought us tea, we moved on by stages to identify the ASA film-speed index, the meter coupling-pin, maximum aperture scale and depth-of-field preview activator.

Sun was setting as we at last gave up for the day and went to dress, as the Brays were coming for supper. Changed into my better clothes while T made final adjustments to the food. Cath came scraged from a fall off her bike; Lou played ping-pong to try the new balls; Dan and I tried the shuttlecocks; the ducklings were on the pond, refusing to be enticed to the well-house for safe keeping overnight, so I put on wellies over my best and waded in to round them up. Sally and John arrived with two ducks, still warm as he'd just killed them. Thelma didn't know how to pluck them and John said she should do it next day, first soaking them in warm water, then burning off the down. And I remembered my grandma flitting across fowls with a lighted taper in the scullery and that long-ago smell of burnt feathers.

Ate cold beetroot soup with sour cream, veal escalopes and apricot tart. Birthdays were simpler, though, when we all rushed out at the last moment for a book token, as my mother still does today. If I dare say this, Thelma cries at the lack of pleasure our family takes in familial sacraments.

Wednesday 1 August

Another couple of hours with the manual and I finally plucked up my courage and loaded a film and wound it forward, watching the frame counter which should have turned but didn't. Exposed two frames and wound again. Still no movement. Wound back, opened the camera to find the film still firmly sealed inside its metal cylinder. No way of reaching it, except with a tin-opener. Lesson learnt: there's no winding film on with an expensive single-lens-reflex-automatic, only with a Brownie, except then there'd be no need as the number was visible through a little red window.

Still, it's the thought that counts.

Thursday 2 August

Mendels arrived to stay with John and Sally, looking after the dogs while the Brays go to London to try and scrounge more money from their children's trust. David and Meg came to supper. At the pond, I showed him where Simeon's son had begun clearing the choking weed by means of a metal hook. Challenged, he was soon doing the same. To thank him for being helpful, I took my turn at hooking, twisting and heaving.

After watching for some minutes, 'You're not doing too well there, Master. Trouble with you intellectual writer-types, no strength of sinew.'

When I let his challenge lie floundering on the bank by turning away, he felt appeased and made amends.

'Let's do it together.'

Some time later a long twine of weed lay drying out among the young oaks.

'That really is a masterpiece. A *morceau du maître*, as the French so wittily say.'

He looked at the camera after supper, gave up and said he thought taking snaps was feeble-minded anyway. He only ever looked at them once before stowing them in a drawer.

In bed that night, I asked Thelma why she'd bought a present I'd never said I wanted. Of course, she was angry and we quarrelled.

Friday 3 August

After an unhappy night, woke at seven and walked through woods busy with the cars and motorbikes of fungi hunters. Tramped in the cool of day, visualising a life on my own. My hands were behind my back till I felt a sudden sharp pain, brought them forward and flicked off a fat horsefly gorging on blood from my middle finger. Every holiday down here is blighted by these creatures that leave a swelling. By Sunday it's almost impossible to write. I've noticed the natives never put their hands behind them. God help the Duke of Edinburgh.

Back at eight for breakfast and Thelma was forgiving and tender, so I didn't leave home but went into the routine for another day.

Tuesday 7 August

Evening: a folklorique display by a visiting Polish dance troupe was to take place in the garden of the *sous-préfecture* in Ribérac. Due to heavy rain that morning, the chosen area was still under water so we were directed to the town cinema, a bleak auditorium with a small stage at one end lit by floats, distorting everything the light fell on, giving a ghoulish tinge to the jolly show. To think all stages used this method until WW2!

The company was about fifty strong, mostly muscular sweaty peasant-types who gave terrific value under trying conditions. Their dances were clearly based on country matters, scything, reaping and at one point hacking at the wooden stage with little hatchets while stamping and shouting.

'*Très solide*,' muttered Thelma.

As each number ended, all fifty had to line up sideways, patiently queuing to exit into the open air by one tiny door normally used for someone to come and sweep the stage behind the cinema screen. One of the footlights exploded and a local artisan, in overall and beret, smoking a Gauloises, crawled on to replace the bulb, the mazurka or czardas galumphing on around him. A Milos Forman film waiting to be shot. My choice for the hero was the gauche youth on double-bass who stared devotedly at the leader throughout.

Saturday 11 August

Reg, Win and my mother arrived in his Cortina. He has good qualities – he's industrious, obliging, always ready to mend the machines our lives depend on. A Proper Man if ever there was. A Doing Daddy. He was soon into his stupefying stories of the car's oil consumption and behaviour on bends, but when I broke my silence to tell him about my own car, it was, 'Well, if no-one wants the bathroom, I'll have a shave.'

The temperature rose and Mum moaned that she was dying of heat, as though the rest of us were bathed in cool breezes. Short of turning off the sun, there was nothing I could do for her. She sat about in the shade clutching her packets of filter-tips and/or sipping vodka flavoured with lime/orange/ginger. I fear for her lungs to see her smoke so much but if she didn't have to reach for an ashtray now and then what exercise would she get?

Reg unloaded the Cortina's boot: tins of beans, ready-made rice pudding, ready-peeled potatoes. He's brought both still and cine-cameras.

'What I got to do one day, Pete, is collect all my prints in albums. I got about four thousand altogether. Make a bonfire of the landscapes, all the scenic pictures, all except the ones with someone standing in front.'

Is his Labour Party view any closer to the good life than the Tories?' That's the question asked by *The Freeway* and the portrait of Reg in that is pretty good.

Reading *Huckleberry Finn* to the children. Often I can't decipher the dialect on the page but spoken aloud it flows like the river that is its driving force. Louise, Dan and Catherine like it as much as I do.

Wednesday 15 August

Reg began fixing strip-lights to the old beams in the barn. Our lightweight alloy stepladder doesn't go nearly high enough so he has to rest it on a chest of drawers. Someone – usually Win – holds the base steady and he goes up there fiddling about, squinting through his bi-focals, cursing in his self-censoring way. 'Blow this something wire!'

Jean-Jacques, our French teacher, and his wife Maureen arrived to stay with their boy Damien. The names these days! The list of Catherine's classmates next term reads like a roll-call of working-class aspirations: Vilma, Julieand, Kimberley, Kristina, Justine, Denise, Terrylee, Lynn and Diane. The boys are more straightforward – Pauls, Kevins, Marks, Michaels and four Stephens, with only the odd Gary or Darren.

Friday 17 August

We swim to keep cool – either in the pool beyond Joanna Bullock's, in the Dronne at Epéluche or Aubeterre or the lake at La Jemaye. The water in every case is only slightly cooler than the air. The *Sud-Ouest* claims the heat-wave has pulverisé all records.

Returned from one of these outings to find Reg propped on the living-room sofa, Win looking worried and Mum smoking and asking why she hadn't been called to help when he fell from the steps and struck his head on the concrete floor. He'd already done this once, Win told us, but managed to cling to a beam till she'd got the ladder in place again. Instead of taking this to heart, he went up again and this time fell in earnest. He'd been unconscious for some minutes and was still deaf in one ear. We helped him to his bed and later he vomited and was rambling on about not having closed a junction-box in the attic.

Saturday 18 August

An English nurse looked in, alerted by some mutual friends. She thought he was making good progress but doubted he'd be well enough to drive home on Tuesday. Win was a model helpmeet, looking after him, making light of his bullying.

Monday 20 August

He's only slightly deranged, shouting in the night, unable to hear at all in one ear, more concerned about the unfinished electrical job than the state of his own brain. I climbed up and closed the junction-box. We had to support him as far as his Cortina in the yard so that he could check that all was well. He worships that machine. Every day he gives me more material for his character in *The Freeway*.

[To make the story short, a local doctor diagnosed *commotion cérébrale*. An ambulance was arranged to take him and Win to Le Havre and another to meet and instal him in Bristol General Hospital. Jean-Jacques was invaluable in all this, doing the necessary French phoning and arguing. My mother would be taken home in Reg's car by a chauffeur supplied by the AA. All she seemed to care about was that she might be late meeting her friend at home. We tried to make her see that Reg's accident, his hearing, the after-effects of concussion, were more serious but to no effect. My portrait of her as Grace in *Joe Egg* wasn't that far out.

The ambulance was a white Citroen hatchback saloon and Reg was taken supine with Win sitting beside him. Soon after that, a driver arrived for Vi, quite unfazed by his journey from Sydenham by Many Forms of Transport and, after breakfasting and washing, was ready to return. Vi went off, happy at least that he was an Englishman, promising to let us know of her safe arrival. A month later we still hadn't heard a word.

Reg never quite recovered. He lost his hearing entirely on one side but there were still twelve years left to him to enjoy life with Win and the Cortina. This deafness finally made driving dangerous and, after a few narrow scrapes, he gave it up, though not without a struggle. Letting go of the car was like an amputation.]

Friday 24 August

Jean-Jacques's family left. The children weren't sorry to see the last of Damien, who'd turned out an enfant terrible. We told them to be tolerant. He was evidently disturbed by whatever had happened in his infancy. All of us found it hard to forgive an action we discovered later: he'd covertly taken a knife and stabbed a number of holes in the inflatable dinghy the kids used on the pond and lake. This made us fear for his future.

During the next few quiet days, I reworked some scenes of *Chez Nous*.

Sunday 26 August

Working in my room while rain fell outside when I heard a car draw up at the roadside, a door being slammed and the clatter of bottles being

[336]

thrown down. For some time we've been angry about the dumping of tins and glass in the hole a few yards from our gateway. We could tell by the Sainsbury's labels the dumpers were English. I jumped up and ran through the house, keen to catch them at it. Arriving at the road, found a French-registered car. Was working out 'Please do not throw your rubbish into our hedge' (*'Er, m'sieur, défense de jeter votre ordure ici'* – or does 'ordure' mean shit?), when I saw that the culprit was our neighbour Belsey. Was so taken aback, I said nothing, only passed the time of day. Later kicked myself black and blue for cowardice.

Tuesday 28 August

Drove to Biarritz, arriving late p.m.

Mike and Shirley Blakemore's house now looks palatial and was full of guests and family. That evening we ate in a brasserie above the beach – crab to start and soufflé au Grand Marnier for afters. Cool Atlantic breezes a relief after the past weeks. It was enjoyable, though these days I always feel constrained with him, on guard. This time I'd made all the overtures and had gone along with the best intentions but still the light badinage suddenly goes too far, turns ugly.

'Are those meant to be sideboards on your face, Pete?'

'I've had them like this for a year or two.'

'They're the only sideburns I've ever seen where you can actually count the hairs.'

It brings to mind the line of Pinter's he most admired, when the rich girl in *The Servant* asks the valet: 'Do you use a deodorant?'

Wednesday 29 August

Broad sands beautiful this morning and the sea rough enough for surfing. Ordinary swimmers and paddlers must stay between two flags where lifeguards can see them, but the surfing freaks go to one side, wait for their wave, jump on a board tied to their ankles and ride in like amphibious heroes from a myth. They make it look easy and I was shocked to find the waves so powerful. The water's warm but the breakers wind anyone who doesn't know how to cope. I backed out, imitating Mike, but he was soon swimming over the waves to the calmer water beyond, then body-shooting in.

'Pete!' he shouted after one visit to the shallows, 'if you see one going to break on you, plunge underneath.'

I realised I was well out of my league, couldn't plunge and began struggling for the shore. Water crashed on my head and pounded my back. I swallowed too much, the brine stinging my mouth, and was relieved when I at last felt beach beneath my feet. Mike was already a long way out and couldn't have seen me if I'd gone under. The life-guards weren't watching this stretch, which is only for strong swimmers. From then on I stayed between the flags.

When he came in, he said he was going back to the house to avoid too sudden exposure to the sun. Thelma urged me to go with him and talk about the script, which was what she said he was suggesting. He agreed without much enthusiasm, and we left Shirley, their son Conrad, Thelma, Sylvia, Louise, Dan and Cath on the beach. On the way back he said, 'Sometimes you can see a bit of topless here, near these steps.'

At first there were none, till I spotted a couple of young women close to the wall, white northern breasts hopefully bared. After staring wide-eyed for some moments, Mike backed out of sight saying, 'My God, d'you realise who they are? Our tenants.'

Though we were only to be there a day, he at once started finding ways to postpone the discussion I'd come for. First a shower, then a meal, then a phone call, then, 'Pete, I must just send a cable about a friend who's arriving tomorrow.' He went out, leaving me alone, and didn't come back for several hours. I'd been involved yet again in one of his intrigues.

[Years later, during a rehearsal of *Privates on Parade*, Joe Melia rounded on him: 'Look, Michael, everyone knows about your adulteries. It's no big secret. Why d'you have to make out they're some huge Ibsenite drama?'

He didn't answer, but the reason was implicit in Joe's question: it was the conspiracy he enjoyed.]

Shirley must have ticked him off later. When he came back, he was a little more forthcoming, though what he had to say was largely destructive. Was he showing pique at not being asked to do *Chez Nous*? That's hard to believe, given his lukewarm response to that play as well.

Eve: to a suburban cinema taken over by an Aussie surfing fanatic who shows his own films there for an audience of the like-minded. But a little tubing goes a long way and an hour or so was too much. This is a brave and enviable élite, pitting themselves against an ocean armed only with a length of wood. Mike's one of them: a Bondi lifeguard, fearless in water, on land a hypochondriac fusspot.

Friday 31 August

Eve: dinner at the Belseys' place.

He dismissed jazz, films, all American culture except James and Eliot, later enlarging this to take in all but Western European.

'I'm only interested in any period inasmuch as it bears on the present. Ergo, only in nineteenth-century art inasmuch as it affects the twentieth. Only slightly interested in eighteenth-century art inasmuch as it affects the nineteenth. I suppose I should try to interest myself in the seventeenth century inasmuch as it affects the eighteenth but frankly I haven't got the time.'

I stirred from slumber now and then to see Elizabeth staring at him nervously as though expecting him to fall apart or explode.

Saturday 1 September

Delivered Deux Chevaux to the Brays for them to keep in running order till we come again in spring. Sally was fresh from an asthmatic *crise* (one of John's favourite words), shoulders high, breathing forcefully through her nose. He showed us his latest picture restoration, done on the vacuum reclining table he wangled from the children's trust.

'It's a bloody Boucher, no question,' he assured us. An eighteenth-century French landscape he'd picked up for F200 in a flea-market. But he'd done so much restoring, we thought it more Bray than Boucher.

Sunday 2 September

To return the children to school earlier, we risked making for home without a ferry booking. Burnt rubbish, closed shutters, locked doors, covered tennis table, folded badminton net, pulled ox-cart into barn, while Thelma immobilised the kitchen, well and plumbing. Rounded up ducks and chickens and left them with Maze for his Christmas dinner. Left keys with Simeon, whose wife gave us a bunch of *immortelles* from beside her banana tree. In the fetid car, they proved anything but everlasting and had to be thrown out before Poitiers.

Stopped for lunch at our usual Routiers, still unfinished. Judging by its dampness, the towel in the toilet was the same one I'd used at Easter. On the gravelled forecourt, three coaches were drawn up, their occupants out for a break in the long journey from Portugal to Paris. Immigrant workers, dodging the draft. Unlike their French drivers, they couldn't afford to eat in the restaurant and had improvised picnics, recreating village life beside the autoroute, the women fetching water, their men smoking and chastising the kids. The drivers recalled them by sounding horns and they drove on northwards, bound for some *bidonvilles* or other slum, with jobs in the Renault factory or worse. Better that, presumably, than being sent to die in some last-ditch colonial conflict.

We arrived Le Havre 9.30, waited two hours in a queue of other people who hadn't booked. Finally the ferry went without us so we joined others in driving on to Calais for the Hovercraft. Just outside town a fog came down that slowed us to 30 m.p.h. and at last to a standstill, as I was tired of staring into a haze of headlamps reflected off the mist. Pulled up on verge and tried to sleep while immense lorries thundered on blindly to Rouen. Thelma took over the wheel at dawn and drove to Calais, where we found that her purse had been lost during the in-and-out of the night. Passed the hat round the car and we, the kids and Sylvia rummaged together enough small change for breakfast. We'd driven 500 miles in a day. Sick and tired, we queue-jumped on to the Hovercraft, a very British sort of vessel, with interior trim like a Vauxhall's, the crew looking like rejects from BOAC. Though the props are noisy and spray spoils the view, we were soon bouncing across at 40 knots and came to rest on Goodwin Sands at Ramsgate.

Monday 3 September

Three expectant employees awaited us at home – Olive Taylor, Mr Thomas and his son, all eager to share the glory of our first response to the improvements. They've transformed the dark and awkward ground floor. Twin doors now slide across a wide opening between front and back. Kitchen cupboard and dividing wall have gone, opening up the playroom which used to be a cramped and stifling boiler-room. So tired, we could hardly stand leave alone smile, but did our best to show how well they'd done.

Later began working through a heap of mail, mostly brown envelopes with brochures from theatres telling me Tom Stoppard's plays are being done throughout the land.

Friday 7 September

Worked in Brompton Square with Finney and Medwin. I read them the first act of *Chez*, not quite reaching the interval. Albert stopped me often to ask a question or suggest a change. I found him almost as sharp and thoughtful as Blakemore. There were frequent telephone interruptions, mostly the missus, Anouk Aimée, on the intercom asking for the dogs or cats to be sent down or up to wherever she was. Sometimes she burst into the room for nothing much and he asked her patiently not to. It was as though she was jealous of his work.

For lunch we were going to the Royal Court to welcome the company of three that's just arrived from South Africa. Thelma came from the hairdresser and Anouk appeared in a white turban and kaftan that looked as though she'd just stepped out of the shower.

'Aren't you coming with us?' I asked.

She was. Another perfect Pooterism.

At Sloane Square we met Athol Fugard and his two actors John Kani and Winston Mshombe. Conversation was a merry blaze but suddenly died and there was Lindsay Anderson asking if there was anybody else he had to shake hands with. A born prima-donna.

David Storey came on to lunch with us. Our first meeting. A deceptively cuddly man I felt could turn prickly on a sixpence. Was amusing about David Mercer's drinking, saying he's always sober inside. I liked his (Mercer's) retort to a black man who spat in his face.

'I'm not going to hit you, not because you're a big Fascist pig who's making it very difficult for me to be liberal, but because I'm a coward.'

Storey also thought Fugard a racist, despite his reputation.

'Did you notice, he was looking for an ashtray for his cigarette and one of the blacks quickly jumped up and passed him one. Not quickly enough, though, and the ash fell on the floor. But who apologised? The black man, for not getting the ashtray there in time.'

P.m.: Read the play aloud, Thelma being Liz and Albert started doing Phil. It began to come alive.

Tuesday 11 September

At lunch there were five generations of Anouk's family, from her grandmother to granddaughter. No wonder poor Albert looks beleaguered, continually picking fights with her.
    'Remember,' she said, 'I was a star before you.'
    'Before I what? Before I was born?'
    'You're so rude, you know that? There's no need to be so rude.'
    The grandma smiles across at me: *'Pas méchant.'*

Wednesday 12 September

Late afternoon met Charles (Wood) in the departure lounge at Heathrow. He's afraid of flying and took a double brandy before boarding. Once in the cabin, we asked each other why we were risking our lives to spend three days in Switzerland without good reason.

[This was my first outing as a literary celebrity. Even now, in my seventies, I can count such episodes on one hand. Nor was I invited out of any respect for my achievement but as a stand-in for Ayckbourn who couldn't make it. Charles, James Saunders and I were all clients of Peggy Ramsay, but – as Mark Twain said of receiving the Légion d'Honneur, 'That is an honour that few escape.']

At Zurich, already pretty pissed, we giggled like girls at the sight of the man sent to meet us, a plump German–Swiss holding up two copies of *Joe Egg*. Charles approached him, reaching in his pocket for francs.
    'Oh, no, please,' said the other, 'I'm not selling these books. They are – oh, you are Mister Nichols, ja?'
    He and Charles shook hands.
    'This is Mister Wood,' said Charles, presenting me.

Which was what we'd planned on the plane. There was no photo of me on the cover and they'd not found copies of any of Charles's. Saunders hadn't met us either and would probably join the fun anyway. But the poor chap looked so confused that I couldn't go through with it, thus spoiling any interest the excursion might have had.

We reached our hotel at midnight. It stood alone on a hillside, dark and inhospitable; once a spa, now partly a farm, which explained the clouds of flies that tormented us throughout our stay. Charles's first floor room was a poky single, mine a double with shower and extensive views over the sloping fields. From close by came the gentle chime of cowbells and from farther the traffic of an autobahn. Had a disturbed night, chasing mosquitoes.

Thursday 13 September

Met a darkly bearded man in the hall who introduced himself in a quiet London voice as Saunders. We three sat at breakfast fighting off the bluebottles and horseflies. James told of his arrival yesterday, by train, at Burgdorf. He'd been so deep in a book he hadn't noticed the appearance of a station, looking up at the last moment to see a man on the platform bearing a card with the one word 'Saunders' in large print. James had quickly grabbed his stuff and struggled off but there was now no sight of the man. As the train began to move away, he'd looked in a passing carriage window to see the same man, being borne away, waving and showing his sign. James phoned the number he'd been given for McHale to be told it was he on the platform and now on the way to Berne.

Our minder turned up, helped us swat some flies and drove us afterwards to a cobbled street in Burgdorf. Here, in a featureless restaurant called The Casino, Saunders at last met McHale, a hearty Irishman. His assistant Christine was the only woman allocated to us. Pleasant and attractive, she wore dark glasses because she was recovering from an eye operation. She soon explained that McHale and she had assumed Charles and I were queer, as Charles had proposed me when Ayckbourn withdrew. A reasonable assumption, which also explained the single and double bedroom. They'd expected us to share mine. But where in the field of assumptions did this leave James?

Monday 24 September

My piano lesson was interrupted by a burst of shouting from the street. The black man was standing on the roof of his minibus waving the branch of a tree and hurling abuse across our back gardens.

'Dese are de houses fucking wanna pool down.'

He's part drunk, part mad. His woman was sitting beside him smoking. She's unhealthy-looking, with signs of alopecia among her dyed-black hair and could be a victim of *folie à deux*. They're the terror of the Lewisham supermarts, always asking for refunds on Lucozade bottles they collect from refuse bins. Sometimes she's dressed as a bride in white, sometimes an Indian in a saffron sari, striding across the heath with her man loping beside her. The postman delivers his National Assistance every week.

Sunday 30 September

Dinner party at home to mark the departure of Ben Morahan to read architecture at Bristol. Other guests: Chris, his father of course, and three other couples of our age. We'd been worried that among these middle-agers, Ben would find no-one to talk to, so invited one of our few *young* friends, Anna Carteret. She turned up late, looking as pretty as ever. Some way through the evening, she came to Thelma in the kitchen saying Chris had asked if he could have her number; what had happened to his wife exactly? Told that he was a widower, she was reassured. Could be a good liaison for a young actress, with the Head of BBC Plays.

Meanwhile Ben talked to David Allford about architecture, so everyone was happy.

Saturday 6 October

Drove to Epwell near Banbury on a misty morning to see Charles and Val Wood's new home. His theatrical background compels him to show himself against changing scenery – first in a Victorian mansion, then a modern penthouse, then a Costwold cottage, with all the props and suitable lighting. 'Horseshoes' is an old forge-cum-pub with low ceilings and jutting beams, poky rooms and inglenook fireplaces.

They walked us through the spacious, drooping garden. Our girls were chasing butterflies with the net we gave Cath for her birthday.

'You're not holding it right,' I told her. 'I saw this Russian writer in America doing it.'

'Well, we aren't Russian writers in America,' she said, as I let their captive tortoiseshell escape. She took the net back and chased them in her own more effective way.

'Our land goes as far as that low wall,' said Val, 'after that is an old dear of eighty-five but we're hoping to get her out. They're all the same. The colonel's got a local in the end of his house and keeps offering him more and more to leave but he's holding out. They're very cunning. They keep you on a string.'

Wednesday 17 October

Gill Frayn rang with bad news. Nicholas Tomalin's been killed in Israel while covering the war that had been sickening us all the week. He'd just got out of a car and his three companions had moved some way off, when a missile struck the vehicle and he was instantly killed. Gill had seen Claire last night (before the news came) and she said she was missing him but was accustomed to that, as wife of a foreign correspondent.

That Malaya Medal he awarded me hangs in my study. We'd last met when we'd tried to buy George and Diana Melly's house next door to theirs. Part of our attraction to it had been the Tomalins' friendliness. Later the agent rang in some embarrassment to say the Mellys had sold it to someone else. I'd read *Private Eye* and knew the Tomalins' reputation as trend-setters of NW3 but it had never been obvious in our meetings.

'How awful that so many should die,' wrote Jane Austen of casualty figures in the Peninsula War, 'but what a blessing that one cares not a jot for any of them.'

One you know is worth all the rest.

[Michael Frayn now lives in Gloucester Crescent too, with his second wife, Claire Tomalin.]

Sunday 21 October

Frayn's been low lately, his plays and novels not catching on as he hoped. Thelma unaccountably thinks we're in a position to cheer him up. She says I have three productions upcoming and he has none. When I say my last few showings have all been flops (the revamped *Ben Spray* on TV, the films of *Egg* and *Health*, productions in Paris and LA), she shrieks that even flops are better than nothing.

So today we walked with him and Gill from Darwin's home in the Kent village of Downe along public footpaths while the sky was alive with small aircraft coming in from all points to land at the flying clubs of Biggin Hill and Farnborough. Riding-school girls came thundering on massive animals. Louise discovered the pleasure to be got from electric shocks and kept grasping the wire fences.

Michael told us Nick's death had upset him more than he'd have expected. He'd combined, he said, the character of decent chap and shit, very fond of a flashy world of fast girls and even faster cars, at the same time as he was deeply attached to his wife and home. Well, aren't we all? He left Claire for one of those Jay sisters and agonised all the time he was enjoying it. Wouldn't say no.

Also disagreed with Michael about Israel, seeing the Balfour Declaration as misguided, taking a pro-Semitic but anti-Zionist position on Jewish resettlement there, while he was clearly very taken with the whole idea. I couldn't pursue this far because, as with the fast girls, I haven't been there. Michael has. To Israel, that is.

Eve: *The Common* on TV was slow and drawn-out. Vivien, knowingly miscast, tried to pull the play in the wrong direction, making us too aware of the woman's history. Had Chris cast her to curry favour with Harold, as their marriage is known to be a rough ride at the moment? She left the other actors with egg on their faces.

A long silence followed the closing credits before Frayn rang to say he'd enjoyed the farce bits but was cool about the rest.

He was the first of not-very-many to ring at all.

Monday 22 October

The Times said it was preachy, the *Guardian* was warmer, saying Vivien had been particularly good. Depressed and alone in my room, I browsed through the first version of the play, a television *film* based on Black-heath Fayre, to be paired with *The Gorge* of 1967. Chris hadn't accepted that, saying inflation in the last five years has made such a project impossible. The play I extracted from it, shot mostly on videotape in a studio at TV Centre, was talky and disparate, too much of the original action done in reported speech. The elements wouldn't mix.

At tea-time, Jean-Jacques and Maureen dropped by to ask when the play's going to be on, as they couldn't bear to miss it. But I wondered: had they seen it?

Eve: Paul Oestreicher, vicar of the Church of the Ascension, fifty yards away, dropped by to tell of an encounter with Minibus Man. He'd called at the vicarage to tell Paul his wife had been taken away by four men in a car and not seen since. While Paul stood at his front door trying to understand his ravings, he spotted a face bobbing in and out of his church opposite. Partly to escape the tirade, he excused himself to go and see if someone wanted succour or sanctuary. It was Minibus Woman, who'd apparently been sheltering there all day with a suitcase, having left 'home'. Her man followed Paul across and at once began shouting and making as if to beat her. Paul calmed them and gradually gathered, mostly from her, that they're married and have a three-year-old child who's in local authority care. They want a home but, if they were given one, Paul wonders, would they then claim the child to live with them and would that be a decent outcome for anyone?

Thelma wonders whether the whole scene wasn't put on for the vicar.

[By his own admission, Paul was hot stuff at the ecumenical side but not so good (or so keen) on pastoral or parochial care. For this reason his was one of the first parishes to appoint a woman as deacon. He was often away recording telly debates on moral issues. One of these at about this time asked 'Can breaking the law ever be justified?' (or: what is the robbing of a bank to the founding of a bank?). One of the speakers saying lawbreaking was never right was Reginald Maudling, company director, who got the sack as Home Secretary when he was shown to be implicated in the Poulson corruption business.]

Wednesday 23 October

Greatly cheered by a kind and flattering letter from Terence Rattigan. He compared *The Common* to Maugham's *Our Betters*, Robertson's *Caste* and even Congreve! Urges me to adapt it for the stage. His best bit is a story prompted by the moment when my teacher looks out of his car into the hostile eyes of a woman waiting for a bus.

'In the days when I could afford to, I bought a Rolls Phantom V, a vast monster with built-in drinks cabinet, sliding tables, telephone, TV, the works. (I bought it to please my driver, Larry Olivier's ex, whom I was nervous of.) One evening, coming up from Brighton, I had the reading light on and was sipping a whisky. I looked out of the window to see a long bus queue shivering in the snow, every member of it looking at me with deep murderous hatred. And what I was reading was *Tribune*. If I hadn't switched off the light at once, the English Revolution would have started right then.'

A good notice in the *Telegraph*, praise from Rattigan on Albany W1 notepaper . . . Where have I gone wrong?

Monday 5 November

Victoria 10 p.m. Waiting in a chilly queue at Customs for the boat-train, we heard a very awff voice asking, 'D'you mind *awfully*? Would you be angels and let me through? I'm most inadequately clad'. We recognised the wife of Our Man in Brussels whom we'd had to meet at the opening of *Health* and also at some evening at the Griggs.

Our waiter in the buffet was either drunk, mad or queer, perhaps all three, had a wonderfully sedate manner and never ceased smiling. He enjoyed waiting, he told us, because of all the lovely people he met – and we were prime examples of the breed.

Outside the carriage window Guy Fawkes bonfires in gardens, parks and waste-lots sped by.

Tuesday 6 November

Missed our rapide at Austerlitz but John Bray waited for the next at Angoulême, bless him, and drove us to his home. Completed the journey by our Deux Chevaux that he'd kept in working order.

[There's only a page about the ten days we spent at Chez Magnou preparing the play set here with the director Robert Chetwyn, designer Michael Annals and photographer John Jefford, so this account is filled out from memory.]

The weather was wonderful, almost continual sunshine, though at twilight the temperature dropped and we all laboured to keep the place warm. Michael was especially good at making fires in the huge hearth.

'This is a doddle,' he said, 'when you've designed as many Cinderella's Kitchens as I have.'

He and I never tired of imitating Blakemore, which didn't appear to irk Bob, though he must have been putting on a brave front. A pleasant, slightly uptight, man, the son of a chauffeur, born in Chelsea.

Michael left us in no doubt about the kind of theatre he hates – exposed brickwork, liberal ideas and Afghan beads – and claims to have spotted all these at Greenwich. The brickwork was beyond dispute and that sort of jewellery could be seen sometimes, but the ideas there are left-wing non-conformist Christian rather than liberal. A common confusion.

Bob and I sat shirtless in the sun, going over the script yet again. This poor little play has had every slight ambiguity examined, all its leaks caulked and barnacles scraped, and is now a watertight commercial entertainment, unsinkable as the Titanic.

[For a while Joan Plowright was keen to play Liz, the home-making wife. The de Filippo comedy she was rehearsing looked to be heading for disaster, would probably close quite soon, and she and Olivier let us know she'd like to be in ours. Then *Saturday, Sunday, Monday* opened to rapturous reviews and ran for a year, so we resumed our search.]

Pat Heywood was finally chosen for Liz, though Memorial (Finney and Medwin) are offering her £100 a week, only twice the national average wage – for playing a lead opposite Albert in the West End! Seen from her viewpoint, she'd be subsidising his life-style, as well as Medwin's Sunningdale weekends and transatlantic flights. I remember waiving my royalties one week during the NY run of *Joe Egg* after Albert had left, later finding one of the items charged against the takings was a first-class jet crossing for Michael – to stay at the Hertford Hotel knocking back Dry Martinis. As Michael (a golfing semi-pro) would have said, 'That's par for the course.' Which is no comfort.

By day Michael Annals ransacked the neighbouring farms for ox-carts, yokes, sabots, agricultural implements and all the other props required in the directions and dialogue. Some were to be bought from well-contented small-holders and shipped home, some photographed by John and copied by craftsmen in London. John also recorded the barn (on which the design was to be based) from every angle so that Michael would have a complete set of photographic views to work from.

My 'idea' had been to have a game or pastime in every scene, the great barn's original purpose of hard labour having been subverted by the affluent new arrivals from England. E.g. sun-bathing, trapezes, ping-pong, photography, the collecting of quaint objects as decorative jokes, and the showing of slides. John had to take exterior photographs that were to be projected as an important part of the action. A crucial plot-point required the absent children to be shown in stills on the screen. But we had no children with us so those from a neighbouring family who walked past our house every morning and evening to and from the village school were drawn in and given sweets and toys. When they got home late and showed off these bribes, their drunken father wouldn't believe they hadn't been stealing – or worse. Alright, so if you didn't nick 'em, how d'you get 'em? What? Who are these weirdoes at Chez Magnou and what did they ask you to do? Pose for pictures? What kind of pictures? Look at me when I'm talking to you!

Whatever they said must finally have convinced him we were fair game because next day he turned up, drunk as always, grinning and asking if we had any little jobs he could do. Or, failing that, did we want the boys and girls to do any more posing?

Monday 19 November

With a gang of middle-class parents, toured the new Comprehensive at Kidbrooke. Next year Louise will be leaving the comfortable un-demanding primary stage for the competitive struggle of secondary school. Gill Frayn organises these visits and wanted Thelma to drum up some working-class parents. So she put it to Olive Taylor, our char, and offered to drive her there and back. Her son is Lou's age and will be moving up too but she couldn't make the meeting, was having her hair done for Club Saturday night and had to buy new shoes. So the usual lot turned out, posh and intelligent, well-informed, walking examples of the value of education. The idea is to persuade People Like Us to stay with state schools right through. Few do, said the headmistress, most children from bright parents drifting off into fee-paying schools as night follows day. So wasn't Olive right? She has no choice, her boy will go wherever he's sent. It's the posh that need persuading.

Our brief inspection of the smart new buildings didn't exactly raise our spirits. A noticeable absence of books, though plenty of lathes. The usual staff shortages – no music teacher in a school called Thomas Tallis. Should we offer Lou as a hostage to fortune?

[In fact, all our children were state-educated, except for two years when Dan had fallen foul of the system, ending up in one of Islington's most socially experimental schools. Even the head teacher advised us to give him a better chance, so for two years he went to Bedales, once a pioneering co-ed, fashionable with both actual and show-business royalty. Though apparently popular there with the likes of Sarah Armstrong-Jones and the offspring of diplomats, he finally asked to go to Sixth Form College instead. That was his roundabout route to university.]

Thursday 22 November

53 bus to the Lyric, arriving onstage to read with Denis Carey, who was up for the part of the French peasant, based on the little man who keeps cropping up when we least expect him at Chez Magnou. He's not only a useful cameo but a crucial plot device, appearing four times, talking continuously but without any written lines from me.

[Denis had been director of the Bristol Old Vic for some years in the 1950s when, as an out-of-work actor, I'd hung about the theatre asking for any parts he hadn't cast. I worked for him a few times, enjoying especially *The Alchemist* and *Henry V*, a production we took to the London Old Vic and the Zurich Schauspielhaus.]

I was embarrassed to be auditioning him, our former positions reversed. Once I'd been the supplicant and he'd been pretending to be a great director. He understood exactly what was required here, improvising fluently in gibberish French while I read Dick's lines. Albert came up onstage at once and said, 'Right, rehearsals begin New Year's Eve to open some time in February. That alright?'

[351]

Actresses came to read, in case we lose Pat Heywood and Geraldine McEwan turns it down. None were right. Some came late or didn't come at all.

Thelma and I had lunch at Biba's, the chic new department store that's replaced Derry and Toms. The original Art Deco foyers and lifts are the pretext for a new look of chromium counters and geometric armchairs. We whizzed up in a brown lift, right out of an Astaire film, to the Rainbow Restaurant where marble floors and a white baby-grand gave promise of being attended by Eric Blore. But the waiters weren't old enough to expostulate like him, only camp boys with bell-bottomed trousers that explained how the floor was kept so shiny.

The arrival of a Zigeuner trio (with boots, balalaika and tambourine) showed that the design motif was Lyons'-Corner-House Revival, though with far better food. Later we went downstairs to look at clothes but it was too dark to risk buying things we could hardly see. Real 1930s shops were at least decently lit. With this and a retrospective of Mary Quant at the London Museum, nostalgia camp has now reached the limit.

[Which has a wistful tone in 2000. How about joining a wartime-type queue to undergo The Blitz Experience at the war museum? Out-of-work miners applying in hundreds to be tour guides at a disused pit? Actors dressed as crossing-sweepers at Ironbridge? The Wigan Pier Visitors' Centre? As a nation, we have nothing much to offer now but parodies of our own past.]

Saturday 24 November

None of the other auditionees quite right so Bob and I pressed Albert to raise his offer to Pat. What's £25 to him that he should weep for it?

Thursday 29 November

Francis Hewlett to stay for a few days. A chance to catch up on almost two years of his humour – breakfast with Loonie Layard, the latest follies of Falmouth Art School, his farcical attempts to rid the world of nuclear weapons, his neighbour Jean Shrimpton telling him of her visit to Tokyo, towering several feet above everyone else, etc.

Friday 30 November

After the Chinese Exhibition at the RA, found long queue at the cafeteria. I put it to Thelma and Francis that the proper Socialist way here was not to overcrowd the People's restaurants but cross the road to Fortnum and Mason. Once seated there, we were encouraged by seeing Richard Crossman at a nearby table, also doing his best to help the great majority by keeping well out of their way.

Evening: a Parent-Teacher's Association meeting. Only six of us turned out on such a cold winter's evening to sit in the draughty hall watching a film of Father Diamond's efforts to revive the spirit of old Deptford. He's recently been promoted (raised, elevated, uplifted, levitated?) to Canon and came in full drag, smoking like a Vatican chimney at election-time, and talking uppishly of the good old days, even doing a few cameos in cod Cockney. His film was all of street parties, old folks' coach-outings (no, charabancs) and Gert-and-Daisy women saying it was a bit of alright. Two other clerics appeared – Stockwood of Southwark and Shepherd of Woolwich – and all three spoke in posh, plummy voices, especially when addressing God, as though He'd only listen to a gentleman.

I must say for this Bill Weedon, the otherwise ambitious and euphemistic headmaster of Morden Mount: he was quite critical afterwards. I spoke in his support, saying perhaps people didn't want to be forced to belong to a community but to enjoy their families and their new lives in hygienic and well-appointed tower blocks. The old spirit, if it ever existed, arose from the general awfulness of life before 1940.

A view that came partly from reading E. Nesbit's stories *Hardings Luck* and *The House of Arden*, set like many of hers in the New Cross area of seventy years ago. Gore Vidal's essay on her has given me the idea of adapting one of these for Greenwich Theatre's Christmas show next year.

Sunday 2 December

Advent service at Church of the Ascension, a cross borne in procession by children, including a shy and simpering Louise. The choir sang out from the gallery and we gave the responses. Later we listened to them by candlelight.

Monday 3 December

Worked on *The Freeway* which suddenly seems forlorn. Is the oil crisis solving the traffic problem, as the Arabs 'hold us to ransom', i.e. ask for more money? Not likely. Surely only a passing scare, these queues at filling-stations and talk of post-offices preparing ration-books. It seems there was rationing at the time of Suez. I rode a bike in those days so didn't notice. When the oil starts flowing from those rigs in the North Sea, they say we'll be *exporting* it. The sheikhs are trying to get what they can while they can.

Tuesday 4 December

Toothache drove me at last to Eisenberg's chair in Blackheath Village.

'Seen anything of Albert lately? I dreamt about him last night. I knew him in Salford as a boy. I remember when he went up to London for his RADA audition. I was on the same train. We shared the guard's van. He was shy of going to do something as pouffy as acting, especially when I told him I was off to labour on a kibbutz in Israel. Yes, your filling's leaking and your gum's infected.'

On the kibbutz he was put in charge of a work-party of tribesmen from Turkestan or some similar Soviet republic.

'They couldn't count so didn't know when they'd packed enough oranges in a box. I had to devise ways of counting to twelve on ten fingers. I'd been educated at Manchester Grammar School. What did I have in common with these exotic illiterates, other than being Jewish? And that turned out to be insufficient so home I came. If the antibiotics don't do the trick, we'll move to Plan B, killing the nerve.'

Thursday 6 December

When Albert rang to tell me we have the Globe Theatre, opening in February, I asked him about his journey with my dentist in the guard's van.

'I don't recall anyone of that name. It certainly wasn't a guard's van because my mother was with me. Dad had told us to enjoy ourselves and given us twenty-seven pounds to have a slap-up time. My sister, who did the letter-writing in our house, couldn't get a hotel as it was

Coronation Year, so Dad grabbed the book and said, "What about this one here? That looks all right." He rang and got us rooms at once. It was the Dorchester, so no wonder. When we got there, we saw the prices: £7–10s–0d a day exclusive of food and drink. We used to eat in Lyons' and take one drink in the hotel at night and gobble down all the crisps and nuts that came with it. Anyway in those days I'd never have heard of a kibbutz.'

Toothache unbearable so I was back in Joe's chair this a.m.

'Did you mention me to Albert?'

'No, we haven't spoken since.'

'No? Well, I doubt if he'd remember me,' he said, after a pause.

I'm the world's worst liar.

After freezing my mouth, he drilled away the rotted filling and started excavating with a probe. At last he held his tweezers before my eyes with a small red streak on the end.

'The first nerve. Came out just right, according to the book.'

More of the same and home, with a mouthful of cloves.

That afternoon, when Sylvia and Olive had gone shopping, we voted for bed. Hardly there when Patsy Grigg rang and chatted about schools and Christmas while I undressed my wife. She made all the right answers, laughed at Patsy's jokes and only said she had to go and look in the oven when her breathing became audibly shorter.

Afterwards I lay staring through the windows at clouds the colour of pigeon breasts which were blown about to become eiderdowns then away altogether leaving a Tiepolo wash of pure blue. Now and then a flight of starlings was thrown from the sky to land on the leafless branches of London planes, chattering and screeching as they do every December, rallying here before making further south – east – north ? . . .

Friday 14 December

Edward Heath's three-day week is a good idea that should have happened years ago, except to those like me who *enjoy* their work. Absurd to support millions of jobless while those in work do it five days a week! Shared out and for shorter hours, the same boring jobs would be less boring. It would probably mean less profits for those in charge, so will never happen, except in this sort of (artificial) crisis.

Once we reached the motorway, the cars were going our way, westward. I stuck to Heath's maximum 50 m.p.h. much of the way, while sports cars zoomed by on the outside lane, many evidently doing a ton. No police. At first the filling stations had queues but by the time we reached Bristol there weren't any. Many of my hometown's streets were unlit, otherwise no signs of crisis. I'd like to give up the car altogether. We don't use it enough to justify the expense. On the journey down we just clocked 12,500 for 18 months. But with petrol scarce, who will buy the thing?

To Bristol Old Vic. They've taken over the Cooper's Hall next door and put in foyers and bars for the Bristol bourgeoisie to sip their sherries in. A grand staircase leading nowhere and two great lustre electroliers reassure us that nothing upsetting is going to happen here.

Sure enough, Shaw's *The Apple Cart* of 1929 won't alarm anyone these days. Some of his predictions were on the nose and about as many missed altogether. In *his* 1980, the workers all have cars, their prosperity based on the enslavement of poorer nations. All right so far, but he assumed those would be British colonies, being essentially Victorian and unable to imagine the empire folding so soon.

O'Toole played Magnus superbly. Shaw always pinned his faith to a Superman, someone as clever as himself, to achieve what democracy couldn't. Higgins, John Tanner, Undershaft, Napoleon. And in real life he looked to Lawrence of Arabia, Mussolini and Stalin.

At Thelma's parents', we toured the new kitchen Reg has created during the past year. Then he showed an album of photographs of various stages of the work. Later we played cards round the dining-table and Millie taught us a new form of whist her friend had learnt on a Mediterranean cruise.

She asked: 'When you were in Milan, Peter, did you see Leonora's Last Supper? It's only in some old shed, very disappointing, but the 3-D was marvellous.'

Reg didn't join the game, sitting aside saying the babble of voices sounded like a Chinese Parliament. The only after-effect of his fall in our barn is deafness in one ear. He says that's been helped a great deal by what he calls his urinade.

Monday 24 December

The prospects for 1974 are brighter now that shortages are going to be forced on this greedy lazy nation. The miners' leaders have sensibly seized their advantage to stage a go-slow and the railworkers are having their traditional Yuletide work-to-rule. I'm enjoying revising *The Freeway* now that traffic *is* at a standstill, though not in the way I'd envisaged.

Nice Christmas Eve party with Gill and Michael Frayn, Lou's form-teacher, Big Chief I-Spy, Bob Chetwyn and his partner Howard Schuman, and Cleo Sylvestre, who ensured Michael's group won the treasure hunt by intuitively solving the clues, with the help of our children.

[Cleo played Nurse Norton through the entire run of *The National Health*. Born of a West Indian mother in Essex, she made a famous response to Enoch Powell's offer of £20,000 to all immigrants to go back where they came from. 'I could get a very nice house for that in Harlow New Town.']

Thursday 27 December

Dinner at the Oestreichers' vicarage. Sherry, vodka and caviar, paella, crème caramel, wine and brandy. Then we sat around a log-fire studying photos the vicar had taken of his wife in the nude, posed against the window of their hotel room in Moscow during an ecumenical gathering of world churchmen. Lore's back was to the camera as she gazed out at a view of St Basil's and the Kremlin.

She'd greeted us at the door wearing a long monastic habit with a tasselled cord around her waist. I made some joke about flagellation, wondering what on earth we were in for.

'Oh,' she said, 'but you'll notice I haven't got the three knots of chastity, obedience and poverty, none of which virtues I possess.'

Both are German by birth but his parents emigrated early to New Zealand where he was born. He's about as Left as the C of E allows and the day before at our house he'd been challenged by a Tory Catholic.

'Do you really want to see a revolution in this country?'

'If you mean,' said Paul in his reasonable, maddening way, 'machine-guns in the streets, I doubt that would be suitable for England. If you mean overturning and rationalising our social order, then yes.'

[The challenger wasn't only right-wing and RC but the English husband of Thelma's Russian teacher, a Soviet refugee whose mother sobbed when she visited Harrod's, as it so reminded her of the good old days.]

Our Christmas visit to the vicarage ended with Paul showing us the walls of his downstairs WC, an unfinished collage in which the Archbishop of Canterbury, Alexander Dubcek, Enoch Powell and Pope John appear cheek-by-jowl with Playboy centrefolds.

Saturday 29 December

Thelma and I shared reading to the children the last lap of *Harding's Luck*, a rattling good story, busy, romantic and realistic – as Nesbit was herself. Time-bends, magic, hidden treasure and a Dickensian feeling for the oppressed. She and husband Hubert Bland were somewhat maverick Fabians after all. Some way from the end, we sensed that Dickie Harding wouldn't stay in the twentieth century but return to James the First's. Dan's face clouded as it used to when we sang 'Danny Boy' and he said 'O, no, horrible end, don't want him to go' and we had to point out that this was better for the boy-hero as, in the former life, he wasn't a cripple and lived in a fine house on the river at Deptford, the House of Arden in fact, which we'll start reading them straight away.

But this is the one to dramatise. So many visual elements: the lame boy, his tramp companion, huge moles called Mouldiwarps, a transformation scene and abrupt changes from poverty to splendour, Edwardian and Jacobean, town and country. Also, if our children's reaction's anything to go by, there won't be a dry eye in the house.

And a promising omen: on page 22: 'It was just like a play at the Greenwich Theatre, Dickie thought.'

This must have been the old Barnard's Music Hall before German bombs and Ewan Hooper.

In bed that night I found this in Maugham's essay on Austen: 'Miss Langley is like any other short girl with a broad nose and wide mouth, fashionable dress and exposed bosom.' Read it to Thelma as a perfect description of herself. She wasn't as amused as I'd expected and went back at once to deciphering her Russian.

Monday 31 December

Drove through quiet uncongested streets to Gray's Inn Road for the first reading of *Chez* in the Welsh Union. An enclave in the heart of town, with the Welsh words for Men and Women lavatories that make you question how anyone needing those words translated could have got so far from Wales. So cold we kept our overcoats on and could see our breath.

The play sounded funnier than I'd expected but the first act read only thirty-five minutes, the second forty-five. Not much to show for two year's work. Albert's part needs building up. Denholm's terrific and Geraldine points her lines superbly. Pat's funny too and the 'aah's I took from Thelma will become more natural when she's practised them a bit.

At midnight we listened for ships' horns from the river they always sound on New Year's Eve, but heard nothing.

1974

Tuesday 1 January

First rehearsals in chilly twilight. Overcoats, scarves, even gloves. Pretending to be sun-bathing in a Dordogne summer when you have numb fingers and a red nose in a Welsh Club in Gray's Inn Road is not in anyone's contract.

Lunches were various fry-ups done in a rotissomat. It was hard to disagree when Denholm complained about England's standards. No French lorry-driver would have eaten such food and no Italian wife would keep her husband if she'd served it. What's happened to our culture?

Thursday 3 January

Arts Council Drama Panel meeting by oil-lamp. I know Heath's Conservative but this is *too* atavistic. Some new members and a few who seldom come – Trevor Nunn, Frank Marcus, Donald Sinden. Crucial item is the future of the Old Vic theatre after the National company leaves it to open its 'concrete ghetto'. Not my words but they sum up the general view. I think it will be great to have a theatre to complement the Festival Hall.

Had to leave for a children's concert at the Purcell Room. Chaotic streets full of cars that had been flushed out by the rail strike and were cruising for a space. I was early, having gone by taxi, and sat watching the hall fill with middle-class mums shepherding their flocks. I began to fear I should be the only man in an otherwise empty row joining in 'Ding-dong merrily' and 'I am a jolly cobbler'. The family arrived at last for a recital that ranged from madrigals to 'Lullaby of Birdland'.

Friday 4 January

Albert says he and Oscar Lewenstein are the only directors of the Royal Court in favour of taking over the Vic. The resident prima donnas – Lindsay Anderson and Anthony Page, to name but a few – don't want their kozy korner broken up or enlarged.

Saturday 5 January

Bob's blocking not so far impressive. Four or five actors are lined up across the stage, down centre, as though the sizeable set is a mere backcloth. Medwin says, 'We don't want them saying we've built the Albert Hall only to do the show in a lobby.'

No work today as Bob is in Brussels talking about another production.

Sunday 6 January

Peggy rang early (from Brighton?) to tell me Mike doesn't want to do *The Freeway*. He asked her to break it to me gently. Why is a call more gentle than a letter? She'll be forwarding his letter now I know the worst.

Monday 7 January

Rehearsals moved to Dean Street and a bleak hall with Selfridge chandeliers above a synagogue. Cold, dark, with bad acoustics, but at least we can eat Italian in the local trattoria. At five, we were expecting another half-hour's work when the caretaker came in, told us our time was up and went without explanation. 'What's this?' Bob asked the stage manager.

'A Jewish half-past-five,' I suggested.

Someone had blundered. A letter from landlords to the management made clear we'd have to quit at five to allow praying to start at five-fifteen. Also, of course, no work at all on Saturday, their Sabbath.

It struck me that a far more useful enterprise than all these theatre institutes and museums they're always raising at the Drama Panel would be a custom-built rehearsal hall like the one BBC-TV has at Acton.

[Still no sign of this 35 years later. In New York, any show with enough money uses the old warehouse block converted for that purpose by Michael Bennett. My last venture in London as director a few years ago saw us trying to breathe life into my play in a Youth Club or Drill Hall in Kennington with echoes like a swimming-bath.]

Wednesday 9 January

Mike's letter made clear it's not myself but my play he objects to. Well, that's a relief.

'I just don't feel strongly enough about it to risk another collaboration.'

I replied – over three pages – saying he'd never much cared for my stuff on first sight and that I believe this to be my best so far so he should give it a try and see if it grows on him.

Thursday 10 January

Traffic into London impossible due to train strikes so Thelma ran me to Greenwich, I crossed beneath the river by the old foot tunnel (the huge lifts still running on electricity!), took a bus to Mile End and from there by tube to the West End.

The Synagogue's caretaker is exceptionally ill-natured, even for a caretaker, one of those born corporals who always get this kind of job. The hall's cold, dark and ugly, and even at midday it's hard to see each other. At four p.m., candles are lit. Today was one of those when Heath has prohibited work. We pressed on for another hour, using torches to light our scripts. At five, the corporal comes to switch *on* the lights to signify the end of the working day. The anomalies of this sort of vengeful measure are more annoying than the actual nuisance. Though we're only rehearsing for a month and a great deal of work (in my case spread over two years) depends on the outcome, we're subject to the same rules as those who do the same jobs every day of their year. Its only practical result is to aggrandise the jobsworths, the Corporal Nyms of life.

[He left quite an impression and re-emerged in the far more sympathetic form of Corporal Len Bonny in *Privates on Parade*.]

Friday 11 January

Another day wasted, as Denholm was recalled for a day's filming.

A note from Peter Hall that though he knows Mike 'doesn't feel able to do your new play', this does not affect his eagerness to see it.

Saturday 12 January

Spent morning working on *The Freeway* while the company were on Wimbledon Common taking stills to be used in the slide-show.

Late afternoon joined them in a Baker Street church crypt, whence they were driven by the Jewish Sabbath.

Monday 14 January

On the stage of the Globe at last. Writing a week later, I can't be sure which method of transport I used on which day, whether bus, ferry, pleasure-boat, underwater tunnel, hot-air balloon or ox-cart. Eventually the railwaymen went back, and London's usual muddle was resumed. On a set for *Private Lives*, they staggered through without books, not a moment too soon. Behind the flimsy flats stood our mossy ox-cart rescued from a field near Ribérac. Geraldine wheeled on the old barrow lent by Belsey. A new member joined the cast: a speckled red hen. They're building a hutch for her on the theatre's roof.

Tuesday 22 January

Went with Medwin to *Evening Standard* lunch at Savoy.

St John Stevas, Minister for the Arts, made a speech in which he compared the life-styles of colliers with those of the acting profession. 'I'd like to know what miners would say if they were expected to be glamorous on the money paid to most of you.' There was one of those momentary but almost audible pauses as people drew breath in astonishment, then a derisive cheer from the left-wing faction.

Olivier got an award for his ten years at the National, a sort of consolation prize for having lost the job to Hall. He must have enough statuettes to fill a sizeable hall and used one recently to chase away a burglar in his Brighton home. Perhaps it had been damaged and this was a replacement. He made a speech which sounded like blank verse, though that may have just been the way he spoke it. Danny La Rue led a standing ovation.

Wednesday 30 January

For a fortnight nothing written here. Spending my days at a place of work and long hours getting there and back is no more than most people do every day of their lives, so that's no excuse. I'm just not used to it.

As well as which, rehearsals are no fun to write about. Gradually, as planned and hoped, the various elements come together. Lines are learnt, photographs come through, props slowly appear, costumes are paraded, sound FX tried out, lines changed. Bob and I have eaten most days in a quiet Italian place nearby where none of the cast disturb us.

Thursday 31 January

First public preview started with applause for the set and a round on Albert's entrance. Pat Heywood, of whom by this time we had such high hopes, was muted and distant. Denholm dried early on and never recovered. Albert plunged about energetically and only Geraldine had the measure of the house, always creating a silence in which to deliver her lines.

A man and woman arrived late to sit beside me, talking and carping throughout.

'Self-conscious,' she would say.

'It's improving slightly,' he'd answer.

During the love scene, the man loudly belched. From the row behind came snoring from another well-fed theatregoer. I finally asked my neighbour if he'd let me listen to the play. The first act raised fewer laughs than I'd expected but the plot carried it along. The second was a long haul to the final scene when snoring and coughing were widespread.

I sneaked out as the curtain fell and walked alone through the streets. But it couldn't be ducked. Back at the Globe, Albert was cooing over the box-office figures. Well, he'd always said it would be fun to do a commercial play for a change after all that art at the Court. Ill-wishers and fair-weather friends touring backstage avoided me. Bob, Thelma and I retired to a pub and agreed it was far from promising, but had no idea what to do.

Saturday 2 February

Thelma woke me with breakfast and the news that she and Lore, the vicar's wife, were going shopping. I said it seemed to me her place was with me on this most miserable of days when I had nothing to do but dwell on next week's failure. I feel certain this is the play that's going to break my run of luck. It doesn't deliver the goods and I'm afraid they'll say so.

The second preview audience was even less responsive, consisting mostly of foreign agents looking for a hit they could get translated. The first half was better done, though Geraldine and Albert were still sizing up the house, Denholm and Pat improving but still under par. The second act's a long decline and the final scene a failure.

Friday we were bidden to lunch by Albert and Michael and I knew they'd be suggesting my ending was wrong, that Dick shouldn't leave but decide he was stuck with the happiness he had. 'You're always saying in your plays that you want to leave Thelma but you never do. That's as interesting as going.'

I said yes, perhaps he should stay, the present ending was a damp squib, but for me there was what Henry James called 'the dear little question of how to do it'. I'd written the scene a dozen times without finding the answer. Albert said I should get off the Librium I was taking and back to my desk. We all pitched in. Michael Medwin's struck me as best: Dick should *intend* to go and try to write a farewell note to his wife. But he can't find the words and keeps going back to the start. Somehow he finds himself holding an egg, remembering the one he's previously broken with ease when he least wanted to. Now he starts pressing on its shell and this time finds he can't. The end might come as he struggles. The egg, nest or family holds. He is what he is.

Next morning I wrote this action down, with the closing line, 'Break, you bastard, break!'

Came to join the family and looked into the street to see a Peugeot 504 Estate parked at 'our' kerb. This is what Thelma had been shopping for, a new car, a good time to buy while I was looking elsewhere. Selling them at the time of petrol rationing must be about as easy as skis in the desert. Yet she got no discounts, not even free seat-belts. And who will buy our old Renault? The new motor, she explains, as we explore it, has room for all the family in three rows of seats and will be better for our long journeys to Siorac. Drove it to Victoria Coach Station to meet my mother arriving from Bristol. On the way home, dropped the new closing page at Bob's place.

Took her that night to the Globe and had to leave her so as to meet Bob and hear his views of the change. Left her in Albert's dressing-room, chatting to him and his dresser, who told me he'd known Barri Chatt and had once done a drag act himself.

[Barri was the famous queen sent out to Singapore to join Combined Services Entertainments as a civilian addition to our armed-forces shows. Or, as I had him say in the character of Terri Dennis in *Privates on Parade* – 'I gave my all for the boys.']

After comparing notes with Bob for an hour, I went to fetch Mum and walked her through Rupert Street market, the pretty stalls alight and fruity in the pitch dark. She'd been surprised, she said, that a male star like Albert had a female dresser. When I put her straight, she refused to believe me.

To relieve our drab theatre façade, Albert had ordered festoons of tinsel and the little lamps that flash around obstructions in the road. Medwin and his wife were in the foyer and I told him his solution had worked – on paper at least.

A little party of friends, some stepping off the Avenue, assembled in the foyer while the house went in. About half an hour after curtain-up, a gruesome twosome arrived – John Van Eyssen and Carl Foreman. They showed no discomfiture at being so late, not even having the grace to say they'd come back another time. Yet they'll have no qualms about starting a bad buzz, after seeing half a preview. Luckily they're both yesterday's men, sinking out of sight together. Foreman's so disagreeable that I actually felt some sympathy with John Wayne on a recent talk-show when he said the Hollywood Commies were putting good people out of work. Because what sort of Commie is Foreman anyway? A millionaire film producer who sees the poor only en route in some limo from his London flat to a chic health farm.

Picked up the new dress Thelma's bought for the first night on Wednesday. New car, dress, presents for cast, star cast in play at the Globe, once the centre of Binkie Beaumont's little empire. Couldn't enjoy any of this, knowing that on Wednesday night all these IOU's would be called in.

After working most of the day on the last scene, Bob and I watched from the back of a packed dress circle. Much the best house and response so far. We afterwards walked through the sordid streets saying there was nothing more we could do, just hope for the best.

Tuesday 5 February

The Hewlett family came to stay – Francis and Liz, Claire, Mark and Francesca. He'd brought the first-night presents for the cast and immediate collaborators: twelve ceramic plaques in his infra-Woolworth style showing a nude girl with a satchel and straw hat in long grass, with a border of 'pop' flowers.

Morning: to Biba's for Claire, now a shy teenager. While the 'women' cavorted among the clothes, Francis and I theorised about the element of Camp in design. Forgot to mention on my last visit here that there's a floor given to joke 'rooms', a parody of the V & A's period interiors. Biba's versions of those are a Tretchikoff room with the Burmese Lady, a greenhouse with overhanging plastic fruit, a lounge in white satinette with plaster ducks in flight across the wall. And there are rugs and carpets just like we had at home, in shades of brown with geometric patterns.

'Look at the prices,' Francis said, 'yet these are sold in every country market but without the inverted commas, the implicit comment that it's smart to take the piss by putting this in a chic London flat. Well, I actually do find these things beautiful. It's the art I grew up in, my natural response is to love it. That green lady holding up the mottled lampshade, that firescreen with the radiating sun in one corner . . . My sister's house is still like that.'

Then on to the V & A and, in a Jacobean panelled room, carved into the ceiling was a flight of ducks. So *plus ça change*.

I skipped the final preview. Just as well, because I'm told it was the worst ever. Evening at home, Francis sketching the kids and cats.

Wednesday 6 February

Awoke to find the world was white again. The first snow of winter had waited for the Hewletts as it had so often in Bristol. These Cornish children believe it's always snowing when they leave home for England. Seeing the sun, knowing the snow wouldn't last long, we dragged our sledge to the park's steepest slope and took great rides down nearly to the wall of the Greenwich theatre, with hard labour in between trudging the thing up the already melting incline. This took the edge off my anxiety as no Librium could have.

Before the show, I delivered our gifts to the dressing-rooms and finally left to see a film, as I'd decided this opening was one I couldn't sit through. The only advantage a playwright has on these occasions: he needn't stick around. But queues at all the best cinemas sent me back. Going in by the stage door, I met Albert waiting in the wings for an entrance.

'How's it going?'

'Okay. Not bad at all.'

I crept into an upper box and looked more at the audience than the play. A full, attentive and interested house. Snowdons in front row of dress circle, Margaret leaning forward, head on hand, Tony slumped back as I'd have been. I saw Harold Hobson (*Sunday Times*) smile once. Thelma was among a sneer of critics, with only Louise between her and Frank Marcus (*Telegraph*). He told me later he only had to look at her to know when to laugh. Elsewhere were the Griggs, Frayns, Mendels, Claude Roy, Brays, Hewletts, most of those who know us.

Afterwards, avoiding everyone, I was caught by Snowdon in a corridor backstage. He asked me if I'd liked his portraits. 'Very nice.' He promised to send prints.

Then there was a party at the Café Royal. Company only, with wives and partners. An enjoyable occasion, like one in a hospital where the patient may die. I had to cut a cake which had iced on it my three associations with Memorial: *Joe Egg*. Comedy, 1967; *Forget-me-not Lane*, Apollo, 1971; *Chez Nous*, Globe, 1974.

And as I stuck the knife in, Albert said 'And it's a plastic cake, so let's have the real one.' This came with a picture of our poster iced in red, green and black. Geraldine did the first cut and deserved to for being so marvellous.

Thursday 9 February

Morning press unanimously good. Once the ghoulish recorder of illness and death, I'd suddenly become a writer of elegant West End hits. 'The present high-water mark of middle-class society drama,' wrote Irving Wardle in *The Times* and praised Bob's production that 'rises to an extraordinary concluding image . . . which strikes me as one of the great endings of modern drama.' Pinero, Coward and Neil Simon were invoked this time instead of Chekhov, Albee and Osborne. A few mentioned – and took the piss out of – Albert's circular letter asking them not to reveal the plot and some spilt the beans, claiming they could find no way to discuss the play without.

Billington (*Guardian*) finished: 'It looks as though we're going to have to wait some time for that first Nichols flop.' Which sounds as though they'd all been hoping.

Enormous relief all round. It looked as though Peggy was right and I have my first real commercial success.

Sunday 10 February

Sundays even better and a great relief to find I was back in Harold Hobson's bad books again after an inexplicable lapse over *Forget-me-not Lane*. Well, he didn't so much review this new play as Albert's letter and scoffed at the plot as being transparent from the word go.

Cushman (*Observer*) says it's 'the best new play in London and the best its author has written'. Not a great compliment coming from someone whose headline for my second was 'Poor Health'. But since then we've met as members of Greenwich Theatre committee and he found I didn't have fangs or fingernails like claws. Critics' views are often affected by such encounters, of which the punters (looking for a likely night out) know nothing. But better such human frailty than a doomed attempt at being impartial.

It's all a game and let's be glad we've been dealt a winning hand again.

Friday 15 February

Drove to Cornwall in our comfortable new car, which Catherine christened near Stonehenge by throwing up over the picnic box.

At a month's distance, as I write this, the details of our delightful week in Falmouth have mostly gone. Sunbathed and picnicked on the beaches in Cornwall's premature spring. All very tropical with its early daffodils, dragon-trees and the exotic greenery in the eighteenth-century garden of the Art College. Francis was busy much of his time trying to save his bit of Cornwall from the worst effects of three million tourists expected to invade them annually as soon as the Midlands motorway's complete.

[The towns and villages suddenly fill with these displaced persons, wandering in search of pleasure, usually spending more time shopping than by the sea they have come to enjoy. Ronald Duncan, the poet and playwright, lives in a cottage with a street frontage. He was in his sitting room reading the paper when a middle-aged couple walked in with their teenage daughter, sat at his dining-table and ordered three Cream Teas. With great restraint, Duncan went to the kitchen, laid a tray, made three teas, served them and went back to his paper while they consumed them. The husband was furious when his money was refused and Duncan told him they'd walked into his home and asked how he'd he like it.]

The Hewletts' son Mark was picking daffodils at slave-rates. Liz was brighter and happier.

It was the perfect way to wind down from the artificial crisis of our opening.

Wednesday 27 February

Seeing more secondary schools for Louise. Her nipples swell and she watches them amazed. She'll soon be menstruating.

Blackheath Bluecoats is a mixed comprehensive – democratic, bustling, brand-new, some of its buildings still incomplete, the classes often given two and three together, the specialist rooms well equipped, with a drama studio as good as Bristol University's. But more exclusive than any grammar.

'I may as well tell you,' said the head, 'there's no point in applying for Louise unless yours is a Church of England family and you're all regular churchgoers.'

We've plumped for Roan Grammar, as it's nearest to home. In Falmouth there's one comprehensive which means what it says. Everyone goes there and it works well. The whole education system is part of the middle-class game called Hierarchy. You move up the board by taking unfair advantage of the other players, jumping over them, buttering up the banker, etc. There's even a *Which* supplement that tells the Paper Lampshade, two-car families about Best Buys among the schools. And it's sold openly!

Thursday 28 February

Approaching last act of the revised *Freeway*. I'm changing the minister who visits the traffic jam on behalf of the government from a faceless civil servant to a Conservative clown, based on Gerald Nabarro. From his obituaries I learnt that he was a working-class or at any rate lower-middle boy who left school at thirteen and built himself consciously into a fake toff, complete with RAF moustache.

We cast our votes for the general election in a local housing estate, Thelma, Sylvia and I putting crosses for Labour in a safe seat, knowing Wilson won't be returned and, even if he is, won't do much better than Heath.

Royal Court: *The Island*, second play by the black Africans Winston Ntshona and John Kani, who have done the only really worthwhile drama for the last year. This was slightly less good than *Sizwe Banzi is Dead*, because Ntshona had the bigger part and is the lesser actor. But Fugard's craft has given them shape and subtlety without losing the natural power of their half-Bantu idiom.

Last thing in bed reading Fisher's *History of Europe*. Post-imperial pre-Papal Rome. The Visigoths at the gates.

Friday 1 March

Election had resulted in a deadlock, with Liberals and others holding the balance of power. Wilson will have to sue for support from Nationalists in Wales and Scotland and from the Paisleyites in Ulster. Glad to be rid of Heath at least.

Eve: To welcome a French producer to *Chez Nous*. I've had a few letters from patrons asking for their money back so it was consoling to see a full house enjoying themselves.

The company manager told me the speckled hen has laid an egg at last. Regulations covering the use of animals in shows require the bird to have a mate, so a cockerel has been ordered.

Thursday 14 March

Well Hall Pleasaunce is all that remains of the house where E. Nesbit spent twenty of her most prolific years. The house is gone but the moat and tudor barn are still (just about) there, just now housing a show of repulsive art.

Once the philandering Fabian husband Bland had died, blind but still a cantankerous male chauvinist, Nesbit couldn't afford to keep the large house going and sold it after her second marriage to the captain of the free Woolwich ferry. Sad to wander in this dull little park under the surviving cypresses and think of her sitting in their shade with Forster, Wells, Shaw, Baron Corvo or Noël Coward who was enthralled by her and called her 'a strange case of a *real* Bohemian'.

[I still find this ménage fascinating and last year drafted a millennium play for the National, set in 1899, a way of illustrating the hopes they had at the advent of the new century and what has happened since. Leading Fabians would appear – even those like the Webbs who may never have visited the house that Wells later described as 'not so much an atmosphere as a web'. But Trevor Nunn at the National showed no enthusiasm for it and, with so many unproduced scripts on my shelves, I nowadays need a positive push or promise before I spend time on a play that requires the sort of resources only found at the NT or RSC.]

Monday 18 March

Claude Roy writes that no-one in Paris is interested in *Chez Nous*. Good. I'll be spared another night in some dusty boulevard house watching a pale shadow of the London show, which by the way has fallen off. The advance is less than before and Albert's name's not enough to counteract poor word-of-mouth. So Peggy was wrong after all.

Thursday 21 March

Knuckle by David Hare. Same sort of excitement I felt at first seeing *Loot* and *Saved*. Mike B. directed. Very well. Stylish, precise, unblinking, an elegant and coherent sermon on the unacceptable face of capitalism. Let's hope to God he doesn't go posh and right-wing like Osborne and Amis or 'artistic' like Pinter.

[No sign of that till lately, when Hare's run of exciting plays slowed down to an old-fashioned trot and finally a slow walk with *Amy's View*, which looked to me like a creaky plea for former values.]

Friday 22 March

Second draft of *The Freeway* done. The idea was to shorten it but, though I've taken a good deal out, I seem to have put as much back. Now I have two equally useful drafts.

Monday 1 April

Fools' Day again. Dad's birthday. Time for making new resolutions.

A weekend of fine weather has lifted all our spirits. London warmer than Naples, Madrid and Mallorca. Spring weddings at our parish church, pretty ceremonies spoilt by arrivals in noisy cars driven by angry-looking men who'd been dragged away from the Grand National.

We played ping-pong at the table on our back lawn and asked each other why our garden doesn't grow. Perhaps a few silver bells or cockle-shells would brighten it up. On either side two avid gardeners produce profusions of blooms from the dusty soil. Yet ours is best for games. How much are we giving up for our children? How old shall I be when they finally leave the nest? When Cath's due to leave off being educated at eighteen, I'll be fifty-six.

The ideal life for me would have been a childless one in a city flat, touring the world's playgrounds with my wife, always making room for literary lunches. Suburban family life precludes that. Does Michael Frayn, who shares our kind of domesticity, go off making travel films in Australia, Sweden, Hungary, Israel, etc., to escape *Blue Peter*, the rumbling dishwasher, the irksome constraints of modern fatherhood? A card from Peggy Ramsay on holiday in Crete reminds me that I've never seen Greece, Turkey, Rome, Naples, the Rhine Valley, Vienna, the Riviera. Easy for two (or one), a military campaign for our family. Our drive in 1962 from Bristol to Yugoslavia in a minivan with baby Louise on a mattress now seems a madcap stunt, done for a bet or charity, but in the event was easy-peasy. With all our new resources – large car, plentiful cash, a mother's help – it should be painless but wouldn't be because babies are passive dolls you carry about like parcels, while growing children are people in their own right, objecting to the food, heat, museums, the lack of a swim, always demanding Coke and crisps.

'Gave a lift to four Americans,' writes Peggy, 'who decorated my car with chains of flowers after they'd said goodbye. Tomorrow to Knossos and culture!'

[There follows a two-page disquisition into the question of how to be both solitary writer and family man. This was the matter that pressed hard on both my fiction and my private thoughts just then. This particular outburst had been brought on partly by reading a biography of Ivy Compton-Burnett. I began making lists of the celibate, childless or homosexual who'd never had to watch *Magic Roundabout* and wouldn't have known a Dalek from an Action Man. Here they were, the great unblessed – Austen, the Brontës, Shaw, James, Forster, the Woolfs, both the Lawrences, Mansfield, Eliot, Auden, Isherwood, Wodehouse, Coward, Angus Wilson, Elizabeth Bowen, Naipaul, Tom Wolfe, Capote, Tennessee Williams . . . Many more had only one son or daughter: Orwell, Osborne, Pinter.

The family men of literature, I claimed, resented their offspring – Tolstoy, Dickens, Waugh. And sometimes their behaviour was vile.]

What a hard bitch Compton-Burnett became and how she enjoyed inflicting pain, though her achievement may in time be seen as supreme. I long to evolve a manner as unquestionable as hers but know it isn't in me. I'm neither intelligent nor educated nor stoical enough. And I live in a more ordinary time. The questions we have to face now don't fall so easily within the province of fiction, but are more about dealing with machinery.

All I have, apart from a gift for mimicry, for hearing voices accurately, is ambition. In my twenties the most I hoped for was to have a play produced. In my thirties, living on television drama, I aimed to write a decent stage play. My early forties have been occupied with the production of four such theatre pieces, all critical and financial successes, on a modest level. I'm sure none of them will survive.

Though it would be easy to go on rehashing my own life into different kinds of stews, I'm now in a position to make a conscious change and want to find a style of speech common to all the characters, not to imitate tones of voice or quirks of diction that are by their nature ephemeral. Of course, Compton-Burnett is the ultimate exemplar.

I've also lost interest in this journal. Twenty years have been described in fits and starts. Perhaps I'll miss this regular exercise but, now that its keeping-up has become a chore, it's better dropped. Lacking notes of the present, I may be forced to invent. What was *really* said doesn't matter. What I *want* to say does.

[Fits and starts was a fair description of how I'd kept it since I began at eighteen. The page-a-day books bought for me as Christmas presents helped maintain the habit. A blank sheet was a reproach, a sign the day had been wasted Now came the first long break, seven months of untouched pages. And from now until 1983 there's either a scrappy, ill-kept record or none at all, especially sad as these were interesting years. So is that why Diary faltered? It seems to confirm the general view that anyone who writes about his or her life on a daily basis should find a better one. I can hardly dispute this, as mine has been most strictly kept in a spell of country retreat and, after that, during the decade I've lived in an upper maisonette with my wife of forty years, a period of fifteen years or more when very little 'happened' to us. Of course, 'eventful = interesting' is a vulgar equation and quiet lives may run deeper, like still waters.

[375]

When the record begins again, there follows a certain amount of catching-up. The colour has been drained from this version of the interim. It lacks the mundane events and routines that properly fill a journal, as they do most lives. I include them only to keep the plot boiling.]

Saturday 9 November

A bright winter's morning. In the bare maple outside my window, a pigeon is jabbing its beak into its wing feathers, gathering a snack of fleas perhaps? Blue sky. White clouds.

In half an hour, John Cox and I will walk down to Greenwich Theatre to discuss the design for *Hardings Luck*, my fusion of two Nesbit novels, which is to be our Christmas production, my third new play to appear this year. *Chez Nous* was a fluke but in the long run not a success. Audiences didn't care for it and stopped coming, despite the starry cast and glowing reviews. Not that it matters much any more but there are signs of a malicious undercurrent that turned opinion against it.

The wait wasn't as long as Michael Billington predicted: only six months, in fact, before *The Freeway* opened at the Old Vic. Then there were no half-measures. This was failure with a vengeance. Another first was the critical unanimity with which it was sunk. *Chez Nous* achieved six months and an irony for me was that it was taken off earlier than planned so that Ayckbourn's plays could find a West End home after their run at the Greenwich Theatre, where it had proved our biggest success to date. I remember a meeting with the puritan Ewan Hooper, our artistic director, in the bar during a performance of it while from upstairs came the huge animal roars of an audience laughing at full stretch.

'Well, we seem to have a hit,' I said.

Ewan shook his head, mystified and disapproving. Giving the people quite this much pleasure was not what had driven him to rebuild and reopen the old music-hall as the only theatre in south-east London.

The Ayckbourn ran for two years at the Globe. *Freeway* will be off by January.

After an experience similar to mine with this one, James Thurber wrote:

'It had only one fault, this play. It was kinda lousy.'

I wish I could feel that in this case. In fact, I always thought it was my best. So did the few people who read it before it went on. Even Michael Blakemore later said his refusal hadn't been due to the script but the state of our partnership. Some chicanery went on while Peter Hall pushed Jonathan Miller into directing it and me into agreeing. We were both persuaded by this amazing man whose political hunger is as huge as his artistic energy. There was an exchange of telegrams between Hall in London and me in Dordogne which ended with my giving in only when he told me that if Miller didn't do it, it wouldn't be done at all, at any rate by the National Theatre. I should have withdrawn it but felt a further wait wouldn't help so topical a story. Jonathan was and still is a friend but he never seemed good casting for this quasi satire which required not his sort of inspired notions but down-to-earth planning and a daily discipline extended over two months of rehearsal. Also a lot of pre-production argument about the text itself, leading probably to several different drafts, as a mutual process of discovery both for me and the director. This is not his style. 'I'm not a script editor,' he told me early on, 'I accept your play as it is.'

'I find it hard to pinpoint why this was such a failure,' he writes in his book on directing.

The play itself was largely to blame. Because I felt strongly about its argument, I failed to see its flaws. A play about a huge traffic standstill has the same inherent obstacle as a novel about a siege. By definition, it lacks movement.

But direction, design and casting didn't help. My idea was a social comedy taking place in a crisis. I wanted a colourful landscape beyond the stranded cars – pastiche-Constable – with a bright blue cyclorama which only darkens at the end when rain's expected. I'd read in a paper that a honeymoon bride, caught in an enormous jam in Florida, described it as 'Like being on a desert island with a lot of happy people'. Our cut-price set had instead a black surround, a promise of gloom and futuristic horrors.

Another serious mistake was the casting of the comedienne Irene Handl in a minor rôle. As soon as I heard, I reminded Peter that it wasn't a starring opportunity and I hoped she knew and accepted that. Of course, he said. But we'd hardly begun when she asked if she could play Joan Hickson's part instead, then started a relentless campaign to be given more lines. Jonathan didn't care for this part of the job any more than our vicar did for the 'pastoral' side. Nothing we did cut any ice. She assumed centre stage, paraphrased every line and, when someone on the book tried to correct her, told them to mind their own business. Joan, in her third play for me, was driven into herself as she saw she was losing a war she hadn't declared.

Despite all this, my faith in the play had not faltered. Not quite blinded but blinkered. I could see all these landmines but kept my eyes fixed on the far horizon of our first night. During the week of previews, Hall decided on drastic surgery and amputated a script that had already been mortally wounded. The company was mostly at a time of life when 'study' (as they call line-learning) is a major anxiety. Once learnt, best held to. So the savage cuts of the preview week left them groggy with doubt and fear.

Even a dress-rehearsal that was like an avant-garde collage didn't shake my confidence. On opening night I stood in the Old Vic foyer modestly receiving the praise of faithful friends, feeling vindicated as I had with *The National Health*. The last pleasure I took from this play was our party at a Turkish restaurant in Deptford and the sight of Jonathan and his fastidious university friends trying not to quail as a belly-dancer shook her bejewelled navel in their faces.

Frank Marcus's 'An unmitigated disaster' was about par for the course. Not one review was *for* it and only one not thoroughly against.

[Plays are blueprints for action. As diagrams they may have qualities that don't work when the ceremonial launch comes. Too much of this play came from *The Gorge* but the encounters between the car-factory shop-steward and the nobleman en route to Glyndebourne were a new and to me amusing element. They brought two ends of the social scale into an unlikely meeting that had actually happened when Reg, Thelma's father, had done some work on John Grigg's car. Both men were written with sympathy but didn't seem so on the stage. In fact, John so resented the portrait that our friendship barely survives.

The play was better served in a radio version in 1991, helped by news bulletins and sound effects.]

As soon as the dailies came out, I left Thelma to face the rest and flew to New York.

An Indian couple befriended me on the plane, the man was ex-RAF and served in Calcutta when I was also there as Aircraftsman Second-class Nichols 2231747. Now he and his wife helped find homes for children orphaned in Vietnam. Utterly Westernised, they drank whisky, smoked Rothmans, bought duty-free goods and hired earphones to hear the film. It was as though they dared not omit any ritual of jet travel.

The woman listened to her phones for a while then turned to me:

'D'you like Country 'n' Western?'

'Not very much, no.'

'Oh, do listen to it sometime. I assure you, it grows on you. Here, listen now.'

Some time later her husband came back from arguing with the cabin crew about his excess baggage and I was able to return her phones with a nod and smile. After lunch they watched two films depicting brutal murders between sequences of car-destruction. From the window-seat I could hardly avoid seeing both screens, though without the sounds of screeching tyres, colliding vehicles and resulting explosions, which the Indians had rented at two dollars each. Whenever anyone walked down the aisle, obscuring the view, she asked them to clear, saying, 'Excuse me' till I thought I'd have to use the emergency procedures.

Arvin Brown wasn't waiting, as he'd promised, and was eventually traced to another terminal. My mistake. Two flights had arrived at once and I'd given his secretary details of the wrong one. A huge black Cadillac hired by the management took us to the Algonquin where he left me to have a nap before dinner at 6.30. I lay wide awake reading Thomas Hardy. The wrong book. I should have chosen something in praise of cities, not *Far From the Madding Crowd*.

The hotel has a famous entrance hall where you can meet and talk but I knew no-one in New York except Arvin. The celebrated bar where Dorothy Parker, Robert Benchley, Alexander Woolcott and the rest used to trade wisecracks is just a bar and quite a small one. Perhaps it's only for us English that they lay on their history so thick. When I go there, I want to see the present, not some second-rate past.

The day's main event took place in Grand Central Station's oyster-bar: a heap of fish that would have sunk a trawler. After we'd nibbled at the edges for a while, Arvin's wife Joyce said she would have asked for doggy-bags but her current dachshund's allergic to seafood.

We walked through the dusk of Saturday evening up Sixth Avenue (a.k.a. 'of the Americas') to 50th Street and across Broadway to the

Circle in the Square theatre in the basement of an office block. A broad staircase leads from the street-level foyer to another classy lobby and finally to an auditorium shaped like a horizontal arch. The playing area pushes halfway through the rows of seats, vanishing into a narrow vomitorium. It's almost as though the architect thought of the stage last. Or only meant them to do long thin plays. I'd never thought of *The National Health* as one of those but it works surprisingly well, erupting into the crowd, the front spectactors able to replace props on beds and lockers when they fall off.

The production's poor-to-middling; it's hard for us to take the accents, that mixture of the Bronx and Sidney which is how Cockney sounds to their ears. Most comments I heard 'at intermission' were hostile.

'This guy seems to have some hang-up about sickness.'

The lack of any mug-shots in the programme meant I could be invisible. I smoked apart on the sidewalk trying not to hear.

The last part of this play is unpleasant beyond the call of duty. I thought of *The Freeway*, which kept its cool and good manners, and of the differing responses these two plays had. Michael did the first so well that few saw through to the unfocused play behind the show.

[But why should audiences tell play from production? They see actors in sets wearing costumes, handling props, skilfully lit, all out to please. Only critics have to worry about content. Was I in the wrong business? The question nagged me till the nineties when I decided the answer was yes, by which time it was too late for me to take up another trade.]

The company only wanted praise and this I tried to give. By the time it was over, all the hullo-goodbye and what-about-*you?*, my biological clock was at 5 a.m. and I thought I might try to sleep. Despite the canyon-echo effects of sirens, garbage disposal, cab-horns, air-con units, what Duke Ellington wrote as Harlem Airshaft, I managed an intermittent doze till 7. Breakfasted off impressive crockery, fresh-squeezed orange-juice served in a silver-plated dish of ice, boiled eggs in a teacup and so on, I walked in bright sunshine to Central Park, where horse-carriages already waited for fares to emerge from the Plaza and cyclists enjoyed the Sunday ban on cars.

In the menagerie, apes and bears seem to have gone native Manhattan, with the same downbeat faces. If they'd spoken (as in those chimp commercials), they'd have said, 'What's your prahblum, bud?' Along the paths, ill-tempered men sold hot dogs, pretzels, burgers, all smelling terrible.

The actors are charming. Rita Moreno is Arvin's tame celebrity this time, the Puerto Rican singer and dancer who made a name with *West Side Story* and consolidated it by an affair with Brando. She's now married to a doctor who's dying of a weak heart. Nurse Sweet is played by a nice Jewish girl with sparkling eyes and a bright smile.

The Browns took me to Greenwich Village where we cruised Washington Square and along streets of Italian markets. Spent nights imprisoned in that hotel bedroom, watching the hours limp by. Rang home when it was England's afternoon and Thelma told me the Sunday reviews had been as bad as the dailies.

Took a bus to Battery Point. The driver looked at my dollar note and said he didn't make change but maybe one of the passengers could. I got on and asked the crowd.

'Sure,' an old man barked back, a cloud of whisky breaking on my face, 'what you want, some cents for the fare?'

He started going through his purse, counting coins.

'Very kind of you.'

'You from outa town?'

I didn't know as yet that this means not only someone from the real America but any stranger, foreigner or member of an alien species.

'No, England.'

'You a limey?'

'Right.'

'I hate the bastards. That's forty cents so far.'

'So why d'you hate us?'

'You should get right out of Ireland, stop killing innocent people.'

'Well, I agree with you. I think most English would.'

Other passengers smiled in mitigation.

'That right? You coulda fooled me. That's ninety –'

'That's enough, thank you.'

'Ten cents makes one dollar. Okay, sir, have a nice day.'

He was an ex-cop, he told me, making an annual visit to his precinct station. He hated New York and never came in if he could help it. I hope the other guys in the NYPD enjoyed his visit.

No smoking in the waiting hall for Staten Island Ferry or on the boat itself. Otherwise the trip was a pleasure, the cheapest outing in town, as everyone kept saying, though Arvin had never done it and Joyce only as a kid. So how long is it since I was at Madame Tussaud's?

I had some small success chatting up Nurse Sweet who volunteered that she'd been shy about stripping off as Ursula in *Lane*. We discussed this in detail and I asked how her career was going. Not well. If this show folded, she'd be back behind the notions counter at Blooming-dale's. But I let it drift without seizing my chance. What's wrong with me? It isn't fear, certainly not fidelity. There was everything to gain, nothing to lose. I hadn't brought my ham sandwich and here was, if not a banquet, a tasty meal. She kissed me on the mouth on parting. Ambitious actress, apparently successful rider. But I left the morning of their last preview.

At Kennedy some London-bound Americans were asked their reason for going.

'It's a fun city.'

'What particularly?'

'Oh, theatre, I guess.'

'And what d'you like least?

'The bombs.'

But why go so far? You can see most plays in Manhattan, eventually. An Ayckbourn opened the same week as mine and a dozen more are on the way.

[The time-honoured trade between the two cities swings like a slow pendulum. As I write, it's turned the other way and London's now seen as a try-out for Broadway. The cheaper costs and more numerous news-paper opinions make it a better alternative to the old outa town try-outs, which were often, oddly enough, at New Haven, though not at Long Wharf but the local Shubert theatre. Our NT relies for much of its revenue on American musicals and plays and the best-known fringe venues try to entice Hollywood stars. One of the RSC's house play-wrights is American.]

Saturday 23 November

Week in Falmouth with the Hewletts. Made itinerary of Cornish curiosities: Truro's twentieth-century Gothic cathedral, Breage's church and its mediaeval paintings, St Buryan's carved screen; the helicopter base awhirl with activity, the great satellite saucers on Gilhooley Down like an advance party of aliens; an Iron Age settlement on a high point above the sea, the walls intact, only the thatched roofs gone; St Austell's china clay pits, their white heaps of waste like a negative print of Rhondda Valley; the fishing villages of Newlyn, Mevagissey, Mousehole and Portloe, often landing their catches as we arrived; the causeway of St Michael's Mount, tourists paddling across as the tide went down; a seal pool where injured animals are kept till they're well enough to be returned to the sea; D.H. and Frieda Lawrence's cottage at Zennor; the model village of Portreath where we saw many of these again, now reduced to Lilliput size, a cathedral as tall as myself.

At the open-air amphitheatre of Mennack, the titles of former productions are carved into the concrete seat-backs – five of Bob Bolt's, none of mine. Apart from one or two pavilions, the scenic backdrop is the Atlantic Ocean, with nothing between until Manhattan which I'd just left. Francis was once asked to design costumes and props for an amateur crack at Andre Obey's *Noah*. He's long known the place as a visitor but no-one had thought to tell him that the players in this production were all pensioners. Among the necessary animal heads, he designed one for the elephant with outstanding African ears. On the first night, a stiff offshore breeze got up, the ears acted like sails and the frail old chap wearing them would have been carried backwards over the cliff had Monkey and Lion not caught his arms and held him down. Every time any other animals saw him moving upstage in an unrehearsed way they got between him and the sea and gently forced him inland.

The treats of this week made us think we should perhaps go and live in the country again.

Sunday 1 December

In the Mackenzies' biography of H.G. Wells, I learnt of the group of like-minded writers living on the Kent coast in the early years of the century and had often thought of driving down to look for Nesbit's last home and simple gravestone. Today managed to assemble and drive the family off early enough and was at Hythe before lunchtime. First impression was of caravan sites and subfusc summer chalets. Sandgate, though, is a cut above and, while I searched for Spade House, which Wells had built for himself and his wife Jane, the kids played on the sea walls and were soaked by enormous waves. The house is far more bunched up than pictures show. Designed by Voysey and built in 1900, it's now a vegetarian guest-house. I was let in by a prim middle-aged man who showed me the awkward dining-room with low ceilings and stucco walls. Sad atmosphere of a Spanish restaurant that serves only salads. The garden's better, right on the cliffs and above the beach, which used to be reached by a vertical railway. There are a few photos of Wells in the hall and a modern curtain embroidered by some disciple with portraits of those who came here in his heyday – Bennett, Shaw, James, Conrad, the Webbs, Stephen Crane – also of Jane and their boys. None of his lovers, but the affaires came later and the Amber Reeves episode was the reason they left it.

[Time's been as unkind to him and his circle as it's been flattering to the parochial snobberies of Bloomsbury. I take their success to be part of the modern love of Theme Parks, the Laura Ashley side of aesthetics. Though Wells backed too many wrong horses, he was at least prepared to lose his shirt. My local library last year had none of his books on its shelves, though half-a-dozen by his acolyte Rebecca West. Discuss.]

Voysey's idea was to get rid of the pretentious suburban villa (like ours in Blackheath) and adapt arts-and-crafts motifs to a large cottage with all mod cons. Ironic that his sloping roofs, gables, dormer windows, high chimney-stacks and pebble-dash became, in a debased form, the pattern for millions of less pretentious suburban villas of the inter-war years. Only one piece of Wells's furniture remains – a garden bench where he wrote in warm weather.

As I went in again, a woman was giving directions on the phone to someone leaving Charing Cross.

'That man suffers from diabetes,' she said after greeting me, 'and hopes that, as Wells did too, a visit to the house might do him some good.'

It was ghostly in a way H.G. would have hated.

At Dymchurch we picnicked by one of the Martello Towers and I afterwards went looking for traces of Nesbit. I had an idea her simple grave was near the miniature railway and we saw from a timetable that a train was due, so fetched the others and stood on the footbridge while the driver halted, got out and held up traffic on the road before puffing the last few yards over a canal bridge. Descending to the platform, we could see that the engine was only five feet high but drew half-a-dozen carriages with perhaps twenty passengers, not bad for a day in mid-winter. Full-sized people stooped on and off and one man boarded with a suitcase, as though going on a proper inter-city trip. On week-days, I suggested to the family, stations of the line were crammed with commuters, solemnly bending low to avoid denting their bowlers, nodding to other regulars, settling in corner seats, folding copies of the *Telegraph* into even smaller shapes than usual. Would straphangers kneel?

Drove across Romney Marsh to Rye, beautiful town on a steep hill. By the time we reached it, the early evening was drawing in and I had a meeting to attend at five. Did a quick scamper, not even finding Lamb House where Henry James lived. He and Wells were unlikely friends and the younger man used to cycle over from Sandgate to visit the elder, an attraction (and finally a repulsion) of opposites. The town is like a film-set, especially those cobbled streets around the Mermaid Hotel.

Since learnt that Nesbit was buried not at Dymchurch but Jesse St Mary. A pretext for a repeat visit. We love literary pilgrimages.

Monday 2 December

John Osborne's doing three shows at Greenwich – directing Max Wall as Archie Rice and after Christmas two new plays of his will follow my Nesbit conflation.

Press show of the first was a terrific evening, even though John's a slack director, the set took no account of the stage's special shape, the ensemble was ragged and it was far too long at three-and-a-half hours. The play's the thing and still marvellous. Though Max is noth-ing like Olivier, he's quite as good in his solos, more convincing and less ambitious. Frankie Howerd behind us and Betjeman in front leaned across us to agree. Afterwards to a party in St John's Wood, at the house of Robyn Dalton, now John's agent. Connie Chapman had played the wife and told us John's indulgent and Max is impossible to act with, as he never does the same thing twice, always a hazard of comedians going straight, used to improvising but not learning.

Osborne sat in a room apart with Thelma and said he remembered me at Frinton-on-Sea being funny as a vicar in *See How They Run* and playing a man three times my age in *The Deep Blue Sea*. But once his sycophantic court joined them, he acted up in that rasping voice, laughing too much. When I mentioned our journey to Wells's house, he said:

'I once spent a dirty weekend in Sandgate.'

Wesker was nice – hairy and feminine, ready to discuss the real problems of writing. The one I daren't raise is now the only serious one for me: that of not being very interested any more.

A young doctrinaire Marxist enjoyed himself in this well-heeled milieu, on the eve of going off to lecture on Socialism at a seminar in Yugoslavia. I agreed to drive them all home to SE12 and, once in the Peugeot, he showed us a bottle of Scotch he'd stolen. Max, Thelma and I couldn't trust ourselves to speak. Robyn may have had a lot of unfair advantages and trampled on a good few other people in her time but we were all too old and hidebound to see this theft as anything but an abuse of her hospitality. The boy's never offered me so much as a light and a world run by him would be hard grind for the rest of us. Someone told me this sort of robbery is now called 'liberation'.

We dropped Max last, at the dismal suburb of Lee Green. While I put the car into gear, we watched him walk away up the side road towards his digs, this famous, once scandalous, little man in a shortie raincoat and trilby, still in rented rooms. The young Socialist's analysis was certainly spot-on: Robyn the agent in St John's Wood, Max the actor in Lee Green? So why *not* pinch her Scotch?

Thursday 5 December

A run of Act One of *Hardings Luck*, dull and old-fashioned.

Luckily, as a Greenwich Christmas outing, it will pass unnoticed by the world at large. The story isn't good enough to stand up to this scrutiny. Her heart was with the middle-class toffs and the boy here is a literary invention. The young man playing him can't act and there's a gap where the hero should be.

[Nicholas Lyndhurst, can't act?]

Friday 6 December

In Lewisham market Thelma had her purse stolen with the freshly-drawn wages for two weeks of Olive Taylor's charring. Hardly surprising, as she often walks along streets with the purse lying on top her open bag.

Monday 9 December

Letter from Chiesman's department store saying an article of ours has been handed in. Her purse, not stolen at all and every penny of the cash intact. Gave £5 to their Christmas party. Human nature exonerated.

Bought an anthology of filth by John Wilmot, Lord Rochester, including the first dirty play I've read. Those with a proven lack of prurience can pore over this in the British Museum where it has lain since 1640. However, Graham Greene's recently republished book on Milord was too hot to handle in the 1930s but now a change of taste means we can all have a look.

Struggled with the synopsis of a play about Combined Services Entertainments, working-titled *Malayan Moonshine*. I must have revised these ideas twenty times and am not sure whether it's any better now but I must start on it soon.

Friday 20 December

A week spent huffing and puffing about the lack of publicity for the Nesbit play. No word appeared in any of the newspaper lists of Christmas shows. TV round-ups included excerpts from pantomimes as far afield as Exeter and Newcastle but none from Greenwich. I've started raging at everyone at the theatre and have watched their well-known ability to weather storms without a change of expression, like Easter Island Statues. Nothing's anyone's fault: it's no-one's job to contact schools or local societies that might have filled seats for the three weeks with party bookings.

Advertising for Osborne's play has continued, despite being sold out for the entire run.

We finally filled the gaps ourselves. Thelma wrote to head teachers and the children and I made posters with felt pens. Mine was the only advert for the show that appeared anywhere in the theatre until yesterday!

Everything else has taken second place to this anger. A bad year ends in a bad play which won't even get the audience usually guaranteed by the festive season. *The Freeway* will have its last dismal showings too.

Wednesday 25 December

Christmas Day. Fourteen of us for the festive dinner: our six (with Sylvia, the mother's help); three from Swansea; Mum, Geoff and Mary from Bristol.

Our mother was smoking and coughing and had complained of various ills since her arrival on Monday. Going to bed, she apologised again for being dull, saying the news of her angina has upset her. As soon as she was tucked up, I told Geoff and Mary that it was news to me too.

'I told you yesterday,' Thelma said.

'You did? I don't remember a thing'

'That's normal. You *never* listen to me.'

'I've been preoccupied.'

So busy with some silly play that I didn't take in that my mother's got angina.

'I suppose she's worried because it's what Dad had for some time before his death,' I said, whereupon Mary began to weave a rich tapestry of surmise about the nature of the condition. I reached for the Medical Dictionary and read out the facts: a thickening of the blood vessels, causing acute pains in the chest and possibly down one arm.

We debated, as dutiful but unloving sons and daughters-in-law, what steps we could take to ease her dis-ease.

[388]

Short of having her live with one of our families, there's very little. She won't accept a ground-floor flat which would save her climbing stairs and straining her heart. Being upstairs makes her feel safer. Thelma thinks she should get out-and-about more. But Mary's tried: she'd sooner sit at home watching telly and weeping. Mary, in fact, sees the telly as the cause of her malaise.

'She comes to us on Saturday and goes home early to watch the box,' she said.

'Perhaps she enjoys it,' I suggested, 'like Bingo. We may think it's a bore but we're different. I think roulette's a bore but millionaires play it day and night. Most people don't know how to fill their lives and any sedative helps. It's like reading three-volume novels or embroidering samplers.'

I didn't really say all that but something on those lines. The similes were aimed at Mary's fondness for Jane Austen.

Dr Patrick Bennett had us over for drinks and told me angina's easily controlled with modern drugs. Sufferers can live twenty years with the condition. At seventy-four, she must expect some dilapidation. Geoff's comment was characteristic:

'With such an empty life, I'm only surprised she's so afraid to die.'

[The angina's passed down to my brother and me. Mum lived into her nineties, still puffing at filter-tips. My own angiogram showed the constricted artery that's not serious enough to cause concern or require the operation with the inflated balloon. I limit my Gauloises to five a day.]

Saturday 28 December

News that Jack Benny's dead.

Monday 30 December

Glad to be writing the last entries of this terrible year. The spasmodic style of this diary reflects the mood. Christmas, never my favourite festival, has been blighted still more by *Hardings Luck*. Perhaps they were right not to advertise. I'd already warned John Cox that the design was too elaborate, would have been fine at Glyndebourne where he's artistic director, but well beyond the Greenwich stage crew, still in the rubber-band and Sellotape era of technology.

[389]

[Always wary of sets that depend on machinery, I urged John and William Dudley not to risk a four-poster bed that had roller-blinds and curtain-devices to effect the time-travel between 1900 and 1600. They scoffed at my cowardice and went ahead. Only during the technical week were they forced to face the fact that I could be right.

Sometimes the overtaxed box of tricks started smoking as a way of warming itself up for action. At first people sitting near the front assumed this was a dry-ice effect but, when they smelt burning oil, soon retreated up the aisles with their coughing children. Recent bombings by the IRA sprang to mind as they hurried their families to the nearest exit.]

Reeling home from the Boxing Day matinée, I found our house thronged with happy friends and family preparing to see the evening show. I warned them not to expect much, but they went all the same and came back full of praise for what had been in fact a public dress rehearsal. John Grigg pronounced it a classic, a new *Peter Pan*. Michael Frayn was clearly relieved to be able to enjoy a play of mine after the last two. The children stared at me as though I'd suddenly grown wings. Even my brother said it seemed to be going alright, in such a way as to suggest that my anxieties had been a play for sympathy.

Over the weekend, the devoted boffins retested the device and put it back for Monday's press night. This was only a third full, naturally, as I dare say no-one had bothered to circulate our details to the papers. We dragooned some volunteers for a second look and called in a few favours from resting actors and friends. 'Right, listen. Play, Greenwich, nineteen-hundred hours, you you and you.' I installed them and left. After a quiet hour at home with a good book, I went back to pick up Thelma and be told that the engine had exploded. The actors had to remember to pull the curtains across by hand at the end and beginning of scenes. Once that was established, things slightly improved.

Not soon enough to save the morning reviews giving us the boot: boring story, too much plot, superfluous narration, unworkable scenery.

Peggy Ramsay rang to say she wouldn't be able to get down to see it this week as she had to go with Ayckbourn to collect his various awards for The Play Of The Year [the one, of course, that had replaced *Chez Nous* at The Globe].

On the front pages of the papers that dismiss my play, the headlines announce five thousand Pakistanis killed by an earthquake in the Indus

Valley. I thought of the scene Val Wood had described, when she had to remind Charles of Vietnamese napalm victims after the reviews for one of his stage failures. Is that a good starting-point for a mean, misanthropic comedy?

[It became *A Piece of my Mind*, opening in London in 1987 on April Fool's, that would have been my father's hundred-and-first birthday, a coincidence he'd have enjoyed.]

I can't feel keen enough on the South-East-Asia concert-party show. A good idea that could work, but so difficult and my whoosh! and pow! are gone after this year. Why try again?

Or look on the bright side: perhaps 1974 has been useful, a change for the worse preceding one for the better. To be rejected may be a step in the right direction, towards another line of work. But what?

1975

Wednesday 1 January

New Year party at the Mendels. Our friend the Jewish cardiologist had hired a Scots Guard to pipe the haggis into his Blackheath dining-room. Another man in kilt and sporran recited:

> Fair fa' your honest sonsie face,
> Great chieftain o' the puddin'-race!
> Aboon them a' ye tak your place,
> Painch, tripe or thairm, etc.,

in dialect so thick I could catch only a word here and there, which is as it should be. The piper replied in Gaelic then began again, marching from the room and playing a reel in the hall for some couple rash (or pissed) enough to try a dance.

While we ate the haggis, I told the reciter he'd done it well. Turned out to be Frank Duncan, an actor with the BBC Rep, who'd borrowed the togs for the evening.

'All this has to be back by midnight or I'll be in rags,' he said.

The piper too had been engaged and was even then hotfooting it to his next gig to earn what he could before the year ended. Duncan said he'd been flummoxed when the piper replied in Gaelic as he doesn't know a word and is only Scottish a long way back and put on the brogue as he had the drag.

Nibs Dalwood in the evening, fresh from Egypt and Lebanon and full of their eastern promise. Massive oil revenues in Beirut have made grotesque fortunes, with which the sheikhs are building palatial banks and art galleries. Naturally Nibs loves the fact that painting and sculpture now represent to the rich a more stable currency than gold. Those social pariahs in the last century, demented solitaries playing their private games with paint and bronze, rejected by every academic authority, came up with a better fiscal bet than anything the stock-brokers could find, except perhaps oil.

'But who, d'you think, has won?' I asked.

Nibs dismissed the question as irrelevant. Van Gogh, Gauguin, Seurat, Cézanne had no choice but to paint. He argued strongly for ambition against the chic new apathy of the young, copping out of a struggle that is, in their view, contesting the wrong prizes anyhow.

'Ambition's what distinguishes us from animals.'

Catherine came back late from *Aladdin on Ice* and flirted with him. She's only ten but already loves cuddling men.

Thursday 2 January

Dinner in an almost deserted Café Royal with Albert and Anouk. Then to Ronnie Scott's to hear George Melly's first set. He's disarming in person and calls himself a stand-up comic who sings the blues a bit. Albert's pressing him to do a show at the Royal Court to raise money to mend the roof.

Saturday 4 January

Card from Biarritz. 'Those of us who are over the hill and failing fast need to stick together. All the best for 1975, Mike and Shirley.'

We saw this as an olive-branch to end the bad feeling that began when we chose to do *Chez Nous* without him. Since then we've both had our setbacks and it seems he's ready for peace. Thelma's reply was better than mine. I invited him to dinner but *she* told him of her new nightdress that splits up the sides as far as her breasts.

Sunday 5 January

Harold Hobson went his own way again, as he's expected to. Today's bark-up-the-wrong-tree is the only good notice of *Hardings Luck*. He linked it with *Joe Egg* and wrote as though he'd been an early champion of that play:

'I vividly remember Joe Melia's superb performance as the distracted father, which would have been unbearably sad had it not been also, legitimately and accurately and, at times, desperately funny.'

[393]

But at the time he wrote: 'Too much in the spirit of a comic turn. He fails too often to remind us that we are watching a troubled and tragic character and not the Staff Room buffoon.'

This brought a call from Joe, beginning, 'Well, Henry Ford was right – history is bunk'.

Wednesday 8 January

French Night at Brompton Square: M et Mme Jean-Pierre Cassel, also a Parisian literary agent and his American wife. Anouk was in her bath-towel get-up, looking as though she'd had no time to dress. She fussed from the moment we arrived. After a meal of veal, artichokes and bananas, she cleared the plates and loaded the dishwasher beside the dining-room, which rumbled all through coffee and conversation. She never appeared again. Nor did Albert get to sit down for quite some time, as she sent him round emptying the ashtrays into a Harrods carrier and then removing the coffee tray. This restaurant-closing routine turned out to be catching, the American woman also doing her bit towards the ashtrays. I began wondering if they'd start putting the chairs upside-down on the table.

Going for a pee at one point, I found our hostess standing in a dark part of the hall pretending to study a list. She pushed open the stair-door for me and when I returned, put out the light, like the gardienne of a WC.

Thursday 9 January

Poor house watching the Nesbit, included Peggy who rushed off shouting, 'I enjoyed it.'

In the bar afterwards, the wealthy Jewish relatives of a moneyed actor in the cast were overwhelming.

'Now tell me, Mister Nesbit,' said a middle-aged aunt, 'what else have you written that I should have seen?'

Friday 10 January

Kenneth Williams rang a.m., in prompt reply to my letter suggesting we should meet.

'I won't come for a meal, no, 'cos I'm undergoing this enormously *sheesh* dental course costing the earth and I can't enjoy anything in my mouth.'

He arrived after dinner, formally dressed and, at first glance, didn't look much older than when we last met – what? – twenty years ago. But his blonde hair was greying at the sides and the skin was no longer as angelic as it had been when I first set eyes on him when we were nineteen and twenty.

[Such a public face, of course, wasn't ever out of mind for long. I must have watched him – or his image – grow old without knowing it. The shock would have been greater for him but he says nothing of it in his diary, only, 'Met his wife and children, Louise and Daniel, there was another little girl but she hardly spoke.' Cath failed to make an impression there – or perhaps didn't try, seeing no chance of a cuddle. 'There was a certain stiffness at first and then we talked easily. I was astonished at his phenomenal memory.']

The children were enthralled as he began performing his journey from Euston to Blackheath, this familiar figure from *Jackanory* now in their own home.

Nothing had changed. And, though I enjoyed the evening, I was struck by the absence of any enlargement in him. He'd appeared complete in every detail at twenty and nothing much has been added or subtracted since. Not surprising his first West End rôle was as one of the lost boys in *Peter Pan*. Still lives in a small flat in the Euston area, as when I last knew him, hardly a mile from where he grew up, and Louie his mum is in the one next door.

'Can't you bring her to tea? I'd love to see her again.'

'Yerrs, well it would 'ave to be a Sunday 'cos during the week she's got the Meals On Wheels she takes round and the hospital visiting and helping with The Old at this club.'

Well, his fantastic vitality had to come from somewhere.

Saturday 11 January

Last day of the Nesbit. Full matinée, but on the whole Hobson's review made no change at the box-office. Curtains still breaking down.

Well, that was a waste of time.

Sunday 12 January

At the Mostyn-Owens', met Tony and Sally Sampson, Mike and Shirley, Hugh and Antonia Fraser. Can't bring myself to speak to this woman that everyone calls Lady, rememering how she not only disliked *Joe Egg* but opposed it on the *Evening Standard* panel. Thelma told me, after a conversation with her, that she professes to admire me. Nothing says we have to kowtow to these people who already have more than their share. Let's at least withhold our approval.

We gave the Blakemores a lift home and they invited us to dinner. A sort of peace was being patched up.

Monday 13 January

Thelma's painting again. It gives her more interest in her life than I've got in mine and the pictures are attractive still-lives or good likenesses.

Men came to convert us – Natural Gasmen, not Mormons, and to continue turning this awkward old villa into a stately home.

Friday 17 January

Albert's said he'll do *Forget-me-not Lane* on BBC-TV in March with Alan Bridges directing. Arthur Lowe refuses to play Charles, no matter how hard they press him. I agree with Thelma that he must be a Freemason and daren't play a scene mocking the initiation. Was Ronnie Barker one as well? He certainly growled about me in a tabloid interview.

Friday 24 January

Alan Bennett says he keeps a diary only when something interesting happens, not every day. In the same radio quiz, Frayn says he can't see how to, as he doesn't know who the reader is. Unnecessary question finally. Oneself, of course, and possibly at some point an interested reader, no more identifiable than that of a novel.

I've lost patience with the army entertainers play yet again. Detailed notes, partly memory, refuse to come to life.

I want to go deeper and describe an adult relationship, not spoil it by an itch to be entertaining or amusing. A serious piece of work. My only hope is based on the brothers in *Hearts and Flowers*. They wouldn't be Geoff and me but two sides of myself, the one moved by ambition and the one who distrusts all kinds of success. Out of this could come a conflict, with neither being 'right'.

Wednesday 29 January

Bridges came to discuss *Lane* and floundered somewhat. Imprecise and grandiose. Over-praised the play. Tried to keep him down to earth.

Doing a preface for the Faber edition of *The Freeway*. Simply cannot write prose. Millions of different ways occur to me to express one thought and it's impossible to decide between them. Have I the sort of mind that can only articulate through different voices in conflict? My piece came out as a petulant counter-attack on the critics' mugging of the play. Fatal.

Reading Meyer's biography of Ibsen. Odd that what he abandoned – vaudeville, asides, monologues – we are bringing back. It seems now there's no need to abandon, rather to reassert, any means native to Theatre.

Friday 31 January

Walked in warm winter sunshine to the dentist in Blackheath village. Outside the Frayns' house, a gang was felling yet another casualty of Dutch Elm Disease. Winter was too warm to kill off the beetles that carry the plague and now it's gone too far to stop except by euthanasia. Four out of ten on the heath and in the park are elms and will have to go. From near Michael's place alone, six beautiful giants are dying and the houses will be exposed in a way no architect could have foreseen.

While he recounted some of this, Joe Eisenberg performed similar too-late surgery on my mouth. Trying to improve the discoloured crown that's capped my injured centre incisor for twenty years, he had fractured the root so that I now wear a temporary plate with a couple of implausible teeth stuck on. He took impressions of my bite and gums to see what bridgework needs to be done to repair his own mistake. Without these auxiliary incisors, my smile looks like a defaced poster.

Wrote to Michael Langham in Minneapolis to ask if he knows of any stints for Visiting Playwright in the Midwest. An article in *Country Life* spoke in glowing terms of the Twin Cities. I only worry over the baking summers and bitter winters when every year the Mississippi doesn't keep rollin' along but freezes solid. The state of Minnesota is as big as France.

Saturday 1 February

Thelma went down with the same flu I've just shaken off. She hopes she'll improve before tomorrow or may have to cancel the visit by Louie and Kenneth Williams. I ranted that she should have said so sooner.

Sunday 2 February

She coped, coughing all through her preparations and thought she'd be alright as long as they went home early.

Louie looked no different but for the white hair. He talked a blue streak, as always, mostly to me, leaving poor Thelma to manage his Mum.

He began with a useful plethora of information about CSE, a great deal about our Sgt-Major Marriott, his gangsterish rackets, gun-running, suicide by cyanide, and how our CO, Major Woodings wooed Marriott's widow at his funeral.

[This sounds almost too like Richard III's seduction of Lady Anne but was authenticated by all who were there. It's described at length in my memoir. My first thought was how fetching a sequence it would make in the show I was assembling but it threatened to be too bizarre and was finally left out.]

When Ken was called in to see Woodings in his room in the officers' quarters, the widow was there drinking his whisky.

[398]

'Now, Sergeant Williams,' Woodings said, 'this is a tough assignment. Your particular party is going up-country to Burma, know what that means? Some of the roughest outposts in the whole of South East Asia Command. And, toughest challenge of all, you're going to be charging admission. Some of those Burma veterans will be paying fourpence to see your show. And you can bet your bottom dollar they won't have forgotten that all the ENSA shows were scot-free. Think you can handle it?'

The imitation – Jack Hawkins crossed with Noël Coward – is hilarious. He thrusts his face close to the listener's and somehow manages to be frightening and funny at once.

An amazing nugget of news: Ken claims that Rae Hammond, the conjurer in our revue *At Your Service*, was a spy, posted to us from the Singapore Intelligence Branch to investigate Marriott's rackets. At once saw I could use this – this man's cover is as a conjuror but he's hopeless because his real game's espionage, not magic.

[I did in earlier drafts but the need to dovetail so many stories and personal histories made me abandon it before the play went into production. I instead made the conjuror a man I didn't meet in CSE but later at Changi. Few of the real CSE people appeared in any guise in the play. Stanley Baxter, one of the real people, told me he was disappointed by that, though also relieved.]

After lunch, I could see Thelma was flagging so when, at about four, Ken said he'd like a walk, I gladly went, leaving Louie at home playing with the kids.

In Greenwich Park, tourists and passers-by spotted him a long way off, sometimes from as far as the Queen's House, shouting 'Hallo, Kenny' and ''Ere, you that Keneth Williams then?' till I thought I should lose my cool and hit one. I asked him how he stood it.

'When I'm alone, I mostly have to speak to them but when I'm with someone I just go on with what I'm saying.'

I hadn't realised the extent of his fame.

After tea, I'd had more than enough and Thelma looked comatose. Finally they told us their taxi had been ordered for eleven. It didn't arrive so we called a local firm and they left at quarter to twelve.

[I'd like to read his own version of this day but the Russell Davies edition leaves it out. Whatever else, it was the start of a new occasional friendship that ran on till two years before his death.]

Wednesday 5 February

Our house filled up – John and Sally Bray with nowhere to stay in London while trying to screw more money out of their daughters' trustees, Sylvia here much of the time, Olive Taylor stays till two, the girls start appearing at three-thirty, Louise first, always rushing to our bedroom, hoping to catch us at it. Then, what with builders and North Sea Gasmen, we've hardly been alone since New Year's Day. And Francis Hewlett came to stay. He and I remembered the occultism of our mothers, their tea-leaf fortune-telling, palm-reading and cards, as well as a whole thirty-nine-articles of taboos and fetishes like spilt salt, broken mirrors, crossed knives and three-on-a-match.

'Mine never made a move without consulting some bloody oracle,' he said.

And all the weird embargos and spells with which they decorated their simple secrets.

'I had an uncle who was fond of cooking and put on an apron when he did. The whisper went round that he was really a woman. I found out the reason years later. He had an anal fissure and had to wear sanitary towels to stop the bleeding.'

Thursday 6 February

Queued at Burlington House for the bi-centenary Turner show, the art event of the year. I hadn't taken a lot of interest as his work's never appealed to me, not being hard-edged enough perhaps. But this would convert any doubter. Not only is he the greatest British painter but an artist to figure in any world league of Beethovens and Tolstoys. The colossal range and output and his later move into Impressionism before the French had even begun.

'They're the only paintings I know that you can *hear*,' said Francis. 'The screams and howls of all those drowning men, the roar of the ocean, the crashing of waves on the deck, the creaking timbers and cracking masts and up above the carnage the mewing of gulls. Cecil B. de Mille pictures.'

A lady water-colourist, after looking at one of these mighty canvases for a while, said to her friend 'Well, of course, oil-paint's so expensive these days. If it wasn't for that, I'd be doing paintings like these.'

Francis and Thelma began inventing equally good excuses for why they weren't producing work on this scale: campaigning for CND, cooking meals for playwright husband, etc.

Just before we left to cross the street to dinner at the Griggs, Pat Norton next door rang to say there was 'activity in the Grove'. This meant 'to do with Sambo', as she was still calling him.

I went to see and found minibus gone, the police just leaving. I asked if they wanted us to open the chains on the little fence the Nortons had put in just before the squatter arrived two and a half years ago. They were terribly respectful, even fawning, and even the black man said 'Sir', when before this he's more often called me a 'rich white bastard' and put a hoodoo on me with his crossed sticks at our front door. Ten minutes later he was gone, leaving only a detritus of irreducible rubbish – some carpet, a broken kettle, a quantity of empty paint-tins. I ought to have made more of him than a sub-plot in *The Common*.

Monday *10* February

Collecting facts and stories for the CSE play. Our conjuror Rae Hammond writes daily with old songs and details of our life there. He's become the unofficial archivist of that brief outpost of showbiz. He's probably so well informed because of his duties as a police spy.

But the BBC series *It Aint Arf Hot, Mum* continues on TV, so should I do it or not? Nothing else is remotely ready as my next.

Tuesday *11* February

After the Grocer, the Grocer's daughter. Margaret Thatcher takes over from Heath as Chief Tory, obviously a good choice for the job.

Wednesday *12* February

Cable from Michael Langham, Guthrie Theater, Minn, Minn. 'Delighted with your proposal. Am exploring possible funding sources and will write at length when I have.'

Wednesday 19 February

Played tennis with Louise, starting in cloud and finishing in bright sunlight. The courts by the Ranger's House are the prettiest I know, the warm brick building behind and high walls of the old garden keeping out the itinerant critics. Claude and Loleh Roy are staying and arrived from London by riverboat. They are so Parisian and chic they wanted to see some East End slums, so we walked under the Thames to the Isle of Dogs. As well as a novelist, critic and translator, Claude's a poet and his eyes lit up when I told him that the name came from sailors, the first sound they heard on returning from a voyage being the baying of hounds from the royal kennels.

[This visit was, of course, before the depressed area became a Development Zone and is now Docklands, an unrecognisable Alphaville of glass towers, elevated railways, wine bars and shopping malls with central atria.]

Tuesday 25 February

At dinner that night, talk turned to sexhibitions. One of the party told us of sex-shows in Bangkok and Copenhagen. In Thailand, he had to walk with a street tout, then ride in a taxi to a side-street far off the beaten track. He'd been told 'Don't worry, we're the wolves here and they're the sheep'. He followed up a staircase and was asked if he wanted a drink. It was hot, of course, so he asked for a beer. A teenage Thai girl and boy came in, neither good-looking, both fully dressed. They stood smiling at him until he asked why they didn't begin. They were waiting for his beer to come. When it arrived, they stripped off and began to screw.

The girl had a lovely body beneath her clothes.

'I was as close to them as I am to you.'

'How did you feel?'

'You don't feel anything much at the time but next day it suddenly explodes in your mind and you think: what have I been *watch*ing?'

He had walked about during the performance and at one point touched the girl's naked breasts. Then he left and was shown back to his taxi, giving small tips all the way.

'Of course, it's a terrible social situation. They're kids from the villages trying to survive in the city.'

It was very different from the Danish operation, which was precisely planned, down to the last kroner, and this guy wasn't the whole audience but was in a party of Japanese men and their wives picked up in a minibus at the airport terminal. The performers were better-looking and did it with faces turned from the audience.

'We were asked not to cough or comment as it put them off. I don't *think* they had an orgasm, just grunted perfunctorily. Perhaps they'd already done a couple of shows that day. We shuffled back to the bus in some embarrassment. An experience haunted by Christian guilt. In Thailand that didn't exist. Despite its horrible mercenary side, it was done with Asian innocence.'

I want to take part, not watch. I'd like an erotic display if I knew the hunger aroused would be gratified. But to watch people eat a hearty meal then be sent back to the hotel with an empty stomach is a torture only a masochist would inflict on himself.

Saturday 1 March

My father always introduced Mum as 'My good lady, Violet Annie Ladysmith', annoying her by telling her age to anyone who remembered that the Boer War siege was relieved 1st March 1900. So today my sister-in-law Mary was giving a surprise party for her seventy-fifth.

Sylvia on holiday, Thelma coping with the kids, so I went alone on the 3 p.m. from Paddington. Only a quarter full, so shifted seats for the first minutes, escaping noisy children, heavy smokers and transistor radios. Settled on the north side facing west, wallowing in the familiar, almost atavistic pleasure of a Bristol journey. A Turneresque exhibition of British weather began at Reading and reached a climax at Swindon, where a lemon sun blazed through black clouds and a double rainbow divided the sky into dark and light. The fainter arc must be a reflection, as the spectrum's reversed.

Temple Meads at dusk and I'd meant to walk to Clifton but a rare Bristol bus was waiting so I joined the queue. Each passenger was given a personal interview by the driver/conductor.

'Woodland Road, my love? What you wanna do is I'll drop you at the Victoriawll Rooms and you got no more than a five-minute walk?'

The 'ell' added to a-ending words and the upward inflexion for a statement where most speech-patterns would have gone down.

'Got a connection at the coach station? That's alright, my lovely. I'll have thee there in good time. Thee's'll catch 'n easy.'

There was none of the aggression of Cockneys or immigrants. Everyone waited while he took his time cashing up.

'Doin' alright tonight, enough for me to go on the beer, this lot.'

His was an anything-but-scenic route, taking in many of the ugly spots of new Bristol. Old Market Street has almost gone, the broadest in the city, where they've replaced the Empire with a Holiday Inn. Lewis's store's still stranded in The Horsefair, prow towards the Floating Harbour as though struggling towards its proper element.

[I wrote and performed a sketch during our last years there telling the horror story of my native city's post-war architecture. The philistine councillor in it explained that this building was the origin of the phrase Ship-shape and Bristol fashion.]

Nineteen of us assembled in Mary's flat above Geoff's jazz record shop, ranging from 85-year-old Auntie Maud to Mary's younger brother Gillie. No old men. They'd all died before their wives. Only Mary's father, the former Royal Navy commander, was still alive and he'd left his wife for another, younger woman. Was there a message for me here?

In old age, he became very religious and penitent, driving my brother to distraction with his notions about Life, a real Ancient Mariner.

'How are you, Alice?' I asked, shaking hands with the great melancholic of our childhood, with her adenoidal voice and down-turned face.

'Not so bad as I was, thanks.'

When Geoff arrived with Violet Annie, we all cheered and she looked more resentful than agreeably surprised, as she should have tried to be. Always a spoilsport these days, she can't ever forget her own threadbare dignity. But perhaps this is the way most of us feel on these occasions, resenting how easily you can be tricked by others. She claimed she'd thought something funny was going on, all along.

Maud was unstoppable – eighty-five not out. Gave up cleaning for Mary at eighty-three as the bus-journey was too much for her. People always do West Country voices as slow and countrified but hers is rapid, almost tripping over itself.

'You remember Jacqueline, Florrie's daughter that used to live out Know-al? Well, she've gone and married a Hindian. A doctor, up Leeds way. But, mind, he haven't got the really black skin. 'Tis like as though 'e've been out in the sun a bit too long? And he haven't got the frizzy hair nor the blubbery lips.'

> [Though the character of Maud in *Born in the Gardens* was a far cry from this real-life Aunt, I helped myself to these lines for Beryl Reid to speak in the play.]

Geoff asked Maud about her conversion. These days we're only ever converted to gas or decimal coinage. Maud and her sister Alice began to answer in that sing-song duologue I've known since infancy, when Mary butted in and would not be stopped.

'They say they're already running out,' she said, 'and bringing it all in from North Africa in lorries.'

After the aunts had gone, Geoff told her he'd been trying to record some of Maud's speech, as it must now be one of the few surviving examples of old Bristol. That way of talking will soon be gone as absolutely as the Empire theatre, the empire itself and Dad's ugly CWS depôt. Geoff had had his tape-machine running behind the sofa.

'Well, I didn't know,' Mary complained.

'How could I tell you without telling Maud? She'd have clammed up.'

Wednesday 5 March

Alan Bridges, directing *Lane* for TV, rang for the first time after promising to speak to me daily. Not an enjoyable talk. Disagreed with almost everything he said. He spoke of my domestic tragi-comedy in terms that would have been hyperbolic for *Hamlet*.

I asked: 'How's Bill Fraser getting on? He seemed excellent at the reading.'

[405]

'Well, you know Bill. That old-fashioned sort of actor who wants to get his business and props straight.'

'I've a good deal of sympathy with that approach. When I was an actor, I did too.'

'Really?'

'And I've found that a lot of those old boys and girls are closer to the author's intention than younger ones who are always trying to tart it up.'

'But one's got to get at the truth. The comedy can come later.'

'Isn't the truth *in* the comedy? Get the comedy right and it'll probably be true. You can't stick it on later like false lashes.'

'Well, in that case perhaps I'm not the right director for you. Comedy's not my strong suit. I'm not simply interpretative but creative.'

'I think interpretation's hard enough without anything else. Getting it right. Surely that's what matters, with a new play anyhow?'

[Despite this being Albert's debut in a TV play, the results of Bridges's creativity were so depressing that the tape was never shown again. I've sometimes asked BBC spies to get me a copy but apparently none exists. It was either wiped (like *Hearts and Flowers*) or possibly kept to be shown on trainee courses as an example of how not to direct comedy.]

Monday 17 March

Rehearsals at Acton. Not as bad as I feared but bad enough. Fraser, who's perfect casting for Dad, doesn't thrive in an atmosphere where every laugh is seen as indecent.

Albert drove me to the tube and I discovered with a shock that the mood suits him well and may be of his own making. They're all wrong, I know, but how to persuade them the serious side won't wash unless the jokes do?

Friday 21 March

Bridges still asks me not to go to rehearsals.

'We want to take it all to pieces tomorrow and show it to you again on Friday.'

Aren't the last few days of preparation a time to put it together? I tried to tell them it was dull, dreary and dead but they were all (except Fraser) in the conspiracy to *interpret* the play, not *do* it.

In the end, I gave up, which was all they wanted of me. 'Write the script and trust us to show you what you meant, though you didn't know it.'

Wednesday 26 March

Teeming rain for the last day of rehearsal, at the White City studios. I left home by train after lunch, leaving Thelma to pack the Peugeot and receive her parents, who are looking after the house while we're in France.

At the gates of TV Centre, groups of sad girls like clowns waited for the Bay City Rollers, screaming tentatively at the arrival of every vehicle.

My play was moving like a juggernaut to its doom, after surviving such crises as Gemma Jones going down with 'flu and Bill Fraser collapsing after overdosing on belladonna. The lack of comedy exposed the people and events as trivial. When I left at half-six, the clowns were still in the drizzle, with their sodden hair and clumpy shoes. They were too despondent to scream when Thelma arrived to pick me up in our car laden with clothes, food, sports gear, books, all the kit for a holiday for six in Siorac.

Thursday 27 March

The Belseys, our nearest neighbours at Siorac, complained that winter was following spring. Cold and wet, with rare sunny intervals. Luckily, though, plenty of wood in the shed, and we've burned most of it during our ten days' stay. As I drove into the yard, the rain still fell and I had to park in the barn so we could unpack in the dry. The power was off and men soon came from the EDF to confess themselves desolated at the inconvenience and promise soon to reconnect. Before long a log was blazing in the great kitchen hearth and Thelma had oil and gaz-lamps lit. In a crisis, she flourishes and I wilt, following Dad in becoming an Im-proper Man.

Our friends had warmed the house, heated the water and wiped away the winter's mildew. The power came back, we ate heartily and fell into our beds after having spent the ferry crossing on reclining chairs, bullied by tannoys. Our state of well-being justified Thelma's optimism.

Friday 28 March

Half a dozen fruit saplings have been planted by our nurseryman, as well as an acacia, a willow and some poplars. Elsewhere an orgy of felling lays bare the woods. The band-saw whines from morn to night. Chekhov's axes are nothing to this mechanised slaughter. On his own, man's only moderately destructive but with power-tools he can wipe out a wood in a week. The Forêt de Double, which slopes away from our house to the horizon, is brought low to provide pulp for the *Sud-Ouest* to bring out more editions reporting the conservationist controversy.

Besley claims the devastation's due to Dignac, the mayor and land-owner, giving much of his property to his only son, a vet in Moussidan, to avoid the prolonged haggle that can happen under Napoleonic law when an estate is divided between hordes of second cousins once removed. In terms of agricultural efficiency, primogeniture wins, okay?

The mayor's a conserving sort of man, almost to the point of atavism and neglect, but his son had no qualms about ordering whole-sale felling of pine, oak and beech to cash in on present prices. He'd no sooner done that than he dropped dead of a heart attack. But the cutting continues, to profit his widow and daughters.

Friday 4 April

Dan ran a high fever for thirty-six hours and swellings in his neck made us think of a recurrence of his mumps. The Brays, coming to dinner, at once said we should call a doctor now that his temperature had stayed so long at 103. Tilney came with us to help our poor French and John drove like a fiend into town in about ten minutes so that I feared at least three more casualties to tax the medical resources of Ribérac. We knocked up an agent at the gendarmerie and he called a doctor. Then we returned at a leisurely pace to Chez Magnou and finished our supper. The young replacement or locum came at eleven and was alarming about hearts and rheumatoid arthritis. Tilney was translating the hard bits but didn't know that 'angine' means tonsilitis and that angina becomes 'angine de poitrine'. We could see our poor son confined to a wheelchair for life, like his eldest sister. He was given a jab in the bum, capsules, anti-biotics, throat-sprays and for good measure that French cure-all, a course of suppositories.

Saturday 5 April

Mlle Boucher, the woman who sold us the house, was brought to meet us one morning by Joanna Bullock, with the little man who works for her on the land beside ours. Joanna embarrassed us both by telling him I'd written him into *Chez Nous*.

Mlle B is a grim-visaged countrywoman of some standing, sharp and selfish, about as beguiling as a stag-beetle. She showed no interest in the present fate of the house where she'd been born and raised but was eager to tell us that the house-agent had swindled us both by helping himself to the field beside ours. He'd told her we wouldn't buy the property unless we got that, while telling *us* it wasn't included in the deal. When she'd asked to meet us and discuss the matter, the agent always told her we were in England. Only when the little *ouvrier* told her of his meeting with us here did she become suspicious and guessed the old crook was keeping us apart so that he could steal the adjacent hectares.

Though I didn't much care for her and the agent's peasant ways, this obsession with land above even money, they were outdone by Mrs B. Her interest in that plot wasn't good neighbourliness, as was later clear when she became the go-between for Mlle B to sell it to a Dutch couple who just had time to build a bungalow before they separated and in turn sold up.

Thursday 10 April

I've been reading about the Malayan emergency for the new play, now retitled *Jungle Jamboree*, which suggests a cheap show and carries undertones of Baden-Powell. The Chambers gives 'jamboree' as 'a great Scout rally' but lists the origin as unknown. Partridge traces it to US, 1872. I always thought it was out of Afrikaans by old *Be Pr*epared himself. Anyway the Boy Scout tinges are right for my view of the Malayan 'war' as described in such accounts as *Jungle Green* by Arthur Campbell MC, an officer with the Suffolks who operated in the Kuala Lumpur region, which shows the viewpoint of the professional soldier. His tone of voice will fit my officer commanding, to set the decent and dutiful viewpoint against the hedonism of the old-queen dancer who becomes his second-in-command.

Montgomery's books are also hilarious – *Forward to Victory* and *The Path to Leadership*, exhortations to soldiers and when all of them had been demobbed, to youth leaders and Mothers' Unions. Sad, funny and frightening all at once.

Friday 11 April

Took John Bray and Thelma for a farewell meal at Mussidan, a treat for her, as she'd fed us all so well throughout the holiday. After we'd ordered the largest meal we reckoned we could eat, Thelma only drank some soup before saying, 'You'll be very cross but can you cancel my order now? I'm not well.'

So John and I, neither of us gourmands, struggled through a whole crab each, a trout, an escalope and the usual afters while she watched us and sipped water. Is she turning from gastronomic promiscuity to voyeurism?

Thursday 17 April

Began writing dialogue for *Jungle Jamboree*. The *Hot Mum* TV sitcom set in a post-ENSA unit in India continues to keep the nation in stitches. But Albert and Michael Medwin egg me on.

'However similar the subject, yours will be your own thing. You can't prevent that.'

The plethora of detail and a huge pool of possible characters do daunt me and I'm not sure if I should try original songs. My first idea was to write only one, the opening chorus, but now perhaps a few more, if only for the show-within-the-show.

Sunday 27 April

In a general scene of commercial recession, it's good to see the Pinter sector holding up well. He's been gilt-edged for about fifteen years now, at any rate as blue-chip as Marks & Spencer, but lately I'd felt his stock wasn't keeping pace with inflationary trends. Lack of diversification didn't help to create confidence. So it has to be a wise decision to merge with several other High Street giants like Gielgud, Richardson & Hall to form an impressive combine called *No Man's Land*, which we saw unveiled last week at the Old Vic. From this showing, it would clearly rally support. Next day's market reports confirmed this and now the Sundays have given us a profile of the founder himself. I learned that he was an evacuee and a conshie. But some other claims in the piece called the whole into question. 'In person, mild-mannered,' for instance.

Jonathan Miller calls HP the Grandma Moses of playwriting. Harold had questioned JM's proposed drag version of *The Importance* by asking for evidence that Wilde wanted it. While we were doing *The Freeway*, JM tried out some casting ideas on me.

'Lauren Bacall,' I echoed, 'as Lady Bracknell? Isn't she American?'

'You see, it's that archetypical contemporary phenomenon, the Gibson Girl, marrying into the English aristocracy, becoming a pastiche dowager but always remaining transatlantic, able to send up the whole game. She'll be brilliant.'

Next time he broached it, he favoured Irene Handl.

'Isn't she Cockney working-class?'

'In fact, she's Belgian and the author of two amusing novels. But yes, the audience perception is Comic Char, which will illuminate that whole area of the arriviste or below-stairs termagant marrying into minor nobility.'

'And what about Lauren Bacall?'

'Hopeless idea. I never pursued that far.'

So there she is, doing it at Greenwich. He dropped in at our house on the second night to tell us he'd fooled the critics again. (But when did he last fool them?) Irene had been so bad in rehearsal that on the last rehearsal, clutching at straws, he'd asked the company to have fun and do it in funny voices. She chose a cod-German and one of the daily reviewers had said it was a revelation and told him more about the play than any other production he'd seen.

[What, I wonder? That Wilde was articulating the subconscious fears of Edwardian society that Germany's new industrial dominance meant the end of British imperial supremacy?]

Sunday 4 May

Can't convince myself that the new play based on my airforce years is *necessary* in the way, say, that *Fanshen* is, David Hare's adaptation of an account of life in a village at the advent of Mao's New China. That is set at the same time as mine but concerns itself with the future.

But why should anyone want to hear about an immature boy who made so little of a real chance? For all I did, I could have spent my national service years in Aldershot, not Bengal, Singapore, Malaya and Hong Kong, where I passed much of my time longing for Bristol! Most of us were virgin soldiers longing for home.

[Not all. I knew men who asked – and got – a posting elsewhere as soon as their native girls got pregnant and started mentioning marriage. This became the central plot of the play I was fumbling with, *Privates on Parade*.]

I've contrived a tangled story based on incidents I observed or heard of and that's exactly how it looks, contrived. Fifty pages so far and no breath of life.

Tuesday 6 May

Having had no takers, we've reduced the house to £39,000. A couple of People Like Us from Maze Hill have made an offer. So which to buy and move to? Nicholas Wollaston (the novelist) has asked if we're still considering his town house in Highbury Terrace (1789) overlooking the pretty park. Yes, but he'll have to come down in price, as we've dropped ours. I'm glad of all this, as change is as good as rest. Or better. Thelma, though, seems glum. She was looking forward to the economic crisis, a return to WW2, turning our back garden into a chicken-run and pig-sty and the front into a potato-patch.

Wednesday 7 May

Saw Orton's *Sloane* revived at the Court. Terrific first act but it spreads too much and had he lived he'd have got over his obsession with false teeth and controlled his impulse to insult women. Given that she's an object of derision for much of the time, Beryl Reid performs miracles.

Who'd have thought Orton was a moralist? Not a disapprover though. He loved it all, he'd have played the same game as the rest as long as his luck lasted. A genuine shocker. Watching his stuff is like having someone walk across your grave, as my mother always said when there was a cold draught.

[*Joe Egg* was one of the last plays he saw. 'It wasn't well written,' says his diary: 'Facetious. It should've been cruel and funny. It was simply flippant and sentimental. "I can't stand this," Halliwell said to me in an undertone, "let's go now." "No," I said, "we must wait for the interval." The play rambled on for about an hour and then we escaped . . . ' They went round to see the end of his *Loot* at the Criterion and Michael Bates was in it and said his wife had been to see mine and hated it. I'd been Sebastian to her Viola in rep and Michael later played 'my father' in *Lane*. Orton watched his own second act, seeming extra-brilliant after mine, he thought.]

Thursday 8 May

Liked our second look at the Wollastons' house. Only snag: the old couple in the basement, sitting tenants since being bombed out in 1940. He walks on a stick and she on swollen legs. The place smells of age and gravy and the rear curtains are never drawn back. They'll stay till the woman's death when the man will go into a home. She told us she's 79 but that she got about alright and there was those worse off than her so she couldn't grumble.

'But she always does,' said Nick's pretty wife, 'for about an hour and a half.'

Nicholas has offered to redecorate for them but they didn't want it. (Fearing he'd raise the rent?). All he's been able to do since buying the house is install a lavatory.

'Before that,' he said, 'they peed in the sink.'

Letter from Langham in Minneapolis saying Ford Foundation will probably pay for my trip. Next April will suit them best. Business manager rang later to ask how much I expected to be paid. Told him: as long as I'm not out of pocket.

[A mistake. Americans take you at your own estimation. I should have asked far in excess of what they'd pay.]

Sunday 11 May

Showed Highbury Terrace to the children. They played on the green with Sylvia while we walked to look at another for sale in Cross Street, noting the general decay of the area. It could go up or down and I'd say down's more likely.

[Another duff prophecy. Islington has become one of the city's prime quarters, a little New York for a generation ravished by America. Tony and Cherie Blair were here before we voted them a new home in Downing Street.]

Alive and pretty in parts and on the Victoria Line. Sized up schools, shops and traffic. All okay. The girls are happy with their nearby schools, Lou's is called 'The Home and Colonial for Girls'. Dan hated the prospect, having played football with some local boys and found them 'thick', which probably means they made fun of him.

Tuesday 13 May

First survey of house talked of settlement, defective plaster and bowing of arched doors, which is what surveyors are paid to do (£135 plus VAT), i.e. get the price down. Basement should be condemned as living quarters. He asks how it's to be repaired before the damp rises, as the old pair are still protected. He values it at ten thousand less than the Wollastons' asking price.

Thursday 15 May

Finished a rough Act One of *Jungle Jamboree*. Promising. Bits certainly come to life. So far only one song. I'd like to do some lyrics that advance the action or deepen the characters.

My swollen foot gives great amusement to Sylvia and Olive. The twelve foolscap pages sent by our surveyor made me wonder what he'd have written about me:

'Comprising of 1 head, 1 torso, 2 arms, hands, legs and feet. The dressings to the frontage are in glass with plastic and metal frames. The front access has been recently in-filled in synthetic fabric on an alloy mounting. Settlement around the first floor has become severe in recent years, the bowing of the lower balcony giving cause for concern, though this is to be expected with properties of this period. Plumbing might need renewal and is not covered by this survey, as we did not seek access.'

Monday 26 May

At page 88 of *JJ*.

A.m. worked on.

P.m. walked with family across heath to Bank Holiday fair, not the genteel Blackheath one run by local do-gooders, that's *Fayre*. This is by travelling showpeople, an unchanging institution: the red-and-white striped backing to the shies has been faded all my life; the serene horses, cockerels and ostriches on their spiral brass columns have always been The Sensation of The Century; chair'o'planes, Ferris wheels, helter-skelters, dodgems. Out-of-date music just audible over the scratchy interference – late Beatles. The kids won five goldfish.

Three couples interested in our house so we're not dropping any further. We're worried that the Wollastons' won't be big enough for us.

[A five-storey Georgian terrace? Not as overweening as it seems. The Blackheath house was larger in actual volume and better-suited to modern family life. Many of the Highbury rooms were poky and could not be enlarged without destroying the original form. Each house in this terrace now fetches over £1 m.]

Thursday 5 June

The referendum Yes or No to Europe. We're so far in now, saying 'no' would be like ringing a doorbell and running away. For which reason alone it would be worth it to see Shifty Wilson's pipe twitching as he thought out his next trick.

The New Staggers printed my comment along with others: I live near the Dover road and certainly don't want any *more* Italian container trucks bringing another load of fold-up bicycles that no-one will ever ride because the streets are crammed with Italian container trucks bringing another load of . . .

If that's the sort of benefit we gain from joining, we're better off being a fifth-rate power.

The vote went 2–1 for staying in.

Monday 16 June

Brought *JJ* to the end of a first draft. Simply don't know whether it deserves a *second*. Thelma enthused – 'The best you've done' etc. But she did that over my flops too. She has to, to keep me going.

[There's little to be said for the job of writer's wife, husband or partner. And the same must go for any artist who works at home. The aim must be to keep the nuisance confined to one space, study or studio, which means praising the resulting work, even though they often dislike it. Mme Bonnard thought Pierre couldn't paint. Mrs Pee-Wee Russell said her old man couldn't play clarinet. If they attempt to say the latest play, book, picture or symphony isn't up to scratch, they risk having the maker hanging about the kitchen and 'getting under their feet'.]

Alan Bates says the girl who played Joe Egg in the film is a chronic sufferer from agoraphobia and rang Peter Medak to ask his help. Since then Alan and Janet have been generously paying for her psychiatric treatment. This expense could perhaps be met by a benefit Sunday performance of the play done by the cast of the film and Alan wanted to know if I'd allow this.

'Would that mean the *director* of the film as well?' I asked and he gave a nervous giggle.

'I suppose it would but Janet's very strong these days.'

'Of course I'd like to help but I'll have to think . . .'

I have said and Peggy agrees we can't allow Medak anywhere near the play, not even for such a good cause.

Tuesday 17 June

Dinner at Frayns'. Met Paul Theroux and wife Annie, residents of nearby Catford. He's a published novelist and I'm reading his *Saint Jack*, a witty fictional memoir by a Singapore ponce. Enviable knowledge of brothels and whores. He'd spent three years teaching in D.J. Enright's Department of English at the university. Hated Lee Kuan Yew and the island.

'Welwyn Garden City on the tropics,' he said with a shudder.

[A garden city was my own description when I arrived there in 1947, but after a year in Calcutta I meant it as praise. Returning in the 80s to research locations for the film of *Privates* and in the 90s, on a stint as Visiting Playwright, I still liked the place and Lee's hygienic reforms. Not that I'd want to stay there longer than the seven weeks of our last visit, but the average Chinese, Malay and Tamil citizen was far better off than they'd been as colonial subjects and always spoke of Singapore with pride.]

Wednesday 18 June

To Glyndebourne in glorious weather for an undress-dress-rehearsal of *The Rake's Progress*. A queer quorum had produced this event – Auden, Kallman, Hockney and John Cox – and it contains what may well be a pouf's paradise: marriage to a bearded lady.

With the LPO playing full blast in the pit, it was all the singers could do to be heard, let alone understood. Stravinsky's music's so interesting, his orchestration so rich, that the poor human voices struggling above it seemed an irritant. With such a lyricist, the words would presumably be worth hearing. As usual, though, I could only make out the recitative. Does *anyone* follow more?

The real pleasure of the afternoon was Hockney's design. Painting was back on the stage, from an opening drop-cloth, with all the contributors' names enclosed in a Hogarth cartoon, to the austere setting for the madhouse. I've longed for this kind of scenery for ages and feel that the fashion for rostra and levels and stairs and sculptural abstractions, all lit like commercials, is encouraged by designers who can't draw. Roger Butlin (who designed *F-M-N-Lane*) sat by me and seemed bewildered by the dazzling success of Hockney's designs, which were for every visual aspect of the show – wigs, pepperpots, undersides of boxes all cross-hatched in a way that imitates Hogarth but looks like no-one but Hockney.

In the interval he stood, with his pop-star hair and glasses talking to his parents from Bradford. I told him how much I was enjoying his marvellous contribution and he said, with engaging openness, that they got better in the second half.

I'm going to insist on painted cloths for the jungle play.

Tuesday 24 June

House agents now say we can have the Robinsons' a few doors from the Wollastons' for £55,000 if we pay their fee of £1,100, a novel way of saying £56,100. It's still advertised in *The Times* for £62,500. I'm glad we shan't be taking on Nicholas and Deidre's place with those sitting tenants, though sorry to let them down because we like them so much. But business is business, chaps. If he'll reduce his asking price, he'll soon sell. The basement we'll get is done to the highest standard and the rest in far better shape than the Ws'.

[We were offered about four houses in this splendid terrace as at this time no-one wanted them. The Robinsons were dress-designers and in the throes of an ugly divorce, from which we profited.]

Sunday 13 July

Empty diary means – for once – full life. No more writing, though I've given thought to the songs in *JJ* and listened to a great many Golden Oldies, as they now call the music of our youth. I've also spent time sitting for my portrait by Thelma. The early sketches were a nasty shock, my nose matching my purple shirt, which she insists is so.

Charles Wood's new play *Jingo* opens soon at the RSC, set in Singapore. Rang him and spoke – first time in eighteen months, hard to believe! – and he told me it's about an army concert party. I shouted 'You thieving bastard!', then he said no, about the island's fall in 1942.

Twice to see tennis at Wimbledon, courtesy of tickets from Eddie Kulukundis, four for Centre Court, four for Number One, admission to Debenture Holders' car park and members' enclosure. Took Dan and Louise and saw Borg, Riessen, Connors, Nastase, Pilic, Wade and Billie-Jean King. Watched final on TV: historic defeat of Connors, bully-boy favourite and champion, by cool black Arthur Ashe, by strategy and pacing. Not often David or the tortoise really pull it off but nice to see. Hope for us all.

Monday 14 July

Lunch at home for Jim Binger, big cheese of Honeywell and prime financial prop of the Guthrie Theater. The Honeywell logo's everywhere, for example on all our central heating parts. It's one of the leading US corporations. He's Chairman of the Board and came to 'fill me in' on my future posting.

> [And, of course, to check that I was a presentable guest, could use a knife and fork, etc. He was hotfoot from coffee with Wilson and Callaghan at No. 10.]

Exceedingly formal and courteous with silver hair and costly clothes, he helped our children sit down, leapt to his feet and bowed when Sylvia, our mother's help, came in and never once used one word where a dozen would do.

'What would be your particular inclination in terms of recreational activities, as distinct from whatever vocational and academic contributions might be expected of you?' was the sort of thing he kept asking.

He was learning English slang and was delighted with 'drop a clanger'. Didn't 'clanger' mean bollock? Was that the sort of language you could pick up at No. 10?

He was sad about the state of our economy and particularly deplored the bolshie attitudes of the work-force in his Clydeside factory. From his potted history of this outpost of the Honeywell empire, it seemed the unrest came from lack of an adequate plant to do the required job. American unions, he said, would never have let their operatives start work without that machinery being in place but in Scotland they were prepared to graft much harder for less pay. So where was the money going that should have gone on better equipment? Well, this suave and civilised man was living in Eaton Square and discovering, as he put it, the many advantages of the British way of life. I did what I could, within the parameters of his politeness, to point out that Clydeside's the most poverty-stricken area in Britain, possibly in Western Europe, but I dare say his answer would have been that, if they wanted to change that, they should work all the harder to encourage chaps like him to bring more jobs and stop griping about the lack of plant. If they didn't, he'd be forced to move the operation some place else like Spain or Portugal where labour was more compliant. No doubt he'd also said this to Wilson, who'd pass it on to the unions involved, after which business would continue on Binger's terms.

And what was the end-product of this Glasgow factory? Computer components, thermostats, tape-recorders? I never quite discovered. He ate our lunch without comment and left at once to be driven off in his limousine to play polo in Cirencester Great Park with Prince Philip.

Tuesday 15 July

Met the TV pundit James Burke at a dinner. Huge head on small body, ideal for filling the screen. He thinks Stoppard's *Travesties* the greatest play ever written. We were booked for it the night after and went with unsmiling faces and clenched teeth, not prepared to give an inch. We knew Tom would charm us if we let him.

I succumbed quite soon but Albert Finney and Celia Gregory, his new friend, held out while Thelma wavered, out of loyalty to me. It's far away Tom's best so far. Funny, inventive, clever, flattering, and finally even serious. It made me ask myself: are the most interesting modern plays always about the *making* of plays? If such an antique hand-made form is to survive, they should probably call attention to the elements of which they're made and suggest other ways they might have come together. With painting and music it happened ages ago – in Cubism and atonalism. No accident that Joyce and Tzara the Dadaist are leading characters in Tom's comedy.

I saw a new play in it: a dramatist in his study trying to write a play. The routines of his working day are inseparable from his memories and inventions, dreams and vengeful fantasies. He must have a proper play to work on. For this I can use a 'straight' story I've been evolving, based on the brothers in my TV *Hearts and Flowers*. Around that

[420]

would be extracts from his diary, old letters, fading photos, recordings, yellowing cuttings, pornography. His wife and children visit his room; others may be as tangible but imaginary; phone-calls, mail, newspapers and bulletins find their way in.

[One of many surprises I've found in editing these journals. This deconstructionalist idea first became a six-part TV serial called *See Me*, which was commissioned and paid for (twice) but never produced. Elements of it were cannibalised many years later (in 1987) for *A Piece of My Mind*. This did reach the stage, a national tour and at last Shaftesury Avenue but only stayed a few weeks. At the time, I tended to agree with the bad reviews (and most of our friends) but now reckon it to be among my better things and want very much to see it revived. It failed with a wide audience because those outside the theatre circle felt excluded.

'I couldn't see,' grumbled my brother, 'what this bloke had to grumble at.']

Also thought of calling my Malayan play *Transvestites*, feeding off Tom's success and getting just in front of his in the alphabetical catalogues.

Friday 18 July

Car took me from home to the old Lime Grove film studios, once the home of Gaumont-British. An old character actor told me: 'We used to call it Gaumont-Yiddish. You could hang a bunch of keys on every nose.' I hadn't been there since my acting days, playing in TV serials – a constable in an early police series, a postman in a village soap-opera. I once played a scene on a li-lo with a scantily dressed girl and had to hide my hard-on from the live cameras.

This time I was in a book progamme to puff the paperback issue of *The Freeway*. God knows, it'll need all the help it can get.

I'd expected a grisly day but we all had a fine old time, treated like stars, drinking BBC wine and eating from a groaning board.

Claude Cockburn arrived with walking-stick soon after me, very posh and funny. An example of how the Communism of that generation was closer to Anarchy. We were well oiled by the time Melvyn Bragg the presenter arrived with the other panellists – Margaret Drabble, Jilly

Cooper and Kenny Everett, but even they couldn't dampen the party spirit. While we were eating, Tom and Clive Exton passed the open doorway and were called in. They'd been writing a play in a week, one of those silly ideas concocted to fill air-time. I'd declined, saying I didn't see how to use the news while it was still new. I teased Tom at the top of my voice about his being a great success and superstar in Bristol even before he'd written any plays and how the Woods used to tell us with bated breath how they'd seen him walking up Blackboy Hill. He smiled at this and invited me to a party this Sunday.

Claude and I were driven along passages and up stairs towards a studio by a pack of pretty women. One, a vision mixer, was anyone's sexual dream, a knock-out with brown skin, voluptuous lips and deep brown eyes. Claude reckoned he hadn't needed his stick when he first came in and before he was knocked sideways by the sight of these delectable women. I praised one to her face and she asked me to a party in Bristol, while I'd be in France *with the family!*

As we entered the dark studio, Claude said, 'There it is, I see it,' and made for a brightly-lit set in the far corner.

'That's *Gardening Club*,' said one of the PAs, going to stop him but too late, as he went flying, stick and all, over an electric cable. No sooner on his feet than he was off to another lighted area, this time *The Verdict Is Yours*.

While being made up, we shared misgivings.

'One always feels this sort of thing is good in principle. Sitting in Ireland, writing, yes, I persuaded myself this may well save civilisation as we know it. Books, after all . . . surely a good thing? But as the hour approaches . . .'

My interview itself was soon done. Bragg and I talked for a few minutes then Margaret Drabble, who'd been all sweetness and light, said:

'Your plays always let people off the hook, don't they? One's left with a slightly cosy feeling. Would you agree?'

'No,' I said and everyone laughed.

'No,' said Bragg, 'just like that?' and I made the mistake of qualifying. I asked them later to edit that out but they wanted 'debate' so it stayed.

It was the fiftieth anniversary of Penguin Books, an indisputable landmark because they account for what literacy my generation has. An animal-trainer had brought a live penguin along.

'Oh, look,' Claude said, 'it's shat on *Watership Down*. What a fine little fellow.'

Then the poor creature bit his keeper and escaped, waddling off round the great hanger at a terrific lick. Floor managers and PR girls gave chase and he careered into the cyclorama before finally being rounded up. This, the true visual event of the day, wasn't caught on camera.

[The man from Penguin told us a fact that I still trot out at parties. What (to that date anyway) is the best-selling Penguin? We all know the top ten – *Odyssey* and *Iliad*, *1984*, *Animal Farm*, *Lady Chatterley*, *Gatsby*, *Watership Down*, etc. – but no-one I've asked has ever got Number One

It's *Aircraft Recognition*, a catalogue of silhouettes and mechanical specifications which earned its place by being bought by almost every citizen during the blitz so that we could tell a Fokker-Wolf from a Messerschmidt.]

Sunday 20 July

Tom's new place is a stockbroker's delight in a huge garden. A marquee covered the celebrated company. We soon joined Clive James who was sitting with his wife Prue at a table with empty seats. Amusing and malicious, with a fixed outback-staring smile. Dealt brusquely with the theatre, which he hates (except for Tom, of course), with every critic but himself, with jazz, TV, I forget what else. The malice was monotonous and I was glad when Tynan joined us and then Mortimer.

Ken told how he'd dealt with the Oxford Union Debate.

'Don't play it their way. Break the rules.'

A toff with a speech impediment had preceded him so Ken began: 'After hearing the last speaker, I'm sure we're all glad to have a roof over our mouths.'

A gag that took some nerve, as he can be stricken with a painful stammer.

Clive and I joined a cricket game and I caught out a boy, realising too late that I shouldn't have. Everyone else was dropping them.

Pooter lives!

Monday 4 August

Chez Magnou: The *Sud-Ouest*'s headlines were all about weather – *toujours la chaleur*. Cognac came top with 36 degrees.

Afternoon: swam in the lake, where the water was a blessing and there was for once no shock walking in.

Back at the house, Louise and I tried our new line and float on the pond and caught six of the less cunning carp, brought them back in a brimming bucket and gave them a bath to swim and clean themselves in. Then they'll be fit to cook.

Night came early. Thunder had been rumbling for some time and now lightning flickered at a distance, coming closer as we ate supper. At twilight sudden gusts of cool air, a landscape brightly outlined against dark cloud, distant sounds distinct as though in hi-fi, then a squall that sent the garden furniture tumbling across the orchard. We ran about rescuing chairs and umbrellas and I parked the Deux Chevaux in the barn. We ate on, through chicken, pork and pig's trotters, but by strawberries and ice-cream it seemed to have missed us. After the kids had been bathed and dressed for bed, we switched off our lights and gathered them to watch the flashing sky. Instantly a small typhoon got up, leaves and twigs that had lain for weeks were whipped into our faces. The doors and shutters slammed. Rain began and we ran to fasten doors and windows in the far rooms. The huge barn-doors were flung open injuring Cath and a friend of Dan's. Sylvia no sooner switched on the lights in the main house than the mains power failed, as always here in a storm. By lamp and torchlight we anchored doors and shutters as best we could, running from house to house through rain that cascaded from the eaves.

The newest bedtime story, *Kidnapped*, had natural sound FX as I shouted it above the din of attic doors and thunder. Reading Stevenson by lightning.

Back in our own house, we lay naked in twin beds with our door open to the yard while the great Romantic spectacle was played out. From the front across the courtyard to our barn or from the rear through own cherry trees over the woods the view was alarming and awesome, a reminder of how little we see of natural extremes. In a metropolis, how can we understand the art or religion of times when there was so little shelter? The first audiences of *Lear* may have walked home (or even watched it, drenched) through such a storm. In London I'd never been aware of the vivid colours of a sustained electric glare. Then came lesser eruptions, like the sudden flares of incendiaries we saw in the raids. A masterly *son-et-lumière*, with a score by Beethoven and décor by Turner.

During one of the most sustained flares, I glanced at Thelma naked on her bed. We'd begun the day by trying, but morning's never our best time. Now we had no trouble. In the glimpses of her face below me, she was looking out at the storm.

[Did the earth move? Diary doesn't say. All but dammit, I should think.]

And here the journal gives out, not to be resumed for six years. The gap supports the view that diaries are written by those with no life to write home about. The years from '76 to '83 were more eventful than any before or since. During this time we moved from Blackheath to Highbury but after only three years sold up again and bought a more modest but still five-storey house in Camden Town. We – the whole family – spent some months in Minneapolis, flying to San Francisco and motoring down Highway One to Los Angeles, passing the Hearst mansion but not having time to stop. We stayed in a downtown Holiday Inn and took the kids to Disneyland. There's a Polaroid snap of us in a garden on Malibu Beach, home of a friend-of-a-friend from the Midwest, a day when we swam in a sea fished by diving pelicans and Rod Steiger dropped in for a drink.

But in London and at Chez Magnou, during 1975-6, I had finished *Jungle Jamboree*, with its ten pastiches of songs of the period. One night at a party I asked Antonia Fraser if she'd prefer *Privates on Parade*. She did and was right. It started an odd compulsion in me to give my plays titles that began with P. This became clear after *Passion Play* (and its unfilmed screenplay *Private View*), *Poppy*, *Piece of my Mind* and the as yet unstaged *Pursued by a Bear*.

The Bristol Old Vic turned down *Privates* on the grounds that my hometown was not yet ready to hear Our Lord referred to as 'Jessica Christ'. The Royal Shakespeare agreed to do it and asked Michael Blakemore to direct. It was good to be preparing a show with him again, though his suggestion of Denis Quilley for the camp captain didn't inspire much confidence. I wanted Stanley Baxter, and failing him Kenneth Williams. Mike rightly said the presence of either would overbalance the play. It wasn't a musical, though it had ten songs and promised to become more of a 'show' as we worked on it. But Quilley? I'd seen him as *Candide* and in revue, so knew he could sing and dance as well as play straight. But wasn't he *too* straight? Certainly not the campest actor around. Mike knew him well, having directed him in O'Neill and *The Front Page* and got his way and everyone who saw it agrees that Quilley's was a dazzling and lovable performance, vestiges of which can be seen in the film that came later.

Mike also brought in Denis King to write tunes for the pastiche songs. This began a partnership that's survived some crises both in our work and personal lives. The beautiful Astrid Ronning who skated her way through the New Haven *Lane* met Denis when we went there for the US premiere of *Privates*. In 1979, she followed him back to London and became Mrs King.

I had already agreed to spend most of 1976 in America, as Visiting Playwright at the Guthrie, with a few minor academic stints at the University of Minnesota. In fact, this split into two spells of some months each, broken by a journey home to check progress on *PoP*. Thirty pages describe the first spell, in summer, when I was joined by Thelma and the children, but of the winter one, when we two were alone, there's no record. It has to be dredged up from the sludge of memory.

There do survive pages or notebooks when a few days, weeks or months show that I was trying to get the motor of this journal turning over again. It coughs and splutters, then the battery goes dead and another long interval follows. One passage in June 1979 reads:

'You can't keep this kind of thing going unless you can be honest and for two of these years I've had something to hide from my wife and family.'

A play finally resulted from all this that tried to show how lying and betrayal can bring deep trouble as well as excitement. Confusion more than pleasure dominated the fictional account. It dealt with passion as suffering rather than as fun. Now, twenty years later, none of it matters except to those of us who were involved. Blood under the bridge. And so it had better remain.

So Denis and Astrid left their spouses to marry each other. Marriages fractured all around us. Michael Frayn left Gill for Claire Tomalin. Mike Blakemore left Shirley for Tanya. Albert and Anouk faced separate futures. Other partnerships survived, sometimes narrowly or after mid-life crises that left the partners feeling shaken and less secure. It may be presumptuous of me to claim that my brother

Geoffrey and Mary, Charles and Valerie Wood, Francis and Liz Hewlett, David and Meg Mendel all weathered storms that in emotional terms were as violent as the night at Chez Magnou. Some of us wouldn't ever be sure again that our decision to continue wasn't as much cowardice as love. Certainly there were elements of both. The final tableau of *Passion Play* suggests not a return of peace but a patched-up truce. Among our circle of friends and relatives, it was as much about our time of life and as any personal history.

Though we were still far from the age when the morning obituaries become compulsive reading, a few of our generation met early deaths. Nicholas Tomalin, of course. Joan Morahan had gone and Christopher had married Anna, whom he met at our house. Tynan, David Mercer, Michael Bates and Nibs Dalwood all shuffled off. The last was the greatest shock. He'd always been so fit and vigorous, gobbling life with enviable greed. In a mountain village in Tito's Yugoslavia, we saw him deal with the language problem in a way that epitomised the artist-technician who had once worked at Bristol Aeroplane Company. He took a pogo-stick from the boot of his Borgward and hopped on it all round the square. He went on to teach bouncing to the local kids. When we drove off, the whole population turned out to wave. His decline was sudden. Within no time he'd succumbed to a rare condition. Ros, his live-in lover, half his age, was appalled at the sight of his embalmed body in the hospital chapel where they'd laid him out. 'What have they done to him?' she cried, seeing the made-up face, rouged cheeks and carmine lips. I used the image in *Born in the Gardens* when the daughter's faced with her father's corpse.

My Minneapolis year began when I flew out alone in the early summer of 1976. From the air Niagara Falls appeared as two white dashes on the vast flatlands of Middle America. After *Joe Egg* had opened on Broadway in 1968, our family had gone as far west as Chicago to visit Thelma's sister, and on to Madison, to stay with Dalwood, who was then with his second wife on a stint at Wisconsin University.

Michael Langham met me at Minneapolis airport, a middle-aged man with a clipped moustache and military manner. He told me Blakemore had left only three days before, having liked the city and theatre and agreed to be considered as Langham's successor when he left in 1978. Tyrone Guthrie had initiated this and the one at Stratford,

Ontario, in his quest for the 'New Architecture' he thought we needed more than new plays, actors or directors. By the end of my year there, I believed he'd been mistaken. Anyway, he began a dynasty of Brits that Blakemore was expected to continue, but the theatre Board decided to put an end to it and appoint an American instead. High time.

I arrived seriously jet-lagged and sleep was impossible in their usual summer night of over 80 degrees, so we sat drinking Scotch in his apartment in a pleasant suburb. In fact, most of the large city looked to me like pleasant suburb. Despite his many years there, Michael had no hint of a local accent, was avid for news of the Test Match and had the manner of an army officer pensioned off under age. Not surprising, as he'd been the second officer of the British Expeditionary Force to be taken prisoner in Europe and remained a POW for the entire war.

Until a rented house became available, I was to stay at the Oak Grove (or 'Grave' as Guthrie had called it), a block of rented suites and apartments about five minutes walk from the theatre. Tatty and run-down, with noisy aircon and chintzy sofas. But Michael had stacked the kitchen with convenience foods, Twinings' tea, Carr's water biscuits, a quart of Scotch and a bar of Callard and Bowser's treacle brittle.

Next day, a Sunday, I met Dick Guindon, the cartoonist who'd be our friend for the coming year. In the preface to his collected drawings, he writes that it isn't easy to do cartoons about Minnesota:

'We are consistently ranked among those states that enjoy the highest quality of life in America and, therefore, the world. What's funny about being the source of the good life?

'We are also the source of the Mississippi River and one form of pneumonia. We have given the world Bobby Dylan, Charles Lindbergh, The Andrews Sisters, F. Scott Fitzgerald and the Los Angeles Lakers. This book will try to deal with some of the reasons why they may have left.'

Dick and Michael took us in turn to meet Ron Ross, a Scottish journalist on the *Tribune* who owns the barn beside M. Maze's house at Siorac-de-Ribérac, along the valley from Chez Magnou, the first of a few coincidences that made me feel all travel in the modern world is a waste of time and effort. We drank daquiris in the plot outside, a not unpleasant sore-throat medicine with no evident alcoholic effect, and later went in to eat Haitian food – peppery chicken, rice and tomatoes with lime juice poured on. I soon learnt it's not the taste or nourishment that matters in the US but how much conversational mileage the food provides and how exotic its pedigree.

Two Valium gave me a good sleep and next day I did the first of some obligatory gigs at the vast state university. At the deserted campus, I was given keys to office and classroom and shown no less than four fully-equipped auditoria (thrust, arena, workshop and proscenium). So much wealth, so much hardware and nothing happening of any note. Enrolment had already been done without me and today I had to sit in the office waiting to see if any more signed on. I browsed through a boxful of student plays. None had made any sense of a personal experience and my prahblum is that anything else bores me.

It was best to have a prahblum, in fact really basic equipment. There aren't drunks but people with a drink problem. Nobody dislikes anyone, they have a problem with him. So you can have a problem with Bartok. It's not 'What are you looking at?', but 'what's your problem?'. The corollary is that there's a possible solution, a happy ending, as in 'No problem!'. In the first place, the cruel climate here must have been a problem, how to keep warm in winter, cool in summer, but that was solved by aircon and central heating. All the downtown stores are linked by elevated glass corridors. The Crystal Court, the first shopping mall we'd seen, was a solution to the climate problem. American Indians (also a first) ride the escalators staring without expression at black pimps and white gays parading the balconies for trade. Old folk sit for hours beneath the potted trees and out-of-towners click their Nikkormats and pose in leather stetsons eating Baskin-Robbins ices.

But technology is always a two-edged sword and the blessing of refrigeration leads to ice-cream which in turn brings about a weight problem. Whole sections of bookshops are devoted to diet. Sex is a problem they face with candour and humour. It's *The Joy of Sex*, a gourmet's guide to lovemaking, rather than the Gideon Bible, that lies at every bedside. A sensible manual of plain fare with spicier dishes for the jaded appetite. *How To Be a Sensuous Woman* was left for us in the house we rented at Dean Boulevard. I found it something of a problem to visualise the middle-aged couples we met tackling some of these recipes, especially with the aid of mirrors.

In my room, I kept the radio tuned to a station relaying classical music all day. My next-door-but-one neighbour Colin Davis was named most mornings. I'd seen him on my last day at home, in his back garden sipping coffee and reading the paper. A Mark Twain style was brought to this channel by a local man called Garrison Keillor, later to become famous with his books on Lake Woebegone.

Dick, Michael and I became buddies, something I knew nothing of at home, and even went on a sort of pub-crawl of run-down bars on the West Bank of ol' man river in a shabby quarter of rooming-houses and warehouse-theatres, one of which was called The Mixed Blood.

This was all a sharp contrast to Kenwood, where we lived, between Lake of the Isles and Lake Calhoun, old quarries now forming a mid-west Lake District. Even Longfellow's Lake Nokoma, the shining big-sea water, is a popular resort. These waters interrupt the relentless grid of streets, numbered from one to infinity north and south as the city spreads, and avenues crossing them alphabetically from Abbott to Zenith, then again from Antoinette to Zarthan, Alabama to Zinran.

Conversations, whether in sleek Minneapolis or duller St Paul, are the kind I have gotten kinda used to at this present moment in time: rational, well-informed but lacking bite, except where Dick's taking part. I'd asked Jonathan Miller about the mid-West before leaving. 'Not enough Jews', he'd told me, but this wasn't true of the Twin Cities where the Walker Art Gallery, Symphony Orchestra and Guthrie Theatre had attracted an unlikely flock to perch for a while in this vast prairie.

I was glad to leave the Oak Grove and cleared my stuff in three journeys, piled on the rear deck of the Chevrolet landing-craft they loaned me for my visit. It had auto-change and assisted steering but was half-a-block long. The traffic's so sedate, other drivers so polite and law-abiding. When Nibs first drove in Wisconsin, he followed the European manner, travelling at forty in a 20-m.p.h. zone, was at once flagged down by cops and barred from driving for his entire stay. Only in their movies are Americans wild and free. During the cold spell, months later, I found the huge car skidding out of control across the icy highway. Somehow I braked it to a halt. Almost at once police were there to squint at my outa-town accent and advise me to ballast the trunk with sandbags.

I was loading some of my gear – a teapot, umbrella and alarm-clock – in the Oak Grove car park one day, en route to our rented house, when one of the Irish members of the company spotted me.

'We got the English guy today,' he shouted. It was a funny way to say 'How English you look!' but I was learning their odd idioms and called back cheerily, 'Absolutely!' At this he froze, turned and made off. He was of the pro-Republican faction and, before knowing quite who I was, had called out that day's good news, that the British Ambassador to Ireland had been killed when his car went over a land-mine.

In St Paul's, we were always prepared for any bar or restaurant to go silent when they heard our voices.

Parties were the norm. The wardrobe master gave one at his place on the banks of Lake Minnetonka. I was being given a lift by the only black (and part Cherokee) woman in the company.

'Gay as hell,' said Dick, 'don't put your hand on her knee, she'll break your arm.'

The cabin stood high on the steep bank, shaded by oak and pine. We lay on lawns sipping wine as the sun set beyond the western margin. Guests arrived late by motor-launch, mooring at a jetty. Candles in brown paper bags were tastefully arranged in a line down to the water, where more floated, glowing orange as darkness came. Despite all this, the occasion fell flat – perhaps they all knew one another too well – and the launch took off again, its light receding across the choppy lake.

'It's like *The Great Gatsby*,' I said.

'Well,' said the host, 'maybe *The Little Gatsby*.'

I was driven to the airport to meet Thelma and the kids arriving by the only form of transport anyone here took seriously. I too learned to look longingly at the sky for arriving and departing planes. When, in the darker months, I went to meet her arriving alone, I lost my way on the lunatic freeway system. Signs suggested 'For west, take east-west high-way at north-south intersection'. As her ETA approached, I gave up these, spotted the flashing lights of a jet and followed it in my Chevvie and was there to meet her as she emerged.

Our next-door neighbours were Chuck and Lee Preston, eccentrics in this society, refugees from a Capra film, indifferent to gadgetry, consumer pressures and competitiveness, having no car and going to work by bus (she to the public library, he a city hostel for derelicts), their house a shabby place full of friends and relatives. A marked contrast to the lakeside mansions where families of four occupied thirty rooms crammed with valuable loot. Every Sunday the Prestons gave brunch in the yard we shared with them and the Bremners the other side. It was at these occasions we met the only native counterparts of the idealistic left-wing we knew in England.

Chuck showed us a report in the Sunday papers of a recent federal enquiry into FBI activities in the Honeywell industrial complex. This company came in for a lot of criticism from anti-war groups for making fragmentation anti-personnel bombs for use on the Vietnamese. The FBI had been directed to break up the gathering opposition but hadn't been able to prevent the protesters buying shares and attending the AGM. They made their views known by speaking from the floor, undermining the whole meeting, and were only finally routed by the Chairman who, with a majority holding, was entitled to close the proceedings whenever he chose. And who should this turn out to be? James Binger, my sponsor, who had come to lunch at Blackheath to vet my suitability.

Passing on an invitation to dine at the Bingers' one Sunday evening, Michael Langham made no bones about what this meant. I was being ordered on parade. It came the same day as Chuck and friends had pointed out the report in the local paper.

Michael, driving us to their home in Wayzata, a well-heeled suburb on Minnetonka, said he hadn't seen the item but that Honeywell was now chiefly known for its weapons. Binger's wife's father had founded Honeywell and had now retired to his home in Florida, leaving his son-in-law in command. Ginny was, Michael said, a rather sweet and reticent woman.

The house was in unimpressive country with views across scrubland of a small pond and no sign of Minnetonka itself. The wardrobe master's place was far more impressive but perhaps millionaires don't have time to look at views. The guests, drinking cocktails beside a swimming-pool, included the publisher of the *Tribune*, Dick and Ross's boss, the director of the Walker Gallery, and a theatrical impresario who was advising Binger on his various holdings in New York, Boston and London. He'd told Michael that his father had just handed him five theatres – three on Broadway and two in Boston.

The matter of the protesters was raised and we were for once in the rare position of taking their message into the enemy camp. Not that it was news to anyone there. And Binger was beset by leftish views and was evidently used to dealing with them. Had this whole 'liberals' lunch been fixed for a day he knew he and Honeywell were to be vilified in the press?

Not long after, we got into some cars and drove to Woodhills Country Club, another bleak place, where Wayzata's best go to pay too much for their steak and fries. I was placed beside Ginny. Her conversation was mostly about how she and Big Daddy were dining at The White House the coming Tuesday. This was said, it seemed, to check the pro-Democratic bias at our end of the table. When he sniffed Ginny's rebuke, the editor changed in a wink and was soon nodding his head off as she praised Gerry Ford. The voice of the turncoat was heard in our land.

Far from shy, Ginny seemed more than able to lead the pack. She'd covered her steak with ketchup before finding it was underdone.

'Michael, is yours done enough?'

'Yes, perfectly, thank you.'

'I'm sure it is. I think you have mine.'

'Surely not.'

'Mine's so rare it's hardly done at all. You want to let me finish yours?'

He dealt with this by a show of English vagueness, which he uses often and with some skill. Ginny turned to me and muttered: 'Well, that didn't get me any place.' She finally stood up, declaring to the company that she had to fly to Florida next day and wanted to sleep.

Another and better party was at the home of another heiress, a nice old house on a point, with every aspect over water. The pretext was to celebrate Langham's birthday. Next day he showed me a box with some tins of soup and spaghetti, bottles of ketchup and salad cream, etc., sent by Heinz Inc. He had to remind me they were a few of their 57 Varieties, sent to everyone of distinction who reaches that age.

At this party, I tried to let my hair down and dispel the idea that I was a stuffy Limey, a tea-drinking crony of the English establishment. I dragged Thelma on to the dance floor and we tried jiving to the Dixieland band (as they still call it here). A couple before us had done an eccentric twist and been loudly applauded. As soon as we entered the lists, the rest left the floor and everyone watched us in icy silence. Thelma wanted to stop but I felt we had to carry through. A rotten moment that still has the power to make us wince. I could have done with a pogo-stick.

In spite of that, that evening was the highlight of our stay, a lavish occasion amid glorious natural scenery on a perfect summer's night. According to Michael, it's always the year's big event and this was even better as the hostess had been dried out at the Ford clinic and no-one had to carry her to bed before the party ended.

The other side of life there was to be seen downtown at the Fairmont Hotel, which our neighbour Chuck was trying to save from the wreckers. A depressing parade of bums, drifters, con-men – black, white and Indian – moves through its lobby. The clerk sits behind a mesh protective screen and takes the money provided by welfare pay-outs which buy these derelicts a night or week or (in one unthinkable case) fifteen years in this flophouse. Chuck calls its Fantasy Hall and says all the inmates are living in some kind of unreality. The middle-aged pimp and his whore wife think they're a respectable married couple with a smart central address. If you've reached the Fairmont, fantasy's not indulgence but necessity. Chuck himself lives on dreams, such as that by diligent application he can turn the Fairmont into a decent family hotel. It's a scene ready-made for an O'Neill or Saroyan or Tennessee Williams.

Mostly we had a happy holiday. Hardly any students turned up for my classes and those only to make up grades. None of them knew anything about drama, though in our few weeks together turned out competent plays, some in the style of Thornton Wilder – 'Well, I don't know about you folks' – many flirting with the obscene – 'Shit, man, I hate to see a faggot jerking off' – but no-one attempted social comedy. They could do with a little. With this in mind, I got them reading *Black Comedy* and *Joe Egg*. Their social scene's as funny as ours but only a few New York Jews are doing it for theatre.

We took the children most days to swim in nearby Lake Cedar. Between beach and house was a level crossing where sometimes enormous trains held up traffic for half-an-hour, long lines of trucks with exotic names from Canada and Mexico passing at walking pace, reminding us of the part played in the States by freight trains. A rail-road strike can still bring industry to its knees.

Sometimes we carried the alloy canoe and paddled from Cedar through channels to Lake of the Isles and on to Calhoun. Or took the bikes along lakeside tracks till our legs ached. Once we paused where some blacks were playing cool jazz by the water to a languid audience of honey-skinned boys and girls who lived in paradise without knowing.

We spent much of one night watching a grain elevator burn down a few hundred yards from our place. The Prestons, of course, said it was arson, the work of developers wanting to clear the ground for a new condominium. They knew because the firemen were having such problems finding the fire hydrants. Just enough water was drawn to limit the damage. In other words, they'd been paid to let it burn, a building with a preservation order. We doubted this. Chuck and Lee were always ready with conspiracy theories about the wicked world. But next day all the news bulletins confirmed their suspicions.

After the family went home at the end of school holidays, I hung around for a week in a condo that had been (and was still called) the Calhoun Beach Hotel. At fifty, I was by far the youngest guest. The others were mostly ageing widows with some kind of tenure bought when their husbands were earning. Some were frail and wandered in mind and body. On occasion I'd rescue one from where she'd been impaled by an elevator door. A nurse would come, wagging a finger, 'Okay, Mrs Nussbaum, you're in the doghouse.' Others were capable of motoring. The parking lot was alive with massive cars that seemed to have no drivers till you looked more closely and saw the little heads with permed coiffures peering out through the steering-wheel. The Calhoun's reception floor smelt of burning hair and there was always a line of ladies waiting at the stylists. There was also mail-call, as in the army, and a huddle of mothers formed every day in the hope of a word from family or friends. A staff-member called their names. I watched one morning as a tough old bird heard her name and pressed forward, saying, 'Here, here, I'm here!', receiving and ripping open the envelope and turning, disillusioned, to the crowd to show the Concessionary Offer: 'Anyone wanna go to the ball*et*?'

I was resented by the company and gave up visiting the theatre. The 'fringe' theatre, Guthrie Two, which I was supposed to run for a season, is a dreary hole without aircon so that in summer it's an oven and no doubt in winter an ice-house. The punters sit on bleachers which means no-one over twenty-five pays a second visit. I didn't myself, so was left with no good reason to stay and Michael released me till he and I were ready to co-direct *The National Health* later that year.

At home Mike and I went on casting *Privates* and finishing the songs. As a family we'd never taken to our elegant Georgian 'row-house' as Americans would call it and were already thinking of selling up. We had a few good times there but somehow the one-sidedness of the terrace, nothing facing us but Highbury Fields, depressed our spirits. It was by far the most beautiful home we've had but never suited.

Leaving Louise (now 15), Dan (13) and Catherine (12) with Thelma's parents, we took off again for the Midwest and stayed the whole time at the Oak Grave. There's no written account of the show Michael Langham and I co-directed and not a lot more in my memory bank. I was surprised at Michael's autocratic way of rehearsing, sitting with his eyes fixed on a prompt copy of the script, gesturing entrances and exits to the actors with both hands held above him and shouting when they failed to follow. It was more like square-bashing than drama. He ran a tight ship and no-one appeared to mind. The company were of that stratum of 'regional' actors, mostly unknown abroad, happy to move from one 'good' theatre to another, a few of them progressing to films or TV, even achieving featured status but rarely if ever becoming stars. Their equivalents at home stand a better chance because of our size and the capital being the centre of theatre, films and TV. They would not have tolerated Michael's methods, which belonged to a previous moment in time. When my own rehearsals became, in his view, too easygoing, he would call the company to order. He must have confirmed the IRA faction in their view of the English as incurable tyrants. It was my first experience of handling a large company (thirty or so) and the actual staging was more Michael's than mine. *The National Health* showed up the limitations of thrust staging. So did Thornton Wilder's farce *The Matchmaker*, where a screen hiding one group of characters from another had to be made transparent so as not to conceal them from half the audience as well. There are no reviews of our show in my desultory scrapbook. I believe it did reasonable business, though nothing like the blinding success of Tahm Star-purred.

I remember mostly the brutal cold, exceptional even for this place of legendary winters. The stock Twin Cities joke is that anyone who's still there in the winter couldn't get their car started in the Fall. Dick Guindon's book has a swaddled man in a grand house under a chandelier telling his wife, 'All in all, this car-starting business has been very good to us. Hasn't it, Rose?'

The lakes always freeze but this December the air was so cold that it was inadvisable to skate as breathing in too deep could freeze your lungs. The nose-hairs became tiny icicles and could cause bleeding. Finally the Oak Grove's plumbing was under permafrost and the lavatories ceased to carry sewage away. After fruitless complaints, residents protested by leaving it in buckets in the corridor outside the manager's office. First thing every day we all went to the parking lot, huddled in scarves, hats, boots and gloves, to get our motors started. We left them running, went inside again, took off some clothes, ate breakfast, listening to Garrison Keillor, and only dared get into the cars after their heating systems had warmed up for half an hour. Lecturing midwestern people about conserving resources is so much wasted breath. Between the hotel and theatre complex there is an urban freeway to be crossed. On the way home one day, emerging on to the great open swathe, heading for the opposite road, I found that my windscreen had suddenly iced over and had to drive blind, only finding my exit by sheer luck.

The smells at the Oak Grove became too bad and before Christmas we flew to Connecticut for a stay with Arvin and Joyce Brown in their pretty pond-side home. The people we mixed with were the opposite of Proper Men, having no idea how to light a fire, pot a Christmas tree or do anything much in that way except barbecue burgers. Chuck Preston had decided to use a real bit of conifer this year but had no idea how to make a bucket heavy enough to support it. Another of Guindon's pictures shows a woman unwrapping her Perma Tree (Already Decorated) from last year's box. 'Arthur,' she says, 'I think the dry cleaners lost some of the bulbs.'

I learned to be grateful for our muggy climate and to be tolerant with our inability to deal with even a slight drop in temperature. After a day or two, I was as thick with the old life as though I'd never left it. Familiar objects, English Usage, a new tolerance from the children after living with their strict grandparents. We seemed hip by comparison.

Rehearsals for *Privates* were well advanced. In the RSC's rooms at Floral Street, Covent Garden, I saw the six-man and one-woman chorus line doing battle over the routines. The rifles were too heavy to be thrown about in the way the choreographer wanted. There was open mutiny.

'You do it then!' said Joe Melia, handing her his gun, 'let's see you.'

Nigel Hawthorne was playing Major Flack, almost the first entirely imaginary character I'd written. I found the actor lurking in ante-rooms, alone and unhappy.

'I feel I may have to throw it in,' he said, 'they've all got songs and dances to do. That's not my thing at all. I'm sorry. I just don't know where I'm going with this. I hate to let you down.'

One morning he appeared with his wonderful performance, as though it had come to him in the post. He joined the rest of them, who had been given lighter rifles. I now only remember the morning in Floral Street when the band played for the first time and Denis Quilley put on a few hints of drag. Trevor Nunn and David Jones came like orderly officers to see what the chaps had put together. And saw that it was good.

As usual, Mike's methods had worked. Fragments that had seemed unconnected, scenes that had been eclipsed by song-and-dance now coalesced in a heart-warming show that had the sweet smell of success.

The plot was confused, not all the pastiches were spot-on – the Brazilian Carmen Miranda never sang a Cuban conga – and it needed half an hour taken out. But, if they could all carry this house of cards to an opening night, we knew we had a hit.

They did, though disaster threatened so often that I was as pessimistic as I'd been over all my shows except *The Freeway*, my only real flop. The family bore the brunt so it was natural for Cath, on the opening, to round on me angrily as the first act ended.

'Well, I can't think what you were raving on about because it's brilliant!'

The audience appeared to think so too and next day and for some time afterwards the reviews were mostly on our side. Some, quoting as many of my jokes as they could squeeze in, complained that there were too many jokes. It was called self-indulgent and clumsy. The actors were often credited with having saved my bacon. But the show packed out for its fifty performances at the Aldwych. Previous engagements meant any more had to be postponed for a year. By the time it was remounted, we'd been given three Olivier Awards, the *Evening Standard* for Best

Comedy and Denis King and I got an Ivor Novello for Best Musical. Denis Quilley and Nigel Hawthorne got gongs for their acting.

Since then I've had every chance to learn that success is transient, especially in Theatre, where nothing remains once the scenery's broken up, except in memory. It was fun while it lasted and gave me new heart to carry on. I wrote *Born in the Gardens* for the Bristol Old Vic, where I'd trained and acted. This commission, to celebrate the bicentenary of this superb theatre, was from Richard Cottrell who'd had to turn down *Privates*. I made it a gift to my home city as well, the fifth of my plays to be set there.

Success apparently lent me some quality I'd lacked till then. Personal fantasies, harboured for many years, now – briefly – became reality and threatened to separate us and our children, events finally fictionalised in *Passion Play*.

As I bring this account to a close, twenty years later, we're still together, our children married with their own, two even divorced. For some time now, I've been discussing the casting of a London revival of *Passion Play*. Like an unmoored ship, this thing has drifted off into open sea. The young director sees no need to discuss the play as though it had any bearing on our real lives. As far as he's concerned, it's fiction. This journal's shown how haphazard my methods are. The plays come together from scraps of experience, remembered jokes, overheard lines, private longings, dependable routines and duties, a long shared history, a sense that (to quote *Joe Egg*), 'Every cloud has a jet-black lining'.

As the world rejoiced to have reached 2000 AD, Thelma and I were more concerned with celebrating our forty years.